THE LIMITS OF THE CRIMINAL SANCTION

THE LIMITS

OF THE

CRIMINAL SANCTION

HERBERT L. PACKER

1968

STANFORD UNIVERSITY PRESS

STANFORD, CALIFORNIA

Stanford University Press
Stanford, California
© 1968 by Herbert L. Packer
Printed in the United States of America
L.C. 68-26780

To Nancy, Annie, and George

Preface

THIS BOOK is an essay rather than a treatise. Whatever usefulness it has does not reside in the learning that it collects. Accordingly, I have avoided the usual compromise between scholarly care and printing costs, which dictates that reference notes be scrupulously assembled and then relegated to the back of the book. Instead I have used footnotes, very sparingly, to provide easy reference to specific quotations or citations in the text, and have written a single bibliographical note (pp. 369–75) to provide a map of the intellectual terrain.

I have accumulated more obligations in the writing of this book than can easily be acknowledged. Some of them are stated in the bibliographical note. For others, especially those incurred when friends and colleagues undertook to criticize part or all of the manuscript, I have to thank Gerald Gunther, John Kaplan, Yosal Rogat, Michael Wald, and especially Sanford Kadish. Grants from the Rockefeller Foundation and the American Council of Learned Societies made possible a year of rumination about the themes of this book, a year that was made memorable by the hospitality of the Dean and Faculty of the University of Pennsylvania Law School. I also wish to thank the Ford Foundation for a grant to the Stanford Law School that helped me finish this book and that is supporting continued inquiry into the problems with which this book is concerned.

My secretary, Peg Dickson, has typed and retyped the manuscript with efficiency and good cheer. The students in my seminar on The Criminal Sanction, Autumn Term 1967, gave the manuscript and its author the kind of redoubtable working over that is both justification and reward for a law teacher's existence. And my friends at the Stanford University Press—Leon Seltzer, Jess Bell, and Elinor Stillman—demonstrated again what scholarly publishing at its best is all about. In short, whatever others can do has been done superbly.

Portions of the book have appeared, in somewhat different form, in *The American Scholar, The Supreme Court Review,* and *The University of Pennsylvania Law Review.* I am grateful to the editors of these periodicals for their editorial assistance as well as for permission to reprint.

My colleagues in the School of Law and in the administration of the University have been patient and tolerant during the gestation. I suspect that they will be as relieved as I by the delivery. My most important debt, happily undischargeable, is acknowledged in the dedication.

H.L.P.

Contents

THE LIMITS OF THE CRIMINAL SANCTION

Introduction: The Argument and Its Audience

THIS IS A BOOK about law and some related subjects; but it is not a specialized book, and I hope that it will be read by people who are not specialists. It is a book about a social problem that has an important legal dimension: the problem of trying to control anti-social behavior by imposing punishment on people found guilty of violating rules of conduct called criminal statutes. This device I shall call the criminal sanction. The rhetorical question that this book poses is: how can we tell what the criminal sanction is good for? Let us hypothesize the existence of a rational law-maker—a man who stops, looks, and listens before he legislates. What kinds of questions should he ask before deciding that a certain kind of conduct (bank robbery, income tax evasion, marijuana use) ought to be subjected to the criminal sanction?

Some people argue that we ought never subject lawbreakers to criminal punishment. Such punishment, they say, is a vestige of our savage past that we ought to abandon in favor of more benign measures of social control, measures that do not involve us in cruelty to our fellow man. Others argue that any act treated by the law of God or Man as being immoral may be properly subject to the criminal sanction. I think both are wrong, although the danger of the moment is that we will overuse the criminal sanction, not that we will abandon it. But both errors need to be combated.

The argument of this book begins with the proposition that

there are certain things we must understand about the criminal sanction before we can begin to talk sensibly about its limits. First, we need to ask some questions about the rationale of the criminal sanction. What are we trying to do by defining conduct as criminal and punishing people who commit crimes? To what extent are we justified in thinking that we can or ought to do what we are trying to do? Is it possible to construct an acceptable rationale for the criminal sanction enabling us to deal with the argument that it is itself an unethical use of social power? And if it is possible, what implications does that rationale have for the kind of conceptual creature that the criminal law is? Questions of this order make up Part I of the book, which is essentially an extended essay on the nature and justification of the criminal sanction.

We also need to understand, so the argument continues, the characteristic processes through which the criminal sanction operates. What do the rules of the game tell us about what the state may and may not do to apprehend, charge, convict, and dispose of persons suspected of committing crimes? Here, too, there is great controversy between two groups who have quite different views, or models, of what the criminal process is all about. There are people who see the criminal process as essentially devoted to values of efficiency in the suppression of crime. There are others who see those values as subordinate to the protection of the individual in his confrontation with the state. A severe struggle over these conflicting values has been going on in the courts of this country for the last decade or more. How that struggle is to be resolved is a second major consideration that we need to take into account before tackling the question of the limits of the criminal sanction. These problems of process are examined in Part II.

Part III deals directly with the central problem of defining criteria for limiting the reach of the criminal sanction. Given the constraints of rationale and process examined in Parts I and II, it argues that we have over-relied on the criminal sanction and that we had better start thinking in a systematic way about how to adjust our commitments to our capacities, both moral and operational.

It is, perhaps, too bad that there is no branch or department of human inquiry to which this book may be safely assigned. It draws on law, on philosophy, on economics, and on some of the behavioral sciences, but it does not pretend to be a technical treatise about any of them. In that sense, it is somewhat old-fashioned. Scholars today are supposed to stick closer to their lasts than was expected of them in the days when we knew less, but knew it about more. The book is somewhat old-fashioned also in that it seeks to apply utilitarian principles to larger problems than those that today seem to interest most professional philosophers. In both substance and method the shades I invoke, not without presumption, are those of Bentham and Mill.

The timeliness of an inquiry into the limits of the criminal sanction hardly needs emphasis. We live today in a state of hyper-consciousness about the real or fancied breakdown of social control over the most basic threats to person and property. "Crime in the streets" is something that we seem unable to cope with. At the same time, and with the same limited resources, we wage ever-more-dubious battle against the use of narcotics, marijuana, and a host of new dangerous drugs. Is there anything that can be said, beyond a simplistic expression of personal bias, about our wide use of the criminal sanction? Are there rational arguments to which rational men can respond rationally? This seems to me to be an important question, and this book is an attempt to give it an affirmative answer.

In the end, this is an argument about the uses of power. The criminal sanction is the paradigm case of the controlled use of power within a society. It raises legal issues that are too important to be left to the lawyers, philosophic issues that are too important to be left to the philosophers, and behavioral science issues that are too important to be left to the behavioral scientists. That is why the argument is addressed, with affectionate respect, to the Common Reader.

PART I

RATIONALE

CHAPTER ONE

The Dilemma of Punishment

TODAY AS ALWAYS the criminal law is caught between two fires. On the one hand, there is the view that punishment of the morally derelict is its own justification. On the other, there is the view that the only proper goal of the criminal process is the prevention of antisocial behavior. As if the problem of reconciling these views were not enough, the second has lately given rise to a new formulation that threatens the very foundations of the criminal law. This new formulation seemingly creates a dilemma for those who do not accept the retributive position yet who do not want to reject the whole concept of the criminal law. In this chapter I will briefly sketch the outlines of this alleged dilemma, and will indicate a way of dealing with the issues it raises. Later I will explore these issues more fully, and will essay an integrated rationale that favors neither punishment for the sake of punishment nor the complete abolition of punishment.

The retributive position is an old one, and its content has not changed much over the centuries. It holds, very simply, that man is a responsible moral agent to whom rewards are due when he makes right moral choices and to whom punishment is due when he makes wrong ones. According to this view, these imperatives flow from the nature of man and do not require—indeed do not permit—any pragmatic justification. There is a perceived sense of fitness in the sight of wrongdoers being made to suffer for their misdeeds. As individuals we have a wholly proper desire to seek revenge when wrongs are inflicted on us; as a society we demand that constituted authority punish those who unjustifiably inflict injury on others or otherwise act in ways we think are wrong. If other benefits are incidentally derived from making the wicked suffer, well and good; but those benefits must not be sought for their own sake. The purpose of punishment is to inflict deserved suffering, and the purpose of the criminal law is to provide an acceptable basis within the social framework for doing so.

The retributive position does not command much assent in intellectual circles, but there seems little reason to suppose that it does not continue to retain a strong hold on the popular mind. The language of punishment is full of its traces. We talk about a criminal "paying his debt to society"; we express satisfaction or dissatisfaction when a criminal "gets what is coming to him" or "gets off lightly." The language of capital punishment is especially rich in examples. The condemned murderer is said to be "paying" for his crime, thereby providing one of the rare instances our law affords of a perfect proportion between crime and punishment. More expressively, if the doomed man dies or commits suicide before he can be executed, he is said to have "cheated the gallows."

Public prosecutors often see themselves as the voice of the community's demand for retribution. The closing argument to the jury in any important criminal trial is heavy with the rhetoric of revenge. And many judges—more openly, it is true, in England than here—conceive of their sentencing function as the expression of society's demand that the criminal expiate his crime. The police use a different set of metaphors: they speak of the criminal sometimes as an animal, sometimes simply as "the enemy." He is seen as a "rat" or a "vermin"—whatever his position in the animal kingdom, he is something to be exterminated. As an enemy he becomes the target in the "war on crime," and the public pronouncements of law enforcement officials leave no doubt that it is a Holy War. The retributive view is summed up in the great Victorian jurist Sir James Stephen's powerful and compelling image: "the sentence of the law is to the moral sentiment of the public in relation to any offense what a seal is to hot wax."[1] Later

---

[1] *History of the Criminal Law in England* (London, 1883), II, 80.

in the same passage Stephen says that the criminal law stands in the same relation to the passion for revenge as marriage does to the sexual passion. Oddly enough, we are more euphemistic today, but the idea is not an unfamiliar one.

To the retributive view there has always been opposed one that we may characterize as utilitarian: it holds that the purpose of the criminal law is to prevent or reduce the incidence of behavior that is viewed as antisocial. This view rejects retribution as a basis for punishment on the ground that suffering is always an evil and that there is no justification for making people suffer unless some secular good can be shown to flow from doing so. The retributive view is essentially backward-looking; it regards the offense committed by the criminal as crucial, and adjusts the punishment to it. The utilitarian view is forward-looking; it assesses punishment in terms of its propensity to modify the future behavior of the criminal and (especially, in the classic view) of others who might be tempted to commit crimes. In its essence, it sees man as a rational, pleasure-seeking creature who can be prevented from engaging in antisocial behavior by the prospect that the pain it brings him will more than cancel out the pleasure. It relies, in a word, on deterrence.

I shall come back to the classic utilitarian view, because it remains, with all its defects, the most useful starting point for an integrated rationale of crime and punishment; but for the moment I want to consider a variant of it that has taken a firm hold in recent years and that seems in a fair way to supplanting the classic utilitarian position in the minds of those most disposed to hold that position. This view, which for convenience I shall call the behavioral, is in complete opposition to the retributive view, and provides the other horn of the seeming dilemma that threatens the existence of criminal law today. Its adherents are vocal and influential. They have or appear to have on their side the lessons of the new learning about human behavior. Their challenge is a simple one: either the criminal law must stand on the retributive position—in which event it will become in time a kind of fossilized remain of a departed era—or it must abandon any attempt to ascribe responsibility for criminal conduct. Crime, guilt, and punishment are meaningless concepts to one who holds this view. He sees the occurrence of the kind of disturbing event that we naïvely call a crime as simply an occasion for social intervention, not the reason for it. Moreover, that occurrence is only one of several possible such occasions, having no characteristic that uniquely compels society to treat it differently from other such occasions. The "commission" of a "crime" is simply one signal among many that a person needs to be dealt with. If this view is right, inquiry into the rational basis for ascribing behavior content to the criminal law is bound to fail. There can be no such basis. Much of this essay is given over to considering whether and to what extent the behavioral view is right.

The behavioral position is considerably more complex than the retributive position. Its four principal bases can, however, be generally stated here. First, free will is an illusion, because human conduct is determined by forces that lie beyond the power of the individual to modify. Second, moral responsibility, accordingly, is an illusion, because blame cannot be ascribed for behavior that is ineluctably conditioned. Third, human conduct, being causally determined, can and should be scientifically studied and controlled. Fourth, the function of the criminal law should be purely and simply to bring into play processes for modifying the personality, and hence the behavior, of people who commit antisocial acts, so that they will not commit them in the future; or, if all else fails, to restrain them from committing offenses by the use of external compulsion (e.g., confinement).

The behavioral view has gained substantial ascendancy in recent years, not so much from the number of its adherents as from their strategic placement for affecting the opinions of others and for modifying public policies. It is a view subscribed to by many if not most psychiatrists, by most practitioners of the behavioral sciences who think about problems of the criminal law, by the overwhelming majority of "professionalized" workers in the correctional field—probation officers, case workers, and the like—and by an increasing number of those popular writers who perform the extremely important function of translating the ideas of the intellectually advanced into current popular terms. Its catchwords—"treat the criminal, not the crime," "punishment is obsolete," "criminals are sick," and the like—are standard fare in large-circulation magazines, and show that the popular culture has absorbed, even it it has not yielded to, the behavioral approach to crime.

The adherents of the behavioral position have something to say about a number of current controversial issues in the criminal law. I will briefly mention only three at this point, simply to demonstrate that the dilemma of the criminal law is a real-life dilemma, not simply a game in the academy.[2]

First, there is the issue of strict liability or liability without fault. An important development in the criminal law of the last century is the creation of offenses—either through enactment by the legislatures or through interpretation by the courts—to prohibit the mere doing or not doing of certain things without regard to the moral blameworthiness of the person who did them. Thus, for example, it has become common to penalize the distribution of impure foods and drugs without reference to whether the seller knew or should have known that they were impure, or the sale of liquor to a minor without reference to whether the seller did or did not make reasonable efforts to discover whether the person he was selling to was a minor. These offenses, involving regulatory or sumptuary laws governing matters far less reprehended than the traditional corpus of crimes of violence or against property, have been treated as a thing apart in the criminal law under some such rubric as "public welfare offenses." Their double divorce from morality—in the morally neutral kind of conduct they concern and in their abandonment of the traditional inquiry into the moral blameworthiness of the offender—has been a comfort to the proponents of the behavioral position in two ways. They have cited these offenses as demonstrating the futility, and indeed the hypocrisy, of the retributionist claim that the criminal law is primarily moral in nature. And they have approved this development in the law as a welcome harbinger of the eventual liberation of the criminal law generally from the crippling and hurtful limitations of the retributive position. In the behavioral view, there is no case to be made against strict lia-

---

[2] All of these points are touched on in Barbara Wootton, *Crime and the Criminal Law* (London, 1963), by far the most lucid and cogent statement of the behavioral position.

bility offenses except on the basis of the retributive hypothesis that they reject. That is one concrete aspect of the dilemma: accept strict liability or be deemed to have embraced retribution.

A second issue concerns sentencing policy. The retributive position holds that punishment must be proportioned to the offense. The graver the offense (on some kind of scale of moral outrage), the more severe the punishment. Nonsense, say the proponents of the behavioral view. Punishment (or treatment, as they usually prefer to call it) should be suited to the needs of the offender and of the rest of the community rather than to the nature of his offense. That is the only way it can look forward to those needs rather than backward to the expiation of his crime. Legislatures can decide in advance on the range of punishment that should be allowable for a given offense, e.g., a minimum of one year of imprisonment and a maximum of ten for, say, burglary. (Even that much in the way of *a priori* limitation would offend hard-core adherents to the behavioral view, who would want to see the correctional authorities left entirely free.) But legislatures have no way of determining how much punishment should be allowable for a given offender. If punishment (or treatment) is to be individualized, there should be large if not complete discretion in the sentencing authority to decide the kind and length of treatment for each offender. In the allocation of sentencing authority, then, the judge should simply turn the offender over to the correctional experts for a completely indeterminate sentence, as opposed to the conventional and traditional procedure by which the judge says to the defendant "Five years" (or whatever), or as opposed to any modification of this procedure whereby limits are placed on the discretion of correctional authorities. To proponents of the behavioral position, any sentence that invokes the nature of the offense rather than the situation of the offender is a throwback to retributive ideas or, at best, to classic utilitarian ideas of deterrence, which these proponents see simply as retribution thinly disguised. Another alleged dilemma, then, which we will have to examine in considerable detail at a later point, is this one: must one either support completely indeterminate sentences or be thought of as a retributionist?

My final instance of the supposed contemporary dilemma is the insanity defense. Traditional criminal law has taken the position that under certain circumstances of mental impairment the actor should not be treated as a criminal. The rationale underlying this position has been confused and inarticulate. For present purposes it is enough to note that adherence to the notion of criminal responsibility universally characterizes the criminal law. In our system, the notion has usually been crystallized in the so-called insanity defense. In its traditional and much-maligned form in the *M'Naghten* rule, this defense requires the acquittal of a person who is too disoriented to understand what he is doing or to know that it is wrong. Under the hammer-blows of modern psychiatric thought, the determinative tests for responsibility have been somewhat modified. But those holding the behavioral view would go further. They see in the insanity defense a principal outcropping of the detested notion of retribution. The inquiry into responsibility is an impossible one, they say. The question of the offender's mental condition becomes relevant not when he is being tried but after it has been determined that he did whatever he is charged with having done, when the question is how he should be dealt with. In short, these critics say that the insanity defense should be abolished. Indeed, they say more. They say that the advance of science into what has heretofore been the sphere of morality, and in particular the acceptance of the concept of psychopathy—which makes the fact of social deviance symptomatic of mental disease—"may well prove to be the thin end of the wedge that will ultimately shatter the whole idea of moral responsibility as a factor in the treatment of anti-social personalities."[3] Once again, the dilemma appears in uncompromising terms: abandon the insanity defense or count yourself a retributionist.

If for any combination of reasons one wishes to reject any of these directives of the behavioral persuasion, he may simply accept the characterization of his position as *pro tanto* retributive. Indeed, there is some evidence that persons who have considered the problem find themselves impelled to accept the dilemma as

[3] Barbara Wootton, *Social Science and Social Pathology* (London, 1959), p. 251.

given. If that is the choice, it is a singularly cheerless one. Either, it seems, one must face up to what will for many be the unpalatable notion that one's views rest on a desire to see other people suffer; or one has to reject the idea of moral responsibility in the criminal law (and, I suppose, in law generally) and see the law as an instrument for treating men "merely as alterable, predictable, curable or manipulable things."[4]

Since I do not believe that this alleged dilemma is real, I see no necessity for impaling myself on either of its horns. The position that I am concerned to articulate and defend in this discussion of rationale can be summarily stated as follows: the prevention of crime is the primary purpose of the criminal law; but that purpose, like any social purpose, does not exist in a vacuum. It has to be qualified by other social purposes, prominent among which are the enhancement of freedom and the doing of justice. The effectuation of those purposes requires placing limits on the goal of crime prevention. Chief among those instrumental limits is this one: a finding of moral responsibility is a necessary although not a sufficient condition for determining criminal guilt and meting out punishment for it.

The position is more quickly stated than defended. The inquiry first requires a very close look at the meaning of the concept of punishment, an enterprise that calls for the drawing of distinctions between punishment and treatment, as well as distinctions among other kinds of sanctions used by the legal system. Chapter Two deals with these matters. Next, Chapter Three describes justifications frequently advanced for the institution of criminal punishment, assesses their merits and shortcomings, and explains why they do not suffice as a satisfactory account of why a moral society should tolerate criminal punishment. Chapter Four attempts a theory of criminal punishment that puts the goals of the criminal law into a larger social context. The remaining chapters of Part I elaborate the minimal doctrinal content of a system of criminal law whose rationale conforms with this analysis.

---

4 H. L. A. Hart, "Punishment and the Elimination of Responsibility," in *Punishment and Responsibility* (London, 1968), p. 183.

CHAPTER TWO

The Meaning of Punishment

INTRODUCTION

The rationale of the criminal law rests on three concepts: offense, guilt, and punishment. Before turning to the content and functions of each, it may be useful to consider the relationships among them.

These three concepts symbolize the three basic problems of substance (as opposed to procedure) in the criminal law: (1) what conduct should be designated as criminal; (2) what determinations must be made before a person can be found to have committed a criminal offense; (3) what should be done with persons who are found to have committed criminal offenses.

The answers that a legal system gives to the first of these questions comprise the "primary norms" of the criminal law: for example, do not murder, rape, rob, or park beside a fire hydrant. The answers that the system gives to the third question comprise the sanctions of its criminal law: if you are found to have committed a criminal offense, you may, for example, be put to death, imprisoned, or deprived of some money. The second question is dependent and instrumental: in order to get from (1) to (3) in any given case, a legal system must provide some criteria for satisfying (2). In that sense, (1) and (3) might be said to be anterior to (2), which may be why Dostoevsky did not call it *Crime, Guilt, and Punishment*.

In order to determine the rationale of the criminal law, we must first inquire what constitutes an "offense," or crime, and what purposes are served by designating offenses, or crimes. That inquiry is relatively easy. Next, there is the concept of "punishment," a word that has largely lost its neutral connotation but one that we cannot avoid using. Here again, we will have to ask what is meant by punishment and what purposes are served by prescribing and imposing punishment. This inquiry is most difficult and complex. We will then be in a position to examine the dependent and instrumental concept of "guilt," which, as will be shown, takes its content from the purposes discerned in the concepts of crime and punishment. At this point it is enough to say that the concept of guilt means something more than a determination that the person charged has engaged in the conduct defined as constituting the offense. The content of the "something more," as we shall see, depends on the functions thought to be served by punishment, and is instrumental in performing those functions.

What we mean by a "crime" or an "offense" is simply conduct that is forbidden by law and to which certain consequences, called punishment, will apply on the occurrence of stated conditions and following a stated process. A crime is not merely any conduct forbidden by law; it is forbidden conduct for which punishment is prescribed and which is formally described as a crime by an agency of government having the power to do so. The standard case presents no problem under this definition. Bank robbery is a crime; breach of contract is not. Marginal questions may and do frequently arise about whether certain kinds of forbidden conduct for which unpleasant consequences may be imposed shall be treated as a "crime" for various purposes (such as the right to a trial by jury) even though they have not previously been formally described as a crime. But the definition of crime is inescapably tautological. Crime is whatever is formally and authoritatively described as criminal. It is not surprising that this definition tells us nothing about what the content of a law of crimes is or ought to be. In order to give a material, as opposed to a formal, definition of crime, one would first have to solve the puzzles about punishment with which the ensuing pages are largely concerned. For that reason we can rest at this point on a formal definition: crime is conduct capable of incurring consequences formally termed criminal.

The question of why we should wish to label conduct as criminal is different from and much simpler than the question of what we hope to achieve by imposing punishments. It is simply, as H. L. A. Hart has put it, "to announce to society that these actions are not to be done and to secure that fewer of them are done."[1] Unlike the case of punishment, in which utilitarian and retributive purposes are at least on the face of it both involved, the defining of crimes serves a purely utilitarian purpose. Punishment, as we shall see, involves among other things the infliction of pain, and thus brings into question the justification of inflicting pain on others. The definition of crime involves no such issue. No one is hurt, except in his self-esteem, by the announcement that it is forbidden to kill another or to smoke marijuana. There is no *a priori* reason why we should not content ourselves with simply announcing that killing or marijuana smoking is forbidden; we might expect that the mere announcement of that fact would to some degree ensure that fewer people are killed or that less marijuana is smoked. Whatever our expectation, the mere announcement that conduct is criminal serves only a secular, utilitarian purpose. It is also worth noting that the aggregation of such announcements serves a somewhat different purpose, also secular and utilitarian: namely, to make it known that certain kinds of conduct are not forbidden, and thereby to assure persons that, whatever other controls may be invoked against them, the criminal law will not concern itself with their conduct.

Crime is the primary norm; punishment is the sanction. Crime without punishment, or at least the threat of punishment, may be impractical, but it is not illogical.

A PRELIMINARY DEFINITION

When a man is sent to the penitentiary after a trial and conviction in a criminal court on a charge of bank robbery, we have

[1] H. L. A. Hart, "Prolegomenon to the Principles of Punishment," in *Punishment and Responsibility* (London, 1968), p. 6.

no hesitation in saying that he is being subjected to punishment. And from this standard case we might be able to extrapolate a rough working definition which, while insufficient for all the functions we might want such a classification to perform, would nonetheless entitle us to conclude that we knew in a general kind of way what was meant by "punishment." The definitions of punishment that have been formulated by philosophers have about them the look of just that sort of extrapolation. But the problems about punishment that are posed for resolution in a highly developed legal system such as ours do not, even in their definitional aspect, yield readily to any such simplistic exercise. Is the deportation of an alien to be classified as punishment? The denaturalization of a citizen who has served in a foreign army? The award of damages in a suit for breach of contract? The enforced hospitalization of a mentally ill person? Of a narcotics addict? The revocation of a driver's license? For repeated traffic violations? For the loss of eyesight? Countless examples could be given in which a major question to be decided by the authority with jurisdiction in a case is whether what is being done is punishment or something else.

Faced with the bewildering multiplicity of occasions on which such questions are posed and the equally bewildering multiplicity of consequences that an answer entails, one might well conclude that any effort to give general content to the concept of punishment is misguided, and that instead the inquiry in each case should be into the specific consequences, if any, that will follow from classifying action as punishment. If nothing depends on the answer, the question is irrelevant. If something depends on it, the answer should be arrived at by weighing the comparative desirability of the consequences thought to flow from possible alternative answers. This method of operation is sometimes referred to as "functional definition." Its explicit articulation, although not its origin, may be traced to the movement known as Legal Realism. It is an indispensable part of a lawyer's equipment, and probably the part soonest and most thoroughly acquired. Ask any moderately bright law student of three months' standing to define "punishment," and his answer will very likely be: "It depends on the consequence." Or, he may misquote

Holmes and tell you that general propositions do not decide concrete cases. (Holmes went on to say in the same passage: "But I think that the proposition just stated . . . will carry us far toward that end.") But the perspective of the law-applier, which is the ordinary perspective of the lawyer, dealing as lawyers do with one problem at a time, is not the perspective of the law-maker, who must generalize in advance. When the question is, as it is for us, what are the uses of punishment, it is no help to be told that the question cannot be intelligibly discussed without considering every possible situation in which calling something punishment will produce consequences different from those produced by calling it something else. And so the attempt must be made to give some general content to the concept.

Recent philosophical discussion has produced a definition of punishment that will serve as a starting point for our inquiry. This definition presents the standard case of punishment as exhibiting five characteristics:

(1) It must involve pain or other consequences normally considered unpleasant.

(2) It must be for an offense against legal rules.

(3) It must be imposed on an actual or supposed offender for his offense.

(4) It must be intentionally administered by human beings other than the offender.

(5) It must be imposed and administered by an authority constituted by a legal system against which the offense is committed.[2]

The last two of these characteristics present no difficulties for our purpose. They are designed merely to differentiate "legal punishment" from punishment inflicted by other human (or divine) agencies, presumably including the conscience of the person being punished. The first three, however, taken separately and as a unit, produce formidable difficulties that have been surprisingly ignored in recent discussions of the subject.

The difficulties that I perceive may be generally suggested by a simple question. Under the definitions given, which of the following actions is not to be regarded as punishment: (1) an award

[2] Hart, "Prolegomenon," pp. 4–5.

of damages against a motorist in favor of the pedestrian whom he has knocked down and injured; (2) an order enjoining the governor of Alabama from interfering with the enrollment of Negro students in the state university; (3) the commitment of a psychotic person to a state mental hospital.

I venture to say that in common usage few would regard any of these actions as punishment. Yet all of them satisfy the first of the criteria in the philosophic definition. The motorist is being forced to pay money; the governor is being prevented from dealing with the situation as he would wish to; the psychotic is being deprived of his liberty against his will. All, surely, are being subjected to "pain or other consequences normally considered unpleasant." The exponent of this definition might point to the second and third criteria as excluding the cases put above. The pain is not being inflicted "for" something called an "offense"; these persons are not "offenders." If we can assume that an "offender" is a person who commits an "offense," then the problem can be reduced to two questions: (1) what is meant by an "offense," and (2) when is punishment "for" an offense?[3]

In common usage the term offense refers to conduct that violates a legal norm. It seems clear enough that the motorist who carelessly runs down a pedestrian has breached a legal norm. So, it would seem, has the governor of Alabama when he interferes with the enjoyment of what has been authoritatively declared to be the legal right of Negroes to have access to the state's educational facilities. And, it may be plausibly maintained, the mentally ill person has subjected himself to the sanction of involuntary commitment by his failure to satisfy the legal requirement that he be able to conduct his affairs without presenting danger to himself or others. Nor can much comfort be derived from reliance on the preposition "for." Whether it means that the conduct in question is the reason why we inflict punishment or simply the occasion for inflicting it, it is undeniable that the

---

[3] Of course, this inquiry can be speedily terminated by that philosophical ploy known as the "definitional stop." My hypothetical cases, so the argument would run, do not involve the commission of "offenses." But I do not suppose that the proponents of the definition of punishment with which we are dealing would assert that "offense" is susceptible to definition by fiat any more than "punishment" is.

driver, the governor, and the psychotic are all being subjected to unpleasant consequences "for an offense." Yet, common sense rebels at the characterization of what is done in any of these three cases as punishment. The definition given is too broad.

The principal difficulty inheres in failure to differentiate the purposes and effects of inflicting pain. Broadly speaking, the legal system brings about the infliction of pain whenever something is done to a person that he would not wish to have done to him. And the occasion for doing so, broadly speaking, is always conduct or status. The standard case of an offense involves conduct: the occurrence of an identifiable, discrete event or events involving human activity. But offenses of status are by no means unknown to the law, including the criminal law. Here we are not talking about an event but about an identifiable human condition: being a vagrant, an alien, a neglected child, or whatever. It seems, then, that we cannot differentiate punishment from other modes of disposition simply by saying that it is pain inflicted for an offense. We have to go further and inquire what the purposes and effects of inflicting pain are thought to be.

PUNISHMENT, TREATMENT, AND OTHER SANCTIONS

When we talk about official infliction of pain, we are dealing with the large issue of sanctions, those rules of the legal order that prescribe the consequences of violating the primary norms that are meant to govern behavior. A definitive classification of sanctions poses problems that still await solution by students of jurisprudence. What I shall tentatively propose here is a fourfold classification of sanctions, distinguished in terms of their dominant purpose or effect. For purposes of this argument, it is important to distinguish carefully between two kinds of sanctions: Punishment and Treatment. These in turn may be distinguished from Compensation and Regulation, which I shall treat much more summarily.

Compensation I shall define as making another person whole following the infliction upon him of an actual or threatened injury. It always involves giving something to the injured person, and consequently always involves an identifiable beneficiary. The standard case is the award of damages to an injured pedestrian. The motorist whose conduct caused the injury is deprived for the benefit of the person he injured. Less obviously, the governor is deprived for the benefit of the Negro students. His freedom of action is restricted so that a threatened injury to others will be averted. The injunction, which binds him, is given to the Negro students. It anticipatorily makes them whole, and thus they are the identifiable beneficiaries.

It is the absence of this factor of benefit to identifiable individuals that serves primarily to distinguish between Compensation and Regulation. At this point, however, a cautionary word: few if any forms of official pain-infliction fall wholly into one or another of these four categories. In fact most involve elements of two or more categories, and attempts to distinguish them come down to inquiries about which category predominates. Examples of difficulties are premature at this point, because we have not yet distinguished the standard cases of Compensation, Regulation, Treatment, and Punishment one from another. For the moment it need simply be remembered that the categories are not pure.

Regulation may be defined as the control of future conduct for general purposes excluding the interests of identifiable beneficiaries. It is public rather than private. It differs from Compensation also in that it is typically administered by agencies of government. In prototype, Regulation resembles one branch of Compensation, the injunction or other special order directing an individual to do or not to do certain things in the future. The difference is that in the case of Regulation there is no identifiable beneficiary. Regulation may be legislative in form, e.g., a general directive that motorists obtain driver's licenses; or it may be adjudicative, e.g., an order by the Federal Trade Commission directing Company X to stop advertising that its cigarettes are good for you. Typically, Regulation can be reinforced by other forms of sanction. A good example is found in the antitrust laws. The government may bring a suit for an injunction against anticompetitive practices. That is a case of Regulation. The same anticompetitive practices may have injured or threatened to injure some other person, who may bring an action for injunctive relief and for damages. The sanctioning method here is Compensation. Finally, the same anticompetitive practices may provide the basis for the government to bring a criminal prosecution in which the responsible persons may be fined and put in jail. This is a case of Punishment.

It is not easy to articulate the distinctions between Treatment and Punishment; yet all would agree that cases can be put that in common word usage would be categorized as Treatment rather than Punishment, and vice versa. There is surely a difference between life imprisonment at hard labor inflicted on a convicted murderer, and the involuntary hospitalization of a person suffering from manic-depressive psychosis. The degree of unpleasantness, or severity, of the sanction is not, however, the differentiating characteristic. Thirty days in jail for disorderly conduct is much less unpleasant than a lifetime in the locked ward of a state mental hospital. Yet common usage will unhesitatingly classify the former as Punishment and the latter (perhaps not quite so unhesitatingly) as Treatment.

What is the difference? I suggest that it resides in two related considerations: (1) the difference in justifying purposes; (2) the larger role of the offending conduct in the case of Punishment. The primary purpose of Treatment is to benefit the person being treated. The focus is not on his conduct, past or future, but on helping him. There is always in the idea of Treatment a calculus of benefit and detriment to the person affected. Typically, this involves the imposition of a short-run detriment, such as the loss of liberty, in the interest of a long-run benefit, such as personal security and, on occasion, the improvement or elimination of the disabling condition. Sometimes the calculus is inadvertently erroneous; sometimes it is knowingly so, or hypocritical. But the calculus is always there. In common parlance, we say that the person being subjected to Treatment is "better off." Whether he is so in fact is an empirical question that should always be pressed as hard as it can be; but the justification for Treatment rests on the view that the person subjected to it is or probably will be "better off" as a consequence. This focus on amelioration carries a concomitant disregard for the offending conduct in which the person may have engaged. The offending conduct, if we want to call it

that, of being mentally ill, or a narcotics addict, or an unvacci-
nated person, will typically bring about the application of Treatment, but the Treatment is not ostensibly for the purpose of
doing anything about the conduct; it is for the purpose of increasing the offender's welfare.

Punishment, on the other hand, has one or both of two justifying aims: the prevention of undesired conduct, and retribution for perceived wrongdoing. But whichever it involves, or in
whatever proportion it may combine the two, the focus is on the
offending conduct. I do not mean by this that we may not consider the needs or deserts of the offender but only that the sine
qua non is the existence or occurrence of offending conduct.

The point at which the notions of Treatment and Punishment
come very close to each other is in the rehabilitative claims for
punishment (or treatment) that constitute a predominant feature
of modern thinking on the subject. But one feature that always
distinguishes a case of Punishment from one of Treatment is the
nature of the relationship between the offending conduct and
what we do to the person who has engaged in it. For example, by
saying that we may deal with a youth who seems likely to fall into
a life of crime either by locking him up or by providing him with
an education, we have not described the essential difference between Punishment and Treatment. If we send him to a school
pursuant to a judgment that he has engaged in offending conduct,
we are subjecting him to Punishment; if we think that he will
be better off in jail than on the streets and proceed to lock him
up without a determination that he has engaged in offending conduct, we are subjecting him to Treatment. Punishment may be
more painful than Treatment (as is usual), or it may be less painful; popular opinion to the contrary, the degree of painfulness
involved does not constitute the difference. The difference is that
in the case of Punishment we are dealing with a person because
he has engaged in offending conduct; our concern is either to
prevent the recurrence of such conduct, or to inflict what is
thought to be deserved pain, or to do both. In the case of Treatment there is no necessary relation between conduct and Treatment; we deal with the person as we do because we think he will
be "better off" as a consequence. We may think that the person

we punish will also be "better off" as a consequence, but that is not why, in any ultimate sense, we do it. We may, for example, wish him to be better off as an intermediate mode of ensuring that certain conduct will not take place; but the ultimate aim is the prevention of the offending conduct, not the betterment of the offender.

I have suggested that Punishment is inflicted for one or both of two purposes: to prevent the occurrence of offending conduct and to inflict the degree of pain that one who engages in such conduct is thought to deserve. Frequently the term Punishment is used in a way indicating that the user thinks it is coterminous with the second of these two purposes, which is frequently spoken of as the retributive purpose of the criminal law. In that usage, all nonretributive or preventive dispositions are spoken of as Treatment, whether imposed in the criminal process or elsewhere. Thus, Lady Wootton criticizes lawyers for being "wholly unable to envisage a system in which sentence is not automatically equated with 'punishment.' "[4]

Lawyers may perhaps be excused for their reluctance to think about the outcome of the criminal process as Treatment or Punishment, according to whether the animating purpose in any particular case is preventive or retributive. As we shall presently see, it can usually be described (as can the criminal law as a whole) as an amalgam of both. But it is enough for present purposes to say that Lady Wootton's inclination to speak of much present-day sentencing as Treatment is not currently useful. Whatever else may or may not be thought of as Punishment, the category is generally thought to include whatever happens to people in the criminal process. The substantive points underlying Lady Wootton's submission, for which she is perhaps the most articulate and lucid spokesman, require extended analysis. The point of word usage does not; for the issues are not such as can be settled by a definitional stop.

Treatment often involves consideration of the betterment of others as well as of the person being treated. We compel smallpox vaccinations to protect others as well as the person we vaccinate. We hospitalize the mentally ill to protect others from harm as

[4] Barbara Wootton, *Crime and the Criminal Law* (London, 1963), p. 50.

well as to protect the persons we hospitalize. The greater our
concern for the interests of others, as compared with our concern
for the interests of the person subjected to Treatment, the more
likely it is that we will not think of what is being done as Treatment. When we get to the point of imposing sanctions primarily
for the purpose of protecting others, we have what I would be
inclined to think of as Punishment, particularly if its imposition
has been triggered, as is commonly the case, by the occurrence of
disturbing conduct. The leading practical example today is the
acquittal of a person of a criminal charge on the ground of insanity followed by his commitment to an institution. His disposition should in our terms be regarded as a case of Punishment,
although not as a case of criminal punishment.[5]

So long as we can tie our concern about a person's future activity to something he has done in the past—some act that he has
committed or some dangerous trait that he has manifested (usually through an act)—and so long as our main concern is with
the protection of others rather than the betterment of the person
being dealt with, it seems to me misleading to call our way of
dealing with him anything but Punishment. It needs to be said,
of course, that in making judgments of this sort we are not bound
by legal labels, but are obligated to examine what has happened
in the particular case at hand. We would be justified in saying,
for example, that while the hospitalization of the mentally ill
must in general be classified as Treatment, the hospitalization
of a certain person to suit the convenience of his family, without
any representation that he will be better off as a consequence, is
Punishment. But word usage is ambiguous on the point. We tend
in common usage to give a narrower meaning to Punishment and
a wider meaning to Treatment than I have suggested may be
analytically appropriate.

The reason for the ambiguity in word usage is not hard to see.
The fact is that Treatment, like Punishment, is triggered by conduct. A decision for Treatment is determined almost invariably
by observing conduct that is thought to indicate a need for Treatment. However, the conduct need not constitute an offense, and
often does not. A man who threatens to kill his wife or himself

[5] See below, p 35.

is engaging in observable conduct, but the conduct does not necessarily constitute an offense for which he is liable to Punishment. To take a more extreme case, a man who has disturbing dreams or who is oppressed by an overwhelming sense of anxiety may alert others to his need for Treatment by pleading for help. Although his pleas constitute conduct, he is not liable to Punishment.

As the behavioral sciences become increasingly useful for measuring and predicting probable future conduct, this nexus between conduct and Treatment may tend to be attenuated. Thus, through such projective tests as the Rorschach it may become increasingly probable that we can predict disturbing conduct before it ever takes place. In some far-off Utopia (or anti-Utopia) whole populations may be subjected to psychological tests that will reveal the need for Treatment before conduct triggers a demand for it. Compulsion, through the legal process, may then be exerted to force possible candidates for Treatment to undergo it. When that day comes, the distinctions between Punishment and Treatment that we have been drawing will be seen in a much clearer light, but the principle will be the same. Treatment will not be "for" conduct any more than it is now. But the Rorschach test will perform the same function that observed conduct now performs: it will be the occasion for invoking Treatment, not the reason for it.

This distinction is blurred in contemporary practice for two reasons. First, as already pointed out, conduct triggers Treatment. But conduct has to be observed, recorded, and established. Somebody has to make an authoritative determination that the conduct has in fact taken place and that it indicates the necessity of Treatment. In other words, there must be fact-finding and law-applying processes to determine whether or not Treatment is indicated. These differ in many ways from the fact-finding and law-applying processes that we use to determine whether or not Punishment is indicated but the two sets of processes have much in common. To a detached observer there may not be any significant difference between a determination that X has committed the offense of public drunkenness and a determination that X is an alcoholic, particularly when the end result of both determi-

nations is a loss of liberty for X. Important as the distinction between the two determinations may be for the purposes of legal
handling, it is undeniably blurred by the similarity in outcome
of the two processes.

The other reason why the distinction is hard to draw is that
a vast range of conduct may be dealt with, at the option of some
decision-maker, either by Punishment or Treatment. The alcoholic may be punished for the offense of drunkenness by being
cured of his disease; or he may be treated and cured without
being punished. The narcotics addict may be punished for illegal
possession of heroin by being sent to an institution where strenuous efforts are made to cure him of his addiction, or he may be
treated and cured without being punished. These things may be
done in the name of Treatment or of Punishment or of both.
Small wonder that there is confusion about what is being done in
any given case.

We are now in a position to observe some of the characteristic
operations of a sanctioning system, and to comment on the mixed
character of particular sanctions. An award of treble damages in
a private antitrust action is, in terms of the categories previously
described, a mixed case of Compensation and Punishment. The
defendant is making the plaintiff whole for the damage he has
caused him. He is also being punished for his breach of the antitrust laws, the Punishment consisting of an exaction beyond what
is necessary to compensate his victim for the injury caused. The
same mixed sanctions are imposed informally when a jury mulcts
a rich motorist who has run down a poor pedestrian for a sum
of damages greatly in excess of what normally would be awarded
as Compensation. If the disparity is acute, the judge may reduce
the award of damages to an amount that he deems fairly compensatory, thereby vindicating the proposition that an ordinary suit
for personal injuries is not the appropriate occasion for the infliction of Punishment. A delinquent taxpayer may be assessed
interest on the amount that he owes, plainly a compensatory exaction designed to make the government whole for the injury
sustained by reason of not having had the use of the taxpayer's
money as soon as it became legally entitled to it. He may also be
assessed, if he has committed fraud, what is revealingly called a

penalty. This may in part be Compensation, to make up to the government the cost of uncovering the fraud, but it is also Punishment, imposed on account of the fraud and in order to ensure that others will not commit fraud in the future.

A REVISED DEFINITION

We can now return to the definition of Punishment with which we started and try to bring it into conformity with the points we have been making. It will suffice, I think, to add to our five original characteristics a sixth, reading as follows: "It must be imposed for the dominant purpose of preventing offenses against legal rules or of exacting retribution from offenders, or both." As amended, the definition serves to exclude those cases of Compensation, of Regulation, and of Treatment that might otherwise fall within the defined category, and to make an intelligible distinction between Punishment and other sanctions used in the legal system.

Before leaving this initial problem of definition, it may be desirable to take account of a very different view of Punishment, one widely held among workers in the correctional and allied fields. This view receives forthright expression in a statement by the English criminologist Herman Mannheim:

Is it an essential element of punishment that it should be an evil? From the point of view of the offender, the answer to the latter question has to be in the negative since individual views as to what constitutes an evil are too different to be met by a comparatively limited choice of penalties. Punishment can therefore be defined only as a form of treatment that is intended to be an evil. Certain modern methods of treating offenders, such as probation or psychological treatment, which are intended to be purely beneficial, can, strictly speaking, no longer be brought under the conception of punishment.[6]

Under this view, a disposition that is intended to be hurtful by those who prescribe or administer it is Punishment and a disposition that is intended by them to be beneficial is Treatment. This view is not easy to accept. In the first place, it is a non se-

---

[6] *Chambers's Encyclopaedia* (new rev. ed., 1967), XI, 362.

quitur to assert that because the judgment of those penalized cannot be taken as definitive, the *only* way of defining a penalty as punishment is by whether or not those who prescribe it intend it to be an evil. Moreover, it is hard to agree that the views of those affected are irrelevant in determining whether how they are treated is an evil. The fact, if it is a fact, that there are more views of what constitutes an evil than there are possible penalties, seems irrelevant to the question whether there is not some consensus among persons affected about whether what is being done to them is an evil.

Mannheim's definition is unacceptable for two reasons: it ignores the element of compulsion, and it makes the distinction between Punishment and Treatment turn on the motives of those who prescribe or administer the disposition of a case. By ignoring the element of compulsion, it understates the consensus that those most directly affected by the disposition are likely to have toward it. Whatever is done to people against their inclination will probably appear to them to be an evil. They may face it with resignation or rebellion, but they will nonetheless perceive it as an evil. Although they may prefer probation or psychological therapy (taking Mannheim's examples) to more severe measures, their ultimate preference would be to be let alone entirely. To send a man for psychological therapy who wishes not to be sent is to subject him to something that he regards as painful and therefore evil, quite apart from whether he or anyone else thinks that such therapy is likely to be helpful.

The other deficiency in Mannheim's position is even more serious. It focuses on what an interested party intends rather than on what a detached observer thinks, thereby depriving the distinction of any pretense to objectivity. If a prison warden thinks that his inmates are better off in his custody than they would be in the world outside, then by Mannheim's definition what he is administering is Treatment rather than Punishment. If the legislature that passes a compulsory commitment statute for narcotics addicts is motivated by hostility toward addicts, commitment is Punishment; if it is motivated by compassion, commitment is Treatment. And if it is motivated by both hostility and compassion? Other objections aside, what use can possibly be made of such a definition?

Other objections cannot be left aside, because they demonstrate that Mannheim's definition not only is unintelligible but leads to quite dangerous consequences. Assuming that our dominant purpose in depriving a man of his liberty is to reduce the likelihood that he will commit further offenses (rather than to make him, as opposed to the rest of us, better off), why should the disposition made of him, however enlightened and humane, be characterized as Treatment rather than as Punishment? Only, it seems, to assuage the feelings of those who carry out the judgment. It is quite understandable that sensitive men involved in what has been called the "grim negativism" of the correctional process should wish to have their activities dissociated from anything as unpleasant-sounding as Punishment. But there are good reasons for denying them that psychic gratification. Their euphemistic language tends to obscure the fact that they are acting against the will of the subject and not primarily for his benefit, and in effect are depriving him of rights that he would enjoy if it were plain that he was being subjected to Punishment. To allow the characterization to turn on the intention of the administrator is to encourage hypocrisy and unconscious self-deception.

The point is, of course, one of word usage. There may be good reasons why words ought not to be used in certain ways, but normally the first requirement of word usage is current intelligibility. Uncertainties about the proper basis for the institution of punishment and doubts engendered by what are thought to be advances in scientific knowledge about the etiology of antisocial behavior, may in the end bring about a shift in people's thinking and in their word usage. Surely Punishment has sufficiently retained the connotation ascribed to it above that it is not quixotic to describe as Punishment all ways of dealing with people that are marked by these features: (1) the presence of an offense; (2) the infliction of pain on account of the commission of the offense; (3) a dominant purpose that is neither to compensate someone injured by the offense nor to better the offender's condition but to prevent further offenses or to inflict what is thought to be deserved pain on the offender. That, at any rate, is the sense in which the word Punishment will be used in this book.

To celebrate this passing of the definitional point, we will now revert to the use of the lower-case "p" in speaking of punishment. A perhaps unnecessary caveat: the definition does not tell us whether a given case is a case of punishment or not. It simply provides criteria for the intelligible discussion of that problem.

CHAPTER THREE

Justifications for Criminal Punishment

INTRODUCTION

Criminal punishment means simply any particular disposition or the range of permissible dispositions that the law authorizes (or appears to authorize) in cases of persons who have been judged through the distinctive processes of the criminal law to be guilty of crimes. Not all punishment is criminal punishment but all criminal punishment is punishment. Punitive damages imposed in a civil suit constitute punishment but not criminal punishment. The deportation of an alien, under our present legal arrangements, is punishment but not criminal punishment. Punishment is a concept; criminal punishment is a legal fact. This important distinction is obscured by loose references in judicial opinions to "punishment" when what is meant is "criminal punishment." For example the deportation of an alien for membership in the Communist Party under a statute that made such membership a ground for deportation after the alien's membership had terminated was upheld by the Supreme Court against the claim, among others, that it constituted ex post facto punishment in contravention of the constitutional prohibition.[1] The Court refused to characterize the deportation as punishment, or so they said. What they were refusing to call it was not punishment considered as a general concept, but rather a particular kind of punishment, criminal or perhaps quasi-criminal. If they

---

[1] Galvan v. Press, 347 U.S. 522, 531 (1954).

had agreed that the deportation was quasi-criminal punishment, it would fall within the prohibition of the ex post facto clause. In legal usage, the term punishment ordinarily has this additional element.

The range of permissible punishments is at the present time very broad, ranging from death, at one extreme, to a suspended sentence at the other. Criminal punishment always includes but is not limited to a formal judgment of guilt. Typically, this judgment is entered when the trier of fact, judge or jury, determines that the defendant is guilty of the offense charged. In a sense this legal usage departs somewhat from common word usage. When Hermann Goering committed suicide in prison following his conviction of war crimes by the Nuremberg Tribunal, it was said of him that he had escaped punishment. It is true that he had escaped the full measure of punishment to which he was potentially subject by the Tribunal's sentence of death. But in contemplation of law, a significant part of his punishment had already occurred, in that he had been found guilty as charged. This idea is not totally foreign to common usage, as can be seen by the plea frequently voiced on behalf of a convicted defendant before sentencing that "he has already been punished enough." And indeed, if he is a respectable member of the community who wants the good opinion of his fellows and of society, he has in a relevant sense already suffered some punishment. Thus the formal announcement of a criminal conviction is itself a form of criminal punishment and one that in many cases may be at least as potent as any other likely to be imposed.

 In my view, there are two and only two ultimate purposes to be served by criminal punishment: the deserved infliction of suffering on evildoers and the prevention of crime. It is possible to distinguish a host of more specific purposes, but in the end all of them are simply intermediate modes of one or the other of the two ultimate purposes. These two purposes are almost universally thought of as being incompatible; and until recently, moral philosophers, who are the arbiters as well as the combatants in this struggle, have tended to assume that one or the other of these purposes must be justifiable to the exclusion of the other. My main point here is that, not simply as a description of existing reality but as a normative prescription for legal action, the institution of criminal punishment draws substance from both of these ultimate purposes; it would be socially damaging in the extreme to discard either. Before arguing this point, however, it may be desirable to elaborate somewhat the description of the two ultimate purposes of punishment.

RETRIBUTION

The retributive view rests on the idea that it is right for the wicked to be punished: because man is responsible for his actions, he ought to receive his just deserts. The view can take either of two main versions: the revenge theory or the expiation theory. Revenge as a justification for punishment is deeply ingrained in human experience, and goes back at least as far as the *lex talionis*: an eye for an eye, a tooth for a tooth, and, we might add, a life for a life. Its marks on the criminal process are similarly deep, the most conspicuous example today being the death penalty for murder. If, as F. H. Bradley has observed, the revenge morality represents the view of the man in the street, then punishment can be seen as a way of satisfying what is essentially a community blood lust. Thus it is an important sociological question whether this view is as widely held today as it was in Victorian England.

It was a distinguished Victorian judge and historian of criminal law, Sir James Fitzjames Stephen, who is known as the most eloquent exponent of the revenge theory, but curiously enough his views have utilitarian underpinnings. To him the punishment of criminals was simply a desirable expression of the hatred and fear aroused in the community by criminal acts. In the famous passage already noted Stephen observed that punishment bears the same relation to the appetite for revenge as marriage bears to the sexual appetite.[2] The figure is an arresting one, but it does not express a pure revenge theory. Instead, it conveys a disguised utilitarian position: punishment is justifiable because it provides an orderly outlet for emotions that, denied it, would express themselves in socially less acceptable ways.

[2] See above, p. 11.

This is but one example of the ways in which an ostensibly retributionist theory may have an implicit utilitarian connotation. We are somehow not content to say that criminals should be punished because *we* hate them and want to hurt them. It has to be because others hate them and would, were it not for our prudence in providing them with this spectacle, stage a far worse one of their own. This kind of hypocrisy is endemic in arguments about the death penalty, but it does not seem to be empirically verified. Lynchings do not, as this theory would lead us to conclude, seem to increase in places that have abolished capital punishment.

The other principal version of the retributive view is that only through suffering punishment can the criminal expiate his sin. Atonement through suffering has been a major theme in religious thought through the ages, and it doubtless plays a role in thought about secular punishment as well. In this view the emphasis is shifted from our demands on the criminal and becomes a question of demands that the criminal does or should make on himself to reconcile himself to the social order. In the absence of assurance that his sense of guilt is equal to the demands made upon it, we help to reinforce it by providing an external expression of guilt.

It hardly matters which aspect of the theory is espoused. The result is the same. The criminal is to be punished simply because he has committed a crime. It makes little difference whether we do this because we think we owe it to him or because we think he owes it to us. Each theory rests on a figure of speech. Revenge means that the criminal is paid back; expiation means that he pays back. The revenge theory treats all crimes as if they were certain crimes of physical violence: you hurt *X*; we will hurt you. The expiation theory treats all crimes as if they were financial transactions: you got something from *X*; you must give equivalent value. Underlying both figures of speech and rendering irrelevant a choice between the figure to be employed is the thought that it is right for punishment to be inflicted on persons who commit crimes. This familiar version of the retributive position, which I shall call the affirmative version, has no useful place in a theory of justification for punishment, because what it expresses is nothing more than dogma, unverifiable and on its face

implausible. The usefulness of the retributive position resides, as
we shall see later, in what it denies rather than in what it affirms.

UTILITARIAN PREVENTION: DETERRENCE

The utilitarian or preventive position, by contrast, has considerable appeal although, as we shall see, it does not suffice as a
justification for punishment. Its premise is that punishment, as
an infliction of pain, is unjustifiable unless it can be shown that
more good is likely to result from inflicting than from withholding it. The good that is thought to result from punishing criminals is the prevention or reduction of a greater evil, crime. There
are many different, and often inconsistent, ways in which punishment may prevent the commission of crimes, but the inconsis-
tencies should not be allowed to obscure the fact that the desired
result is the same in every case.

The classic theory of prevention is what is usually described
as deterrence: the inhibiting effect that punishment, either
actual or threatened, will have on the actions of those who are
otherwise disposed to commit crimes. Deterrence, in turn, involves a complex of notions. It is sometimes described as having
two aspects: after-the-fact inhibition of the person being punished, special deterrence, and inhibition in advance by threat or
example, general deterrence. These two are quite different although they are often confused in discussion of problems of punishment. For example, it is sometimes said that a high rate of
repeat offenses, or recidivism as it is technically known, among
persons who have already been once subjected to criminal punishment shows that deterrence does not work. The fact of recidivism
may throw some doubt on the efficacy of *special* deterrence, but
a moment's reflection will show that it says nothing about the
effect of *general* deterrence.[3] An even more preposterous argument is sometimes heard to the effect that the very existence of
crime or (more moderately but equally fallaciously) the increase
in crime rates is evidence that deterrence does not work. Unless
we know what the crime rate would be if we did not punish

[3] In the interest of clarity I shall reserve the term "deterrence" for general deterrence and shall use "intimidation" for special deterrence.

criminals, the conclusion is unfounded. It may well be that some forms of punishment, through their excessive severity, produce a net increase in the amount of crime, but that is a very different issue (although one often confusingly invoked by people skeptical of the deterrent efficacy of punishment). Since these same people are typically proponents of rehabilitation as a goal of punishment (also, be it noted, in the interest of prevention) and since punishment is not the less punishment for being rehabilitative in purpose, it is evident that the argument is beside the point. As so often in debates on this issue, the problem of how severe given forms of punishment should be is confused with the problem of whether punishment is itself justifiable. It cannot be too often emphasized that the severity of punishment is a question entirely separate from that of whether punishment in any form is justifiable.

The idea of deterrence as a mode of crime prevention is often derided on psychological grounds. Criminals do not, so these critics say, pause to reflect upon possible consequences before committing a crime; they act upon obscure impulses that they can neither account for nor control. We may agree that the criticism is probably well-founded, but it is not applicable to very much of what is comprehended by the idea of deterrence. If the term deterrence (like most such high-level abstractions) is to have any functional utility, we must recognize that it does not describe a simple entity. The "one word–one meaning" fallacy is nowhere more pernicious than when words so broadly connotative as deterrence are used as if they described things rather than clusters of ideas.

The modern psychological criticism of deterrence turns out on inspection to be based on a very simple model, one almost might say a caricature, of what is signified by the term. The model is Jeremy Bentham's, and it is a model of great, although not unlimited, usefulness. It assumes a perfectly hedonistic, perfectly rational actor whose object it is to maximize pleasure and minimize pain. To such an actor contemplating the possibility of a criminal act the decision is based on a calculus: How much do I stand to gain by doing it? How much do I stand to lose if I am caught doing it? What are the chances of my getting away with it? What is the balance of gain and loss as discounted by the chance of apprehension? The purpose of criminal punishment, on this model, is to inject into the calculus a sufficient prospect of loss or pain to reduce to zero the attractiveness of the possible gain.

The psychological critics reject the reality of this model.[4] In doing so, they substitute for it a model of man as governed by largely unconscious drives that impel him to act quite without regard to any rational principle of pleasure-seeking. That model, like the Benthamite model that these critics deride, is useful; but like the Benthamite model, it does not come close to exhausting the possibilities of human existence. The psychological model, if I may call it that, represents the criminal as murderer—and not as murderer for profit but as perpetrator of the crime of passion. He is the man who kills on impulse because he hates his father, he is sexually inadequate, he lacks control, and so forth. The polemics of the psychological critics are full of case histories that conform to this model. No one would deny their reality, but they do not tell the whole story. The Benthamite model may well be a more nearly accurate representation of the acquisitive criminal: the burglar, the embezzler, the con man. Perhaps the purest modern instance is the man who cheats on his income tax. While we should not overlook the significance of irrational drives in even such carefully planned crimes as these often are, it still seems clear that they have a rational hedonistic component. The Benthamite model has considerable relevance to cases of this sort, which—although they do not necessarily dominate the field of criminal activity—cannot safely be ignored.

My point, of course, is not that the Benthamite model of deterrence explains everything, but rather that it explains something about human behavior. The criminal law is a human institution that needs to take account of as many possibilities of human action as seem inherent in the human condition. Bentham gave us a hold on a piece of reality. That hold should not be abandoned simply because it is partial, especially if one concludes that complete views of reality are unattainable.

All that I have been concerned to show so far is that even the

---

[4] E.g., Walter Bromberg, *Crime and the Mind* (New York, 1965); and Gregory Zilboorg, *The Psychology of the Criminal Act and Punishment* (New York, 1954).

caricature of deterrence resulting from a restriction of the idea
to the dictates of rational hedonism has some validity as a basis
for punishment. But much more needs to be said about the
cluster of ideas validly subsumed under the heading of deterrence. The warning given by the threat of punishment as reinforced by the occasional spectacle of its actual infliction has a
wider meaning than Bentham's model suggests. One need not
see man as an isolated atom, intent only upon making rational
choices that will advance his own pleasure, to see deterrence at
work. Let us expand our view to take account of what we know
of man as a creature whose impulses are subjected from birth to
the manifold processes of socialization and whose reactions to
situations in which he finds himself are largely automatic. To
deny on that view the reality of deterrence is to call into doubt
many of our hypotheses about the socializing capacity of human
institutions such as the family, the school, the peer group, the
community. Or, equally implausibly, it is to single out one social
institution—the criminal law—and deny to it the compulsive
force that we ascribe to every other institution that conditions
human behavior.

Our hypotheses about the operation of general deterrence
should be broadened to include also the effect of punishment—
and indeed, of all the institutions of criminal justice—on the
totality of conscious and unconscious motivations that govern
the behavior of men in society. On the conscious level, moral
norms are learned and the learning is reinforced by threats of
unpleasant consequences that will follow if those norms are disregarded. The degree to which the norms are accepted depends
largely on the vividness with which coercive threats are made.
And it is not merely the physical unpleasantness of punishment
—loss of life, loss of liberty, loss of property—that makes the impression. Feelings of shame resulting from the social disgrace of
being punished as a criminal are feared also. And it is not only
Bentham's rational hedonists who are touched by the power of
deterrence, but all those who are sufficiently socialized to feel
guilty about breaking social rules and whose experience has led
them to associate feelings of guilt with forms of punishment. It
may be conceded that it is the law-abiding whose moral systems
are affected in this way by the force of deterrence. But to say that

is not to minimize the force of what is being done, unless we are prepared to say that the threat of punishment, involving as it does both physical and psychic pain, has no role to play in making people law-abiding and in keeping them that way.

At least as much importance attaches to the effect of the threat of punishment on behavior governed by unconscious motivations. On this level, "threat" becomes a much subtler and more complex concept than either the rational hedonists or their critics have been prepared to recognize. The existence of a "threat" helps to create patterns of conforming behavior and thereby to reduce the number of occasions on which the choice of a criminal act presents itself. Every one of us is confronted daily by situations in which criminal behavior is a possible alternative. Sometimes the presentation is sufficiently vivid that we think about it and reject the criminal alternative. More frequently and more significantly, we automatically and without conscious cognition follow a pattern of learned behavior that excludes the criminal alternative without our even thinking about it. Indeed, the arguments for the efficacy of deterrence may become stronger the more one departs from a rational free-will model and the more one accepts an unconsciously impelled, psychological determinism as an accurate description of human conduct. There seems to be a paradox in the rejection by some psychologists of the idea that the threat of punishment (itself reflecting a legal model) can induce people unconsciously to adopt patterns of law-abiding behavior. Guilt and punishment are, after all, what the superego is all about.

The socializing and habit-forming effects of the threat of punishment are not limited to simple, literal observation of threats being made and carried out. There is heavy symbolic significance in the operation of the criminal sanction; for the process of ascribing guilt, responsibility, and punishment goes on day after day against the background of all human history. The vocabulary of punishment (itself heavily influenced by legal concepts and models) with which we become acquainted beginning in early childhood impresses us—some more than others—with the gravity of antisocial conduct. The ritual of the criminal trial becomes for all of us a kind of psychodrama in which we participate vicariously, a morality play in which innocence is protected, injury requited, and the wrongdoer punished. It is not simply the threat of punishment or its actual imposition that contributes to the total deterrent effect but the entire criminal process, standing as a paradigm of good and evil, in which we are reminded by devices far more subtle than literal threats that the wicked do not flourish. These public rituals, it is plausible to suppose, strengthen the identification of the majority with a value-system that places a premium on law-abiding behavior.

When the criminal is seen caught in the toils of this process, any desire people may have that he suffer reinforces the values against which he has offended. In this sense, the retributive and utilitarian justifications for punishment tend to coalesce. The sense of fitness (which, as Holmes wryly remarked, is unqualified only with respect to our neighbors) that we feel at the spectacle of merited suffering becomes a prop for our own sense of identification with law-abidingness. This is, then, an important part of the utility of punishment: not, as the simplistic notion goes, that criminal justice prevents lynching by satisfying community passions for revenge, but rather that blood lust properly tamed reinforces individual rectitude. The symbols change and not all of them are essential; we get along well enough without wigged barristers. But the symbolic richness of the criminal process is a powerful deterrent, something we too often forget especially when desiccating reforms are advanced in the name of the "treatment" of offenders.

When the threat of punishment is removed or reduced, either through legislative repeal or (as ordinarily occurs) through the inaction of enforcement authorities, conduct that has previously been repressed (in two senses of the word) tends to increase. We are so familiar with the phenomenon that there may be no more convincing demonstration than this of the effectiveness and complexity of deterrence. When, for example, laws repressing certain kinds of sexual conduct are no longer enforced with any regularity, the conduct in question is promoted, not merely because people feel that a threat has been removed but also, and probably more significantly, because the subtle process of value reinforcement through the rites of criminal stigmatization comes to a stop.

I have elaborated the elements of deterrence theory because the idea of deterrence has fallen into considerable and undeserved disrepute. I do not want, however, to overestimate the importance of its role in any rational penal system. Deterrence has its limits, and inattention to those limits has doubtless helped to discredit it. To start with the most obvious point, deterrence is not the only mode of prevention available to us, and any ultimate appraisal of its role in a system of crime prevention must wait upon a comprehensive presentation of other possible modes, and an examination of the extent to which they use techniques and work toward goals inconsistent with those peculiar to deterrence. Beyond that, it is clear that the deterrent role of the criminal law is effective mainly with those who are subject to the dominant socializing influences of the day. That it is effective with them is its strength. That it is not effective with others is its countervailing weakness. Deterrence does not threaten those ① whose lot in life is already miserable beyond the point of hope. It does not improve the morals of those whose value systems are closed to further modification, either ② psychologically (in the case of the disoriented or the conscienceless) or ③ culturally (as in the case of the outsider or the member of a deviant subculture). And, where the prohibited conduct is the expression of sufficiently compulsive drives, deterrence is made possible, if at all, only by cruelly rigorous enforcement, widespread repression, and a considerable drain on human and economic resources—a price we may well shrink from paying.

limits

SPECIAL DETERRENCE OR INTIMIDATION

A second utilitarian justification for punishment is its asserted propensity to reduce or eliminate the commission of future crimes by the person being punished. Again, the concept rests primarily on a rational, hedonistic model of behavior. Once subjected to the pain of punishment, so the theory runs, the individual is conditioned to avoid in the future conduct that he knows is likely to result again in the infliction of pain through punishment.

No aspect of preventive theory has been subjected to such a

barrage of criticism in recent years as has the idea of intimidation. The criticism centers on what is thought to be a conclusion
emerging from empirical study of recidivism among offenders.
Although there is much disagreement over specific figures and
even more over their significance, it is universally recognized
that persons who have served prison sentences have a high rate
of reconviction, perhaps as much as fifty per cent. Superficially,
this well-documented fact does appear to raise substantial questions about the efficacy of intimidation. Yet, as we shall see, there
are reasons not to reject out of hand its usefulness in crime prevention.

First, there is the obvious but frequently overlooked fact that
we do not know how much higher the recidivism rate would be
if there had been no criminal punishment in the first place. It is
not unreasonable to suppose that the rate would probably be
somewhat higher if persons who committed crimes were free to
continue committing them without being punished. Second, the
argument against intimidation often confuses the severity of
punishment with the fact of punishment. By singling out those
who have been subjected to the relatively severe sanction of imprisonment, the generalization ignores the effect of such punishment measures as probation and suspended sentences on persons
who commit crimes. As we have previously pointed out, the very
fact of criminal conviction is itself a form of punishment, particularly to the relatively law-abiding citizen. To be detected in the
commission of crime and then subjected to the stigma of a criminal conviction may in itself have a strong impact on the future
behavior of the offender. The studies we have on the subject
seem to demonstrate that those subjected to the relatively less
severe sanctions of probation or of early release from prison on
parole have a lower rate of recidivism than do persons subjected
to more severe punishment. A related point is that by and large
those who are selected for severe punishment are less likely to
conform with standards of law-abidingness. They are the more
experienced, more hardened criminals who are for one reason or
another not amenable to intimidation.

It should also be noted that recidivism rates appear to vary
greatly for different types of crime. We need far more specific

research than we have yet had on this point, but it does seem clear that "crime" is much too vague an entity to be studied wholesale as the basis for any conclusions about the efficacy of intimidation. There may well be types of offenses (or types of offenders) that are relatively immune to the influence of intimidation. Once such categories are established by empirical evidence rather than, as now, by hunch, the role of intimidation in a system of punishment for such offenses will need to be reevaluated. But we are certainly not in a position now to say that the concept has no utility. Finally, it must be remembered that punishment may serve, and ordinarily will serve, more than one intermediate goal of prevention. Even if intimidation does not seem to be, standing alone, a sufficient justification for punishment, that is no reason to reject the contribution it may make to crime prevention if preventive goals are pursued in the name of such other justifications as deterrence and rehabilitation. To take only one example, there is no hard line separating the effects of rehabilitation and intimidation. The convict who goes straight after his release may do so because he is a "better" man, but he may also do so because he is the same old man under better control. If he refrains from committing further crimes at least in part because he does not want to be punished again, it would take a very lofty view of human nature to assert that he has not been "rehabilitated."

Perhaps the most cogent criticism of intimidation derives from observation of the effect of inhumane punishment on offenders. The combination of the corrupting influence of criminal associations in prison with the feelings of bitterness, hatred, and desire for revenge on society that are engendered by inhumane treatment in a backward prison may well produce a net loss in crime prevention. Whatever feelings of intimidation are produced on the prisoner by the severity of his punishment may be outweighed by the deterioration of his character in prison. His punishment may contribute to the effect of deterrence on others, but in the process he is lost to society.

This antinomy embodies one of the great dilemmas of punishment, reflecting the conflict among intermediate justifications that have the common ultimate goal of crime prevention. Punishment must be severe enough to exert a restraining effect on others, but not so severe as to turn the person being punished into a more antisocial creature than he was before. We will have more to say at a later point about the issue of severity. It is enough now to note that we have not as a society displayed much imagination in this regard. Severity has been by and large equated with brutality; and we have neglected the possibility that not everything that men fear and wish to avoid must necessarily have a brutalizing effect on them if they are exposed to it. Until we have devised measures that avoid this dilemma, we are wise to be cautious in our reliance on intimidation as a guide to penal action.

BEHAVIORAL PREVENTION: INCAPACITATION

The simplest justification for any punishment that involves the use of physical restraint is that for its duration the person on whom it is being inflicted loses entirely or nearly so the capacity to commit further crimes. By contrast with the idea of general deterrence, about whose empirical basis there is continuing disagreement, the empirical basis for incapacitation is clear beyond argument. So long as we keep a man in prison he will have no opportunity at all to commit certain kinds of crimes—burglary, obtaining property by false pretenses, and tax fraud are three of the many types precluded in this way. And his opportunities to commit certain other kinds—such as assault or murder—are greatly diminished by confinement. Of course, such extreme forms of punishment as execution and solitary confinement for life can assure total and near total incapacitation. In a society that was single-mindedly devoted to the repression of crime as a paramount objective of social life, incapacitation would be the most immediately plausible utilitarian justification for the punishment of offenders. On further inspection, however, its plausibility diminishes.

We may start by noting that incapacitation differs radically from general deterrence as a mode of crime prevention and that, in consequence, it must be justified on different bases. Deterrence operates according to the nature of the offense. The personal

characteristics of the numerous people who are every day punished for committing crimes cannot be known by the public, to
whom the deterrent threat is addressed. The threat of punishment or the spectacle of its imposition creates general awareness
that people who do certain kinds of things will be punished if
they are caught, no matter what their personal characteristics
are. Incapacitation has a much subtler and more attenuated relationship to the nature of the offense. To the extent that there
is any connection at all, it rests on a prediction that a person who
commits a certain kind of crime is likely to commit either more
crimes of the same sort or other crimes of other sorts. This latter
prediction does not seem to figure largely in the justification for
incapacitation as a mode of prevention. To the extent that we
lock up burglars because we fear that they will commit further
offenses, our prediction is not that they will if left unchecked
violate the antitrust laws, or cheat on their income taxes, or
embezzle money from their employers; it is that they will commit
further burglaries, or other crimes associated with burglary, such
as homicide or bodily injury. The premise is that the person may
have a tendency to commit further crimes like the one for which
he is now being punished and that punishing him will restrain
him from doing so.

Incapacitation, then, is a mode of punishment that uses the
fact that a person has committed a crime of a particular sort as
the basis for assessing his personality and then predicting that
he will commit further crimes of that sort. It is an empirical
question in every case whether the prediction is a valid one. To
the extent that the prediction is valid, utilitarian ethics can ap-
prove the use of punishment for incapacitative purposes, on the
view that the pain inflicted on persons who are punished is less
than the pain that would be inflicted on their putative victims
and on society at large if those same persons were left free to commit further offenses.

It will be seen that this proposition is highly dubious when
applied to the issue of whether all of the people who commit a
certain kind of offense should be punished for it. How can we
say in advance that the quantum of pain likely to be caused by,
let us say, murderers as a group if they are left unpunished would

exceed the quantum of pain imposed on them by punishment? If we could be sure that they as a group are likely to cause significantly more deaths or bodily injuries than the population at large, we would have the beginnings of a rationale for punishing them as a group in the name of incapacitation. We may have such a basis for offenses that can be shown to be highly repetitive, but we do not have an *a priori* basis for saying it about offenses in general. The incapacitative justification, then, when addressed to the question whether people who commit a certain kind of offense should be punished for it, is no stronger than the empirical evidence available that offenses of that kind are likely to be repeated.

Just as the deterrent and incapacitative modes of punishment differ in their effects, so do they differ as operational criteria for lawmakers. A legislature that is seeking to determine when punishment is justifiable must decide according to the nature of the offense (which is knowable in advance) rather than according to the personality of the particular offender (which is not). How reliable is the prediction that people who are once detected in the commission of a certain kind of offense will go on committing that kind of offense? Some persons commit burglary under circumstances that indicate they are unlikely to do so again. Others are known to be making a career of it. We can hardly say in advance which is which.

There are kinds of conduct that are typically repetitive. Persons who commit theft because they suffer from kleptomania are apt to go right on doing so. Narcotics offenders, if they happen to be addicts, are by definition likely to repeat their offenses. We have learned that there is a typical syndrome involved in the writing of bad checks. It is an activity of such a compulsive sort that repeat performances are highly probable. In cases of this sort, the empirical basis for making the kind of prediction upon which the incapacitative rationale necessarily rests is quite strong. But note the paradox that this involves. The case for incapacitation is strongest in precisely those areas where the offender is least capable of controlling himself, where his conduct bears the least resemblance to the kind of purposeful, voluntary conduct to which we are likely to attach moral condemnation. Baldly put, the incapacitative theory is at its strongest for those who, in retributive terms, are the least deserving of punishment. That is not, of course, enough to disqualify it as a basis for punishment. It does, however, suggest a certain tension between the concept of blameworthiness as a prerequisite of punishment and the dictates of the incapacitative claim. Perhaps the way to dissolve that tension is to abandon blameworthiness as a condition for the imposition of punishment. That is the thrust of the behavioral theory that presents one horn of the criminal law's contemporary dilemma. Incapacitation as a basis for punishment seems particularly attuned to the demands of the behavioral position.

Another noteworthy feature of the incapacitative theory is its implication for the question of severity. If it is justifiable to lock someone up to keep him from committing further crimes, for how long is it justifiable to do so? One answer may be: until we are reasonably sure that he will no longer commit crimes of that sort. But when is that? In the case of crimes that stem from a personality trait of the offender, we may confidently expect that he will go on committing the offenses in question until the personality trait changes. If we cannot give the hopeful answer: until he is reformed, then we must say: so long as he remains a danger. But that may well be for the rest of his life, if by "danger" we mean a person with a propensity to commit certain kinds of criminal acts. The logic of the incapacitative position drives us to say that until the offender stops being a danger we will continue to restrain him. What this means, pushed to its logical conclusion, is that offenses that are universally regarded as relatively trivial may be punished by imprisonment for life. It means that, at least, unless we have some basis for asserting that lengthy imprisonment is a greater evil than the prospect of repeated criminality.

The problem is by no means academic. The laws of many states contain so-called habitual offender provisions, the general thrust of which is that upon conviction for two or more offenses at different times the offender may be sentenced to an extended term of imprisonment, sometimes for life. To the extent that there is a coherent rationale for laws of this sort, it rests upon the prediction of continued dangerousness that justifies the incapacitative theory of punishment.

Another difficulty with the incapacitative position is its irrelevance to many forms of criminal conduct. Consider the case of perjury. A witness in a civil trial is persuaded to give false testimony so that his friend, who is seeking damages for injuries suffered in an automobile accident, may win his case. The falsity is detected, and the witness is tried and convicted for having committed perjury. What is to be done with him? Presumably he will be, or at least may be, sent to prison. If incapacitation were the sole justifying basis for punishment, it would seem peculiar to imprison this person. He may have shown a propensity for telling lies under oath (although even that is disputable), but it is hardly likely that he will have the occasion to do so again. It is simply ludicrous to say, "We will send you to prison for three years so that we can be sure that at least for those three years you will not commit any futher acts of perjury." Whatever the justification for punishment in this case, it clearly does not rest on the need to restrain the prisoner from committing further crimes. Or consider the use of the criminal sanction to enforce compliance with tax laws. A doctor takes fees in cash that he does not report on his income tax return. This is discovered, and he is tried and convicted for income tax evasion. It strains credulity to suggest that we are sending him to prison for a year so that during that time he will not be able to cheat on his income tax. Even if we lived in a Gilbert and Sullivan sort of universe in which that was the stated reason for punishing tax evaders, we would still face the strong moral objection that alternative, less severe methods of prevention would be just as effective, or nearly so. A rule, for example, that the tax returns of all persons who had been once convicted of income tax evasion would automatically be submitted to detailed audit would probably have the same effect.

Even crimes for which punishments are generally thought to rest at least in part on the incapacitative ground may not, on reflection, reveal much of a basis for invoking that ground. The man who murders his rich aunt so that he will accelerate his inheritance under her will is not imprisoned (or executed) in order to keep him from murdering other people. Indeed, murderers in general have been shown to be among the least recidivistic of offenders. Once released from prison they have a very low rate of reconviction for any criminal offenses, let alone for murder. The justification for punishing such persons must rest on other grounds.

It appears, then, that incapacitation does not present a claim as a sufficient basis for imposing punishment. Of the utilitarian grounds for punishment, only general deterrence has so far been shown to present any such claim. The most that can be said for incapacitation is that it may provide an additional basis for punishment in cases where reasonable evidence concerning the nature of either the particular offender or his kind of offense suggests that he would repeat that offense or commit others if he were not imprisoned.

BEHAVIORAL PREVENTION: REHABILITATION

The most immediately appealing justification for punishment is the claim that it may be used to prevent crime by so changing the personality of the offender that he will conform to the dictates of law; in a word, by reforming him. In that ideal many have seen the means for resolving the moral paradox of the utilitarian position: that punishment is an instrumental use of one man for the benefit of other men. Perhaps "resolving" is too strong a word. After all, the goal sought by the rehabilitative ideal is not reform for its own sake or even for the sake of enabling its object to live a better and a happier life. We hope that he will do so, but the justification is a social one: we want to reform him so that he will cease to offend. He is still being made use of. Whatever moral truth inheres in Kant's famous imperative—"One man ought never to be dealt with merely as a means subservient to the purpose of another. . . . Against such treatment his inborn personality has a right to protect him"—is not made inapplicable by the benevolence of the reformer. Perhaps all we can say is that the ideal of reform mitigates the harshness of the paradox. We are helping society, true. But we are doing so by helping the offender.

It has become fashionable to reject the unpleasant word "punishment" when talking about rehabilitation. For reasons I have given in some detail, this emerging linguistic convention is a misleading one. However benevolent the purpose of reform, however better off we expect its object to be, there is no blinking the fact that what we do to the offender in the name of reform is being done to him by compulsion and for *our* sake, not for his. Rehabilitation may be the most humane goal of punishment, but it is a goal of *punishment* so long as its invocation depends upon finding that an offense has been committed, and so long as its object is to prevent the commission of offenses.

What are the significant characteristics of a system of punishment based on the goal of rehabilitation? Principally, such a system is—like incapacitation—offender-oriented rather than offense-oriented. If rehabilitation is the goal, the nature of the offense is relevant only for what it tells us about what is needed to rehabilitate the offender. To be sure, that relevance is greater than is commonly supposed. In the present state of our knowledge about the human personality and the springs of human action we cannot afford to ignore what a man has done as an index of the kind of man he is and, consequently, of what measures are required to make him better. Still, what he has done is only one measure, and a rough one at that, of what he is. The rehabilitative ideal teaches us that we must treat each offender as an individual whose special needs and problems must be known as fully as possible in order to enable us to deal effectively with him. Punishment, in this view, must be forward-looking. The gravity of the offense, however measured, may give us a clue to the intensity and duration of the measures needed to rehabilitate; but it is only a clue, not a prescription. There is, then, no generally postulated equivalence between the offense and the punishment, as there would be in the case of the retributive or even the deterrent theory of punishment.

It follows from this offender-oriented aspect of the rehabilitative ideal that the intensity and duration of punishment are to be measured by what is thought to be required in order to change the offender's personality. Unlike the related goal of incapacitation, the inquiry is not into how dangerous the offender is but rather into how amenable to treatment he is. If a writer of bad checks can be cured of his underlying disorder only by five years of intensive psychotherapy, then that is what he is to receive.

And, of course, no one knows at the outset how much of what kind of therapy will be needed in his or anyone else's case, so it cannot be said in advance what the duration of his punishment will be. It ends whenever those in authority decide that he has been rehabilitated. Of course, if he does not yield to treatment and is thought to present a danger, he will not be released. The two goals always go hand in hand. No rehabilitationist has ever been heard to say that offenders whom we are incapable of reforming should be released when this incapacity becomes manifest. Indeed, some of them eagerly embrace the view that incorrigible offenders must be kept in custody for life, if necessary. They have not been concerned to inquire too closely into the criteria of necessity. In its pure form, the ideology seems to call for cure or continued restraint in every case. Incapacitation, then, is the other side of the rehabilitative coin. It may well seem a dark underside.

There are two major objections to making rehabilitation the primary justification for punishment. The first probably comes very close to settling the matter for present purposes. It is, very simply, that we do not know how to rehabilitate offenders, at least within the limit of the resources that are now or might reasonably be expected to be devoted to the task. The more we learn about the roots of crime, the clearer it is that they are nonspecific, that the social and psychic springs lie deep within the human condition. To create on a large scale the essentials of a society that produced no crime would be to remake society itself. To say this is not to suggest that the goal of so improving society is not worthwhile, or that there is any superior social goal. It is merely to suggest that this is a task to be undertaken in the name of objectives and using techniques that far transcend the prevention of undesirable behavior. One trouble with the rehabilitative ideal is that it makes the criminal law the vehicle for tasks that are far beyond its competence. Surely the point does not require laboring that a general amelioration of the conditions of social living is not a task that can be very well advanced in the context of the institutions and processes that we devote to apprehending, trying, and dealing with persons who commit offenses.

Rehabilitation after the fact, which is all we can realistically propose, suffers simply from a lack of appropriate means. The measures that we can take are so dubiously connected with the goal that it is hard to justify their employment. We can use our prisons to educate the illiterate, to teach men a useful trade, and to accomplish similar benevolent purposes. The plain disheartening fact is that we have very little reason to suppose that there is a general connection between these measures and the prevention of future criminal behavior. What is involved primarily is a leap of faith, by which we suppose that people who have certain social advantages will be less likely to commit certain kinds of crimes. It is hard to make a good argument for restraining a man of his liberty on the assumption that this connection will be operative in his case. It is harder still if he already possesses the advantages that we assume will make people less likely to offend.

We know little about who is likely to commit crimes and less about what makes them apt to do so. So long as our ignorance in these matters persists, punishment in the name of rehabilitation is gratuitous cruelty. In truth, the threat of punishment for future offenses as extrapolated from the experience of suffering punishment for a present offense may be the strongest rehabilitative force that we now possess. To the extent that a man is rendered more prudent about committing offenses in the future by reason of unpleasantness suffered on account of offenses past, he may be said to be rehabilitated in as meaningful a sense of the term as we can generate from present-day experience. For the gross purposes of the criminal law, a man is better when he knows better. As already suggested, intimidation and rehabilitation have more affinities than present fashions in penal thought accord them.

There is, of course, no reason to suppose that our lamentable ignorance about how to reform offenders is a condition that will persist forever. Indeed, there are measures available today that illustrate in a gross kind of way the claims that rehabilitative theory may be able to make tomorrow. One example is the prefrontal lobotomy, a neurosurgical procedure that has the effect among others of reducing the kind of aggressive drives that impel one toward criminal activity. Of course, it is not a very selective procedure; although it reduces drives, it does not discriminate among ways in which the drives find expression, so that the patient who has undergone this procedure is as unlikely to do anything useful as he is to do anything destructive. Nonetheless, if he does have a reduced drive toward criminality it seems fair to say that, insofar as we are interested in reducing the propensity to commit offenses, the patient has been rehabilitated. In terms of the immediate goal sought, it is irrelevant that rehabilitation has been accomplished at the cost of a profound alteration in his personality of a sort that he (and the rest of us as well) has not invited and would probably prefer not to undergo.

Let us suppose, though, that the side effects of some yet-to-be-discovered means of changing the human personality are not such as we would consider objectionable. To put it another way, suppose that the existing empirical objection to the rehabilitative ideal is removed. Should that ideal be permitted to dominate our punishment system? It is with this question that the second major objection to rehabilitation as the primary goal of punishment emerges. If people can be changed for the better without suffering effects that would generally be considered unfortunate, is there any moral case against compelling them to undergo measures designed to produce such change, given the predicate that they have by their past behavior demonstrated a readiness to commit offenses of a sort whose future occurrence will now be reduced? It may be enough to measure our present fumbling efforts against that millennial prospect and assert that until it arrives the question is academic. It may also be that when the day of the good-behavior pill comes, we will be on the one hand so insensitive to such interferences with the personality and on the other hand so eager to enjoy the increased security that its wholesale administration to offenders promises that questions of this order will seem as academic then as they do now. But if we consider the moral dimensions of the question, the answer is by no means clear. Is it quixotic to assert that man has a right to be bad? Perhaps that right will appear to have little substance when the means of change is more readily at hand than it is today. Yet I have serious doubts on this point, and I am impelled to ask whether a theory of punishment that requires acquiescence in compelled personality change can ever be squared with long-cherished ideals of human autonomy.

SUMMARY: THE LIMITS OF PREVENTION

I have so far dealt with rehabilitative theory on the assumption that what is claimed for it is primacy as a goal of punishment, and I have been concerned to point out certain difficulties that stand in the way of accepting this superficially attractive proposition. Before leaving this aspect of the subject, I should like to comment on a claim frequently advanced by proponents of the behavioral view (which we can now see as the advocacy of rehabilitation and incapacitation as complementary goals of punishment). This claim, briefly stated, goes back to the polarity described at the beginning of this discussion: that there are only two views and that one must choose between them. On the one hand, this claim asserts, there is the demand for vengeance, which we call retribution. It is backward-looking to the offense rather than forward-looking to the offender; it is punitive rather than preventive, it is predicated on metaphysical notions about "responsibility" for the offense that bear no relation to the social justifications for punishment. On the other hand, there is the behavioral position, which, as we have seen, can be characterized as an attempt to deal with the prevention of crime by changing the offender or his situation: primarily, through reforming him, secondarily, through incapacitating and intimidating him.

The attitude of proponents of the behavioral position toward deterrence is ambivalent. They do appear to recognize that deterrence, to the extent that it operates, serves preventive goals. But they question whether it does operate, point out that empirical evidence of its operation is lacking, and assert that in the absence of more solid factual demonstration than we now have available, the claims of deterrence should be subordinated to claims for individual treatment of offenders based on the concepts of rehabilitation and incapacitation. Some go further: they assert that deterrence is simply vengeance thinly disguised. To punish a man with the vague hope that doing so will serve to deter others is simply a rationalization, so the argument runs, for a desire to inflict pain on him because he deserves to suffer for his misdeeds. Why not come right out and admit it, these critics say: if punishment is imposed for any purpose other than to make the offender a better man or to protect society against him, it is socialized vengeance and should be rejected by any society that calls itself civilized.

It is doubtless true that there are times when the utilitarian claims of deterrence are used to mask a desire to inflict what is thought to be deserved suffering. The debate over the death penalty is a notable example. Those who support capital punishment on essentially retributive grounds continue to couch their argument in deterrence terms in spite of the lack of evidence to support the claim. But to cite this kind of aberration as evidence that the deterrent position is retributive is to confuse the issue in two ways. First, the argument about the severity of punishment is confused with an argument about the justification for any punishment at all. Second, the assertion is made that because an argument can be misused it has no validity, an obvious non sequitur. A commercial pornographer may favor freedom of speech solely because it enables him to ply his trade unmolested by the law, but this does not in any way prejudice the arguments on the merits for freedom of speech.

The fact that punishment involves suffering is a moral embarrassment. But it is just as much an embarrassment to the behavioral position as it is to the claim that punishment is justified because it deters. The case for incapacitation is every bit as capable of being a mask for vengeance as is the case for deterrence. Life terms for habitual offenders are urged because of an asserted need to protect society from their depredations. Indeterminate commitments for sexual psychopaths and narcotics addicts are urged on the same ground. Our experience with measures of this kind—their genesis in demands for action when the community is shocked by a heinous crime, their operation as wastebaskets for the socially undesirable—suggests that they are just as capable of serving as outlets for feelings of revenge as are undisguised pleas to make the offender pay. Indeed, these claims may be less defensible than a straightforward plea for revenge. To the morally unacceptable urge to punish they add the morally degrading spectacle of widespread hypocrisy and self-deception. And they present a social danger that measures we might reject if they were acknowledged to be based on the urge for revenge will be accepted when put forward in the more plausible guise of scientific utility.

The same danger is latent in the case for rehabilitative measures. Given the lack of any solid empirical basis for supposing that we know how to reform, given the fact that measures of reform may entail just as severe restrictions on personal liberty as measures employed for deterrent or even retributive ends, the danger is equally present that in the name of humanitarian goals we will commit ourselves to measures that are in large part, albeit covertly, inspired by the demands of vengeance. And there is the additional danger that, because such measures are being taken in the name of humanity, we will be less quick to recognize and defend against encroachments on libertarian values.

The proponents of the behavioral position often seem oddly obtuse in the face of modern knowledge, such as it is, about the unconscious springs of human conduct. One would suppose that they of all people would be alert to the ambivalent quality of human motives, especially when they involve large-scale interference with the freedom of others. Helping others rather than punishing them sounds attractive. Substituting amelioration for suffering sounds high-minded. Thinking of crime as evidence of pathology rather than of depravity sounds advanced. But who can be sure that the urge to punish and the urge to cure may not have a common source in some dark recess of the human psyche? At the very least, what is called for is a little trepidation, a little self-doubt, a little awareness of how great a leap is needed to get from the theoretic dictates of the behavioral view to a set of working institutions and processes for dealing with deviant conduct.

I do not make these points in a spirit of disparagement. They are no more telling against the advocates of the behavioral position than is their criticism of the claims of deterrence. But they are no less telling, either. All that I have been concerned to show is that any unitary theory of punishment is inadequate and that all theories—not simply deterrence—that start from the utilitarian premise suffer from the same moral embarrassment. In the words of a distinguished lawyer-philosopher: "[Punishment is] at best, a needed but nonetheless lamentable form of societal control."[5]

I have been concerned to examine in detail the ambiguities in utilitarian theories of punishment precisely because I believe that those theories provide the most satisfactory starting point we possess for an integrated rationale of criminal punishment: one that gives a satisfactory account of the general justification for punishment and that provides a basis for determining both what kinds of conduct and what kinds of people should be subjected to the criminal sanction. Having in mind the ambiguities of the utilitarian position, let us now consider whether a satisfactory integrated theory of punishment can be devised.

[5] Richard Wasserstrom, "Why Punish the Guilty?" *University* (Spring 1964), p. 14.

CHAPTER FOUR

Toward an Integrated Theory of Criminal Punishment

THE POSITION that I propose to elaborate and defend in this chapter can be stated summarily as follows:

(1) It is a necessary but not a sufficient condition for punishment that it is designed to prevent the commission of offenses.

(2) It is a necessary but not a sufficient condition of punishment that the person on whom it is imposed is found to have committed an offense under circumstances that permit his conduct to be characterized as blameworthy.

To locate this position among the various justifications for punishment that we have been examining: it rejects the retributive position insofar as that position views the infliction of punishment on a blameworthy offender as a sufficient justifying condition; it rejects the behavioral branch of the utilitarian theory insofar as that position views the tendency of punishment to prevent crime by reforming or incapacitating the offender as a sufficient justifying condition; it accepts the classical utilitarian theory as the proper starting point for a justifying theory; it views utilitarianism as inadequate to serve all the purposes that ought to be served by an integrated theory of punishment.

My reasons for adopting this position may well start with a reiteration of the point made at the end of the last chapter: punishment is a necessary but lamentable form of social control. It is lamentable because it inflicts suffering in the name of goals whose achievement is a matter of chance. It may be useful at this point to sum up briefly the reasons why the achievement of those goals is a matter of chance.

Deterrence is the only utilitarian goal of punishment that affords a generalized *a priori* justification for the infliction of punishment. It is the only goal we can accept in advance for punishing all crimes committed by all persons, without scrutinizing the facts of the particular case in which punishment may be imposed. Yet acceptance of its existence, let alone its efficacy, involves a leap of faith. In contrast, intimidation, incapacitation, and rehabilitation are all partial and fragmentary goals, and their relevance in any given case is always at issue. Although it is easier to make an empirical assessment of their effectiveness than to do the same for deterrence, they involve difficult moral puzzles, central among which is: what is the calculus by which one determines whether punishment in their name serves or disserves even the limited goals of crime prevention, let alone the range of goals that a legal system is designed to achieve?

If we could be sure that the threat of criminal punishment averts more harm than is caused by the infliction of even that minimum of punishment needed to keep the threat credible, or if we could be equally sure about the outcome of the same calculus applied to the claims for individualized measures of intimidation, incapacitation, or rehabilitation, we mght—I do not say that we would—be able to assert that the preventon of crime is a sufficient justification for the infliction of criminal punishment. But we cannot be sure. Instead, we are forced to recognize the moral ambiguity of punishment even when taken on its own terms for the narrow utilitarian objective of reducing the incidence of criminal behavior. And for that reason, limits need to be placed on the adoption of the utilitarian stance, whether in its classical form of reliance on deterrence or in its modern, behavioral form of reliance on individualized measures of intimidation, incapacitation, and reform. There are other reasons, which we shall come to shortly, for skepticism about the utilitarian stance, reasons having to do with values that transcend the goal of crime prevention. The point being made here meets the utilitarian crime prevention argument on its own ground: if the utilitarian calculus yielded a clear answer, it might be justifiable to ignore the issue of moral blameworthiness or culpability in setting forth the rationale, and hence the limiting doctrines, of the criminal law. But it does not, and we cannot.

I shall not try to define culpability, but shall merely identify what kind of thing or quality is meant by it in this discussion. It is, in any event, better described than defined. By culpability, I mean those aspects of human conduct, as defined by the legal system, that serve, or ought to serve, as excuses for exemption from criminal punishment. These include, as is conventionally recognized, states of mind. They also include the interaction between conduct as it occurs in human events and conduct as a legal construct. In Chapters Five and Six the nature of these aspects is elaborated in some detail. Up to a point, of course, the absence of such aspects may also, although it need not, satisfy the utilitarian that a particular instance of human conduct does not call for punishment in the interest of preventing crime. That is particularly true of the individualized measures of punishment applied after the fact. A man who is shown to have committed a homicide through an accident for which he was not at fault does not present a case for social protection through measures of incapacitation or reform. But when we consider the *a priori* justification for punishment—its propensity to deter others from committing offenses—it is far from clear that a willingness to entertain such excuses serves the end of crime prevention.

The argument runs as follows. If people are to be deterred from engaging in criminal conduct by the punishment of those who have done so in the past, it is important that the imposition of punishment be as nearly certain as possible. An important source of uncertainty arises when persons who have engaged in criminal conduct are allowed to present excuses, because it is possible that false excuses may be presented and believed. The prospect that this holds out to others who may be contemplating criminal conduct results in "utilitarian losses"; therefore, the demands of utility require that excuses not be entertained. The idea of strict liability in the criminal law, to the extent that it has any coherent intellectual basis, rests on notions of this kind.

So long as deterrence is viewed in the narrow, crude, *in terrorem* sense employed by Bentham and still prevalent in utilitarian thought, the argument has considerable force. If all that is at stake is the propensity of punishment to scare people, if our image of man is exclusively that of the rational hedonist who will do anything that promises to enhance his well-being if he thinks he can get away with it, then it is hard to answer the argument that permitting excuses weakens the deterrent efficacy of the criminal law. But if deterrence (or prevention) is more broadly conceived as a complex psychological phenomenon meant primarily to create and reinforce the conscious morality and the unconscious habitual controls of the law-abiding, then the flank of the old argument may be turned. Punishment of the morally innocent does not reinforce one's sense of identification as a law-abider, but rather undermines it. A society in which excuses were not allowed would be a society in which virtue would indeed have to be its own reward. What could be more certain to undermine one's sense that it is important to avoid the intentional or reckless or negligent infliction of harm upon others than the knowledge that, if one inflicts harm, he may be punished even though he cannot be blamed for having done so? If we are to be held liable for what we cannot help doing, there is little incentive to avoid what we can help doing. One may as well be hanged for a sheep as a lamb.

Losses may and will occur through the acceptance of false excuses. But the calculus cannot end there. These losses must be weighed against the damage that will be done to the criminal law as carrier of our shared morality unless its reach is limited to blameworthy acts. Unjust punishment is, in the end, useless punishment. It is useless both because it fails to prevent crime and because crime prevention is not the ultimate aim of the rule of law.

Law, including the criminal law, must in a free society be judged ultimately on the basis of its success in promoting human autonomy and the capacity for individual human growth and development. The prevention of crime is an essential aspect of the environmental protection required if autonomy is to flourish. It is, however, a negative aspect and one which, pursued with single-minded zeal, may end up creating an environment in which all are safe but none is free. The limitations included in the concept of culpability are justified not by an appeal to the Kantian dogma of "just deserts" but by their usefulness in keeping the state's powers of protection at a decent remove from the lives of its citizens.

The case for an essentially preventive view of the function of criminal law is unanswerable; anything else is the merest savagery. But a purely preventive view, reinforced as that view is today by a scientific and deterministic attitude toward the possibilities for controlling human conduct, carries the danger that single-minded pursuit of the goal of crime prevention will slight and in the end defeat the ultimate goal of law in a free society, which is to liberate rather than to restrain. Human autonomy is an illusion if we make it conditional on human perfection. As Holmes once observed, law, like other human contrivances, has to take some chances. I see an important limiting principle in the criminal law's traditional emphasis on blameworthiness as a prerequisite to the imposition of punishment. But it is a *limiting* principle, not a justification for action. It is wrong to say that we should punish persons simply because they commit offenses under circumstances that we can call blameworthy. It is right to say that we should not punish those who commit offenses unless we can say that their conduct is blameworthy. In the next three chapters we shall examine the minimal doctrinal content of a criminal law based on this view.

The rationale that I have sketched is a transitional one. As we find ourselves gaining more nearly exact knowledge about the sources and control of deviant behavior, the pressure from the behavioral position upon this rationale will become very strong and may prove to be irresistible. The more confidently we can predict behavior and the more subtly we can control it, the more powerful will be the temptation to relax the constraints that inhibit us at present from aggressively intervening in the lives of individuals in the name of crime prevention. But the millennium will not announce itself with unmistakable clarity. And skeptics about its advent may then as now find some merit in a limiting rationale for the criminal sanction.

In this survey of the general justifying aims of criminal punishment I have taken a somewhat skeptical attitude toward the claim that the rehabilitation of offenders is a sufficient justification for imposing punishment. My skepticism is based on two distinct but related grounds: first, the great uncertainty, indeed ignorance, that presently attends our efforts to reform offenders; second, the injustices, greatly increased by our uncertainty and ignorance, that may be done to offenders who are treated differently because of assumed differences in the needs to which their penal treatment is supposed to respond. I should make it clear, if I have not already done so, that my skepticism is limited to reliance on rehabilitation as an *a priori* justifying aim of punishment; it does not extend to questions about how particular offenders should be dealt with once we have determined on other grounds that the institution of criminal punishment is morally justifiable. The place for operation of the rehabilitative ideal is not in determining whether punishment is justified; neither is it in determining what kinds of conduct should be made criminal. However, once a decision to punish has been made and justified on other grounds, the rehabilitative ideal should be fully used in deciding what kinds of punishment should be imposed. To put it another way, the rehabilitative ideal deserves consideration in evaluating not the propriety of punishment but its severity.

It seems desirable to make clear also the extent of the difference between the views I have been setting forth and what I conceive to be the essence of the retributive position. That position views the imputation of blame or culpability to the offender as in itself a sufficient justification for the imposition of criminal punishment. This view is sometimes expressed forthrightly; at other times it is masked by assertions that punishment on the basis of moral fault strengthens the moral fiber of the individual being punished, or constitutes education for good citizenship, or something of that sort. That kind of assertion has a pharisaical ring to it made less attractive, if anything, by its Pollyanna-ish overtones. Punishment is not a virtue, only a necessity.

The view I take of the role of culpability in the justification for punishment is an instrumental one. I see this limitation on the utilitarian position as desirable not for any inherent quality that it possesses but because it serves ends that I think require attention in a criminal system. It does so in several different ways.

First, it establishes a firm basis for resisting the attenuation of the offense as a component in the definition of punishment. Without an offense—a more or less specifically defined species of conduct —there can be no basis for imputing blame. A man may be a danger to others, or in need of help, or any other equivalent in the current cant that denotes an inconvenient human being whom we would like to get out of the way; but unless he has committed an offense, unless he has done something rather than merely been something, we cannot say that he has been culpable. And, it follows from the view taken of culpability as a necessary condition, that he cannot be found guilty through the criminal process and subjected to criminal punishment. A strictly preventive view would rightly see this limitation to offenses actually committed as nonsense. If we have solid grounds for thinking that a person is disposed to the commission of offenses, why wait until he has done so to punish (i.e., rehabilitate and/or restrain) him? The instrumental use of culpability through the ascription of legal guilt prevents this dissolution of the nexus between offense and punishment. Of course, the important practical question is not whether the nexus is to be dissolved, but rather how far and in what ways it may be relaxed, a subject to which we will return in the next chapter. It is enough now to note that there are solid arguments for keeping the offense in sharp focus, and the culpability restriction is a good means of doing this.

Another aspect of this instrumental case for culpability is that there is a rough correspondence between the dictates of the culpability limitation and aspects of the desirable operation of the criminal sanction. People ought in general to be able to plan their conduct with some assurance that they can avoid entanglement with the criminal law; by the same token the enforcers and appliers of the law should not waste their time lurking in the bushes ready to trap the offender who is unaware that he is offending. It is precisely the fact that in its normal and characteristic operation the criminal law provides this opportunity and this protection to people in their everyday lives that makes it a tolerable institution in a free society. Take this away, and the criminal law ceases to be a guide to the well-intentioned and a restriction on the restraining power of the state. Take it away is precisely what you do, however, when you abandon culpability as the basis for imposing punishment. While it may often serve the state's purposes not to interfere with its citizens unless they have acted with foresight, on many occasions their foresight or lack of it may seem immaterial. If we leave to a purely utilitarian calculus the decision whether a man's innocence or ignorance shall count for him, the answer on any given occasion will be uncertain. Only by providing the shield of a culpability requirement can this desirable aspect of the criminal law be preserved.

Finally, the singular power of the criminal law resides, as I have argued, not in its coercive effect on those caught in its toils but rather in its effect on the rest of us. That effect, I have tried to show, is a highly complex one. It includes elements of coercion and of terror: if I do as he did, I too shall suffer for it. But it also includes conscious and unconscious moralizing and habit-forming effects that go far beyond the crassness of a narrowly conceived deterrence. If it is not thought enough of a justification that the law *be* fair, the argument may seem appealing that a criminal law system cannot attract and retain the respect of its most important constituents—the habitually law-abiding—unless it *is seen to be* fair. And whatever fairness may be thought to mean on the procedural side, its simplest (if most neglected) meaning is that no one should be subjected to punishment without having an opportunity to litigate the issue of his culpability. Even imagining a system in which, once forbidden physical conduct has taken place, no excuses are listened to is enough to show the importance of making culpability a necessary condition of liability to punishment.

I have emphasized in these pages the moral ambiguity of punishment as well as its inevitability. We cannot avoid punishment, nor can we ever feel entirely happy about it. One virtue of the criminal law is that it brings the problem of punishment out into the open. Alternative sanctions that involve many of the same pitfalls may appear superficially attractive because they seem to permit avoidance of the issues of punishment. The issues are still there, although in a less direct and therefore less striking form. Even if by a stroke of the pen we could wipe out the criminal law as a legal institution, we would sooner or later have to confront the triad of Crime, Guilt, and Punishment, and to decide whether we wanted to make them part of a sanctioning system.

It is to the ambiguity, rather than the inevitability, that I want to return in a final word. What should we conclude from this effort to expose the ambiguity that lies at the heart of the case for punishment? If this social institution is indeed necessary but lamentable, what does this mean to the rational legislator, that mythical reader of these words? First, it suggests that he pay careful attention to the limits imposed by the rationale of the criminal law, that he understand them and accept them, not grudgingly as a nuisance or an interference with important practical goals, but willingly as a means of preventing this human agency from becoming tyrannical and in the end destructive. Second, it suggests the need for careful scrutiny of the institutions and processes of criminal justice, and in particular, an assessment of their strengths and weaknesses as modes of crime prevention. Finally, it suggests that the rationale of the criminal law conceals important clues to the central issue with which our rational legislator is concerned: what are the criteria that he should take into account in determining what kinds of behavior should be treated as "criminal."

CHAPTER FIVE

Culpability and Conduct

INTRODUCTION

In the field of criminal law, traditional scholarship has carried on the useful and indeed essential job of doctrinal explication and analysis. Much important work has been done, particularly in recent years, to make clear and precise what had developed in a random and inchoate fashion. These studies have brought to light the continuities underlying the various judicial and legislative statements about the criminal law. They have shown that apparently isolated rules, like claim of right as a defense to larceny, are simply instances of the general excusing condition of mistake, which appears in a whole range of offenses, from murder to writing bad checks. An essay like this one is now possible because this work of explication and analysis has already been done.

These pages do not represent, nor should they be mistaken for, another attempt to state with technical accuracy what is known as the "general part" of the substantive criminal law. Rather, they set forth a model of the minimal doctrinal content of a criminal law belonging to no particular time or place. It is a criminal law whose doctrinal content derives from the rationale outlined in the preceding chapters, one that pursues the central goal of prevention of socially undesirable behavior, as limited by restrictions of culpability. As will be seen, the minimal doctrinal content has more to do with the limitation than it does with the central goal.

In this chapter and the next two I will try to examine, briefly and nontechnically, some representative doctrines. A technical treatise on the criminal law would examine many more in greater detail, although with less attention to their overtones. The only claim I make for these instances—and it is not an immodest one—is that taken as a whole they raise all the *basic* problems posed by criminal law doctrine. They are presented here for two reasons: first, they reveal the operational consequences of the rationale we have been discussing; second, they exemplify the effects of such a rationale on the prudential limits of the criminal law, which is the main concern of this book. These doctrines express the criminal law's compromise between the inevitability and the ambiguity of punishment. They give content to the three main ideas—Crime, Guilt, and Punishment—that underlie the criminal law. I do not claim that my account of these doctrines is strikingly original, although it departs in some respects from accepted analysis. The originality, such as it is, inheres in the view that they are joined and should be judged by their common propensity to adjust the dictates of crime prevention to the demands of a legal system that makes individual freedom the prime value.

In conventional criminal law terms, the cluster of doctrines to be dealt with in this chapter is summed up by the maxims *nullum crimen sine lege* and *nulla poena sine lege*: no one may be convicted of or punished for an offense unless the conduct constituting that offense has been authoritatively defined by an institution having the duly allocated competence to do so. These maxims have a constitutional counterpart in this country: first, through the explicit prohibition of Article I, Section 9, clause 3, that "No Bill of Attainder or ex post facto Law shall be passed"; second, through the judicially developed cluster of prescriptions generally referred to as the "void-for-vagueness" doctrine. For present purposes, we need not consider what the source of these notions in positive law happens to be. What we need to do instead is simply to describe these ideas, to ask what values they express, and to consider their relevance to the operation of the criminal law.

By dissociating the ideas from their largely fortuitous legal origins and organizing them more systematically, we can come up with the following approximation:

(1) No one may be subjected to criminal punishment except for conduct.

(2) Conduct may not be treated as criminal unless it has been so defined by appropriate lawmakers before it has taken place.

(3) This definitional role is assigned primarily and broadly to the legislature, secondarily and interstitially to the courts, and to no one else.

(4) In order to make these prescriptions material and not merely formal, the definitions of criminal conduct must be precisely enough stated to leave comparatively little room for arbitrary application.

CONDUCT AS A PREREQUISITE

It may hardly seem a startling notion that the criminal law, or law in general for that matter, is concerned with conduct—people's actions (including their verbal and other expressive actions) and their failures to act. Yet there is nothing in the nature of things that compels this focus. The criminal law could be concerned with people's thoughts and emotions, with their personality patterns and character structures. It is true that if this rather than conduct was the focus, it would still be expedient in most cases to ascertain these essentially internal characteristics through inquiry into conduct. But if these internal characteristics were the focus, conduct would simply be evidence of what we are interested in rather than the thing itself; and we would not hesitate to use other evidence to the extent that it became available. If, for example, we could determine through projective tests like the Rorschach or through other and more sophisticated forms of psychological testing that a given individual was likely to inflict serious physical injury on someone, someday, somewhere, and if we viewed conduct as a prerequisite rather than as merely evidentiary, we would presumably not hesitate to inflict punishment on that person for his propensities, or, as the old cliché has it, for thinking evil thoughts. We might rationalize this simply by saying that we were punishing him for the offense of having flunked his Rorschach test, but we would then be acting on a somewhat Pickwickian definition of "conduct."

Why do we not do so? The obvious historical answer is that,

aside from a few antiquarian anomalies such as the offense of imagining the King's death, we have not been sufficiently stirred by the danger presented or sufficiently confident of our ability to discern propensities in the absence of conduct to use the instruments of the criminal law in this fashion. For some it may be enough to rejoice that historically this was so and to rest on that historical accident for the present and the future, but I think that a further answer is required. This answer turns, in my view, on the idea of culpability, that necessary but insufficient condition of criminal liability that is an important part of our integrated theory of criminal punishment.

Among the notions associated with the concept of "culpability" are those of free will and human autonomy. I do not mean this in any deep philosophical sense but in a contingent and practical social sense. It is important, especially in a society that likes to describe itself as "free" and "open," that a government should be empowered to coerce people only for what they do and not for what they are.

If this is important for law generally, it is *a fortiori* important for that most coercive of legal instruments, the criminal law. Now, this self-denying ordinance can be and often is attacked as being inconsistent with the facts of human nature. People may in fact have little if any greater capacity to control their conduct (some say in part, some say in whole) than their emotions or their thoughts. It is therefore either unrealistic or hypocritical, so the argument runs, to deal with conduct as willed or to treat it differently from personality and character.

This attack is, however, misconceived. Neither philosophic concepts nor psychological realities are actually at issue in the criminal law. The idea of free will in relation to conduct is not, in the legal system, a statement of fact, but rather a value preference having very little to do with the metaphysics of determinism and free will. The fallacy that legal values describe physical reality is a very common one. We shall encounter it in its most vulgar form in connection with the so-called insanity defense. But we need to dispose of it here, because it is such a major impediment to rational thought about the criminal law. Very simply, the law treats man's conduct as autonomous and willed, not because it is, but because it is desirable to proceed as if it were. It is desirable because the capacity of the individual human being to live his life in reasonable freedom from socially imposed external constraints (the only kind with which the law is concerned) would be fatally impaired unless the law provided a *locus poenitentiae,* a point of no return beyond which external constraints may be imposed but before which the individual is free— not free of whatever compulsions determinists tell us he labors under but free of the very specific social compulsions of the law. The law is full of such points of no return. One way (worth trying but never essayed, so far as I know) of analyzing the structure of criminal law would be to locate its prescriptions along a spectrum of points of no return. We shall encounter a few of them shortly, particularly when we consider offenses of status and the general theory of criminal attempts. For our present purpose it is enough to note that the basic *locus poenitentiae* of the criminal law is the limitation of its ambit to the realm of conduct.

Conduct should not be confused, as it sometimes is, with the infliction of harm. We are simply forcing the criminal law onto a Procrustean bed when we attempt to assimilate the diverse kinds of conduct with which it may be concerned to the occurrence of harm. The infliction of harm may well be a useful classifying device, serving for some analytic purposes to distinguish certain kinds of crime from others; and it may afford an important prudential criterion of limitation for the scope of the criminal sanction; but the use of the term "harm" to embrace all of the kinds of conduct that have been or rationally might be comprised within a criminal code is at best illusory. What is the harm inflicted by an unsuccessful attempt to kill someone who does not even know that he is in danger? Or by driving in excess of the speed limit without becoming involved in an accident? Or by possessing tools that are adapted for committing burglaries? Yet attempted murder, reckless driving, and possession of burglar's tools are all well-established examples of criminal conduct. And even the most ardent proponents of the "harm" theory have never charged that calling these forms of conduct criminal is inconsistent with any important legal principle. As we shall see, there may be prudential reasons cautioning against resort to some criminal proscriptions because they do not describe harms; but in principle precursor offenses such as these are just as much cases of conduct as are those harm-inflicting offenses that may ensue from them. The problems that offenses of this sort raise are essentially definitional problems, as we shall see in succeeding sections. That does not disqualify them from congruence with the first and most basic requirement of the criminal law: that the subject with which it deals is conduct.

It may seem anomalous, particularly to those with some training in the conventional doctrines of the criminal law, that we should fasten here on conduct as a limitation on culpability. The orthodox view is that culpability is primarily a matter of the actor's mental state, rather than of the conduct in which he engages. Indeed, it is those offenses whose commission is established by proof of conduct irrespective of the offender's mental state that are referred to as offenses of strict liability and that are denounced, and rightly so, as being incompatible with culpability limitations. And yet, the paradoxical fact is that the limitation of criminal punishment to conduct constitutes the first and most important line of defense against erosion of the idea of culpability, for it keeps the criminal law from becoming purely the servant of the utilitarian ideal of prevention.

A clue to why this is so is afforded by the universally recognized doctrine that conduct that occurs while the actor is in an unconscious state—sleepwalking, epileptic seizures, automatism —may not be dealt with criminally. Conduct must be, as the law's confusing term has it, "voluntary." The term is one that will immediately raise the hackles of the determinist, of whatever persuasion. But, once again, the law's language should not be read as plunging into the deep waters of free will vs. determinism, Cartesian duality, or any of a half-dozen other philosophic controversies that might appear to be invoked by the use of the term "voluntary" in relation to conduct. The law is not affirming that some conduct is the product of the free exercise of conscious volition; it is excluding, in a crude kind of way, conduct that in any view is not. And it does so primarily in response to the simple intuition that nothing would more surely undermine the individual's sense of autonomy and security than to hold him to account for conduct that *he* does not think he can control. He may be deluded, if the determinists are right, in his belief that such conduct differs significantly from any other conduct in which he engages. But that is beside the point. *He* thinks there is a difference, and that is what the law acts upon.

There are forms of legal coercion whose invocation does not formally depend upon conduct. The rapidly developing body of law dealing with the civil commitment of the mentally ill affords a conspicuous example, and is an instructive contrast to the criminal law. By and large, the criteria for invoking social intervention on mental health grounds treat conduct in a very attenuated way or reject it altogether. Under prevalent civil commitment processes, persons are deprived of their liberty on the ground that they are "mentally ill," are "in need of treatment" or are "dangerous." Without at this point engaging in speculation about whether this is good or bad, we can readily perceive that it is different from the basis on which the criminal law proceeds. While observations of the individual's conduct—his perceived abnormal or bizarre behavior—will typically trigger a decision to intervene and bring about civil commitment, the conduct is not the formal cause of the commitment but simply evidence showing the existence of the formal cause, or criterion, that society relies on in making the decision to commit. As we have seen, there will be many occasions on which the coerced civil commitment of a person for mental health reasons satisfies the definition of punishment. And these present a series of dilemmas whose dimensions we will have to explore when we consider alternatives to the criminal sanction. For present purposes, however, it is enough to note that in this particular the criminal law is far more respectful of human autonomy than is the law dealing with mental health. It is so at the cost, if cost it be, of taking a less single-mindedly preventive view of its aims.

The underlying rationale of civil commitment is purely preventive and forward-looking. It seeks to protect the patient and those around him by restraint and by rehabilitation. It seeks, when it is not purely custodial, to make the patient a better and happier person, both for his own sake and for the sake of those with whom he comes into contact. A criminal law that was purely preventive and purely utilitarian would in fact look much more like civil commitment. The difference is culpability, and it is not a difference that enables us to distinguish between prevention and punishment. It is a difference that serves to protect, in the case of the criminal law, values concerned with freedom, with autonomy, and with security. And the restriction of criminal punishment to conduct serves as its first line of defense.

It will be objected that the criminal law does not in fact now deal only with conduct. There is a strong tradition in Anglo-American law of treating certain kinds of status, such as vagrancy, as criminal. To be a person "without visible means of living who has the physical ability to work, and who does not seek employment, nor labor when employment is offered him" (in the words of a now-repealed California statute) may perhaps be characterized as engaging in a kind of omissive conduct: but common sense rebels at the use of the word "conduct" to describe a condition that does not "take place" but rather exists without reference to discrete points in time. It must be acknowledged that when the law makes the status of vagrancy or the status of "being a common drunkard" (that phrase redolent of Elizabethan England) a criminal offense, it is departing from the restriction to conduct. Laws of this sort are in fact very much on the way out. Courts are giving them a helpful push on the road to oblivion under the rubrics of constitutional anathema: void-for-vagueness, cruel and unusual punishment. As we shall see, these labels refer to certain additional values that are independently fatal to offenses of status, and we will consider the relation of those values to the definition of offenses later in this chapter. But for the moment let us focus on the relevance of these interesting anomalies to the limitation of criminal punishment to definable conduct.

Offenses of status can best be understood as embodiments of the preventive ideal at a time when the criminal law offered no alternatives. Their demise is the result, whatever the rubric under which it is accomplished, of the development of alternatives that have permitted us the previously unavailable luxury of recognizing that such offenses are anomalies in the criminal law. There has always been pressure to rid the community of people who are perceived as dangerous, threatening, or merely odd. That pressure, until fairly recently, has had to find its outlet almost entirely in the criminal law. But the extraordinary expansion of the concept of illness, and especially of mental illness, that has taken place during the last century has furnished us another set of outlets. Now we can afford to insist on the doctrinal purity from which crimes of status represent so marked a lapse. The Supreme Court vividly illustrated this point recently in *Robinson v. California*,[1] holding unconstitutional a California statute making it a crime to be addicted to narcotics. The Court's rather cryptic rationale was simply this: the legislature may not make it a crime to be sick. But unless addiction to narcotics is viewed as an illness, the argument fails. It is not without significance that the Court took it for granted that narcotics addiction is an illness. The question, of course, is not whether it "is" an illness but rather how it is perceived. What would Chief Justice Marshall have said? Times change, habits of thought change, our use of words changes, and the legal process changes with them. We can now afford the luxury of restricting the substantive content of criminal law to conduct, leaving status and prediction to other legal processes. As we shall see, that does not solve the ultimate problem but only shifts it.

Thus we see that limiting criminal punishment to cases of conduct *pro tanto* detracts from the utilitarian goal of prevention and is, in fact, the first in a long series of trammels that the rationale of the criminal law places on a purely preventive orientation. The conduct limitation is the main distinction between criminal law and civil commitment, although the difference does not make the outcome of either process any the more or the less a form of punishment. Finally, the conduct limitation in the criminal law has been powerfully reinforced by the development of alternative legal processes for dealing with the prevention of future undesired behavior.

THE PRINCIPLE OF LEGALITY

Academic discussions of the criminal law give central importance to the prohibition against the retroactive definition and punishment of crime. *The* first principle, we are repeatedly told,

[1] 370 U.S. 660 (1962).

is that conduct may not be treated as criminal unless it has been
so defined by an authority having the institutional competence
to do so before it has taken place. Why should this be so? Perhaps the most conventional answer is that people are entitled
to know what they are forbidden to do so that they may shape
their conduct accordingly. There is a core of good sense in that
assertion, but as we shall see, it is overly simplistic and in some
respects misleading. A more sophisticated answer is that this kind
of prohibition against ex post facto lawmaking, as the reprehended practice is conventionally termed, is necessary in order
to secure evenhandedness in the administration of justice and to
eliminate the oppressive and arbitrary exercise of official discretion. This answer invites exploration and refinement, for it
too is not without its flaws.

It may be useful to start by pointing out that insistence on the
principle of legality has something of an academic ring to it today.
The principle may be essentially sound, and the all-but-universal
compliance with it that characterizes the administration of the
criminal law in this country and (to an only slightly lesser extent)
in Great Britain may be the loftiest of tributes to the civilized
state we have achieved, but the fact remains that the issue is a
rather sterile one today. Except for such cataclysmic events as
the abandonment of the principle in Hitler's Germany and the
riposte of the victorious Allies at Nuremberg, examples that can
justly be termed clear-cut are very hard to come by. And those
few that do occur turn out on examination to involve the issue
of whether the legislature has a monopoly on the institutional
competence to define crimes (to which we shall turn in the next
section) rather than the question whether someone, be it court
or legislature, must decide before particular forms of conduct
occur what is to be treated as criminal.

The reasons for the seeming disappearance of the problem are
not hard to discern. There are today practically no forms of conduct society might wish to punish that cannot be dealt with by
some general or specific proscription of the criminal law. And,
it seems, legislative sentiment for defining new crimes crystallizes
much more quickly than does generalized public pressure. The
wave of recent statutes making it criminal to possess the halluci-

nogenic drug LSD provides a recent instance. No one thought it strange that these statutes, without exception, were drafted so as to become effective in their criminal aspect at a date somewhat later than their passage. No one complained that this prospectivity—indeed, prospectivity plus, since statutes usually become effective immediately upon completion of the enactment process—would result in thousands of LSD takers' escaping their just punishment. We simply do not think that way.

Legislation like that enacted in response to the use of LSD is comparatively rare nowadays. The great bulk of criminal legislation in recent years—the annual grist of our legislative mills—has fallen into one of three categories: highly detailed and particularistic proscriptions of conduct already reachable through some broader enactment; extensions of the time thrust of the criminal law that make it apply to preparatory conduct, further back from the ultimate apprehended harm; and changes (usually increases) in the punishment for given offenses. None of these forms of enactment can be regarded as a response to the kind of pressure that threatens to breach the principle of legality. The principle is so secure today that, to understand what it is all about, we must try to imagine how it would have looked a century or more ago.

An instructive example is the development of the law of theft in eighteenth-century England, as classically described by Jerome Hall.[2] His general theme is the response of the criminal law to the increasing complexity of property relationships in the nascent commercial and urban society of that day. The law of theft, as it had developed to that point, reflected an agricultural society in which the principal danger that one ran from the acquisitive conduct of others was that they would make off with one's moveable possessions. The central offense against property was larceny: the taking and carrying away of another's possessions with the intention to deprive him permanently of their enjoyment. Proscriptions against obtaining property through fraud were limited to cheating accomplished by the use of false weights or tokens, conduct which the ordinary prudent man could not guard

---

[2] *Theft, Law, and Society,* 2d ed. (Indianapolis, 1952), chap. 2.

himself against. The increasing impersonality of the marketplace had not yet forced reexamination of the idea that the ignorant or credulous buyer had only himself to blame if he got defrauded. And theft through breach of trust—what we call embezzlement— had not yet become a criminal offense, except in the very limited situation of a servant's appropriation of goods entrusted to him by his master, which was assimilated to the offense of larceny by creating the fiction that the servant did not have lawful "possession" of the goods but only "custody." This stratagem preserved the notion that trespassory taking (one against the master's possession) was essential to the law of larceny. The very idea of creating a fiction for this seems dependent on the principle of legality; but let us take it as given that the law of England in 1770 was, very roughly speaking, as stated above, and let us then consider two actual legal developments that pose testing cases for the received doctrine about the principle of legality.

The first of these relates to the law of fraud.[3] A man named Pear rented a horse from a stable on the representation that he wished to ride it to Surrey and back again. Instead, he kept the horse; and he was charged with larceny by the defrauded stabler. The case gave the judges a lot of trouble. How could the offense be larceny when Pear came into possession of the horse lawfully? Where was the trespassory taking? Clearly, Pear was a horse thief; but had he committed a criminal offense? The judges' recognition that conduct of this sort posed a serious threat to commercial relationships prevailed over their scruples about expanding the ambit of the law of larceny. As was typical in the development of Anglo-American law, in this moment of tension a fiction was conceived. Pear's felonious intention, whenever it came into his mind, related back to the moment he rented the horse and made his taking of it trespassory. The way was opened for the wholesale development of the law of fraud. Obviously, if Pear's implied representation to the stabler that he would bring the horse back at the end of the rental period could count as the equivalent of a trespassory taking, then any false pretense could do so. Ironically, the judges had overlooked a statute passed by Parliament years earlier that could have been read as creating the

3 Rex v. Pear, 2 East's P.C. 685 (1779).

offense of obtaining by false pretenses. Later on, the judges of England recognized the possibilities in this statute, and the law of false pretenses as we now know it began to be developed. Pear's Case became a historical anomaly, chiefly notable for the creation of a totally irrational distinction, which has plagued generations of law students but has no other redeeming social importance, between the offenses of obtaining by false pretenses and larceny by trick. But its relevance for our purpose is this: by judicial decision Mr. Pear was adjudged a felon for conduct that did not seem to be criminal when he engaged in it.

Contrast the happy fate of one Bazeley, a teller employed by the Bank of England.[4] A customer handed him a hundred-pound banknote, to be deposited in his account. Bazeley pocketed the banknote. When the defalcation came to light, he was prosecuted for larceny. Once again, where was the trespassory taking? The escape hatch of Pear's Case was not available. Under well-established property law concepts, the money belonged to the bank once it was accepted for deposit. And because the larceny could not be from the customer, it had to be from the bank. There would have been no problem if Bazeley had put the banknote into the cash drawer, even for a moment, for then it would have been in the possession of the bank, and his appropriation of it would have been a trespassory taking in the category of larceny by servant described earlier. But the bank never got possession of "its" banknote. Therefore, no larceny. Mr. Bazeley was acquitted. And Parliament, aroused by the threat posed to public confidence in the safety of England's greatest financial monument, passed the first embezzlement statute, directed at embezzlements from the Bank of England. Ten years later a stockbroker named Walsh converted to his own use some securities entrusted to him by a customer. He was prosecuted and, like Bazeley, acquitted.[5] The act of Parliament applied to bank tellers, not to stockbrokers.

The question that all this suggests is: why should Pear be convicted, but Bazeley and Walsh acquitted? This historical excursion may tell us something about the principle of legality

---

[4] 2 East's P.C. 571 (1799).
[5] 168 E.R. 624 (1812).

that does not clearly emerge from a purely abstract and theoretical discussion of it. To begin with, all three men engaged in conduct that was recognized by the mores of the day, if not by formal legal proscription, as wrong, unjustifiably hurtful to others, and therefore to be discouraged. Because of deficiencies in the received criminal law of the day, it could not plainly be said that any of the three committed a crime. The court in Pear's Case resorted to a fiction in order to "interpret" his conduct as falling within the law of larceny. The Bazeley and Walsh courts found themselves unable to formulate an interpretation that would bring the conduct in question within the scope of the law as received. It may perhaps be argued that Pear's judges were false to the values thought to be served by the principle of legality; still, all three adhered formally to the principle. Even though Pear's Case is generally regarded as being one of the most sweeping and (by those who dislike that sort of thing) unjustifiable pieces of judicial legislation in Anglo-American legal history, the judges who decided it did everything in their power to convince their audience that their decision adhered to the principle that a man could be punished only for crimes already, so to speak, on the books. Why? Why didn't those judges come right out and say: we are treating Pear as a criminal even though what he did was not recognized as being criminal when he did it. And why didn't the judges in Bazeley's case create the offense of embezzlement? Or, after the first restricted embezzlement statute was passed, why didn't the judges in Walsh's case use it as an analogy for dealing with a situation that differed only in the occupation of the embezzler from what Parliament had already proscribed?

Can it be argued with a straight face that Pear, Bazeley, and Walsh had some kind of reliance interest in the existing state of the criminal law that the courts were bound to recognize? Suppose all three had consulted lawyers before acting as they did and had been told, as they surely would have been, that the criminal law did not apply to their conduct. They knew that what they were doing was wrong. Why should the legal system accord any weight to their shysterish expectation that the law would not apply to them? Is there any more than this to the first argument that is always advanced in support of the principle of legality: that people are entitled to fair notice of what the law requires so that they may plan their lives accordingly? Only this: if people are to be punished for conduct that is not criminal when engaged in but that is universally recognized to be wrongful, what is to safeguard people from being punished for conduct that is neither criminal when engaged in nor universally recognized to be wrongful? The "fair notice" rationale has little or nothing to do with cases like Pear's, Bazeley's, or Walsh's. Indeed, it has nothing to do with any of the instances of what are regarded as deviations from the principle of legality in Anglo-American legal history. The creation of genus rather than species crime—usually under the guise, be it said, of "discovery" or "interpretation"— has always been in response to situations in which the community's sense of security and propriety was deeply offended by the conduct in question. The "fair notice" rationale is a prophylactic rationale for tomorrow's hard case rather than for today's easy one. It represents a reaction that is one of the most characteristic and ingrained responses in the human situation and therefore in the law: if we let you do this, how do we know that you won't use it as a justification for doing something we wouldn't want you to do? Call it "bad precedent," "slippery slope," "entering wedge" or what you will, the instinct it expresses is a deep-seated one. And it is, in my view, only as an expression of that instinct that the "fair notice" rationale for the principle of legality becomes intelligible. It is not, in the cases in which it is advanced, that *this* man—Pear or Bazeley or Walsh—is being unfairly taken by surprise. It is that if we let you do this to these fellows, who so richly deserve it, how do we know that you won't do it to us?

Seen in this light, the "fair notice" rationale becomes a thinly disguised version of the second and more sophisticated rationale of the principle of legality, which is that it is necessary in order to prevent abuses of official discretion. This argument, too, is not without its difficulties. Even if the principle of legality is strictly observed, in the sense that no conduct is subjected to criminal punishment in the absence of an existing law making the conduct criminal, there is ample scope for the exercise of official discretion in an arbitrary and abusive kind of way. The principal techniques available for this purpose involve "interpretation" of the "existing law." If the law is articulated with some degree of generality—and it is in the nature of law that elements of indeterminacy will always be present, no matter how rigorous the effort to eliminate them—cases may be brought within it that involve just as much "unfair surprise," just as much abuse of official discretion, as if there had been no formal statement of the law anterior to the conduct in question. This possibility, which is an everyday reality in a complex legal system such as ours, cannot be eliminated by simple reliance on the principle of legality as it is commonly understood. Instead, its control requires the development of rather more sophisticated doctrines and of an adequate institutional structure for applying these doctrines. The doctrines have to do with the allocation of law-making and law-applying competences and with the distinction between "law-making" and "law-applying." Without such doctrines, the principle of legality is a somewhat forlorn hope for safeguarding the values it assertedly serves.

The principle of legality, as it is commonly understood, postulates a seemingly plausible model of the institutional framework within which the criminal process operates. According to this model, there are two necessary institutions, one to make the law, the other to apply it in the specific case at hand. We call the first a legislature and the second a court, and we assume that each tends only to its own set tasks. The model is such a familiar one that it is easy to overlook two interesting facts about it: this division of function is highly atypical in the context of the Anglo-American legal system; and it is not very descriptive of the way in which Anglo-American criminal law has actually evolved. Until the development of specialized administrative institutions —a development practically confined to this century—that require both legislative creation and constant legislative servicing, the great bulk of legal decision-making in the Anglo-American legal system went on through the work of the courts in the adjustment of disputes that came before them. The rules of decision for particular cases, regardless of the fictions that the courts invented to deny it, were evolved after the fact. The texture of the law of torts, of contracts, and of property contains far more judge-made, retrospective strands than it does legislative, prospective strands. And the same is true of the criminal law, except for the formal differences that *after* centuries of retrospective law-making by judges, the results of their work have been put into prospective codes by legislatures. Thus the process of judicial law-making in the criminal field has, except in the most interstitial kind of way, come to a halt.

In view of these historical facts, we can see a kind of aberrational aspect to the principle of legality that requires further exploration. Leaving aside historical questions of how it came to pass that the principle of legality, for all its incompatibility with the genius of Anglo-American law, came to be enshrined in our jurisprudence, we need to inquire whether and to what extent observance of its dictates serves the purposes of the criminal law as we have discerned them. In order to do this, we will have to pay attention to two problems that we have so far failed to treat as problems: what functions are performed by the allocation of "law-making" and "law-applying" competences to different legal institutions? And what, exactly, do we mean by "law-making" and "law-applying"?

THE ALLOCATION OF COMPETENCES

One possible model of a criminal law system would leave the invocation of the process entirely to the initiative of the persons who claimed to have been injured by the conduct complained of. This is of course precisely the way in which the system for the redress of injuries between private persons works, even today. On this model, if *A* killed *B*, *B*'s family, or whoever else was thought to have a sufficient interest to assert, would summon *A* to appear before a tribunal for the purpose of adjudicating his guilt. The tribunal, if satisfied of *A*'s guilt, would do what it does in civil cases today—award damages against *A* in favor of the complainant—but it would go on to impose some form of punishment on *A*, in the interest of preventing such conduct by *A* and others through the modes of deterrence, restraint, and reform. Would such a system serve the ends of a system of criminal law? Plainly it would not. Leaving aside practical difficulties, such a common-law, privately oriented criminal system would exhibit a basic deficiency, in that enforcement would be so sporadic and happenstance that the goal of prevention would not be served. People who were injured would often not complain: because they would be too busy, too lazy, too brave, too timid, or whatever. Or, though they might wish to complain, they might be unable to do so because they did not know the identity of the person who injured them. Or, though they suspected that they had been in some way injured, they might not even be sure enough of that fact to complain.

It is plain, then, that the objectives of criminal law in a complex, urbanized society like ours—one in which individuals are largely anonymous—require a set of institutions for detecting the commission of offenses, apprehending offenders, and determining whether they should be held for the adjudicative process. In short, it is essential to have police and prosecutors. But it is also essential to have checks on the exercise of discretion in the initiating phase of criminal prosecution when such prosecution is set in motion by an arm of the state rather than by private complainants. And it is here that we can see the real importance of the principle of legality in the criminal law today; for this principle operates primarily to control the discretion of the police and of prosecutors rather than that of judges.

In the judicial process the principle of legality is not essential to guarding against abuses of discretion because other checks accomplish the same thing. Courts operate in the open through what has been described as a process of reasoned elaboration. They have to justify their decisions. It is not enough to say: this man goes to jail because he did something bad. There is an obligation to relate the particular bad thing that this man did to other bad things that have been treated as criminal in the past. The system of analogical reasoning that we call the common-law method is a very substantial impediment to arbitrary decision-making. The fact that courts operate in the open according to a system of reasoning that is subjected to the scrutiny of an interested audience, both professional and lay, militates against any but the most marginal invasions of the values represented by the principle of legality.

By contrast, the police and the official prosecutors operate in a setting of secrecy and informality. Their processes are subjected to public scrutiny in only the most sporadic and cursory ways. Although some courts (particularly low-level courts in large cities faced with the necessity for dispensing assembly-line justice) at times behave with the informality and lack of articulation that characterizes the police and prosecutors, no one has ever discovered a police or prosecutorial organization that behaves like a court. When judges deviate from the model of openness, evenhandedness, and rationality, it is recognized and deplored as a deviation from their ideal role. But no one expects the police or the prosecutors to behave the way a court is supposed to behave; that is simply not their role, and they are not subjected to even the minimal psychological constraints that flow from self-perceived deviation from an acknowledged role.

The principle of legality, then, is important for the allocation of competences not between the legislative and judicial branches, but among those who initiate the criminal process through the largely informal methods of investigation, arrest, interrogation, and charge that characterize the operation of criminal justice. Part II of this book is devoted to an analysis of these methods. Their relevance here is simply that they exist and that their existence poses problems in the exercise of power to which the principle of legality is an important response.

Does this mean, then, that the conventional focus of the principle of legality, which is on defining the respective roles of legislature and courts, is distorted? Does it really make no difference whether the operative law is "made" by legislatures, declaring certain kinds of conduct criminal before they occur, or by courts, looking backward at the conduct whose criminality they are called upon to adjudicate? Not at all. The conventional focus is perfectly correct although not, as we have seen, for conventional reasons. It is correct because in a system that lodges the all-important initiating power in the hands of officials who operate, as they must, through informal and secret processes, there must be some devices to insure that the initiating decisions are, to the greatest extent possible, fair, evenhanded, and rational. Most of these devices, as we shall see in Part II, are in the nature of post-audits on the decisions taken by the police and prosecutors. But the most important single device is the requirement, enforced through the medium of collective expectation, that the police and prosecutors confine their attention to the catalogue of what has already been defined as criminal. It is, of course, theoretically possible that such a catalogue might simply comprise a digest of all the cases previously determined by judges to be criminal. But even if nothing else were at work to preclude this, the dictates of rational Weberian bureaucracy would insure that the catalogue would look much more like the generalized, prospective statements of positive law in the legislative style than like a digest of judicial decisions.

More is at work, of course, than the dictates of rational bureaucracy. If criminal law can be made *a posteriori,* by judges, rather than *a priori,* by legislatures, then the enforcement officials are under strong temptation to guess what the judges will do in a particular case. This temptation cannot be eliminated, as we shall shortly see, but it can be minimized through the habits of thought acquired by enforcement officials who work under the principle of legality. To take a modern instance, consider the problem of dangerous drugs such as LSD. If judges had as broad a lawmaking power as legislatures do, any policeman who thought that taking LSD was a bad thing that should be treated as criminal and any prosecutor who agreed with him could combine to put the criminal process in motion against people who took LSD. And if they could find one judge (among hundreds in a jurisdiction) who agreed with them, they could obtain a criminal conviction. And if a majority of the members of the appellate court in the jurisdiction agreed with them, they would carry the day.

In fact, nothing of the sort has occurred, despite the sentiment, probably greater among law enforcement officials than among the public at large, for the suppression of LSD. Aside from a little informal harassment of the kind that no legal system can effectively preclude, members of the deviant subculture composed of LSD takers remained free to follow their bent until legislative bodies began declaring, according to their mode of operation that, henceforth or from a certain day forward, anyone who takes LSD will be committing a crime. This kind of certainty and regularity is particularly to be prized when the initiation of legal sanctions is in official rather than private hands.

I do not, of course, mean to suggest that deviations from this principle do not occur. They do, rather more freely in Great Britain than in this country, but with decreasing frequency and ever-louder protests. A good example is the furor over the decision of the House of Lords in the famous case of *Shaw* v. *Director of Public Prosecutions.*[6] After the passage of the Street Offenses Act, which put a severe crimp into the streetwalking activities of London's prostitutes, the enterprising Mr. Shaw hit on a new way to advertise the wares that could no longer be hawked in person. He compiled a list of names, addresses, and telephone numbers, which he published as the *Ladies' Directory.* He was convicted of the judge-made offense of conspiring to corrupt public morals, and the House of Lords affirmed his conviction, thereby vindicating judicial power to make forms of conduct criminal that were not criminal before. Now, it is of course arguable that the House of Lords did not make a new law but applied an old one. That is the rhetoric of the prevailing opinions, and certainly the distinction is a difficult one to make. But the point of Mr. Shaw's story is that even so modest a lawmaking increment as this (if that is what it was) by England's highest judicial tribunal caused a storm of controversy that has even yet not abated. Courts do not altogether refrain from this sort of thing, but they think twice before they do it; and they do it so seldom that every instance is likely to become a *cause célèbre.* Shaw's case is hardly to be compared with Pear's in the magnitude of the departure made, but the sensibilities of the twentieth century are far more tender on this point than were those of the eighteenth.

VAGUENESS, STRICT CONSTRUCTION, AND PREVENTIVE DETENTION

Our examination of the institutional pressures that give the principle of legality its contemporary vitality reveals that the legislature is the principal lawmaker in a modern system of crimi-

---

[6] [1961] 2 Weekly L.R. 897.

nal law and that the court acts as lawmaker only in a subordinate
and interstitial way. But how does the system make this division
of power work? In order to understand the means available for
maintaining an appropriate allocation of roles to legislature and
court in a system of criminal justice, it is necessary first to reject
the delusively simple notion that we can clearly separate these
roles. As we shall see, there is a penumbral zone that is of great
importance in the administration of the criminal law.

Legislative law governing criminal conduct consists of generalized directions as to what people are forbidden to do in the
future: it is a crime to swear falsely in a judicial proceeding as
to some fact material to the proceeding. Judicial law consists of
particularized statements attaching legal consequences to particularized past conduct: Alger Hiss was guilty of perjury because
he falsely swore that he had not passed secret documents to an
agent of a foreign power in testimony before a grand jury that
had legitimate grounds for inquiring whether he had done so.
The legislature's job is law-making; the court's job is fact-finding
and law-applying. It all seems very simple until we ask whether
what the court did in Pear's case was to make law or to apply it.
The question is, of course, unanswerable in categorical terms.
It can only be dealt with by assessing the generality of the legislative enactment.

Let us suppose for a moment that a legislature, contemplating
the momentous problem of drafting a new criminal code, decided
to solve its problem by a single grand enactment: whoever does
anything bad shall be punished as justice may require. When a
court is called upon to decide whether John Jones, who hit his
neighbor over the head with a hammer during the course of an
argument, has violated the statute, is the court making law or is
it applying law? The question is absurd, of course. In a sense,
the court is doing both. But the significant question, which is
concealed by categorical treatment of law-making and law-appli-
cation, is: how great a degree of freedom is the court allocated in
deciding whether to treat John Jones's conduct as criminal? The
extremity of the example makes the issue clear. But the same
kind of issue is presented whenever the necessarily general, necessarily indeterminate directives of the legislature are used to de-

termine the after-the-fact conduct of the agencies of criminal law enforcement, including the police, the prosecutors, and (most visibly although not perhaps most importantly) the courts. It hardly needs argument that the hypothetical criminal enactment just proposed—whoever does anything bad shall be punished as justice may require—does violence to the principle of legality. As the example shows, it is not enough that the law formally being applied is law in existence at the time the conduct complained of occurred. Devices are needed to ensure that the amount of discretion entrusted to those who enforce the law does not exceed tolerable limits. Both the working out of the devices and the decision about what limits are tolerable are functions that fall to the courts. It is, of course, no accident that they fall to the courts; neither, however, is it the result of any omnicompetent lawgiver's deliberate plan. It is, very simply, an institutional necessity. The legislature cannot do the job, because the job may be operationally defined as the work left over after the legislature has done its job. Those who enforce the law cannot do the job because no man may be the judge in his own case. (A good definition of a police state would be a system in which the law enforcers were allowed to be the judges in their own cases.)

The devices worked out by the courts to keep the principle of legality in good repair comprise a cluster of doctrines that give the criminal law much of its distinctive content. For our purpose it is enough to identify and describe two of these doctrines, which fairly represent the values involved. They are the void-for-vagueness doctrine and the doctrine requiring the strict construction of penal statutes. The vagueness doctrine is a fairly recent product of American constitutional law, but the canon of strict construction has a lengthy common law history. Because of their differing origins, these two doctrines are not usually thought of as related. As we shall see, they have an intimate connection and may most usefully be thought of as contiguous segments of the same spectrum.

Under the vagueness doctrine in its starkest form, the court says to the legislature: you have given so much discretion in picking and choosing among the various kinds of conduct to which this statute may be applied that we will not let it be applied at all. That is unquestionably the response that an American court would give to the prosecution of John Jones under the hypothetical bad conduct statute discussed above. In fact, the vagueness doctrine has been most frequently and most stringently invoked in a limited class of cases: those in which the threat of enforcement discretion has been perceived as impinging on constitutionally protected values such as freedom of speech and of the press. As a constitutional limit on legislative delegation to enforcement agencies, the doctrine has thus been used infrequently to safeguard the values with which it is directly concerned; instead, it has developed as an instrumental doctrine rather than one having independent force. Vagueness is bad, so the Supreme Court's decisions seem to teach us, not because it is as a general proposition wrong for the legislature to give away its offense-defining power to the law enforcement agencies and the judges but because it is wrong to do so when certain values that the Court is particularly interested in protecting (like freedom of speech) seem to be threatened by the delegation. Because of this skew, the actual operation of the doctrine has led to rather anomalous results. For example, it is hard to imagine a more complete throwing up of the hands by the legislature than this one: it is a criminal offense to sell goods "at unreasonably low prices for the purpose of destroying competition or eliminating a competitor." Yet this provision, Section 3 of the Robinson-Patman Act, was recently upheld, albeit without enthusiasm, by a divided Supreme Court in the *National Dairy* case.[7]

In this book, however, it is not the actual operation of doctrine with which we are primarily concerned. Indeed, it is not for us a matter of moment that the vagueness doctrine is a constitutional doctrine, except possibly as it serves to explain why the Supreme Court has been so chary in applying it. Rather, our concern is with its theoretical relevance to a system of criminal law. It is a doctrine that is properly addressed in the first instance to the legislature, an injunction to take care in the framing of criminal statutes that no more power be given to call conduct into question as criminal, with all the destruction of human autonomy that this power necessarily imports, than is reasonably

---

[7] United States v. National Dairy Products Corp., 372 U.S. 29 (1963).

needed to deal with the conduct the lawmakers seek to prevent.

The other doctrine with which we are concerned here—the canon of strict construction of penal statutes—may perhaps be viewed as something of a junior version of the vagueness doctrine. It too is a court-evolved doctrine, and so takes the form of a statement by the court to the legislature about a case pending before the court. It says: "the language you have used in this criminal statute does not convey a clear intention to cover the case before us. Therefore this man, who may well have done something that all of us would like to treat as criminal, must go free." Courts have, for a variety of reasons (by no means confined to the rationale sketched here), traditionally been quite insistent on maintaining a high standard of compliance with this policy of clear statement—so much so, indeed, that the results in a particular case must sometimes appear quite strange.

Consider the famous case of *McBoyle* v. *United States*.[8] A federal statute made it an offense to transport a stolen "motor vehicle" in interstate commerce. McBoyle transported a stolen airplane. Justice Holmes, speaking for a unanimous Supreme Court in reversing the conviction, said that the statute should not be "extended" to cover aircraft "upon the speculation that, if the legislature had thought of it, very likely broader words would have been used." One might well conclude that in this case the Court was being overly restrictive, just as one might conclude that in *National Dairy* they were being too permissive. From one viewpoint the court was trying to educate (or perhaps to punish) the legislature for not being sufficiently precise in its use of language.[9] A more spacious view would see the decision in *McBoyle* as a symbolic affirmation of the values inherent in the principle of legality. Courts can't very well make symbolic gestures in a vacuum. If the Supreme Court had affirmed McBoyle's conviction the case would now be forgotten, no matter how persuasive its statements about the need for legislative precision.

The trouble with these doctrines as they conventionally ex-

---

[8] 283 U.S. 25 (1931).
[9] In fact, the lesson was so badly learned that Congress amended the statute in a way that excluded stolen boats. There are dangers in this flagellant use of statutory interpretation.

press themselves in the law is that they come at the wrong point
in the process. They are only superficially judicial doctrines, although that is the guise in which they make their appearance.
They are no more than empty words unless they are recognized
and acted upon by the legislature, which creates crimes, and by
the law enforcement officers, whose uneasy role it is to interfere
with human autonomy so as to subject to the criminal process
those who have engaged in conduct of the sort the legislature is
concerned to prevent.

In retrospect, we can see that the entire doctrinal web we have
been talking about is necessitated by one basic fact about the
rationale of the criminal law: that its accommodation of competing demands of order and freedom begins with the limitation
of its application to conduct. Although it seeks to control the
future by shaping the ways in which people behave and by intervening in the lives of people who display antisocial propensities,
the criminal law limits its effect and its intervention to the *locus
poenitentiae* of what has in fact observably taken place in the
past. This self-denying ordinance is what makes the criminal law
tolerable as a means of social control in a free and open society.
The other doctrinal consequences of the rationale of the criminal
law sketched in earlier chapters of this book, fundamental though
they surely are, pale into insignificance beside this one.

Everything that has been said in this chapter about the allocation of competence to create categories of criminal behavior and
about the principle of legality with its instrumental doctrines
of void-for-vagueness and strict construction shows that this body
of doctrine serves the single, important function of confining the
criminal law to conduct. A purely behavioral criminal law would
brush this limitation aside as irrational. It would take advantage
of every means devisable by human ingenuity to look into the
future, to deal with propensities before they expressed themselves
in action, i.e., to prevent bad occurrences in the future without
regard to past conduct. And such a criminal law would have no
place in it for the strict separation of institutional competences
or for the principle of legality and its attendant doctrines. It is
no accident that the current constitutional attack on status crimes
is based on the vagueness doctrine; for status crimes represent

one of the most clear-cut instances in our received criminal law of a purely behavioral emphasis on prediction. The function of this now-discredited body of law is to subject to control people who have not engaged in any identifiable bad conduct but who are thought likely to do so in the future.

Considerable tension exists between the goal of prevention and the idea that the criminal law's reach is limited to conduct. Conduct belongs to the past; it consists of identifiable, discrete events. We know it experientially and historically; and law that deals with it must develop methods of proof that are akin to the historian's. Ranke's ideal—to know the past *wie es eigentlich gewesen ist*—could just as well be the motto of the criminal courts. But prevention is a goal that speaks to the future in, as we have seen, a variety of modes—deterrence, incapacitation, rehabilitation. We cannot know prevention; we can only predict it. Our faith is in conduct as a predictive clue, perhaps our best one. But it is only a clue, and there is always a temptation to ignore it in favor of other clues that may seem to be less limiting. That temptation is not very strong in the case of deterrence as a mode of prevention, because deterrence uses a man's past conduct not as a predictor of what he will do in the future but as an occasion for demonstrating to others what will happen to them if they engage in similar conduct. Deterrence thus minimizes the tension between past and future. Incapacitation and rehabilitation do not let us off that lightly. There is no other way to influence the future behavior of the world at large than to reinforce the idea that certain kinds of *conduct* are to be discouraged. The method of deterrence has no concern with such vague concepts as dangerousness. But conduct, which is at the center of the idea of deterrence, is at best a means to an end when what we have in mind are the distinctively behavioral modes of prevention that we call incapacitation and rehabilitation. If we can predict tendencies and propensities without respect to identifiable conduct, if we can prevent conduct from taking place and thereby avoid the constrictions of historical proof, why not do so? The temptation is always there, and the history of the criminal law is full of examples of how easily we yield to it. Some of them are outright violations of the principle of legality. Some of them have been treated historically as if they are not even though in substance they are. Others represent reasonable accommodations to the principle of legality. It may be instructive to look briefly at a few points on the spectrum of preventive detention.

The prototype of the outright violation is the arrest "for investigation" or "on suspicion." The ideal of the law of arrest is that no person may be deprived of his freedom, even momentarily, unless there is probable cause to believe that he has committed a crime. But that ideal is flouted in practice hundreds of times every day. People who arouse the suspicion of the police that they may be up to no good are taken into custody—sometimes only for a few minutes, sometimes for days or even weeks—out of a variety of preventive motives. The most nearly respectable such motive is that upon interrogation it will turn out that these people have in fact committed an offense for which they can be duly charged, even though the formal grounds for arrest are lacking. But many more—perhaps the bulk—of arrests on suspicion do not have a motive with even that degree of pseudo-legality. Rather, such arrests reflect the view that these people may engage in bad conduct in the future and that, if they are harassed in advance, both their opportunity and their incentive to engage in criminal conduct may be reduced. Known gamblers, narcotics addicts, and prostitutes in our large cities are particularly vulnerable to this kind of preventive detention. And, as we shall see, the more difficult it is to detect their offenses after they are committed, the stronger is the temptation to subject them to preventive detention in advance of putative occurrence.

Preventive detention can be accomplished under the guise of punishment for crimes committed if the definition of the crime is sufficiently vague and elastic. The classic instance is the offense of vagrancy. If it is an offense to wander about without lawful business and without visible means of support, then there is warrant for arresting and incarcerating people ostensibly because they are "vagrants" but in fact because they are likely to commit offenses unless restrained. A very common variation on this theme is the use of a vagrancy prosecution as a lever for inducing transients to "move on" to another locality, so that their future crimes, if any, will be committed elsewhere. The perspective of any given set of law enforcement officials is parochial. To them, "prevention" means prevention in the locality for which they are responsible. And so the vagrancy laws are used to push crime problems from one place to another.

Vagrancy laws, and other crimes of status, are currently in very bad odor. In the case mentioned earlier, a California law making it a criminal offense to be addicted to the use of narcotics was declared unconstitutional by the United States Supreme Court on the ground that it is "cruel and unusual punishment" to make it a crime to suffer from the illness of addiction.[10] Following this lead, several lower courts have held that statutes making it an offense to be a common drunkard are similarly defective. Whatever the constitutional basis, it seems clear that laws of this sort, like the offense of vagrancy itself, are incompatible with the principle of legality because they give law enforcement agencies undue discretion in defining conduct as criminal, to the extent that they require conduct at all, and because they are essentially devices for effecting preventive detention.

We may expect the gradual disappearance of crimes of status to put increased pressure on other devices for facilitating preventive detention, both criminal and noncriminal. As we have already seen, the conduct dealt with by the criminal law is not exclusively conduct that results in the ultimate harm apprehended. We do not wait to incarcerate drunk drivers until they have killed someone; the criminal law punishes drunk driving as well as vehicular manslaughter. We do not wait to incarcerate people who break into houses for the purpose of committing theft until they actually steal something; the law punishes burglary as well as larceny. Indeed we do not even wait until a burglary is actually committed if we are lucky enough to catch a man who possesses tools that are usable for burglary and for nothing else. These offenses, all dealing to some extent with preparatory conduct that may lead to some ultimate harm, are perfectly consistent with the minimal requirements of the principle of legality. All of them, however, do involve preventive detention in a very real sense. And all of them raise questions about how

[10] Robinson v. California, 370 U.S. 660 (1962).

far back from the ultimately apprehended act the criminal law should reach to proscribe preparatory conduct.

The principal doctrinal device that traditional criminal law has relied on for dealing with preparatory conduct, and therefore for introducing some measures of preventive detention into the criminal law, is the so-called inchoate crime: attempt, conspiracy, and solicitation. It is worth examining one of these—attempt— in a brief, nontechnical way to see what light it sheds on the response of criminal doctrine to the pressure for some measures of preventive detention.

The law of attempts is explicitly addressed to the problem of conduct that has not reached the ultimately apprehended harm. In this explicitness, it differs from such offenses as reckless driving and burglary, which are formally self-contained even though, as we have seen, they represent an effort to deal with conduct before it has ripened into an ultimate harm. But in the law of attempt, this aspect of incompleteness is out in the open. The gist of attempt is that the actor has tried to do something but has not succeeded. Now, all of us frequently make moves in the direction of criminal activity, thereby satisfying this essential element of the attempt concept. It is, therefore, instructive to note the doctrinal mechanisms whose function it is, baldly put, to keep from making criminals of us all.

To begin with, there is no such thing as a general crime of attempt. There are only attempts to commit particular crimes. If I take steps to marry my first cousin in a jurisdiction that does not treat such marriages as incestuous, we can be standing at the altar with the preacher about to conduct the marriage service, and I still will not have committed attempted incest. Here we see in operation the most basic limiting aspect of the law of attempts, its dependence on the principle of legality for its legitimacy. Contrast this dependence with the broad sweep of status offenses, as well as of the explicitly outlawed arrest on suspicion, and the durability of the conduct limitation in the criminal law becomes manifest.

Next, the law of attempts requires a high order of proof that the actor really was engaged in conduct that would have led to an offense but for some mischance, rather than in suspicious-seeming but intrinsically innocent activity. This assurance is given in two ways: first, by insisting on a showing that the actor had a purpose to bring about the forbidden result; second, by requiring proof that his conduct brought him a substantial distance on the road to achieving his objective. The books are full of cases in which defendants who bought guns, sent threatening letters, laid in wait, and did a variety of other menacing things were exonerated because the actions in question were held to have been too remote from the intended objective to constitute the conduct component of the offense of attempt. Indeed, modern analysis has rejected as too restrictive much of the enshrined dogma about how close one might come and still not be guilty of an attempt. The point for our purposes is not who was right—the old judges or their new critics—but rather that the criminal law has in fact displayed a very high degree of finickiness about penalizing conduct that falls short of a completed offense. One may well think, as I do, that much of the dogma of the law of attempts is sheer nonsense, and still respect the soundness of the instinct that has set up a barrage of obstacles to the free use of the attempt device. What we can see at work in this branch of the criminal law is an almost instinctive rejection of the ultimate implications of preventive detention.

The law of attempts represents an uneasy compromise with the pressure for preventive detention. It is a compromise that falls so far short of what would be demanded if the idea were given full sway in the criminal law, as those holding the behavioral view would like to see done, that we can see in it a paradigm of the criminal law's essentially self-denying ordinance: we will concern ourselves with prevention of future antisocial conduct, but we will do so only when we can anchor the necessary prediction to something specific and concrete that the actor has done in the past. If pressures exist—and they assuredly do—for more sweeping recognition of the idea of preventive detention in the law, those pressures must find outlets other than the criminal law and, optimally, other than the sanction of punishment. As we shall see, these pressures do find other outlets, notably in the rapidly proliferating laws relating to the "civil commitment" of the "mentally ill." As we shall also see, these laws, in their basic concept and in their administration, do not avoid the ubiquitous problem of punishment. But that is another story. For reasons already given, it is important to hold the line in the criminal law, even if we wish or are forced to give scope to the idea of preventive detention elsewhere.

CHAPTER SIX

Culpability and Excuses

INTRODUCTION

In the preceding section we have seen how important it is to make conduct a necessary condition for the imposition of criminal liability. The values underlying the integrated theory of punishment require that some more or less specific act or omission, prescribed in advance by a governmental authority having the institutional competence to do so, serve as the basis for the intervention of the criminal process in the life of the accused. In this chapter we will explore the reasons why conduct is a necessary but not a sufficient element for criminal liability.

Let us start with a few simple examples. (1) Arthur is discovered standing over the corpse of Victor, a smoking revolver in his hand. He readily admits to having killed Victor but asserts that Victor had attacked him with a knife and that he, Arthur, had feared for his own life. (2) Barry, while eating dinner in a restaurant, notices that it has begun to rain. On leaving the restaurant he takes a raincoat with Vincent's name stenciled inside the collar from the coatrack near the door. Vincent has Barry arrested. Barry admits that the raincoat is not his own, but asserts that he had seen it hanging there for the past six months and had thus supposed that its rightful owner had abandoned it. (3) Charlie, a narcotics addict, leaves the country for a vacation trip to Mexico. On his return to the U.S. he is stopped at the border by

immigration officers who recognize him as a trafficker in narcotics. There is a statute making it an offense for a narcotics
addict to leave the country without registering with the immigration authorities. Charlie asserts that he never heard about this
statutory requirement.

In each of these three cases there is no doubt that the actor's
conduct answers to the description of conduct proscribed by a
duly promulgated criminal statute. Under conventional criminal
law doctrine it is, however, perfectly clear that Arthur and Barry
are not guilty of a crime if their excuses are believed. Charlie's
excuse, on the other hand, will in all likelihood not count in his
favor. In conventional terms, Arthur and Barry lacked *mens rea,*
and Charlie did not. As we shall see, the distinction is not intelligible; our theory of punishment turns out to require that
attention be paid to the excuses of all three. But it is far from
self-evident that any of the excuses need be entertained.

Before tackling the difficult question of whether and to what
extent factors other than the actor's conduct should be taken into
account in determining his criminality, it may be helpful to look
briefly at the linguistic problem posed by terms like "mental element" and *mens rea* (law Latin for "guilty mind"). At the outset, it has to be stated that the unitary impression conveyed by
terms such as these is misleading. There is no such thing as *the*
mental element or *mens rea* of a particular crime, let alone of
crime in general. These terms are simply shorthand statements
for a cluster of concepts having to do with states of mind or their
absence, experienced by people whose conduct is arguably criminal. When we speak of Arthur's having the *mens rea* of murder,
we may mean any one or more of the following things: that he
intended to kill Victor; or that he was aware of the risk of his
killing Victor but went ahead and shot him anyhow; or (more
dubiously) that he ought to have known but didn't that there was
a substantial risk of his killing Victor; or that he knew it was
wrong to kill a fellow human being, or that he ought to have
known it; or that he didn't really think that Victor was trying
to kill him; or that he did think that, but only a fool would have
thought it; or that he was not drunk to the point of uncon-
sciousness when he killed Victor; or that even though he was

emotionally disturbed he wasn't grossly psychotic, etc., etc. Depending on the facts of the case and on the particular aspect of the facts on which one happened to be focusing, one might have any of these statements in mind when saying that Arthur had the *mens rea* of murder.

There are, very generally speaking, two analytic approaches to the question of *mens rea*. The first, which we may call the positive approach, attempts to identify particular states of mind and to attribute them to each of the material elements constituting the definition of particular criminal offenses. This positive approach has been carried to a high degree of analytic rigor in the American Law Institute's Model Penal Code, which identifies four grades of mental elements—purpose, knowledge, recklessness, and negligence. It then attributes these four mental elements to three material elements—the actor's physical conduct, the surrounding circumstances, and the result of the conduct. In this analytic framework, what we might ordinarily think of as "defenses"—self-defense, for example—are included as material elements of the offense that must be accompanied by an appropriate mental element. Thus, in Arthur's case, the analysis might proceed somewhat as follows. Arthur knowingly engaged in the physical conduct of pulling the trigger. He had knowledge of the relevant attendant circumstances: that he was pointing the gun at Victor, that Victor was a live human being, that the gun was loaded, etc., etc. He either intended the result of Victor's death or at least was reckless (consciously disregarded a substantial risk that it might occur) about it. Now, the facts of Arthur's case seem fairly cut-and-dried. The crucial question is whether what would otherwise be a plain case of murder is to be treated either as some lesser homicidal offense or as a noncriminal homicide because of Arthur's alleged belief that his life was in danger. Here, depending on what the evidence showed, one might conclude that Arthur didn't really believe that his life was in danger (if, for example, no knife was found in Victor's possession) and that the defense therefore failed on that ground; or that he did entertain such a belief but on unreasonable grounds; or that he did entertain such a belief and it was neither reckless nor negligent of him to do so. Whether Arthur would be found guilty of murder would thus depend upon two things, both of them "mental": what mental element the law required for a successful plea of self-defense and what one concluded on the basis of the evidence about Arthur's alleged belief that his life was being endangered by Victor. The analytic framework does not, of course, tell us whether or not Arthur should be treated as having committed a criminal offense; it simply enables us to analyze in an orderly way whether according to a given set of legal definitions Arthur's conduct is criminal and, if so, what crime he has committed. Its great virtue is that it reveals the complexity of the idea of mental element, and demonstrates that there is no such thing as *a* state of mind for a particular offense but rather a combination of states of mind, each bearing on a different element of the offense, including the so-called defenses.

The other analytic approach to *mens rea*, which we may call the negative approach, views the definition of criminal offenses as what H. L. A. Hart has termed "defeasible": a man who kills another is guilty of murder, *unless* he did not kill intentionally or recklessly, or *unless* he believed that his life was in danger; a man who takes another's property is guilty of theft *unless* he was unaware that the property was that of another, *unless* he thought the owner was making him a gift; a man who leaves the country without registering as required by law is guilty of an offense *unless* he did not know that he was required to register. In this analysis, the mental element is perceived as relating exclusively to matters of justification, excuse, or mitigation. If you kill someone, you are guilty of murder unless you did so accidentally, or unless you did so under provocation, or unless you did so in self-defense. The proponents of this analytic approach argue that the positive approach is overly rigid, and that it is in any event impossible to identify in advance all of the possible excuses (all of which depend upon some state of mind or other) that may serve to exculpate or mitigate conduct that would otherwise be viewed as criminal.[1]

There is much learned disputation about the comparative merits of these two approaches. The positivists, if I may use that term, accuse the negativists of being sloppy; the negativists ac-

---

[1] E.g., Peter Brett, *An Inquiry Into Criminal Guilt* (London, 1963), chap. 4.

cuse the positivists of being rigid. The dispute is academic, in the pejorative sense of the word. Which approach one takes, or what combination of the two approaches one takes, depends on the analytic function that is being served at the moment. If one is engaged in drafting a criminal code, which must prescribe precisely what has to be proven to convict of crime and precisely what distinctions separate one crime from another when the same external facts are present (as, for example, in differentiating murder from manslaughter), there can be no doubt that the positive approach is much the superior. If, on the other hand, one is attempting to discern after the fact the true inwardness of judicial decisions, particularly in a criminal law system that does not include a highly developed set of legislative prescriptions, it seems equally plain that the negative approach is superior. It is no accident that the positive approach is adopted in the masterly legislative construct underlying the American Law Institute's Model Penal Code. Nor is it an accident that those British philosophers who have advanced our understanding of the rationale of the criminal law by subjecting the work of British judges to linguistic analysis have relied on the negative approach. For each, the approach taken was the better tool for the job at hand. What is unfortunate, because so easily avoidable, is the notion that a choice has to be made once and for all between the two approaches, regardless of the job each is being conscripted to perform.

In the pages that follow I shall be relying mainly on the negative approach to the problems of *mens rea* because that approach focuses on the categories of justification and excuse (such as necessity, duress, and mistake) that comprise the minimal doctrinal content of a criminal law whose rationale is based on the integrated system developed in earlier chapters. The concept of defeasibility is central to this analysis. It views certain defined forms of conduct as being prima facie criminal unless the conduct takes place under certain circumstances having to do with the actor's state of mind. Our central inquiry will be what those circumstances are and why they should be viewed as relevant to a determination of criminality.

It is an obvious but generally overlooked point that this assortment of excuses (using that term loosely to cover all the cir-

cumstances of defeasibility that affect a determination of criminality) is concerned totally with the actor's state of mind and not
with the physical conduct in which he has engaged. If we let
Arthur off, it is not because he did not kill Victor; if we let
Barry off, it is not because he did not take Vincent's raincoat; if
we let Charlie off, it is not because he did not leave the country
without registering as a narcotics addict. This is not, of course,
to assert that *mens rea* is concerned only with excuses. If there
were such a one-to-one relationship, the connection would be
clearer than it is. All excuses involve *mens rea*; but not all *mens
rea* problems involve excuses. The other category of *mens rea*
problems, with which we are not concerned at this time, relates
to grading: the determination of the comparative severity of
punishment for different but related offenses. For example, if
one kills another intentionally, most criminal codes will tend to
prescribe a more severe punishment than if one kills another
negligently. If one takes another's automobile intending to keep
it permanently, most criminal codes will tend to prescribe a
more severe punishment than if one takes it intending only to
use it for a limited period of time and heedless of whether or not
the rightful owner is likely to regain possession of it. And so on.
These, again, are discriminations that turn entirely upon the
ascription of some sort of *mens rea* to the actor.

To sum the matter up, there are two kinds of *mens rea* problems in the criminal law: problems concerning excuses and problems concerning grading. These two categories exhaust the whole
of the subject. We are concerned at this point with the first and
not the second because we are interested in the preconditions of
criminal liability rather than in the distinctions between ways
of dealing with people who have committed crimes. And because
it is functionally appropriate to do so, we will therefore use the
language of the negative rather than the positive approach to
mens rea.

THE GENERAL RATIONALE OF EXCUSES

Why should the criminal law pay any attention to excuses? If
people engage in conduct that, in its externals, conforms to a de-

scription of what is forbidden by a criminal statute, why should they be allowed, under any circumstances, to escape punishment by invoking an absence of *mens rea,* an excuse? By recurring to our earlier discussion of the justifications for punishment we may begin to get a handhold on this problem, but it will very quickly become apparent that the answer is by no means clear. The exercise will be a useful one, I think, because it throws much additional light on the inadequacy of either a utilitarian or a retributive explanation, standing alone, for the institution of criminal punishment.

The question to be considered is this: suppose that Victor really was threatening to take Arthur's life, and suppose that Arthur really did apprehend the danger that he was in, why should a system of criminal justice pay any attention to those facts when it is clear that Arthur has intentionally killed Victor? The retributive answer—that Arthur has not acted wickedly—is less unsatisfactory than the affirmative justification for punishment on retributive grounds. The idea that the "guilty" must be punished without regard to social consequences is much more difficult to accept than is the proposition that the "innocent" must not be punished—again without regard to social consequences. Still, the retributive answer begs the question of the standard by which guilt or innocence is to be judged. And its disdain for social consequences weakens the force of the position for anyone who views the criminal law as an instrument of social policy rather than as a set of categorical imperatives.

In a utilitarian view, the answer at first blush seems more plausible. None of the preventive aims of punishment will be served by treating Arthur's conduct as criminal. Deterrence could not have operated on him if he really thought that killing Victor was necessary to save his own life. As Hobbes pointed out: ". . . no Law can oblige a man to abandon his own preservation. And supposing such a Law were obligatory; yet a man would reason thus, *If I doe it not, I die presently; if I doe it, I die afterwards; therefore by doing it, there is time of life gained;* Nature thereof compells him to the fact."[2] By the same token, one who kills from ne-

---

[2] *Leviathan* (Facsimile of 1651 ed., Oxford, 1958), p. 157.

cessity has not demonstrated homicidal dangerousness; his conduct shows no more than that when his own life is endangered he will take the life of the man who threatens him. Consequently, he does not require restraint or reform in the interest of social protection. However, this argument is unconvincing. It asserts that punishing Arthur serves no utilitarian goal; but all it demonstrates is that punishing Arthur serves no utilitarian goal so far as he is concerned. It does not dispose of the possibility that punishing Arthur may serve a utilitarian goal where others are concerned. And indeed it might. The punishment of Arthur involves the threat of punishment to others. If we excuse Arthur because he really saw himself as threatened, we may incur two kinds of "utilitarian losses." We may present others with the incentive to fake the same excuse, and we may leave at large homicidally dangerous people who have successfully faked the excuse.

The problem is put in a clearer light if we ask what we mean by saying that Arthur "really" believed that Victor was about to kill him. What we mean is that we believe that he believed it. We believe it not as a matter of faith, but because we have been shown evidence that makes us believe it—Arthur's own protestations, what we can discover about his character based on past conduct and reputation, whether Victor was in fact armed, how the incident appeared to eyewitnesses (if any), and so on. All of this takes time and effort, the expenditure of which must (in a utilitarian universe) be justified. In the end the decision is not a matter of fact but only one of probability. And if we require (as the criminal law typically does) that the prosecution satisfy the trier of fact to a very high degree of probability that the hypothesis of a simulated excuse is excluded by the evidence, then we offer a warm invitation to Arthur (and to others) to make a run at deceiving us. And if this is true for an excuse like self-defense, which requires only a relatively objective historical investigation, how much truer it is of an excuse like insanity, which (as we shall see) is an impossible tangle of fact and value. From a utilitarian viewpoint, the argument against according excuses a dispositive effect is a very strong one. The countervailing consideration—that the misery produced by laws that did not recognize excuses would outweigh the benefits of greater compliance with the law—is at best speculative. And its force may be somewhat blunted by the observation that in a developed legal system there might be found devices for summary administrative mitigation of punishment in "deserving" cases. At any rate, if all we are concerned with is the prevention of crime, there is no utilitarian calculus clearly showing that excuses ought to be recognized.

If we focus for a moment on the behavioral branch of the utilitarian position, the case against excuses becomes even stronger. In that view, it will be recalled, considerations of deterrence are minimized, and the goals of punishment vis-à-vis the individual offender are seen as paramount. This might superficially appear to militate in favor of excuses because, as we have seen, in classic utilitarian terms the fatal weakness of excuses is their relaxation of deterrence. However, the behavioral position sees the occurrence of criminal conduct simply as the occasion, not the justifying reason, for the intervention of the criminal process. Its emphasis is predictive; it seeks to identify dangerous persons and subject them to restraint and reform. Now, there is nothing about the fortuity of homicide in self-defense that demonstrates lack of dangerousness. The actor's past conduct is only one of many clues to how he may behave in the future. If we are going to use past conduct as the basis for intervention—a basis that the thoroughgoing advocate of the behavioral view would regard as irrational —then why adopt the wasteful procedure of screening out some of the potentially dangerous on the basis of a largely irrelevant criterion? If Arthur killed Victor, let's have a look at Arthur and decide what to do with him. And let's have that look not in a courtroom, where we are trammeled with a lot of legal mumbo jumbo, but rather in the Reception and Diagnostic Center of the State Department of Corrections, where we can apply all our scientific knowledge to deciding what kind of fellow Arthur is and what we ought to do with him. In short, convict first and ask questions later. If this argument is plausible from the behavioral standpoint in the case of self-defense, think how much more plausible it is in the case of an excuse like insanity. The conclusion seems inevitable that there is no place in the behavioral-utilitarian scheme of things for recognizing excuses in the criminal law.

The reasons for recognizing excuses do not, then, have much to do with the prevention of antisocial conduct. They have to do with other values that, to put it bluntly, interfere with absolute efficiency in the prevention of antisocial conduct. They have to do with preserving human autonomy and with maximizing the opportunity to exercise choice. They have to do also with maintaining an appropriate distance between the state and the individual, with minimizing the appropriate occasions for state intervention into the way the individual lives his life. This point about intervention perhaps requires some amplification. The doctrines and rules of the criminal law are not designed merely to enable a court to decide whether or not it is appropriate to subject an individual to criminal punishment. They are also designed to guide officials in all phases of the criminal process before the trial in deciding whether and to what extent they should intervene. The law of excuses is at least as important in telling a prosecutor when to prosecute as in telling a judge and jury when to convict. And, even though we do not usually think of the police as exercising much judgment about the niceties of the law of excuses, that law may also tell the policeman when he should refrain from arresting. Take the simple case of a man who drives through a traffic light on his way to the hospital with his critically ill child. It would hardly be enough for the system to exonerate that man on his appearance in traffic court. The operationally significant moment for him is when the policeman who flags him down decides that instead of giving him a ticket he will give him a motorcycle escort to the hospital. Although it may seem somewhat odd to put it this way, what the policeman is doing in these circumstances is making an ad hoc application of the law of excuses.

The point of this discussion is that the case for excuses in the criminal law rests most securely on claims for the protection of human autonomy that quite transcend the calculus of crime prevention. Our best reason for not punishing people who are not "culpable" is simply that culpability is an appropriate criterion for limiting the reach of state intervention. The concept of culpability is not a metaphysical construct that defies rational analysis, as some proponents of the behavioral position assert. It is a handy tool left lying around by the retributionists that can be used to advance certain goals of the criminal law: not those that have to do with preventing antisocial behavior, but those that have to do with limiting the damage done to other important social values as the criminal law goes about its inevitable but ambiguous business.

There is no *a priori* reason why any given kind of excuse should or should not be recognized by the criminal law. Rather, it is a matter of judgment whether the utilitarian losses that inevitably attend the recognition of an excuse are outweighed by the gain in freedom from state intervention, especially when such intervention diminishes the individual's capacity to make moral choices. A few exercises in this kind of judgment-making will help to give content to the idea of culpability as a limiting criterion for the imposition of criminal punishment, and will also show how a criminal law based clearly on the rationale proposed in earlier chapters is necessarily a very complicated instrument of public policy. In examining the content and rationale of a few representative excuses, we will start with the one that appears to rest most solidly on a pure utilitarian basis and then proceed along what may be thought of as a spectrum of decreasing utilitarian justifications until we arrive at a point where nonutilitarian considerations can be seen to play a clearly controlling role.

NECESSITY

In the early days of Anglo-American criminal law, the law of homicide distinguished between two kinds of noncriminal killings, "justifiable" and "excusable." Their procedural incidents have long since ceased to have any significance, but the two concepts have considerable utility in analyzing what we have been referring to generically as "excuses" in the criminal law. Briefly put, the distinction is this: conduct that we choose not to treat as criminal is "justifiable" if our reason for treating it as noncriminal is predominantly that it is conduct that we applaud, or at least do not actively seek to discourage; conduct is "excusable" if we deplore it but for some extrinsic reason conclude that it is not politic to punish it. The policeman who kills an armed robber who is trying to kill him is not merely let off from punishment; he will most likely end up with a promotion, or at least with a letter of commendation in his file. On the other hand, the same policeman who kills a sixteen-year-old boy who he mistakenly supposed was escaping from the scene of a robbery may be (somewhat reluctantly) exonerated from a charge of murder; but it is unlikely that his career will be advanced by the incident. Under conventional criminal law doctrines both policemen are the beneficiaries of what we have been generically referring to as "excuses," but it seems clear that the reasons supporting this result in the two cases must be very different.

The strongest utilitarian case for withholding punishment arises in the situation in which the actor's conduct results in a greater quantum of good (or a lesser quantum of bad) than would any other course of action open to him, including inaction. This utilitarian precept arises from the perception, intuitive but usually not articulated, that life is full of dilemmas, in which no matter what is done something undesirable will result. If we cannot maximize gains, then the principle of utility tells us that we must minimize losses. The policeman kills the kidnapper to save his innocent victim. The lost alpinist breaks into a mountain cabin to take refuge from the storm. The fire-fighters destroy property in order to confine the forest fire. The ambulance driver runs through a red light in order to rush a critically ill person to the hospital. In each case, the actor is confronted with a dilemma, in the sense that whatever he does will result in a loss. In each case, the choice he makes involves the breach of some positive rule of the criminal law. Yet we intuitively sense that it would be wrong to punish him for doing so. Why?

In the first place, it seems foolish to make rules (or to fail to make exceptions to rules) that discourage people from behaving as we would like them to behave. To the extent that the threat of punishment has deterrent efficacy, rules such as these would condition people confronted with dilemmas to make the wrong choice, either through action or inaction. And the actual imposition of punishment would serve no useful purpose since we assume these people are not in need of either restraint or reform. Furthermore, the threat of punishment would in at least some of these cases be inefficacious because of the strength of the impulse to make the right choice. This is obviously so where one's own life is at stake, as in the case of the lost alpinist; but it is also true of all cases where there is a great disparity between the choices, one which could be lessened only by the severest threat of punishment. To the extent that the threat of punishment worked, it would produce bad results; to the extent that it failed to work it would expose the criminal law to highly merited ridicule.

The conventional criminal law, perhaps quite wisely, has tended to treat each such situation as it arises and to prescribe detailed and specialized rules for its solution, the leading example being the very highly developed set of rules in the law of homicide dealing with self-defense, defense of others, crime prevention, and the like. For our purposes, however, these can all be reduced to a single simple prescription: if one who is confronted with a choice of evils makes the "right" choice, and that choice involves conduct that would violate some criminal law, he is excused from that violation. It is of course crucial to this position that someone other than the actor determines that his choice was the "right" one. In a legal system, this decision is confided in the first instance to law enforcement officials: to police, who must decide whether an arrestable offense has been committed, and to prosecutors, who must decide whether to charge the accused with crime, thereby initiating the more formal phases of the process. Ultimately, however, the validity of the choice-of-evils excuse must be passed on by a competent adjudicator—a judge or jury. There has to be, in short, a series of post-audits, which involves the expenditure of resources and which, like all human activities, admits of the possibility of error. It is on these considerations, as we have already seen, that the countervailing utilitarian argument against recognizing this or any other excuse rests. The counterargument is obviously less convincing in this case than in the case of any other excuse that one can think of. The reason is that the avoidance of this particular set of possible utilitarian losses can be achieved only at a cost that is uniquely excessive. Not only would we subject to punishment people for whom punishment is not needed; we would also discourage conduct that we would wish positively to encourage. There is no other kind of excuse of which that is true. We might well conclude, then, that here the utilitarian argument can stand on its own.

However, that argument is surely strengthened by the addition

of the negative aspect of the retributive position. We may cavil
for many reasons at the idea that it is right to punish the wicked;
but how can one disagree with the proposition that, if it is wrong
to punish the non-wicked, it is surely wrong to punish the good.
Remember that we are talking about individual cases in which
it is thought that the actor did the right thing. Although there
may be a small residual doubt whether that is an adequate utilitarian reason for not punishing him, there can be no stronger case
for precluding punishment on the basis of the retributive position. There is something of a tension between arguments for
punishment that turn on general justifications, like deterrence,
and arguments that turn on justifications for punishment in a
particular case. The choice-of-evils situation demonstrates the
resolving power of the retributive position, which can be seen
as operating most effectively in the context of the particular case.
It is not enough to say that no useful purpose would be served by
punishment in the particular case; arguments about utility have
a peculiar inconclusiveness when thus framed. More is required:
we must be able to say that it is wrong to punish in the excluded
case. The basis for doing so is nowhere clearer than in the case of
an appropriate choice of evils, where the actor has demonstrated
not merely an absence of blameworthiness but positive moral excellence.

Not every man confronted with a dilemma of the kind we have
been discussing makes the right choice. Or, to put it more realistically, there are many situations in which it is very difficult to
say what the right choice would be. Consider, for example, the
plight of the army officers who were confined in prisoner-of-war
camps during the Korean conflict and who were induced to make
propaganda broadcasts for the enemy by means of threats that
they and the men in their charge would be mistreated if they did
not. Charged with various offenses against the military code, they
offered in defense that they had been compelled to act as they did.
Leaving aside the technical niceties of the defense, let us suppose
that the tribunal concluded, on the basis of hindsight, that the
officers had made the wrong choice: that their judgment had been
infected by considerations of personal safety and comfort to which
an army officer should not succumb; that the danger they appre-

hended was exaggerated; that they should have temporized instead of giving in; and so on. Let us say that the tribunal nonetheless concluded that, although the officers had not behaved as one would ideally wish them to, they had not displayed any unusual weakness in giving in: they had exhibited the degree of fortitude anticipated (although less than that hope for) of men in their situation. Should they be excused on that ground? Or, consider the following case.[3] A man driving down a narrow, winding mountain road comes upon a disabled car completely blocking the road. In it are five people. He steps on the brake which, to his horror, does not hold. His possible choices are either to run off the road, thereby surely killing himself, or to plough into the disabled car, with a substantial likelihood of killing its occupants. He chooses the latter course, and all five occupants of the car are killed in the ensuing crash. Charged with manslaughter, he pleads duress. Clearly, he made the "wrong" choice: there is no measure of the value of lives but a quantitative one, and he chose to sacrifice five to save one. Yet no honest judge or juror could say that confronted with the same dilemma he would have done otherwise.

The question may be put whether there is any point in the law's setting up standards that the average man cannot comply with. The utilitarian answer, though assumed by many writers to be clear, is at best ambiguous. Note that we are now dealing with conduct which, unlike that in the case of a successful necessity plea like self-defense, is undesirable. We have no incentive to use the law to encourage people to make wrong choices. The argument must rest on the notion that punishment in such cases is inefficacious because it cannot deter the actor who finds himself confronted with a dilemma. Although this is true, it by no means follows that preclusion of excuse might not compel a somewhat sterner sense of self-discipline in one who confronted an arguably ambiguous choice of this kind. Beyond that, there is the utilitarian loss involved in letting an occasional false excuse of this sort slip by; and there is an even greater loss resulting from the expenditure of considerable time and effort in adjudicating the

[3] See Monrad G. Paulsen and Sanford H. Kadish, *Criminal Law and Its Processes* (Boston, 1962), pp. 376–77, for a similar example.

many claims of this sort that would be presented, only a small percentage of which would be likely to show much merit. Why should the occasional instance of criminal conduct compelled by duress not be treated simply as a "hardship case" for informal exculpation by law enforcement officials or, failing that, for whatever mitigating weight correctional authorities might think it deserved, thereby eliminating it from the formal fabric of the criminal law?

The answer, if it is accepted at all, is expressed in terms that do not focus on the criminal law's function to prevent antisocial conduct. The law that exacts more of an individual than its framers could give under the same circumstances is simply hypocritical. No one who saw such a law in action could have anything but contempt for it. Now, it would be easy to say that this consideration is essentially utilitarian, that it focuses on the diminution in respect for and compliance with law that would result from such open hypocrisy. But that argument smells of the lamp. It would be hard to demonstrate that this sort of knowledge about the doctrinal niceties of the criminal law could ever become so widely diffused in the community as to have a significant impact on public attitudes toward the law. Only those comparatively few persons who are familiar with and sensitive to the operation of justice would be more than transiently affected by the knowledge that duress was not a defense. And even with them, it is marvelous how quickly the familiar is seen as the inevitable. No, the appeal here is to the sense of injustice, to use Edmond Cahn's fine phrase. It is hypocritical and therefore wrong to punish a man for conduct that he could not have kept from engaging in without exposing himself to the perils of some heroic act. And it is in consequence wrong not to allow people an opportunity to litigate that issue. It is only because we choose to indulge our sense of moral fitness that we recognize this particular excuse. Its recognition is more problematic than in the case of necessity (the "right" choice of evils). But its established, if somewhat tenuous, place in our criminal law demonstrates anew the relevance of the integrated theory of criminal punishment for the criminal law.

APPARENT NECESSITY: THE ROLE OF "MISTAKE"

We have so far been considering "real" excuses: claims that a state of affairs existed which a subsequent observer concludes really did exist at the time of the allegedly criminal conduct. To put it differently, we have focused on cases in which externally verifiable reality and the actor's perception of that reality seem congruent. We must now ask what difference it ought to make when this congruence is shown to be missing.

To return to Arthur's claim that he killed Victor in self-defense, let us suppose that our investigation of the facts leads us to conclude that Victor wasn't really trying to kill Arthur; Arthur merely thought that he was. And, to eliminate a problem that is more relevant to grading than to criminality, let us suppose that Victor was carrying a toy gun, which he playfully pointed at Arthur and which Arthur quite reasonably mistook for the real thing. One important reason for recognizing the choice-of-evils excuse is immediately eliminated: we have no interest whatever in promoting mistakes. The question is rather whether we want to tolerate them. If, as in the case we have hypothesized, the mistake is "reasonable," the most immediately apparent justification for tolerating it is that a reasonable mistake, by definition, would not induce people in general to act differently, especially when their sense of self-preservation impelled them to act as they did. In this sense, the argument for excusing mistakes about necessity is much the same as the argument for recognizing the "wrong" choice in a dilemma. If the actor has behaved like a reasonably prudent but unheroic man, it would be hypocritical for other reasonably prudent but unheroic men to punish him.

However, the force of the crime prevention argument against recognizing excuses is much greater in the mistake situation than it is in situations of genuine necessity. For in the latter, the possibility of simulating an excuse is somewhat kept in check by the requirement that the excusing condition "really" existed. If the door is to be opened to the excuse that "I thought my life was in danger, even though I concede now that it really wasn't," it seems inevitable that far greater utilitarian losses will become possible. The calculus produces no clear answer.

And yet, we may flinch at the thought of branding as a murderer a man whose offense consisted of a perceptual error that made it seem necessary to resort to deadly force in order to defend his life. It hardly seems enough to tell him that he may not be punished quite so severely as other homicides. He ought to be exculpated, and in any civilized legal system he will be exculpated. The reason that tips the balance is that he has not done anything for which he deserves to be punished.

The traces of utilitarian rigor that continue to impede full recognition of this excuse can be seen most clearly in the treatment of people who kill or injure another in the mistaken belief that their action was necessary to prevent harm to a third person. The judge-made criminal law of the eighteenth and nineteenth centuries easily came to the conclusion that this kind of mistake should be excused when the person being protected stood in a special relation to the actor, such as being a member of his immediate family or some other dependent like a body servant. This assimilation of defense of others to self-defense probably stemmed from a recognition that it would be futile to expect people not to act on appearances when their emotions were as strongly aroused as they would be by an attack on a close relative. But the law developed more ambiguously in cases in which the aid was rendered on behalf of a stranger or, at any rate, one who was not a near relation. While some decisions recognized the excuse of apparent necessity, others took the position that the actor who came to the defense of another did so "at his peril," and could not avail himself of the defense if the alleged victim was not "really" in danger.

The problem is exemplified by a recent New York case in which a man came upon a struggle between a teen-aged boy and two middle-aged men.[4] The boy was being dragged by the men and was struggling ineffectually and tearfully. His would-be rescuer attacked the two men, and in the melee one of the men's legs was broken. The injured man thereupon drew a gun, announced that he was a policeman, and put the defendant under

4 People v. Young, 210 N.Y.S. 2d 358, rev'd, 11 N.Y. 2d 274 (1962).

arrest. It turned out that the two middle-aged men were plain-clothesmen who were engaged in arresting the boy for disorderly conduct, a fact of which the would-be rescuer was ignorant. Charged with assault on the policeman, he argued that his belief in the necessity of action to rescue the boy was an excuse. The issue sharply divided two appellate courts in New York, the Appellate Division holding that the excuse was valid and the Court of Appeals that it was not, both by divided votes. The judges who voted to recognize the excuse stressed the importance of not discouraging people from coming to the assistance of their fellow human beings. Those who voted against allowing the excuse stressed the importance of safeguarding the police from improvident attacks by people who didn't know the facts. In the utilitarian terms in which the argument was conducted it is a standoff. In behavioral terms, there is no case whatever for not convicting the defendant. It will be time enough after he has been studied to see whether his Good Samaritan proclivities mask an assaultive personality. In retributive terms, the answer is equally clear in the other direction: if there was no blameworthiness inherent in the defendant's faulty perception of the situation, his conduct was no more reprehensible than it would have been had he been correct in seeing the two middle-aged men as aggressors and the boy as their innocent victim.

The integrated theory of criminal punishment requires that the excuse be recognized. The moral quality of an act inheres not in the act but in the actor's frame of mind with respect to it. That rule is to be preferred which maximizes the actor's capacity to make value choices by what he understands to be moral criteria. No man can measure the comparative utility of the two rules; but their comparative morality is clear and ought to prevail so long as comparative utility is honestly in doubt. No less is demanded of a body of law that makes even a merely instrumental use of moral condemnation as a sanctioning device.

STRICT LIABILITY: DECLINE OF "MISTAKE"

When we leave the area of the dilemmatic choice, which comprises what is technically known as the law of justification and excuse, "mistake" becomes the operational signal for invoking a vast range of excuses. Indeed, the idea of mistake underlies the whole question of *mens rea* or the mental element, with the dubious exception of the insanity defense (which, as I shall argue subsequently, is most usefully viewed as something other than a problem of *mens rea*). When we say that a person, whose conduct in other respects fits the definition of a criminal offense, lacked the requisite *mens rea*, what we mean is that he made a mistake about some matter of fact or value that constitutes a material element of the offense.

A few examples will show that the question of mistake pervades the entire criminal law. Arthur is charged with homicide and claims that he thought the man he shot at was really a deer. Barry is charged with stealing a raincoat that he claims he thought was really abandoned property. Charlie is charged with possessing heroin; he says he thought the white powder in the packet was talcum powder. Dan is charged with bigamy; he says that he thought his first wife had divorced him. Evan is charged with statutory rape; he claims the girl told him she was over the age of consent. Frank is charged with selling adulterated drugs; he says that so far as he knew the drugs conformed to requirements. George is charged with failing to file his income tax return; he says that he didn't know about the income tax. Harry is charged with carrying a concealed weapon; he claims he didn't know it was against the law to do so.

Under existing law Arthur, Barry, and probably Charlie will be listened to. That is, the trier of fact will decide whether each of them really did make the mistake he claims to have made. If it is believed that he did and (ordinarily) if the mistake is thought to be "reasonable," no crime has been committed. As recently as fifteen years ago Dan's mistake was simply ignored; however, he might be excused in some jurisdictions today if his claim is believed. Evan is probably out of luck, although there is a developing trend in his favor. Frank, George, and Harry might just as well save their breath; their exculpatory claim of mistake will not be listened to.

If all this seems confusing and arbitrary, that is only because it is confusing and arbitrary. Traditional criminal law has fallen into the deliberate, and on occasion inadvertent, use of strict liability or liability without fault. For our purposes strict liability can be defined as the refusal to pay attention to a claim of mistake. In a behavioral-utilitarian view of the criminal law there is, as we have seen, good reason to ignore the defense of mistake. But if the preventive goal of criminal law is to be limited by the negative implication of the retributive position, as we have concluded it should, then mistakes must be considered and, if found relevant and believable, accepted as excuses.

The story of how traditional law slipped into an easy reliance on strict liability, to the detriment of its essential doctrinal content, need not concern us here. However, it may be instructive to consider one famous case in which the Supreme Court of the United States contributed to the erosion of *mens rea,* because it shows that important values may be sacrificed as easily through inadvertence as through design. The narrow issue in *United States* v. *Dotterweich*[5] was whether the president of a company that shipped misbranded or adulterated products in interstate commerce was a "person" who had done so under the Food, Drug, and Cosmetic Act, notwithstanding the fact that he had nothing to do with the shipment. Buffalo Pharmacal Company, a drug wholesaler, purchased drugs from manufacturers, repackaged them under its own label, and shipped them on order to physicians. Dotterweich and the company were prosecuted for two interstate shipments alleged to be adulterated or misbranded. The first consisted of a cascara compound that conformed to specifications but whose label included reference to an ingredient that had, a short time before, been dropped from the National Formulary. One infers that the old labels were still being used. The other shipment was of digitalis tablets that were less potent than their label indicated. The company did not manufacture these tablets, but merely repackaged them under its own label. So far as appears, there was no way short of conducting a chemical analysis of the tablets for their seller to know that they were not what their label declared them to be. The jury found Dotterweich guilty but for "some unexplainable reason" disagreed as

[5] 320 U.S. 277 (1943).

to the company's guilt. Dotterweich was sentenced to pay a fine and to "probation for 60 days." Under the statute he could have been sentenced to a year's imprisonment. The court of appeals reversed, on the ground that the statute should not be read as applying to an individual agent of the principal (here the company), since only the principal was in a position to exculpate itself by obtaining a guaranty of nonadulteration from its supplier. Since there appeared to be no statutory basis for distinguishing between a high corporate agent, like Dotterweich, who might have obtained such a guaranty, and a shipping clerk or other menial employee who might have actually made the forbidden shipment and who would not necessarily be covered by the statutory provision protecting people who obtained a guaranty, a divided court of appeals concluded that Dotterweich's conviction could not stand.[6]

It will be noticed that the answer to the question whether this was indeed a "forbidden shipment" was dealt with rather cursorily. The court of appeals held merely that "intention to violate the statute" was not an element of the offense. The shipments in question were illegal under the statute, and that was that. Whether Dotterweich (or anyone else) had failed to take reasonable precautions was not put to the jury. Negligence as a possible mode of culpability was overlooked.

The court of appeals opinion had at least the merit of keeping separate two questions that it would confound analysis to blur: first, whether whoever was responsible for the shipment could be held criminally liable, notwithstanding the absence of culpability on his part (the issue of "strict liability"); and second, whether Dotterweich could be held criminally liable, notwithstanding his own lack of connection with the shipment (the issue of "vicarious liability"). It is obvious that the second issue is dependent on the first; if no one committed a crime, there was no crime for which Dotterweich could have been held vicariously liable. The underlying issue was whether the statute imposed strict liability.

The opinion for the Court, by Mr. Justice Frankfurter, did not

6 United States v. Buffalo Pharmacal Co., 131 F. 2d 500 (2d Cir. 1942).

make the essential distinction between the issues of strict and vicarious liability. It is not paraphrasing unfairly to say that the Court held that since the liability was strict it was also vicarious. But the premise that the Act dispensed with *mens rea* and imposed strict liability was assumed rather than examined:

The prosecution to which Dotterweich was subjected is based on a now familiar type of legislation whereby penalties serve as effective means of regulation. Such legislation dispenses with the conventional requirement for criminal conduct—awareness of some wrongdoing. In the interest of the larger good it puts the burden of acting at hazard upon a person otherwise innocent but standing in responsible relation to a public danger. *United States* v. *Balint*, 258 U.S. 250. And so it is clear that shipments like those now in issue are "punished by the statute if the article is misbranded [or adulterated], and that the article may be misbranded [or adulterated] without any conscious fraud at all. It was natural enough to throw this risk on shippers with regard to the identity of their wares. . . ."[7]

It is well to note that this offhand passage is precisely all that the opinion had to say on the *mens rea* issue, despite the fact that this was the first time the Supreme Court had before it the construction of the mental element in this important federal criminal statute. It is also well to note the primitive and rigid view of *mens rea* that the quoted passage reflects. "Conscious fraud" and "awareness of some wrongdoing" are impossibly high standards, the opinion seems to say, and that leaves only strict liability. Did the company or its responsible agents behave recklessly or negligently with respect to the possibility that these shipments were not up to standard? Perhaps it was inexcusably careless not to have destroyed the old cascara labels and prepared new ones. Perhaps not. But could not the lower courts have been told that this question should be submitted to the jury? The case posed an obvious opportunity for framing a more discriminating set of standards for the mental element, but the opportunity was forgone.

Next, let us consider the areas in which the minimal doctrinal content of the criminal law has been eroded. There are four cate-

---

[7] 320 U.S. at 280–81.

gories to be considered in determining how responsive the traditional common law has been to the notion of *mens rea*. These may be characterized as:

(1) Basic offenses dispensing in whole or in part with *mens rea*.
(2) Negligence as a mode of culpability.
(3) The barrier of *ignorantia legis*.
(4) Public welfare offenses.

Basic Offenses. The usual examples are sexual offenses, notably "statutory rape" and bigamy. These are universally regarded, in their traditional manifestations, as examples of strict liability in the criminal law. They serve as the basis for an assertion that might otherwise seem surprising, that there is no adequate operational distinction between offenses that dispense entirely with *mens rea* and offenses that dispense with *mens rea* only partially, or with respect to only one material element of the offense. Indeed, there is no such thing as a "strict liability" offense except as a partial rather than a complete discarding of *mens rea,* for there is always some element of any offense with respect to which a mental element is attached. In both the statutory rape and bigamy situations, it is the exclusion of *mens rea* with respect to the "circumstance" element of the offense that results in the imposition of strict liability: in the case of statutory rape, the circumstance that the girl is under the age of consent; in the case of bigamy, the circumstance that one or both of the parties is not legally free to remarry. Although there is an encouraging trend of contrary decisions in the bigamy field, it probably remains the majority rule in this country that a good-faith belief that one is legally free to remarry is not a defense to a charge of bigamy. Indeed, this view apparently has constitutional sanction. In the area of statutory rape, the strength of the traditional strict liability view has not been appreciably diminished.

These examples are familiar ones. It might perhaps be thought that they represent rather unusual exceptions to a generally pervasive principle of applicability of *mens rea*. Actually, the contrary is true. Two conspicuous examples arise in the area of homicide. Both the felony-murder and the misdemeanor-manslaughter rules, insofar as they have independent force and are not simply instances of the more general operation of homicide doctrines, reflect the imposition of strict liability as to the homicidal result. If a robber is automatically to be held for the death of an accomplice who is shot by their intended victim, or if a person commits a battery that leads to the unforeseen and reasonably unforeseeable result of the victim's death, liability for the homicide rests upon the refusal to consider *mens rea* as to the result.

The standard rejoinder to the argument that strict liability is being imposed in such a situation is that habitually given in the sex-offense cases. It comes down to the assertion that, since the underlying conduct is "wrongful," the actor must take all the consequences of that conduct, whether or not he foresaw or desired them. But it begs the question to assert that one who has intercourse with an underage girl, even though he is ignorant of her age, is to be held for statutory rape because his underlying conduct is "wrongful." The question is whether he should be held for an offense to whose elements he did not advert as well as for an offense to whose elements he did advert. The fact that various limitations have been worked out to prevent some of the most absurd consequences of rigid adherence to this "at peril" notion should not distract attention from its incompatibility with the spirit of *mens rea.*

Negligence. If a man purposely or recklessly brings about a forbidden harm, we have no hesitation in saying that he had the requisite *mens rea* with respect to his conduct. But if he negligently brings about the forbidden harm, a different problem is presented. Negligence is not readily transformable into a state of mind. It is, by definition, the absence of a state of mind. Negligence is, in short, an extension rather than an example of the idea of *mens rea* in the traditional sense.

There are those who argue that negligence as a mode of culpability has no place in the criminal law, because the threat of punishment for causing harms inadvertently must be either inefficacious or unjust or both.[8] Whatever the merits of this philosophic position, it is plain that negligence has a very strong foothold in the criminal law. It finds its most explicit formula-

[8] E.g., Jerome Hall, *General Principles of Criminal Law,* 2d ed. (Indianapolis, 1960), pp. 135–41.

tion in the statutes penalizing negligent homicide in the driving of an automobile. But its hold on the criminal law is far more pervasive than this. Negligence suffices as a mode of culpability whenever the question asked with respect to the actor's perception is not whether he knew but whether he should have known. In the case of homicide, the difference between negligent inadvertence to the risk of death and conscious advertence to that risk is, very roughly speaking, the dividing line between manslaughter and murder. But beyond this, murder itself is sometimes treated as an offense that may be committed negligently, either by applying an external standard to the actor's perception of the risk or by applying an external standard to his perception of the basis for some excuse, such as self-defense. To the extent that we subject persons to liability for this most serious of offenses on the basis of an external standard, we are retreating very far from a doctrinal purist's stance. But even if murder by negligence is rejected as anomalous, we must face the challenge that negligence as a mode of culpability cannot be reconciled with the principle of *mens rea*.

It has been suggested that negligence has closer affinities with strict liability than it has with those modes of culpability that reflect subjective awareness on the part of the actor.[9] However, there are important differences between a legislative determination that all instances of a certain kind of conduct are unacceptable and a jury's determination that a particular instance of such conduct falls below a previously established community standard. The decisive difference is that the legislature cannot and does not foresee the infinite variation of circumstance that may affect the jury's view of a particular case. If there is an issue of fault for the jury to adjudicate, the line between subjective and objective fault—between "he knew" and "he should have known"—is a very shadowy one. Often, a judgment that "he knew" will simply reflect an inference from "he should have known." Conversely, a judgment that "he should have known" may contain the further unarticulated statement: "and we think he probably did know but we aren't sure enough to say so." There simply isn't a definite

9 Richard Wasserstrom, *Strict Liability in the Criminal Law*, 12 STAN. L. REV. 731, 741–45 (1960).

line between imputations of subjective awareness and those of objective fault: they are points on a continuum. The jury's opportunity to make an individualized determination of fault may focus indifferently upon one or the other. Putting the issue in this light, it seems plausible for the criminal law to employ a negligence standard on occasion, although not as a matter of course, without being charged with having abandoned the substance of *mens rea*. To put it another way, it seems to me proper to view negligence as an extension of rather than a departure from the values associated with the *mens rea* concept.

Ignorantia Legis. The principle that ignorance of the law is no excuse is deeply embedded in our criminal law. If the criminal law faithfully reflected prevalent community standards of minimally acceptable conduct, there would be no difficulty in reconciling the principle *ignorantia legis* with the requirements of *mens rea*. Yet, the proliferation of minor sumptuary and regulatory offenses, many of them penalizing conduct under circumstances in which the fact of illegality can scarcely be known to a first offender, creates a sharp problem. Sometimes a legislature specifies that awareness of the law's requirement is a necessary ingredient of guilt. More often it does not. Courts rarely remedy the deficiency by fashioning a doctrine that distinguishes sensibly between innocent and guilty conduct in contravention of an esoteric legal proscription.

It has been suggested by the framers of the Model Penal Code that a limited defense should be available to persons accused of crime if they can show a good-faith belief that their conduct does not legally constitute an offense, owing to lack of publication or reasonable availability of the enactment.[10] It is not entirely clear how broad this defense is meant to be. I should like to read it as establishing a negligence standard for the defense of ignorance or mistake of law. If read (or expanded) in this way, the proposal would go a long way toward resolving the *ignorantia legis* paradox. If we assume that an actor is unblameworthy in failing to know that his conduct violates a particular enactment (a condition that will ordinarily obtain only if either he or the enactment

[10] American Law Institute, MODEL PENAL CODE §2.04 (3), and Comment, pp. 138–39 (Tent. Draft No. 4, 1955).

is a stranger to prevailing standards in the relevant community), then criminal punishment is objectionable for precisely those reasons that obtain in respect to strict liability.

Public Welfare Offenses. Ever since Francis B. Sayre gave the phrase currency, this category of offenses has been treated by commentators as the main "exception" to the principle of *mens rea* and by courts as a convenient pigeonhole for any crime construed to dispense with *mens rea.* Perhaps the principal significance of the public welfare offenses lies in their open flouting of *mens rea,* as opposed to the rather more covert erosions that have gone on in the main body of the criminal law. Despite the enormous body of judge-made law that affirms dispensing with the mental element in violations of food and drug regulations, liquor regulations, traffic rules, and the like, few courts have explicitly considered and avowed the propriety of applying distinctively "criminal" sanctions to minor infractions. On the contrary, these offenses have been treated as something different from traditional criminal law, as a kind of hybrid category to which the odium and hence the safeguards of the criminal process do not attach. However limited in application the departure from *mens rea* may be in this category of offenses, it cannot be doubted that acceptance of this departure has been a powerful brake on the development of a general theory of *mens rea* in the criminal law.

This discussion of the "exceptions" to *mens rea* is intended to suggest that in every one of the cases enumerated at the beginning of this section the defense of "mistake" should be entertained and, if found warranted by the facts, accepted. This conclusion follows, however, only if what we are confronted with is a case in which the criminal sanction is fully appropriate. Here we are touching on a major thesis of this book, namely, that the criminal sanction should not be applied to trivial infractions such as minor traffic offenses, to cite perhaps the most conspicuous example of current misuse. The culpability issue highlights this point. Treating every kind of conduct that the legislature unthinkingly labels as criminal with the full doctrinal apparatus of culpability would place an intolerable burden on the courts. Yet our principles compel us to entertain *mens rea* defenses whenever the consequences of a criminal conviction are severe, whenever we are using the full force of the criminal sanction. A line must be drawn that does not depend simply upon the fortuitous use of the label "criminal." Labels aside, the combination of stigma and loss of liberty involved in a conditional or absolute sentence of imprisonment sets that sanction apart from anything else the law imposes. When the law permits that degree of severity, the defendant should be entitled to litigate the issue of culpability by raising the kinds of defenses we have been considering. If the burden on the courts is thought to be too great, a less severe sanction than imprisonment should be the maximum provided for. The legislature ought not to be allowed to have it both ways.

A CAVEAT ON THE INSANITY DEFENSE

There is no more hotly controverted issue in the criminal law than the question of whether and, if so, to what extent and according to what criteria "individuals whose conduct would otherwise be criminal should be exculpated on the ground that they were suffering from mental disease or defect when they acted as they did. What is involved specifically is the drawing of a line between the use of public agencies and public force to condemn the offender by conviction, with resultant sanctions in which there is inescapably a punitive ingredient (however constructive we may attempt to make the process of correction) and modes of disposition in which that ingredient is absent, even though restraint may be involved."[11] This is the way the framers of the Model Penal Code put the issue, and their statement could hardly be improved upon.

The question of criteria has been the focus of legal debate, with much learned disputation about the merits and demerits of the traditional *M'Naghten* rule, the irresistible impulse test, the *Durham* rule, and the Model Penal Code formulation. In this brief discussion I shall not deal with these important issues but only with the prior question: why an insanity defense? Specifically, must the minimal doctrinal content of the criminal law provide for such an excusing condition? I believe that at the present time it must; but I disagree with those who assert that the dictates

[11] MODEL PENAL CODE, Comment, p. 156 (Tent. Draft No. 4, 1955).

of utility require it. In a purely preventive view of the function of the criminal sanction, the case for an insanity defense is weak indeed. That case rests securely, indeed inescapably, upon limits that are imposed through the dictates of culpability as reflected in the integrated rationale of criminal punishment.

Let us begin by considering the consequences of a verdict of not guilty by reason of insanity. We shall assume what is largely although not entirely the case today, that such a verdict does not operate to release the person from custody but instead, either automatically or through procedures customarily invoked, operates to deprive the person of liberty through confinement in an institution called a mental hospital. Let us also assume, what is often but not always the case, that the institution in question is in most respects very like a prison, that the person's confinement there is not marked by a notably therapeutic regime, and that his release is determined in part by a judgment of the seriousness of the conduct for which he was tried and in part by an estimate of his propensity to repeat that or similar conduct. These are assertions that require far more discriminating investigation than they have received, but we shall treat them as proven. For many people, their assumed existence demonstrates the absurdity of the insanity defense. Why not abolish it, ask these critics, relieve the criminal process of the need to litigate the issue, and let the disposition of mentally ill offenders be attended to after conviction, without regard to labels.[12]

The argument is appealing but specious. We must put up with the bother of the insanity defense because to exclude it is to deprive the criminal law of its chief paradigm of free will. The criminal sanction, as I have pointed out before, does not rest on an assertion that human conduct *is* a matter of free choice; that philosophic controversy is irrelevant. In order to serve purposes far more significant than even the prevention of socially undesirable behavior, the criminal sanction operates *as if* human beings have free choice. This contingent and instrumental posit of freedom is what is crucially at stake in the insanity defense. There must be some recognition of the generally held assumption that some people are, by reason of mental illness, significantly im-

12 See, e.g., J. Goldstein and J. Katz, *Abolish the "Insanity Defense"—Why Not?* 72 YALE L. J. 853 (1963).

paired in their volitional capacity. Again, it is not too important whether this is in fact the case. Nor is it too important how discriminating we are about drawing some kind of line to separate those suffering volitional impairment from the rest of us. The point is that some kind of line must be drawn in the face of our intuition, however wrongheaded it may be, that mental illness contributes to volitional impairment.

How we perceive volitional impairment is a culturally conditioned matter. There is nothing immutable about it; nor is there anything immutable about the law's reaction. For example, we presently regard epilepsy as resulting in so great a loss of consciousness that volitional capacity is utterly destroyed. If a person engages in criminal conduct while in an epileptic fit, we say that he was incapable of performing a voluntary act and we acquit him. Unlike an insanity acquittal, this decision operates to release the person from further custody. It is as if he hadn't committed the act at all. At the other extreme, we recognize that cultural deprivation of a kind associated with urban poverty may in a very real sense restrict the individual's capacity to choose and make him more susceptible to engaging in antisocial conduct than the "average" member of society. However, we regard those constraints as too remote to justify an excuse on the ground that the person could not have helped acting as he did. Perhaps some day the law will take a culturally differential as well as a physiologically differential view of volitional impairment. It has not yet done so, however. The insanity defense is somewhere between these two extremes, which helps to explain why it is so controversial and why we are so ambivalent about recognizing it. This too may change. If some forms of mental illness are shown to have a chemical basis, or some other explicitly physiological origin, we may abandon the ambivalent reaction of acquittal-*cum*-detention. This is, of course, the sheerest speculation. The point is that our attitudes toward volitional impairment can change, and the criminal law can change with them. As matters stand, however, to impose the moral condemnation of a criminal conviction on a person who is thought to have acted in a state of severe volitional impairment would be to abandon the notion of culpability in its most crucial use.

This emphasis on volitional impairment may seem quixotic to

those who are familiar with the debate over criteria for the insanity defense. The *M'Naghten* rule, which remains the standard adhered to in most American jurisdictions, is both attacked and defended on the ground that it confines its attention to the impairment of cognitional capacity. This is, as Professor Abraham S. Goldstein has definitively shown, a misreading of the *M'Naghten* rule's development and practical application.[13] But it is unimportant for present purposes whether, as I agree with Professor Goldstein, both the attack and the defense are misconceived. If *M'Naghten* or any other rule focuses on the impairment of cognitive capacity, on the actor's ability to understand the nature and quality of his act, the question remains: why does it focus on that capacity? It seems to me quite clear that this is a purely instrumental focus. We are interested in the impairment of cognitive capacity not for its own sake but for a further purpose. We excuse a man who does not understand not because he does not understand but because his lack of understanding renders him incapable of making a meaningful choice. Cognition is not the complement of volition; it is its precursor.

The insanity defense cannot be viewed as an excuse in the ordinary sense. It would be more useful to say that its successful invocation is a direction to punish but not to punish criminally. The forced incarceration of a person in a mental institution because he has signaled his dangerousness by committing what would ordinarily be an offense is clearly a form of punishment, as we have defined it. However, it is not criminal punishment; for although it is imposed to prevent the commission of further offenses, it is not imposed to express community condemnation of the original offense. This, as we have seen, is what distinguishes criminal punishment from other forms, and it is precisely what is lacking in the case of the insanity defense. He was, as the saying goes, "sick not bad."

The asserted analogy (or even identity) with *mens rea* that has been pressed by both attackers and defenders of the insanity defense is a red herring. The insanity defense has no more to do with *mens rea* than does the defense of infancy; at most such

[13] *The Insanity Defense* (New Haven, 1967), chap. 4.

defenses involve what might be called "constructive *mens rea*." The attackers of the insanity defense assert that, like any *mens rea* defense, it should lead to total acquittal.[14] They say that to acquit on the ground of insanity is to say that the actor did not have the requisite purpose, knowledge, recklessness, or negligence with respect to a material element of the offense charged and, that being so and no offense having been proven against him, he should be unconditionally discharged. Since we are obviously not willing to do that, they say the defense is a sham and should be abolished. Others, equally wrongheadedly, assert that the insanity defense must be preserved *because* it is an aspect of *mens rea*. To make either assertion is to confuse the idea of culpability, which is implicated in the insanity defense, with technical culpability requirements, which are not.

Some color of plausibility is lent these assertions by the existence of the peculiar defense of "partial insanity" or "diminished responsibility," particularly in the law of homicide. The idea there is that mental illness might be adduced to show that the actor lacked the state of mind required for a particular degree of homicidal crime as, for example, premeditation and deliberation in first-degree murder. That would have the effect, if accepted by the trier of fact in the particular case, of reducing what would otherwise be first-degree murder to second-degree murder or even to manslaughter. This defense bears no relation to the insanity defense, which is not at all addressed to particular elements of the offense but rather to the actor's general mental condition. The "partial insanity" defense is simply a useful ploy to avoid conviction for an offense that might incur the death penalty.

In sum, the insanity defense is not implied in or intrinsic to the complex of mental element defenses that make up most of the law of culpability. It is an overriding, *sui generis* defense that is concerned not with what the actor did or believed but with what kind of person he is.

[14] This proposition is at least hypothetically advanced in Goldstein and Katz, p. 865.

CHAPTER SEVEN

Proof and Proportionality

THE STANDARD OF PROOF

The doctrinal safeguards of conduct and culpability would not mean very much unless they were protected from erosion in the daily wear and tear of the criminal process. It is all very well to insist on adherence to doctrine in the legislative proscription of criminal conduct; but doctrine in the books is not doctrine applied. Who will apply it, and by what standard? The answer to the "who," as will become clear when we examine the workings of the criminal process, is threefold: the judges, as they preside over criminal trials; the prosecutors, as they decide what cases they will press; and the defense lawyers, as they try through both formal and informal means to secure the best possible outcome for their clients. The standard, which is our present concern, requires the consideration of doctrines about proof.

A criminal case, or any lawsuit for that matter, necessitates making a judgment about past events. Like any historical reconstruction, such a judgment is not a matter of certainty but rather one of probabilities. We can never know the past in even the contingently certain way in which we "know" whatever we immediately perceive. In ordinary civil litigation—disputes about commercial transactions, the ownership or use of property, personal injury and property damage—we are satisfied to let the decision about past events turn on a balance of probabilities. Or, as the law of evidence puts it, the plaintiff's case fails unless he proves the facts required to support his claim by a preponderance of the evidence.

A tougher standard prevails in the criminal law, attesting to the seriousness with which we view invocation of the criminal sanction and at the same time creating unique difficulties of administration. We traditionally say that the defendant's innocence is assumed and that his guilt must be proved beyond a reasonable doubt. It is useless to try to define "reasonable doubt." What it suggests is not a quantifiable standard but an adjudicative mood. If there is any hesitation, which reflection does not dissipate, in deciding that what "really" happened accords with the legal requirements for finding the defendant guilty of the offense with which he is charged, then the jury must acquit him. It probably should also follow, although courts have vacillated about this, that the judge who feels such hesitation should not allow the jury to decide the case, but should instead direct a verdict of acquittal, or if he does let the jury decide, should thereafter set aside their verdict. But comparatively few criminal cases get to that stage. The crucial application of the standard, therefore, is made by the prosecutor when he decides whether a person who has been arrested should be formally charged with an offense. The prosecutor must in effect estimate the probative force of the evidence that he can muster for the trial, consider how that evidence is likely to stand the challenge of cross-examination or of what he knows may be said on the other side, and conclude whether he is likely to be successful in meeting the standard of proof beyond a reasonable doubt. He must, in short, make a prediction and then act upon it. This prediction, itself an assessment of probability, will be differently made by different prosecutors, depending upon factors ranging from sanguinity of temperament and degree of conscientiousness to the importance of the case and the pressure from the public. But every prosecutor must somehow make this prediction in every case. It is a formidable barrier to arbitrary prosecution; it is also a formidable barrier to easy conviction.

The high standard of proof, itself a part of the minimal doctrinal content of the criminal law, has an important bearing on those aspects of the doctrinal content having to do with "excuses": proof of the *mens rea,* or mental element, in criminal cases. If those doctrines are to have any vitality, they must be recognized as part of what the prosecution must prove beyond a reasonable doubt, just as much as the reconstruction of external events is accepted as a part of that burden. This recognition cannot be effective unless the concept of guilt is seen as a complex of elements rather than a single entity. Specifically, the prosecution must be required to prove beyond a reasonable doubt each element of the offense charged against the defendant, and proving these elements must be taken to include disproving any excuses that may be relevant. If the defendant claims that he killed in self-defense, the prosecution must prove beyond a reasonable doubt that he did not kill in self-defense. If he claims that he mistakenly thought that the property he took was abandoned rather than the property of another, or that he mistakenly thought his first wife had divorced him, or that he mistakenly thought anything else that, if true, would constitute an excuse, then that claim must be disproven beyond a reasonable doubt in order to establish criminal guilt. The difficulty that this requirement imposes should not be underestimated. It means that the prosecution must prove a negative, always a difficult thing to do, and furthermore, that it must prove a negative relating not to objective fact, but rather to the defendant's state of mind.

It is this practical difficulty of proof rather than any well-defined conceptual position that has led to the substantial incursions of strict liability into the criminal law. Even if all that has to be proven is negligence—that the defendant's mistake was an unreasonable one—the burden on the prosecution is one that it would prefer not to assume. But there is no way out. If culpability means anything in the criminal law, which is to say, if "criminal" means anything, the nonexistence of excusing conditions must be demonstrated in order to establish guilt. This does not mean, of course, that the prosecution must undertake to negate all conceivable excuses in every case. It need do so only if there is evidence supporting the excuse, whether it appears in testimony presented by the prosecution or in that presented by the defense. To put the matter in the terms employed by the law of evidence, the defense has the production burden and the prosecution has the persuasion burden.

I have been asserting that the dictates of an integrated theory of criminal punishment require that the nonexistence of excusing conditions be proven by the prosecution beyond a reasonable doubt. This is far from universal practice in the criminal law today. Excuses about which we are peculiarly ambivalent, such as the insanity defense, are often left to the defendant to prove. And recognition of a novel defense like mistake of law is only transitionally achieved by allowing the defense to be presented while requiring the defendant to carry the burden of proving it, or by setting a less severe standard than proof beyond a reasonable doubt for the prosecution's negation of the defense. But these devices are compromises with the principle of culpability, compromises that will not endure. The more clearly we see the requirements that the peculiar character of the criminal sanction lays upon us, the less willing we will be to permit this kind of temporizing with basic principle. Recent legislative revisions of the criminal law attest to the predictive truth of this observation. In the context of our examination of the criminal sanction the point is obvious: the standard of proof and especially its universalization to include excuses are powerful curbs on unwise, sweeping use of the criminal sanction.

PROPORTIONALITY AND PUNISHMENT

The final element of minimal doctrinal content is also the most complex. It concerns the relationship between the seriousness of offenses and the severity of their punishment, and the expression of that relationship in the structure of the criminal law. In a purely behavioral view of the criminal sanction, the question would not arise. In that view it is exclusively the offender, and not at all his offense, that counts. Punishment would be completely individualized. No principle would dictate that the law's structure reflect gradations in the seriousness of offenses. Antisocial conduct would be dealt with ad hoc according to an estimate of two and only two factors: the need to incapacitate the offender and the possibility of rehabilitating him. The situational murderer might be released as soon as he had been diagnosed as being unlikely to reoffend; the violent psychopath and the incorrigible writer of bad checks might find themselves side by side in lifelong detention.

A strictly classic, Benthamite utilitarian view would point to a different but equally simple solution. The principle of "economy" in the imposition of pain would dictate that just enough punishment, and no more, to deter offenders from committing any given category of offenses should be allotted to that category. The schedule or tariff of punishments might be quite detailed. The animating principle, however, would be simplicity itself: the greater the temptation, the greater the punishment.

The underlying principle of retributive punishment would be equally simple although, again, different. It would dictate that punishments be commensurate with the degree of culpability manifested in particular offenses, with perhaps some mitigation allowed for less than normal wickedness on the part of particular offenders. There would, as in the case of the classic utilitarian view, be a schedule of punishments, but it would be constructed on a very different principle (although, perhaps, with quite similar results).

The integrated theory of punishment to which we are committed requires an integrated approach to the goals of punishment, recognizing that the tensions among the goals cannot be wholly resolved. It must borrow from all perspectives, recognizing that none can be wholly definitive. Punishments must be individualized but within limits, limits having to do both with the need for deterrence and with judgments about comparative morality, as well with the relative difficulties of predicting future behavior. The question is one of emphasis or, perhaps, it is a question of what the starting point should be.

The starting point must, I believe, be determined by the exigencies of providing a legislative framework for a system of criminal punishment. Let us assume what is presently the fact and what is likely to remain so for some time to come: the standard mode of criminal punishment is imprisonment. The question then becomes: what is the best allocation of competences to make decisions about sentencing? What can the legislature best do, and according to what criteria? What can the court best do, and according to what criteria? What can the correctional authorities best do, and according to what criteria?

The legislature cannot prescribe how many years, months, and days each person convicted of each offense should spend in prison. It can know only about offenses, not about offenders. The judge who sentences the offender knows about both, but he is not in the best position to determine how many years, months, and days the individual offender should serve. He can only predict how the offender is likely to respond to punishment; what will actually happen to the offender, what changes of personality he may or may not undergo, are things that lie in the future. The correctional authorities are in the best position to make the concededly speculative assessment about the future behavior of the particular offender because they are the only ones who know how the correctional process has affected him. So it is they, or a releasing agency informed by them, who ought to make that determination. But the people at that end of the process are in the worst position, not the best, to determine where on the scale of severity the range of punishment that may be inflicted for a given offense shall fall. The judge, who has a view of the deterrent and retributive factors based on his knowledge of the facts of the case, is in a better position to make that judgment. And the legislature, which has the entire spectrum of criminal behavior in view, is in the best position. Clearly, then, each of these agencies has a part to play, but the nature of these parts should be determined by an estimate of the agencies' respective strengths and weaknesses.

The legislature should be responsible for classifying offenses according to some criteria of seriousness and providing ranges of punishment for each such offense. In practice, this means determining maximum terms of imprisonment, and possibly minimum terms as well. There is no end to the permutations and combinations that can be achieved by manipulating minimum and maximum terms. One could have a different set for each offense and still not come close to exhausting the available combinations. Many existing penal codes exhibit just this multiplicity of terms. In California, for example, there are some 45 different sets of maxima and minima applying to felonies alone. This proliferation far exceeds the capacity of the legislature to make rational discriminations of seriousness, by whatever criteria. The Model Penal Code has proposed that for offenses requiring imprisonment for more than a year (felonies) there should be only three legislative categories, carrying maxima of five years, ten years, and life imprisonment. One can argue about whether three categories are quite enough (New York's recent revision calls for five), but it is evident that legislative judgment cannot extend much further. The legislative decision, then, should be limited to classifying conduct that it has chosen to treat as criminal into a comparatively small number of rather gross categories. Leaving aside offenses (like minor traffic offenses) for which a fine is the usual penalty and which should not be classified as criminal at all, the first question facing the legislature is whether to classify an offense as a felony or a misdemeanor. These categories are not inevitable, and, indeed, there may be arguments against the usefulness of short-term (less than one year) imprisonment, which is the customary dividing line between felony and misdemeanor. If the decision is in favor of long-term imprisonment, then the legislature must decide which of a very limited number of categories to place the offense in, depending on how serious it is felt to be.

The judge's function, rightly viewed, is to decide whether the legislative prescription shall be followed in the individual case or whether special circumstances relating to the particular offender should result in some mitigation, or possibly aggravation, of the legislatively determined norm in his case. The mitigating devices should include some or all of the following: dispensing with imprisonment (probation and/or suspended sentence), reducing the grade of the offense (with consequent reduction in potential length of imprisonment), and reducing the maximum of the statutory term. The aggravating device should be (by as simple a scheme as possible) increasing the length of the term that the offender may have to serve. This might be done because of special circumstances such as the commission of prior offenses or multiple offenses, indicating that this offender posed a greater threat than the run of persons committing his particular offense. This limited job of individualization by the judge would then leave to the correctional authorities and the parole boards the job of deciding precisely how long each offender should be required to serve within the limits of the punishment prescribed by the legislature and assigned by the judge.

The allocation of competences sketched above follows in rough outline the consensus among students of the subject reflected in the sentencing provisions of the Model Penal Code. Oversimplified as this account has been, it indicates how very complicated the problem becomes in a system that attempts to pursue (as I have argued it must do) more than one goal of punishment. Armed with even this fragmentary an understanding of the complexities of the sentencing problem, let us return to our point of major concern: the criteria that the legislature ought to take into account in determining the relative severity of criminal punishment for different kinds of offenses. And, to simplify matters, let us assume what in fact comes very close to being the case, that the only distinctively "criminal" punishment available is imprisonment. The question then becomes: what quantities of this punishment should be allowed in respect to what offenses for administration by the other participants in the sentencing process? Remember that we have precluded ourselves from ignoring the nature of the offense and allowing differentiations to be made solely on the basis of the personal characteristics of the offender. The legislature cannot content itself with saying, as extreme advocates of the behavioral position would have it say, that the permissible range for all offenses committed by all offenders shall be one day to life. What discriminations shall it make, and on what principles, assuming that it writes on a clean slate?

The very idea of discriminating among offenses necessarily implies proportion. Whether deterrence or incapacitation or a blend of the two is the object in mind, it is inescapable that the starting point for this kind of legislative effort is the idea that some offenses are to be taken more seriously than others and that the severity of the available punishment should be proportioned to the seriousness with which the offense is viewed. It makes no difference for this purpose whether seriousness is thought of as representing primarily moral obloquy or potential for social damage, although it may make a difference when the actual proc-

ess of assigning punishment to offenses gets under way. The point
is that different offenses are perceived differentially, regardless of
why they are perceived differentially.

Two questions now emerge: where on the scale of severity shall
we pitch the upper and lower limits of punishment; and how shall
we allot punishments to offenses as between the upper and lower
limits. If, for example, we decide that the most important value
to be protected by the criminal law is the physical integrity of the
individual, would there be any reason not to assign the most
serious possible punishment to all invasions of physical integrity,
ranging from murder to a slap in the face? To put the matter that
way forces us to recognize that values as general as the one just
stated are too gross to be of much use in this kind of inquiry. Even
though we posit the protection of physical integrity as the supreme value, we do not see the various threats to that integrity
as being equally serious. Indeed, we do not regard all threats to
life itself as calling for the most severe measures of deterrence and
incapacitation. Armed robbery and drunken driving are not
likely to be placed on a par, even if the latter is thought likely
to result in a greater number of deaths.

Proportionality implies more than a simple differentiation
among modes of conduct. It also implies a pyramidal effect. Those
things that are more serious are, generally speaking, rarer than
those things that are less serious. There are fewer murders than
assaults. There are fewer robberies than thefts. There is less reckless driving than there is illegal parking. And there are fewer
offenses that we regard as requiring the utmost severity than there
are offenses requiring only moderate severity, which, in turn, are
less frequent than those we are satisfied to treat with relative
leniency. This proposition may be tested by inspecting any criminal code or, better yet, by inspecting the actual punishment assigned to offenders. As to the former, the Model Penal Code (as
we have observed) divides all felonies into three degrees, punishable respectively by maximum terms of life imprisonment, ten
years, and five years. There are only four felonies of the first degree under the Code and twelve felonies of the second degree, but
there are 32 felonies of the third degree. To put it differently,
there are only 16 felonies for which a maximum prison term of

ten years or more is authorized. When the actual practice under an existing set of arrangements is examined, the same pyramidal effect can be observed. In 1965 there were 4,830 persons who received their first release on parole from California prisons. Of these, precisely one per cent (48 persons) had served a prison term of more than ten years. Another seven per cent (360 persons) had served more than five years but not more than ten. The rest had served less than five years. (And half of the prisoners held for more than ten years had been convicted of murder.)

What these examples demonstrate is that the range of theoretical severity is small, and the range of practicable severity even smaller. Since the overwhelming majority of persons convicted of felonies cannot as a practical matter be held for very long terms in the prison system, the legislature must content itself with a relatively narrow range of discriminations for the great mass of offenses. Assuming that all of the most serious offenses—crimes on the order of murder, rape, kidnapping, armed robbery, and the like—have been allocated the severest punishment, only marginal differentiations are available for dealing with the great run of offenses. Thus the principle of proportionality and its concomitant pyramidal effect sharply limit the flexibility of the criminal sanction as a device for dealing with a wide range of antisocial conduct.

PART II

PROCESS

CHAPTER EIGHT

Two Models of the Criminal Process

INTRODUCTION

People who commit crimes appear to share the prevalent impression that punishment is an unpleasantness that is best avoided. They ordinarily take care to avoid being caught. If arrested, they ordinarily deny their guilt and otherwise try not to cooperate with the police. If brought to trial, they do whatever their resources permit to resist being convicted. And even after they have been convicted and sent to prison, their efforts to secure their freedom do not cease. It is a struggle from start to finish. This struggle is often referred to as the criminal process, a compendious term that stands for all the complexes of activity that operate to bring the substantive law of crime to bear (or to keep it from coming to bear) on persons who are suspected of having committed crimes. It can be described, but only partially and inadequately, by referring to the rules of law that govern the apprehension, screening, and trial of persons suspected of crime. It consists at least as importantly of patterns of official activity that correspond only in the roughest kind of way to the prescriptions of procedural rules. As a result of recent emphasis on empirical research into the administration of criminal justice, we are just beginning to be aware how very rough the correspondence is.

At the same time, and perhaps in part as a result of this new accretion of knowledge, some of our lawmaking institutions—particularly the Supreme Court of the United States—have begun to add measurably to the prescriptions of law that are meant to govern the operation of the criminal process. This accretion has become, in the last few years, exponential in extent and velocity. We are faced with an interesting paradox: the more we learn about the Is of the criminal process, the more we are instructed about its Ought and the greater the gulf between Is and Ought appears to become. We learn that very few people get adequate legal representation in the criminal process; we are simultaneously told that the Constitution requires people to be afforded adequate legal representation in the criminal process. We learn that coercion is often used to extract confessions from suspected criminals; we are then told that convictions based on coerced confessions may not be permitted to stand. We discover that the police often use methods in gathering evidence that violate the norms of privacy protected by the Fourth Amendment; we are told that evidence obtained in this way must be excluded from the criminal trial. But these prescriptions about how the process ought to operate do not automatically become part of the patterns of official behavior in the criminal process. Is and Ought share an increasingly uneasy coexistence. Doubts are stirred about the kind of criminal process we want to have.

The kind of criminal process we have is an important determinant of the kind of behavior content that the criminal law ought rationally to comprise. Logically, the substantive question may appear to be prior: decide what kinds of conduct one wants to reach through the criminal process, and then decide what kind of process is best calculated to deal with those kinds of conduct. It has not worked that way. On the whole, the process has been at least as much a given as the content of the criminal law. But it is far from being a given in any rigid sense.

The shape of the criminal process affects the substance of the criminal law in two general ways. First, one would want to know, before adding a new category of behavior to the list of crimes and therefore placing an additional burden on the process, whether it is easy or hard to employ the criminal process. The more expeditious the process, the greater the number of people with whom it can deal and, therefore, the greater the variety of antisocial conduct that can be confided in whole or in part to the criminal law for inhibition. On the other hand, the harder the process is to use, the smaller the number of people who can be handled by it at any given level of resources for staffing and operating it. The harder it is to put a suspected criminal in jail, the fewer the number of cases that can be handled in a year by a given number of policemen, prosecutors, defense lawyers, judges and jurymen, probation officers, etc., etc. A second and subtler relationship exists between the characteristic functioning of the process and the kinds of conduct with which it can efficiently deal. Perhaps the clearest example, but by no means the only one, is in the area of what have been referred to as victimless crimes, i.e., offenses that do not result in anyone's feeling that he has been injured so as to impel him to bring the offense to the attention of the authorities. The offense of fornication is an example. In a jurisdiction where it is illegal for two persons not married to each other to have sexual intercourse, there is a substantial enforcement problem (or would be, if the law were taken seriously) because people who voluntarily have sexual intercourse with each other often do not feel that they have been victimized and therefore often do not complain to the police. Consensual transactions in gambling and narcotics present the same problem, somewhat exacerbated by the fact that we take these forms of conduct rather more seriously than fornication. To the difficulties of apprehending a criminal when it is known that he has committed a crime are added the difficulties of knowing that a crime has been committed. In this sense, the victimless crime always presents a greater problem to the criminal process than does the crime with an ascertainable victim. But this problem may be minimized if the criminal process has at its disposal measures designed to increase the probability that the commission of such offenses will become known. If suspects may be entrapped into committing offenses, if the police may arrest and search a suspect without evidence that he has committed an offense, if wiretaps and other forms of electronic surveillance are permitted, it becomes easier to detect the commission of offenses of this sort. But if these measures are prohibited and if the prohibitions are observed in practice, it becomes more difficult, and eventually there may come a point at which the capacity of the

criminal process to deal with victimless offenses becomes so attenuated that a failure of enforcement occurs.

Thus, a pragmatic approach to the central question of what
the criminal law is good for would require both a general assessment of whether the criminal process is a high-speed or a low-
speed instrument of social control, and a series of specific assessments of its fitness for handling particular kinds of antisocial behavior. Such assessments are necessary if we are to have a basis
for elaborating the criteria that ought to affect legislative invocation of the criminal sanction. How can we provide ourselves
with an understanding of the criminal process that pays due
regard to its static and dynamic elements? There are, to be sure,
aspects of the criminal process that vary only inconsequentially
from place to place and from time to time. But its dynamism is
clear—clearer today, perhaps, than ever before. We need to have
an idea of the potentialities for change in the system and the
probable direction that change is taking and may be expected to
take in the future. We need to detach ourselves from the welter
of more or less connected details that describe the myriad ways
in which the criminal process does operate or may be likely to
operate in mid-twentieth-century America, so that we can begin
to see how the system as a whole might be able to deal with the
variety of missions we confide to it.

One way to do this kind of job is to abstract from reality, to
build a model. In a sense, a model is just what an examination of
the constitutional and statutory provisions that govern the operation of the criminal process would produce. This in effect is the
way analysis of the legal system has traditionally proceeded.
It has considerable utility as an index of current value choices;
but it produces a model that will not tell us very much about
some important problems that the system encounters and that
will only fortuitously tell us anything useful about how the system actually operates. On the other hand, the kind of model that
might emerge from an attempt to cut loose from the law on the
books and to describe, as accurately as possible, what actually
goes on in the real-life world of the criminal process would so
subordinate the inquiry to the tyranny of the actual that the
existence of competing value choices would be obscured. The

kind of criminal process we have depends importantly on certain value choices that are reflected, explicitly or implicitly, in its habitual functioning. The kind of model we need is one that permits us to recognize explicitly the value choices that underlie the details of the criminal process. In a word, what we need is a *normative* model or models. It will take more than one model, but it will not take more than two.

Two models of the criminal process will let us perceive the normative antinomy at the heart of the criminal law. These models are not labeled Is and Ought, nor are they to be taken in that sense. Rather, they represent an attempt to abstract two separate value systems that compete for priority in the operation of the criminal process. Neither is presented as either corresponding to reality or representing the ideal to the exclusion of the other. The two models merely afford a convenient way to talk about the operation of a process whose day-to-day functioning involves a constant series of minute adjustments between the competing demands of two value systems and whose normative future likewise involves a series of resolutions of the tensions between competing claims.

I call these two models the Due Process Model and the Crime Control Model. In the rest of this chapter I shall sketch their animating presuppositions, and in succeeding chapters I shall show how the two models apply to a selection of representative problems that arise at successive stages of the criminal process. As we examine the way the models operate in each successive stage, we will raise two further inquiries: first, where on a spectrum between the extremes represented by the two models do our present practices seem approximately to fall; second, what appears to be the direction and thrust of current and foreseeable trends along each such spectrum?

There is a risk in an enterprise of this sort that is latent in any attempt to polarize. It is, simply, that values are too various to be pinned down to yes-or-no answers. The models are distortions of reality. And, since they are normative in character, there is a danger of seeing one or the other as Good or Bad. The reader will have his preferences, as I do, but we should not be so rigid as to demand consistently polarized answers to the range of questions posed in the criminal process. The weighty questions of public policy that inhere in any attempt to discern where on the spectrum of normative choice the "right" answer lies are beyond the scope of the present inquiry. The attempt here is primarily to clarify the terms of discussion by isolating the assumptions that underlie competing policy claims and examining the conclusions that those claims, if fully accepted, would lead to.

VALUES UNDERLYING THE MODELS

Each of the two models we are about to examine is an attempt to give operational content to a complex of values underlying the criminal law. As I have suggested earlier, it is possible to identify two competing systems of values, the tension between which accounts for the intense activity now observable in the development of the criminal process. The actors in this development— lawmakers, judges, police, prosecutors, defense lawyers—do not often pause to articulate the values that underlie the positions that they take on any given issue. Indeed, it would be a gross oversimplification to ascribe a coherent and consistent set of values to any of these actors. Each of the two competing schemes of values we will be developing in this section contains components that are demonstrably present some of the time in some of the actors' preferences regarding the criminal process. No one person has ever identified himself as holding all of the values that underlie these two models. The models are polarities, and so are the schemes of value that underlie them. A person who subscribed to all of the values underlying one model to the exclusion of all of the values underlying the other would be rightly viewed as a fanatic. The values are presented here as an aid to analysis, not as a program for action.

Some Common Ground. However, the polarity of the two models is not absolute. Although it would be possible to construct models that exist in an institutional vacuum, it would not serve our purposes to do so. We are postulating, not a criminal process that operates in any kind of society at all, but rather one that operates within the framework of contemporary American society. This leaves plenty of room for polarization, but it does require the observance of some limits. A model of the criminal process that left out of account relatively stable and enduring features of the American legal system would not have much relevance to our central inquiry. For convenience, these elements of stability and continuity can be roughly equated with minimal agreed limits expressed in the Constitution of the United States and, more importantly, with unarticulated assumptions that can be perceived to underlie those limits. Of course, it is true that the Constitution is constantly appealed to by proponents and opponents of many measures that affect the criminal process. And only the naive would deny that there are few conclusive positions that can be reached by appeal to the Constitution. Yet there are assumptions about the criminal process that are widely shared and that may be viewed as common ground for the operation of any model of the criminal process. Our first task is to clarify these assumptions.

First, there is the assumption, implicit in the ex post facto clause of the Constitution, that the function of defining conduct that may be treated as criminal is separate from and prior to the process of identifying and dealing with persons as criminals. How wide or narrow the definition of criminal conduct must be is an important question of policy that yields highly variable results depending on the values held by those making the relevant decisions.[1] But that there must be a means of definition that is in some sense separate from and prior to the operation of the process is clear. If this were not so, our efforts to deal with the phenomenon of organized crime would appear ludicrous indeed (which is not to say that we have by any means exhausted the possibilities for dealing with that problem within the limits of this basic assumption).

A related assumption that limits the area of controversy is that the criminal process ordinarily ought to be invoked by those charged with the responsibility for doing so when it appears that a crime has been committed and that there is a reasonable prospect of apprehending and convicting its perpetrator. Although police and prosecutors are allowed broad discretion for deciding not to invoke the criminal process, it is commonly agreed that

[1] See above, Chapter Five.

these officials have no general dispensing power. If the legislature has decided that certain conduct is to be treated as criminal, the decision-makers at every level of the criminal process are expected to accept that basic decision as a premise for action. The controversial nature of the occasional case in which the relevant decision-makers appear not to have played their appointed role only serves to highlight the strength with which the premise holds. This assumption may be viewed as the other side of the ex post facto coin. Just as conduct that is not proscribed as criminal may not be dealt with in the criminal process, so conduct that has been denominated as criminal must be treated as such by the participants in the criminal process acting within their respective competences.

Next, there is the assumption that there are limits to the powers of government to investigate and apprehend persons suspected of committing crimes. I do not refer to the controversy (settled recently, at least in broad outline) as to whether the Fourth Amendment's prohibition against unreasonable searches and seizures applies to the states with the same force with which it applies to the federal government.[2] Rather, I am talking about the general assumption that a degree of scrutiny and control must be exercised with respect to the activities of law enforcement officers, that the security and privacy of the individual may not be invaded at will. It is possible to imagine a society in which even lip service is not paid to this assumption. Nazi Germany approached but never quite reached this position. But no one in our society would maintain that any individual may be taken into custody at any time and held without any limitation of time during the process of investigating his possible commission of crimes, or would argue that there should be no form of redress for violation of at least some standards for official investigative conduct. Although this assumption may not appear to have much in the way of positive content, its absence would render moot some of our most hotly controverted problems. If there were not general agreement that there must be some limits on police power to detain and investigate, the highly controversial provisions of the Uniform Arrest Act, permitting the police to detain a person

2 Mapp v. Ohio, 367 U.S. 643 (1961); Ker v. California, 374 U.S. 23 (1963).

for questioning for a short period even though they do not have grounds for making an arrest, would be a magnanimous concession by the all-powerful state rather than, as it is now perceived, a substantial expansion of police power.[3]

Finally, there is a complex of assumptions embraced by terms such as "the adversary system," "procedural due process," "notice and an opportunity to be heard," and "day in court." Common to them all is the notion that the alleged criminal is not merely an object to be acted upon but an independent entity in the process who may, if he so desires, force the operators of the process to demonstrate to an independent authority (judge and jury) that he is guilty of the charges against him. It is a minimal assumption. It speaks in terms of "may" rather than "must." It permits but does not require the accused, acting by himself or through his own agent, to play an active role in the process. By virtue of that fact the process becomes or has the capacity to become a contest between, if not equals, at least independent actors. As we shall see, much of the space between the two models is occupied by stronger or weaker notions of how this contest is to be arranged, in what cases it is to be played, and by what rules. The Crime Control Model tends to de-emphasize this adversary aspect of the process; the Due Process Model tends to make it central. The common ground, and it is important, is the agreement that the process has, for everyone subjected to it, at least the potentiality of becoming to some extent an adversary struggle.

So much for common ground. There is a good deal of it, even in the narrowest view. Its existence should not be overlooked, because it is, by definition, what permits partial resolutions of the tension between the two models to take place. The rhetoric of the criminal process consists largely of claims that disputed territory is "really" common ground: that, for example, the premise of an adversary system "necessarily" embraces the appointment of counsel for everyone accused of crime, or conversely, that the obligation to pursue persons suspected of committing crimes "necessarily" embraces interrogation of suspects without the intervention of counsel. We may smile indulgently at such claims; they are rhetoric, and no more. But the form in which they are

[3] See below, pp. 175–86.

made suggests an important truth: that there *is* a common ground of value assumption about the criminal process that makes continued discourse about its problems possible.

Crime Control Values. The value system that underlies the Crime Control Model is based on the proposition that the repression of criminal conduct is by far the most important function to be performed by the criminal process. The failure of law enforcement to bring criminal conduct under tight control is viewed as leading to the breakdown of public order and thence to the disappearance of an important condition of human freedom. If the laws go unenforced—which is to say, if it is perceived that there is a high percentage of failure to apprehend and convict in the criminal process—a general disregard for legal controls tends to develop. The law-abiding citizen then becomes the victim of all sorts of unjustifiable invasions of his interests. His security of person and property is sharply diminished, and, therefore, so is his liberty to function as a member of society. The claim ultimately is that the criminal process is a positive guarantor of social freedom. In order to achieve this high purpose, the Crime Control Model requires that primary attention be paid to the efficiency with which the criminal process operates to screen suspects, determine guilt, and secure appropriate dispositions of persons convicted of crime.

Efficiency of operation is not, of course, a criterion that can be applied in a vacuum. By "efficiency" we mean the system's capacity to apprehend, try, convict, and dispose of a high proportion of criminal offenders whose offenses become known. In a society in which only the grossest forms of antisocial behavior were made criminal and in which the crime rate was exceedingly low, the criminal process might require the devotion of many more man-hours of police, prosecutorial, and judicial time per case than ours does, and still operate with tolerable efficiency. A society that was prepared to increase even further the resources devoted to the suppression of crime might cope with a rising crime rate without sacrifice of efficiency while continuing to maintain an elaborate and time-consuming set of criminal processes. However, neither of these possible characteristics corresponds with social reality in this country. We use the criminal sanction to cover an increasingly wide spectrum of behavior thought to be antisocial, and the amount of crime is very high indeed, although both level and trend are hard to assess.[4] At the same time, although precise measures are not available, it does not appear that we are disposed in the public sector of the economy to increase very drastically the quantity, much less the quality, of the resources devoted to the suppression of criminal activity through the operation of the criminal process. These factors have an important bearing on the criteria of efficiency, and therefore on the nature of the Crime Control Model.

The model, in order to operate successfully, must produce a high rate of apprehension and conviction, and must do so in a context where the magnitudes being dealt with are very large and the resources for dealing with them are very limited. There must then be a premium on speed and finality. Speed, in turn, depends on informality and on uniformity; finality depends on minimizing the occasions for challenge. The process must not be cluttered up with ceremonious rituals that do not advance the progress of a case. Facts can be established more quickly through interrogation in a police station than through the formal process of examination and cross-examination in a court. It follows that extrajudicial processes should be preferred to judicial processes, informal operations to formal ones. But informality is not enough; there must also be uniformity. Routine, stereotyped procedures are essential if large numbers are being handled. The model that will operate successfully on these presuppositions must be an administrative, almost a managerial, model. The image that comes to mind is an assembly-line conveyor belt down which moves an endless stream of cases, never stopping, carrying the cases to workers who stand at fixed stations and who perform on each case as it comes by the same small but essential operation that brings it one step closer to being a finished product, or, to exchange the metaphor for the reality, a closed file. The criminal process, in this model, is seen as a screening process in which each successive stage—pre-arrest investigation, arrest, post-arrest investigation, preparation for trial, trial or entry of plea, convic-

---

[4] See President's Commission on Law Enforcement and Administration of Justice, *The Challenge of Crime in a Free Society* (Washington, D.C., 1967), chap. 2.

tion, disposition—involves a series of routinized operations whose success is gauged primarily by their tendency to pass the case along to a successful conclusion.

What is a successful conclusion? One that throws off at an early stage those cases in which it appears unlikely that the person apprehended is an offender and then secures, as expeditiously as possible, the conviction of the rest, with a minimum of occasions for challenge, let alone post-audit. By the application of administrative expertness, primarily that of the police and prosecutors, an early determination of probable innocence or guilt emerges. Those who are probably innocent are screened out. Those who are probably guilty are passed quickly through the remaining stages of the process. The key to the operation of the model regarding those who are not screened out is what I shall call a presumption of guilt. The concept requires some explanation, since it may appear startling to assert that what appears to be the precise converse of our generally accepted ideology of a presumption of innocence can be an essential element of a model that does correspond in some respects to the actual operation of the criminal process.

The presumption of guilt is what makes it possible for the system to deal efficiently with large numbers, as the Crime Control Model demands. The supposition is that the screening processes operated by police and prosecutors are reliable indicators of probable guilt. Once a man has been arrested and investigated without being found to be probably innocent, or, to put it differently, once a determination has been made that there is enough evidence of guilt to permit holding him for further action, then all subsequent activity directed toward him is based on the view that he is probably guilty. The precise point at which this occurs will vary from case to case; in many cases it will occur as soon as the suspect is arrested, or even before, if the evidence of probable guilt that has come to the attention of the authorities is sufficiently strong. But in any case the presumption of guilt will begin to operate well before the "suspect" becomes a "defendant."

The presumption of guilt is not, of course, a thing. Nor is it even a rule of law in the usual sense. It simply is the consequence of a complex of attitudes, a mood. If there is confidence in the reliability of informal administrative fact-finding activities that take place in the early stages of the criminal process, the remaining stages of the process can be relatively perfunctory without any loss in operating efficiency. The presumption of guilt, as it operates in the Crime Control Model, is the operational expression of that confidence.

It would be a mistake to think of the presumption of guilt as the opposite of the presumption of innocence that we are so used to thinking of as the polestar of the criminal process and that, as we shall see, occupies an important position in the Due Process Model. The presumption of innocence is not its opposite; it is irrelevant to the presumption of guilt; the two concepts are different rather than opposite ideas. The difference can perhaps be epitomized by an example. A murderer, for reasons best known to himself, chooses to shoot his victim in plain view of a large number of people. When the police arrive, he hands them his gun and says, "I did it and I'm glad." His account of what happened is corroborated by several eyewitnesses. He is placed under arrest and led off to jail. Under these circumstances, which may seem extreme but which in fact characterize with rough accuracy the evidentiary situation in a large proportion of criminal cases, it would be plainly absurd to maintain that more probably than not the suspect did not commit the killing. But that is not what the presumption of innocence means. It means that until there has been an adjudication of guilt by an authority legally competent to make such an adjudication, the suspect is to be treated, for reasons that have nothing whatever to do with the probable outcome of the case, as if his guilt is an open question.

The presumption of innocence is a direction to officials about how they are to proceed, not a prediction of outcome. The presumption of guilt, however, is purely and simply a prediction of outcome. The presumption of innocence is, then, a direction to the authorities to ignore the presumption of guilt in their treatment of the suspect. It tells them, in effect, to close their eyes to what will frequently seem to be factual probabilities. The reasons why it tells them this are among the animating presuppositions of the Due Process Model, and we will come to them shortly. It is enough to note at this point that the presumption of guilt is descriptive and factual; the presumption of innocence is normative and legal. The pure Crime Control Model has no truck with the presumption of innocence, although its real-life emanations are, as we shall see, brought into uneasy compromise with the dictates of this dominant ideological position. In the presumption of guilt this model finds a factual predicate for the position that the dominant goal of repressing crime can be achieved through highly summary processes without any great loss of efficiency (as previously defined), because of the probability that, in the run of cases, the preliminary screening processes operated by the police and the prosecuting officials contain adequate guarantees of reliable fact-finding. Indeed, the model takes an even stronger position. It is that subsequent processes, particularly those of a formal adjudicatory nature, are unlikely to produce as reliable fact-finding as the expert administrative process that precedes them is capable of. The criminal process thus must put special weight on the quality of administrative fact-finding. It becomes important, then, to place as few restrictions as possible on the character of the administrative fact-finding processes and to limit restrictions to such as enhance reliability, excluding those designed for other purposes. As we shall see, this view of restrictions on administrative fact-finding is a consistent theme in the development of the Crime Control Model.

In this model, as I have suggested, the center of gravity for the process lies in the early, administrative fact-finding stages. The complementary proposition is that the subsequent stages are relatively unimportant and should be truncated as much as possible. This, too, produces tensions with presently dominant ideology. The pure Crime Control Model has very little use for many conspicuous features of the adjudicative process, and in real life works out a number of ingenious compromises with them. Even in the pure model, however, there have to be devices for dealing with the suspect after the preliminary screening process has resulted in a determination of probable guilt. The focal device, as we shall see, is the plea of guilty; through its use, adjudicative fact-finding is reduced to a minimum. It might be said of the Crime Control Model that, when reduced to its barest essentials and operating at its most successful pitch, it offers two possibilities: an administrative fact-finding process leading (1) to exoneration of the suspect or (2) to the entry of a plea of guilty.

Due Process Values. If the Crime Control Model resembles an assembly line, the Due Process Model looks very much like an obstacle course. Each of its successive stages is designed to present formidable impediments to carrying the accused any further along in the process. Its ideology is not the converse of that underlying the Crime Control Model. It does not rest on the idea that it is not socially desirable to repress crime, although critics of its application have been known to claim so. Its ideology is composed of a complex of ideas, some of them based on judgments about the efficacy of crime control devices, others having to do with quite different considerations. The ideology of due process is far more deeply impressed on the formal structure of the law than is the ideology of crime control; yet an accurate tracing of the strands that make it up is strangely difficult. What follows is only an attempt at an approximation.

The Due Process Model encounters its rival on the Crime Control Model's own ground in respect to the reliability of fact-finding processes. The Crime Control Model, as we have suggested, places heavy reliance on the ability of investigative and prosecutorial officers, acting in an informal setting in which their distinctive skills are given full sway, to elicit and reconstruct a tolerably accurate account of what actually took place in an alleged criminal event. The Due Process Model rejects this premise and substitutes for it a view of informal, nonadjudicative fact-finding that stresses the possibility of error. People are notoriously poor observers of disturbing events—the more emotion-arousing the context, the greater the possibility that recollection will be incorrect; confessions and admissions by persons in police custody may be induced by physical or psychological coercion so that the police end up hearing what the suspect thinks they want to hear rather than the truth; witnesses may be animated by a bias or interest that no one would trouble to discover except one specially charged with protecting the interests of the accused (as the police are not). Considerations of this kind all lead to a rejection of informal fact-finding processes as definitive of factual guilt and to an insistence on formal, adjudicative, adversary fact-finding processes in which the factual case against the accused is publicly heard by an impartial tribunal and is evaluated only after the accused has had a full opportunity to discredit the case against him. Even then, the distrust of fact-finding processes that animates the Due Process Model is not dissipated. The possibilities of human error being what they are, further scrutiny is necessary, or at least must be available, in case facts have been overlooked or suppressed in the heat of battle. How far this subsequent scrutiny must be available is a hotly controverted issue today. In the pure Due Process Model the answer would be: at least as long as there is an allegation of factual error that has not received an adjudicative hearing in a fact-finding context. The demand for finality is thus very low in the Due Process Model.

This strand of due process ideology is not enough to sustain the model. If all that were at issue between the two models was a series of questions about the reliability of fact-finding processes, we would have but one model of the criminal process, the nature of whose constituent elements would pose questions of fact not of value. Even if the discussion is confined, for the moment, to the question of reliability, it is apparent that more is at stake than simply an evaluation of what kinds of fact-finding processes, alone or in combination, are likely to produce the most nearly reliable results. The stumbling block is this: how much reliability is compatible with efficiency? Granted that informal fact-finding will make some mistakes that can be remedied if backed up by adjudicative fact-finding, the desirability of providing this backup is not affirmed or negated by factual demonstrations or predictions that the increase in reliability will be x per cent or x plus n per cent. It still remains to ask how much weight is to be given to the competing demands of reliability (a high degree of probability in each case that factual guilt has been accurately determined) and efficiency (expeditious handling of the large numbers of cases that the process ingests). The Crime Control Model is more optimistic about the improbability of error in a significant number of cases; but it is also, though only in part therefore, more tolerant about the amount of error that it will put up with. The Due Process Model insists on the prevention and elimination of mistakes to the extent possible; the Crime

Control Model accepts the probability of mistakes up to the level at which they interfere with the goal of repressing crime, either because too many guilty people are escaping or, more subtly, because general awareness of the unreliability of the process leads to a decrease in the deterrent efficacy of the criminal law. In this view, reliability and efficiency are not polar opposites but rather complementary characteristics. The system is reliable *because* efficient; reliability becomes a matter of independent concern only when it becomes so attenuated as to impair efficiency. All of this the Due Process Model rejects. If efficiency demands short-cuts around reliability, then absolute efficiency must be rejected. The aim of the process is at least as much to protect the factually innocent as it is to convict the factually guilty. It is a little like quality control in industrial technology: tolerable deviation from standard varies with the importance of conformity to standard in the destined uses of the product. The Due Process Model resembles a factory that has to devote a substantial part of its input to quality control. This necessarily cuts down on quantitative output.

All of this is only the beginning of the ideological difference between the two models. The Due Process Model could disclaim any attempt to provide enhanced reliability for the fact-finding process and still produce a set of institutions and processes that would differ sharply from those demanded by the Crime Control Model. Indeed, it may not be too great an oversimplification to assert that in point of historical development the doctrinal pressures emanating from the demands of the Due Process Model have tended to evolve from an original matrix of concern for the maximization of reliability into values quite different and more far-reaching. These values can be expressed in, although not adequately described by, the concept of the primacy of the individual and the complementary concept of limitation on official power.

The combination of stigma and loss of liberty that is embodied in the end result of the criminal process is viewed as being the heaviest deprivation that government can inflict on the individual. Furthermore, the processes that culminate in these highly afflictive sanctions are seen as in themselves coercive, restricting, and demeaning. Power is always subject to abuse—sometimes subtle, other times, as in the criminal process, open and ugly. Precisely because of its potency in subjecting the individual to the coercive power of the state, the criminal process must, in this model, be subjected to controls that prevent it from operating with maximal efficiency. According to this ideology, maximal efficiency means maximal tyranny. And, although no one would assert that minimal efficiency means minimal tyranny, the proponents of the Due Process Model would accept with considerable equanimity a substantial diminution in the efficiency with which the criminal process operates in the interest of preventing official oppression of the individual.

The most modest-seeming but potentially far-reaching mechanism by which the Due Process Model implements these antiauthoritarian values is the doctrine of legal guilt. According to this doctrine, a person is not to be held guilty of crime merely on a showing that in all probability, based upon reliable evidence, he did factually what he is said to have done. Instead, he is to be held guilty if and only if these factual determinations are made in procedurally regular fashion and by authorities acting within competences duly allocated to them. Furthermore, he is not to be held guilty, even though the factual determination is or might be adverse to him, if various rules designed to protect him and to safeguard the integrity of the process are not given effect: the tribunal that convicts him must have the power to deal with his kind of case ("jurisdiction") and must be geographically appropriate ("venue"); too long a time must not have elapsed since the offense was committed ("statute of limitations"); he must not have been previously convicted or acquitted of the same or a substantially similar offense ("double jeopardy"); he must not fall within a category of persons, such as children or the insane, who are legally immune to conviction ("criminal responsibility"); and so on. None of these requirements has anything to do with the factual question of whether the person did or did not engage in the conduct that is charged as the offense against him; yet favorable answers to any of them will mean that he is legally innocent. Wherever the competence to make adequate factual determinations lies, it is apparent that only a tribunal that is aware of these guilt-defeating doctrines and is willing to apply them can be viewed as competent to make determinations of legal guilt. The police and the prosecutors are ruled out by lack of competence, in the first instance, and by lack of assurance of willingness, in the second. Only an impartial tribunal can be trusted to make determinations of legal as opposed to factual guilt.

In this concept of legal guilt lies the explanation for the apparently quixotic presumption of innocence of which we spoke earlier. A man who, after police investigation, is charged with having committed a crime can hardly be said to be presumptively innocent, if what we mean is factual innocence. But if what we mean is that it has yet to be determined if any of the myriad legal doctrines that serve in one way or another the end of limiting official power through the observance of certain substantive and procedural regularities may be appropriately invoked to exculpate the accused man, it is apparent that as a matter of prediction it cannot be said with confidence that more probably than not he will be found guilty.

Beyond the question of predictability this model posits a functional reason for observing the presumption of innocence: by forcing the state to prove its case against the accused in an adjudicative context, the presumption of innocence serves to force into play all the qualifying and disabling doctrines that limit the use of the criminal sanction against the individual, thereby enhancing his opportunity to secure a favorable outcome. In this sense, the presumption of innocence may be seen to operate as a kind of self-fulfilling prophecy. By opening up a procedural situation that permits the successful assertion of defenses having nothing to do with factual guilt, it vindicates the proposition that the factually guilty may nonetheless be legally innocent and should therefore be given a chance to qualify for that kind of treatment.

The possibility of legal innocence is expanded enormously when the criminal process is viewed as the appropriate forum for correcting its own abuses. This notion may well account for a greater amount of the distance between the two models than any other. In theory the Crime Control Model can tolerate rules that forbid illegal arrests, unreasonable searches, coercive interrogations, and the like. What it cannot tolerate is the vindication of those rules in the criminal process itself through the exclusion of evidence illegally obtained or through the reversal of convictions in cases where the criminal process has breached the rules laid down for its observance. And the Due Process Model, although it may in the first instance be addressed to the maintenance of reliable fact-finding techniques, comes eventually to incorporate prophylactic and deterrent rules that result in the release of the factually guilty even in cases in which blotting out the illegality would still leave an adjudicative fact-finder convinced of the accused person's guilt. Only by penalizing errant police and prosecutors within the criminal process itself can adequate pressure be maintained, so the argument runs, to induce conformity with the Due Process Model.

Another strand in the complex of attitudes underlying the Due Process Model is the idea—itself a shorthand statement for a complex of attitudes—of equality. This notion has only recently emerged as an explicit basis for pressing the demands of the Due Process Model, but it appears to represent, at least in its potential, a most powerful norm for influencing official conduct. Stated most starkly, the ideal of equality holds that "there can be no equal justice where the kind of trial a man gets depends on the amount of money he has."[5] The factual predicate underlying this assertion is that there are gross inequalities in the financial means of criminal defendants as a class, that in an adversary system of criminal justice an effective defense is largely a function of the resources that can be mustered on behalf of the accused, and that the very large proportion of criminal defendants who are, operationally speaking, "indigent" will thus be denied an effective defense. This factual premise has been strongly reinforced by recent studies that in turn have been both a cause and an effect of an increasing emphasis upon norms for the criminal process based on the premise.

The norms derived from the premise do not take the form of an insistence upon governmental responsibility to provide literally equal opportunities for all criminal defendants to challenge the process. Rather, they take as their point of departure the notion that the criminal process, initiated as it is by government

[5] Griffin v. Illinois, 351 U.S. 12, 19 (1956).

and containing as it does the likelihood of severe deprivations at the hands of government, imposes some kind of public obligation to ensure that financial inability does not destroy the capacity of an accused to assert what may be meritorious challenges to the processes being invoked against him. At its most gross, the norm of equality would act to prevent situations in which financial inability forms an absolute barrier to the assertion of a right that is in theory generally available, as where there is a right to appeal that is, however, effectively conditional upon the filing of a trial transcript obtained at the defendant's expense. Beyond this, it may provide the basis for a claim whenever the system theoretically makes some kind of challenge available to an accused who has the means to press it. If, for example, a defendant who is adequately represented has the opportunity to prevent the case against him from coming to the trial stage by forcing the state to its proof in a preliminary hearing, the norm of equality may be invoked to assert that the same kind of opportunity must be available to others as well. In a sense the system as it functions for the small minority whose resources permit them to exploit all its defensive possibilities provides a benchmark by which its functioning in all other cases is to be tested: not, perhaps, to guarantee literal identity but rather to provide a measure of whether the process as a whole is recognizably of the same general order. The demands made by a norm of this kind are likely by their very nature to be quite sweeping. Although the norm's imperatives may be initially limited to determining whether in a particular case the accused was injured or prejudiced by his relative inability to make an appropriate challenge, the norm of equality very quickly moves to another level on which the demand is that the process in general be adapted to minimize discriminations rather than that a mere series of post hoc determinations of discrimination be made or makeable.

It should be observed that the impact of the equality norm will vary greatly depending upon the point in time at which it is introduced into a model of the criminal process. If one were starting from scratch to decide how the process ought to work, the norm of equality would have nothing very important to say on such questions as, for example, whether an accused should have the effective assistance of counsel in deciding whether to enter a

plea of guilty. One could decide, on quite independent considerations, that it is or is not a good thing to afford that facility to the
generality of persons accused of crime. But the impact of the
equality norm becomes far greater when it is brought to bear on
a process whose contours have already been shaped. If our model
of the criminal process affords defendants who are in a financial
position to do so the right to consult a lawyer before entering a
plea, then the equality norm exerts powerful pressure to provide
such an opportunity to all defendants and to regard the failure
to do so as a malfunctioning of the process of whose consequences
the accused is entitled to be relieved. In a sense, this has been the
role of the equality norm in affecting the real-world criminal
process. It has made its appearance on the scene comparatively
late, and has therefore encountered a system in which the relative financial inability of most persons accused of crime results in
treatment very different from that accorded the small minority
of the financially capable. For this reason, its impact has already
been substantial and may be expected to be even more so in
the future.

There is a final strand of thought in the Due Process Model
that is often ignored but that needs to be candidly faced if thought
on the subject is not to be obscured. This is a mood of skepticism
about the morality and utility of the criminal sanction, taken
either as a whole or in some of its applications. The subject is a
large and complicated one, comprehending as it does much of the
intellectual history of our times. It is properly the subject of another essay altogether. To put the matter briefly, one cannot improve upon the statement by Professor Paul Bator:

> In summary we are told that the criminal law's notion of just con-
> demnation and punishment is a cruel hypocrisy visited by a smug
> society on the psychologically and economically crippled; that its
> premise of a morally autonomous will with at least some measure of
> choice whether to comply with the values expressed in a penal code
> is unscientific and outmoded; that its reliance on punishment as an
> educational and deterrent agent is misplaced, particularly in the case
> of the very members of society most likely to engage in criminal con-
> duct; and that its failure to provide for individualized and humane
> rehabilitation of offenders is inhuman and wasteful.[6]

---

[6] *Finality in Criminal Law and Federal Habeas Corpus for State Prisoners*, 76
HARV. L. REV. 441, 442 (1963).

This skepticism, which may be fairly said to be widespread among the most influential and articulate contemporary leaders of informed opinion, leads to an attitude toward the processes of the criminal law that, to quote Mr. Bator again, engenders "a peculiar receptivity toward claims of injustice which arise within the traditional structure of the system itself; fundamental disagreement and unease about the very bases of the criminal law has, inevitably, created acute pressure at least to expand and liberalize those of its processes and doctrines which serve to make more tentative its judgments or limit its power." In short, doubts about the ends for which power is being exercised create pressure to limit the discretion with which that power is exercised.

The point need not be pressed to the extreme of doubts about or rejection of the premises upon which the criminal sanction in general rests. Unease may be stirred simply by reflection on the variety of uses to which the criminal sanction is put and by a judgment that an increasingly large proportion of those uses may represent an unwise invocation of so extreme a sanction. It would be an interesting irony if doubts about the propriety of certain uses of the criminal sanction prove to contribute to a restrictive trend in the criminal process that in the end requires a choice among uses and finally an abandonment of some of the very uses that stirred the original doubts, but for a reason quite unrelated to those doubts.

There are two kinds of problems that need to be dealt with in any model of the criminal process. One is what the rules shall be. The other is how the rules shall be implemented. The second is at least as important as the first. As we shall see time and again in our detailed development of the models, the distinctive difference between the two models is not only in the rules of conduct that they lay down but also in the sanctions that are to be invoked when a claim is presented that the rules have been breached and, no less importantly, in the timing that is permitted or required for the invocation of those sanctions.

As I have already suggested, the Due Process Model locates at least some of the sanctions for breach of the operative rules in the criminal process itself. The relation between these two aspects of the process—the rules and the sanctions for their breach—is a purely formal one unless there is some mechanism for bringing them into play with each other. The hinge between them in the Due Process Model is the availability of legal counsel. This has a double aspect. Many of the rules that the model requires are couched in terms of the availability of counsel to do various things at various stages of the process—this is the conventionally recognized aspect; beyond it, there is a pervasive assumption that counsel is necessary in order to invoke sanctions for breach of any of the rules. The more freely available these sanctions are, the more important is the role of counsel in seeing to it that the sanctions are appropriately invoked. If the process is seen as a series of occasions for checking its own operation, the role of counsel is a much more nearly central one than is the case in a process that is seen as primarily concerned with expeditious determination of factual guilt. And if equality of operation is a governing norm, the availability of counsel to some is seen as requiring it for all. Of all the controverted aspects of the criminal process, the right to counsel, including the role of government in its provision, is the most dependent on what one's model of the process looks like, and the least susceptible of resolution unless one has confronted the antinomies of the two models.

I do not mean to suggest that questions about the right to counsel disappear if one adopts a model of the process that conforms more or less closely to the Crime Control Model, but only that such questions become absolutely central if one's model moves very far down the spectrum of possibilities toward the pure Due Process Model. The reason for this centrality is to be found in the assumption underlying both models that the process is an adversary one in which the initiative in invoking relevant rules rests primarily on the parties concerned, the state, and the accused. One could construct models that placed central responsibility on adjudicative agents such as committing magistrates and trial judges. And there are, as we shall see, marginal but nonetheless important adjustments in the role of the adjudicative agents that enter into the models with which we are concerned. For present purposes it is enough to say that these adjustments are marginal, that the animating presuppositions that underlie both models in the context of the American criminal system relegate the adjudicative agents to a relatively passive role, and therefore place central importance on the role of counsel.

One last introductory note before we proceed to a detailed examination of some aspects of the two models in operation. What assumptions do we make about the sources of authority to shape the real-world operations of the criminal process? Recognizing that our models are only models, what agencies of government have the power to pick and choose between their competing demands? Once again, the limiting features of the American context come into play. Ours is not a system of legislative supremacy. The distinctively American institution of judicial review exercises a limiting and ultimately a shaping influence on the criminal process. Because the Crime Control Model is basically an affirmative model, emphasizing at every turn the existence and exercise of official power, its validating authority is ultimately legislative (although proximately administrative). Because the Due Process Model is basically a negative model, asserting limits on the nature of official power and on the modes of its exercise, its validating authority is judicial and requires an appeal to supra-legislative law, to the law of the Constitution. To the extent that tensions between the two models are resolved by deference to the Due Process Model, the authoritative force at work is the judicial power, working in the distinctively judicial mode of invoking the sanction of nullity. That is at once the strength and the weakness of the Due Process Model: its strength because in our system the appeal to the Constitution provides the last and the overriding word; its weakness because saying no in specific cases is an exercise in futility unless there is a general willingness on the part of the officials who operate the process to apply negative prescriptions across the board. It is no accident that statements reinforcing the Due Process Model come from the courts, while at the same time facts denying it are established by the police and prosecutors.

CHAPTER NINE

The Models in Operation: From Arrest to Charge

INTRODUCTION

We turn now to some details of the Crime Control and Due Process Models. The criminal process bristles with problems; it would take a book to provide even so much as an introduction to their full range. The aim in this and succeeding chapters in Part II is a far more modest one: simply to look at a representative selection of problems that occur at various stages of the process, with an eye toward advancing in several ways the argument of this essay. First, and most simply, this is an effort to convey a sense of the extraordinary complexity of the criminal process, no matter which model one visualizes as corresponding to reality; even the Crime Control Model is a formidable consumer of human resources. Second, it is an attempt to point up the appearance throughout the process of recurrent themes of the two models that oppose each other and that pose the limited number of basic choices that can shape the real-life structure of the process. Finally, this assortment of instances will serve to document an assertion made earlier: that the present real-world criminal process tends by and large to resemble the Crime Control Model, but that the current trend is pushing it a significant distance across the spectrum toward the Due Process Model.

There are various ways of dividing up the criminal process for purposes of description and analysis. We shall view it as consisting of three major stages or periods: the period from arrest through the decision to charge the suspect with a crime; the period from the decision to charge through the determination of guilt; and the stage of review and correction of errors that have occurred during the earlier periods. From the first period I have chosen five problems to illustrate the contrasting requirements of the two models: arrests for investigation, electronic eavesdropping, detention and interrogation after a "lawful" arrest, the sanction for illegally secured evidence, and the problem of access to counsel, which assumes special significance during this first, or preliminary, period. From the second period I have selected three problems: the decision to charge, with special emphasis on the issue of whether and to what extent there should be an "outside" scrutiny of the decision; pre-trial detention; and the plea of guilty. From the third stage I have selected problems of direct appeal and collateral attack that raise issues of equality of access to the courts, of the special problems of criminal justice in a federal system, and of retroactivity in the application of changed norms in the criminal process. Finally, I have written a postscript on the pervasive and strategically crucial problem of access to counsel.

The themes here dealt with could be illustrated by many other problems of the criminal process, including the use of police decoys and informers, discovery in criminal cases, the presentation of the insanity defense, and the institution of trial by jury. Concerning each of these, and others as well, it can be asserted with some confidence that the antinomies of the two models reveal themselves in the same or similar form as in the problems chosen for discussion and also that conclusions about the current situation and trend of the real-world process would be substantially the same.

ARRESTS FOR INVESTIGATION

Normally, the first stage of the criminal process as it directly affects the suspect is the act of taking him into physical custody. Once the police think that a crime has been committed and that they have identified the person who committed it, they will want to take him into custody so that his guilt may be presumptively established (typically by having him identified by the victim or some other witness or by inducing him to confess) and he may be held for further proceedings. Sometimes the police will want to detain a person even though he is not suspected of having committed any specific offense, either because they think he is a generally suspicious character who on investigation will likely turn out to have done something criminal, or because they think that police intervention may prevent the commission of an offense, or because they hope that by harassing him in this way they can induce him to stop engaging in some undesirable activity of which he is suspected or to leave the locality.

The act of taking a person into physical custody is ordinarily spoken of as an arrest. The term "arrest" carries important legal consequences with it, so that great controversy attends the question whether certain forms of physical restraint—such as stopping a person on the street for questioning or taking him to the station house for a brief period of questioning without then and there intending to prefer any particular charge against him—are "really" arrests. Because our discussion of the competing norms will refer to a number of different kinds of restraining conduct that may or may not be thought of as desirable depending on the dictates of the particular model, there is no reason not to refer indifferently to all of them as arrests, with the understanding that the term is used as a physical description, not as a designation of an operational legal norm.

Two crucial issues arise at this stage of the process: (1) on what basis are the police entitled to make an arrest and (2) what consequences, if any, will flow from their making an "illegal" arrest. These are issues that divide our two models, and that may in addition be thought of as representing a paradigm of the kind of division that will occur over numerous other issues that arise in the process of investigation and apprehension.

The Crime Control Model. Of course the police should be entitled to arrest a person when they have probable cause to think that he has committed a particular criminal offense like murder, or rape, or burglary; but it would be absurd to suggest that an arrest is permissible *only* in that situation. The slight invasion of personal freedom and privacy involved in stopping a person on the street to ask him questions or even taking him to the station house for a period of questioning and other investigation is necessary in a wide variety of situations that only by the exercise of hypocrisy could be described as involving "probable cause." As one example, people who are known to the police as previous offenders should be subject to arrest at any time for the limited purpose of determining whether they have been engaging in antisocial activities, especially when it is known that a crime of the sort they have committed has taken place and that it was physically possible for them to have committed it. For another example, anyone who behaves in a manner suggesting that he may be up to no good should be subject to arrest for investigation: it may turn out that he has committed an offense, but more importantly, the very fact of stopping him for questioning, either on the street or at the station house, may prevent the commission of a crime. As a third instance, those who make a living out of criminal activity should be made to realize that their presence in the community is unwanted if they persist in their criminal occupations; periodic checks of their activity, whether or not this involves an arrest, will help to bring that attitude home to them.

In short, the power of the police to arrest people for the purpose of investigation and prevention is one that must exist if the police are to do their job properly; the only question is whether arrests for investigation and prevention should be made hypocritically and deviously, or openly and avowedly. It only causes disrespect for law when there are great deviations between what the law on the books authorizes the police to do and what everyone knows they have to do.

The police have no reason to abuse this power by arresting and holding law-abiding people. The innocent have nothing to fear. It is enough of a check on police discretion to let the dictates of police efficiency determine under what circumstances and for how long a person may be stopped and held for investigation. But if laws limiting police discretion to make an arrest are thought necessary, they either should provide very liberal outer limits so as to accommodate all possible cases or, preferably, should require nothing more explicit than behavior that is reasonable under all the circumstances.

The question of appropriate sanctions for breach of whatever rules are devised to limit police arrest powers is, as a practical matter, at least as important to the ends of crime control as is the nature of the substantive rules themselves. The most appropriate sanction is discipline of the offending policemen by those best qualified to judge whether his conduct has lived up to professional police standards—his superiors in the police department. Discipline by his superiors may make him a better policeman; in cases where that seems improbable, he should be dismissed from the force. Civil remedies for the arrested person administered in the ordinary courts are also a possibility, although they are less likely to serve the end of educating the erring police officer. The one kind of sanction that should be completely inadmissible is the kind that takes place in the criminal process itself: dismissal of prosecution or suppression of evidence. That kind of sanction for police misconduct simply gives the criminal a windfall without affecting the conduct of the erring police. As Cardozo put it, "the criminal is to go free because the constable has blundered."[1] This is particularly inept in the light of the fact that rules for the governance of police conduct are apt to be quite technical, leading to a certain number of good-faith mistakes. The policeman who made the mistake may never know or be only dimly aware that his conduct resulted in a criminal's going free. His own conduct is much more likely to be changed by measures that affect him personally and that do not have the fortuitous effect of conferring benefit on the criminal and thus of reducing the effectiveness of law enforcement.

There are, generally speaking, two kinds of devices for giving the police adequate scope in making arrests for investigation. The first is what might be called the direct method: explicitly providing broad powers to stop and question persons, irrespective of whether they are reasonably suspected of having committed a particular crime. The second is the indirect method: framing broad enough definitions of criminal conduct to give the police the power to arrest on the orthodox "probable cause" basis a wide variety of people who are engaged in suspicious conduct. Vagrancy laws, disorderly conduct laws, and laws making it a crime not to give an account of oneself in response to police in-

[1] People v. Defore, 242 N.Y. 13, 21 (1926).

terrogation are all examples. It is not too important which of these methods is used; often a combination of the two will produce the desired result.

Due Process Model. It is a basic right of free men—basic in the sense that his other rights depend upon it—not to be subject to physical restraint except for good cause. The only measurable standard of cause is the time-honored prescription that no one may be arrested except upon a determination that a crime has probably been committed and that he is the person who probably committed it. Normally, such a determination should be made independently by a magistrate in deciding whether to issue a warrant, but in situations of necessity, it may be made by a police officer acting on probative data that is subject to subsequent judicial scrutiny. Any less stringent standard opens the door to the probability of grave abuse, as repeated investigations of police practices have shown. A society that covertly tolerates indiscriminate arrest is hypocritical; but one that approves its legality is well on the way to becoming totalitarian in nature.

It is far from being demonstrable that broad powers of arrest for investigation are necessary to the efficient operation of the police. The argument that they are necessary is open to a serious charge of inconsistency, since it is also argued that changes in the law are necessary to bring it into conformity with prevalent, though unacknowledged, practices. If arrests for investigation are actually now tolerated on a wide scale, it makes no sense to assert that legalizing them is necessary to keep efficiency from being impaired. In the end, however, arguments about what is required by efficiency are wide of the mark. A totally efficient system of crime control would be a totally repressive one, since it would require a total suspension of rights of privacy. We must be prepared to pay a price for a regime that fosters personal privacy and champions the dignity and inviolability of the individual. That price inevitably involves some sacrifice in efficiency; consequently an appeal to efficiency alone is never sufficient to justify any encroachment on the area of human freedom. It must be shown that efficient law enforcement will be so heavily impaired by failure to adopt the proposed measure that the minimal conditions of public order necessary to provide the environment in which individuals can be allowed to enjoy the fruits of personal freedom will in themselves cease to exist or be gravely impaired. No one has been able to show that we are at or near that point.

The practical consequence of enlarging police authority to detain individuals for questioning is not likely to be that all classes of the population will thereupon be subjected to interference. If that were the consequence, the practice would carry its own limiting features, because the popular outcry would be so great that these measures could not long be resorted to. The danger is rather that they will be applied in a discriminatory fashion to precisely those elements in the population—the poor, the ignorant, the illiterate, the unpopular—who are least able to draw attention to their plight and to whose sufferings the vast majority of the population are the least responsive. Respect for law, never high among minority groups, would plunge to a new low if what the police are now thought to do sub rosa became an officially sanctioned practice.

The need, then, is not to legalize practices that are presently illegal but widespread. Rather, it is to reaffirm their illegality, and at the same time to take steps to reduce their incidence. This brings us to the question of sanctions for illegal arrests. To the extent possible, these sanctions should be located within the criminal process itself; because it is the efficiency of that process that they seek so mistakenly to promote, the process should penalize, and thus label as inefficient, arrests that are based on any standard less rigorous than probable cause. As a minimal requirement, any evidence that is obtained directly or indirectly on the basis of an illegal arrest should be suppressed. Beyond that, any criminal prosecution commenced on the basis of an illegal arrest should be dismissed, preferably with prejudice, but at the least with the consequence that the entire process, if it is to be reinvoked, must be started over again from scratch and all records, working papers, and the like prepared in the course of the first illegal proceeding impounded and destroyed.

Most illegal arrests do not result in criminal prosecution (one of their undoubted vices), and are therefore not amenable to sanctions imposed in the criminal process itself. A variety of devices should be marshaled to provide effective sanctions against arrests for investigation. The ordinary tort action against the policeman has been demonstrated to be of very limited usefulness. It should be supplemented by provision for a statutory action against the governmental unit employing the offending policeman, with a high enough minimum recovery to make suit worthwhile. Since an important public service is performed by attorneys who bring suits against errant police officers, there should also be provision for allowing adequate attorney's fees in cases where the action is successful. Measures of this kind will give governmental units a stake in proper police activity and an incentive to discourage illegal activity that they do not now have. Direct disciplinary measures against the offending police officer are also desirable, but it is unrealistic to expect them to be initiated by a departmental authority. Outside scrutiny is needed, both to insure that the law is being impartially enforced and, what is perhaps even more important, to reassure the general public that the police are not a law unto themselves. To this end, there is need for civilian boards (i.e., boards not dominated by police) to which complaints about illegal police activity may be directed and which can at least initiate, if not conduct, disciplinary proceedings in cases where preliminary investigation shows that the complaint may have merit.

The Situation and the Trend. The legal authority of the police to stop persons on the street, search them for weapons, and require them to answer questions about their identity is ambiguous. There is no doubt that the police, like any other person, may accost others and ask them questions. The question is what the police may do if the person refuses to stop or to answer questions. There is no authoritative holding on whether the police may constitutionally be authorized to restrain a person who refuses to stop and answer questions if they do not have probable cause to arrest. The question is a difficult one to raise, because it can rarely be shown that a particular piece of evidence used against a criminal defendant was obtained as a result of an assertedly illegal "stop." In addition to being difficult, the question is of central importance. The hundreds of thousands of contacts between police and citizen that take place every day, ranging from friendly inquiries to threatening encounters, occupy a kind of legal no man's land. There may well be a significant distinction between a brief period of on-the-street interrogation to check an identity or "freeze" an emergency situation and the further and coercive step of taking a suspect to the station house for a period of questioning to see whether reasonable cause exists for his arrest. Both of these devices occupy the middle ground between complete immunity from police interference with freedom of movement on the one hand and arrest (in the orthodox sense of being taken into custody on reasonable cause to answer to a charge of crime) on the other. The problem of determining whether there should be any middle ground and, if so, what it should be is a neat paradigm of the problem of coercion in a free society.

There have been a number of attempts to establish a middle ground through legislation. The Uniform Arrest Act, first proposed in 1941, would give the police officer the power to "stop any person abroad who he has reasonable ground to suspect is committing, has committed, or is about to commit a crime, and may demand of him his name, address, business abroad, and whither he is going." It goes on to provide that any person so questioned who fails to give a satisfactory account of himself may be "detained" for further questioning and investigation at the police station, the period of such "detention" not to exceed two hours. The Act has been adopted by only three states,[2] and has apparently been construed out of existence in one of them. It is silent on the question of remedies available to a person wrongfully detained under its provisions.

The so-called "stop-and-frisk" law passed in New York in 1964 has similar provisions for on-the-street questioning, but it does not provide for further detention. It also allows a police officer to search any suspicious person he stops for weapons if he "reasonably suspects that he is in danger of life and limb," and provides that the officer may take the weapon or "any other thing [he finds] the possession of which may constitute a crime." After the questioning, the officer must either return it "if lawfully possessed" or "arrest such person" (presumably for the illegal pos-

2 Delaware, New Hampshire, and Rhode Island.

session). This last provision was construed to uphold a conviction for narcotics possession based on the discovery of heroin in the pocket of a man stopped and searched for weapons, and, as so construed, was upheld as constitutional by the New York Court of Appeals.[3]

Most recently, a proposed solution has been presented by the draftsmen of the American Law Institute's Model Code of Pre-Arraignment Procedure. It provides for a twenty-minute "investigative stop" on the street or in any other place in which the police may be lawfully present, during which they may stop, question, and search for dangerous weapons any person who either is thought to have knowledge about a crime that has been committed or is observed in circumstances that suggest that he either has committed or will commit an offense. If nothing turns up that would justify an arrest, the police must tell the person so detained that he is free to go at the expiration of the twenty-minute period. A very few minor offenses are excluded from the crimes for which this investigative stop may be used: misdemeanors punishable by less than thirty days' imprisonment, vagrancy, and loitering. Otherwise its spectrum is as broad as the criminal law itself. The draftsmen of this code, which is incomplete, have not yet indicated the range of sanctions they plan to make available for curbing abuses of this authority by the police.

"There is no doubt that it is common police practice to stop and question suspects as to whom there are no sufficient grounds for arrest."[4] Professor Frank Remington, the knowledgeable commentator who expressed that opinion, goes on to say that while the factual situation is no doubt clear, it is not easy to document. It is also clear that many persons so stopped who do not give a satisfactory account of themselves are taken to the station house for further investigation. A recent study of "arrests for investigation" in the District of Columbia, where the police use this term to describe the act of taking into custody without probable cause, showed that in a one-year period there were 3,743

---

[3] People v. Sibron, 18 N.Y. 2d 603 (1966), *rev'd,* 88 Sup. Ct. 1889 (1968). See below, p. 185.

[4] Remington, *The Law Relating to "On the Street" Detention,* 51 J. CRIM. L.C. & P.S. 386 (1960).

such arrests.[5] This figure represented less than one per cent of the total arrests in the District—415,925—during the period. But since such arrests are apparently made only for investigation of felonies, the more relevant figure is the percentage of arrests for felonies that fall into the category of arrests for investigation. Here the percentage is 28, or about one in every four felony arrests. Most such arrests were made on the street, but a substantial proportion were made in the suspects' homes.

The present sanctions for illegal arrest are essentially as follows: exclusion in a criminal prosecution of evidence obtained by a search conducted incident to an illegal arrest; tort action against the offending police officer; and complaint to the police department which, with rare exceptions, disposes of the complaint through departmental channels and without "civilian" scrutiny. Since very few illegal arrests culminate in a criminal prosecution, judicial control through exclusion of illegally obtained evidence is not a very effective sanction. It remains the best we have, however, since the others are almost totally ineffective.

The pressure to find a middle ground between the rigorous standards that prevail for a technical "arrest" and the total abdication of standards represented by the District of Columbia practice just described has become quite intense. And this pressure has given rise to a number of criminal prosecutions that have at last afforded the Supreme Court a chance to begin developing constitutional doctrine on the subject of arrests for investigation. The Court appears to have concluded that some middle ground is necessary, that neither the pure Due Process nor the pure Crime Control model will do in this situation. In a series of very recent cases, it has begun what is likely to be a lengthy process of adapting the imperatives of the Fourth Amendment to what it sees as the needs of law enforcement. In one of these cases, *Terry v. Ohio*,[6] the Court upheld a conviction for carrying a concealed weapon based on evidence secured through an on-the-street detention and weapons search of a man who was observed by the

[5] Commissioner's Committee on Police Arrests for Investigation, *Report and Recommendations* (Washington, D.C., 1962), p. 8.
[6] 88 Sup. Ct. 1868 (1968).

police to be acting suspiciously. There was no question, as the Court made clear, but that the police did not have reasonable cause to make a technical "arrest" at the time they stopped and searched the suspect. The Court's reasoning laid heavy stress upon the importance of permitting a police officer to make a weapons search for his own protection. The obvious problem presented by this rationale is that the police may be tempted to make searches for incriminating evidence in the guise of self-protective weapons searches.

In two other cases decided on the same day as *Terry*, the Court managed to avoid for the moment the question whether evidence other than weapons found on persons who had been stopped and frisked could be introduced into evidence against them. In *Sibron* v. *New York*,[7] involving possession of narcotics that had been found in the suspect's pocket during a purported weapons search, the Court held that the circumstances did not warrant the officer's making a self-protective search for weapons. In the companion case of *Peters* v. *New York*, where the charge was possession of burglar's tools, the Court concluded (rather questionably) that the search that turned up the tools was incident to a lawful arrest; as a result the question of the constitutionality and admissibility of evidence under the *Terry* standard was simply avoided. In both New York cases the police had acted under the authority of the New York stop-and-frisk law. The Court refused to pass on the validity of that law, holding instead that the reasonableness of police conduct of this sort must be judged under the Fourth Amendment.

If the previous course of constitutional adjudication in the field of criminal procedure offers any guide, we can now expect a series of highly particularistic decisions from which bits of language will be plucked by advocates of the two opposing positions as evidence that the norms are moving their way. The stop-and-frisk cases fall far short of giving blanket approval to investigative arrests of the indiscriminate kind that were documented by the District of Columbia Report already described. Still, it appears that first blood in this battle has been drawn by the proponents of the Crime Control Model; these cases make it unlikely

7 88 Sup. Ct. 1889 (1968).

that many local governments will direct their police departments to stop making arrests for investigation, as the District Commissioners did in the wake of the Report.

The problem of arrests for investigation is now more visible than it has ever been before. The gap between the Supreme Court's first tentative resolution of the problem and the pure Due Process norm is a substantial one. It is no more substantial, however, than the gap between the Court's stance and the Crime Control norm or, indeed, between the Court's stance and what we know of present-day practice. The increase in visibility generated by empirical investigations and by newly awakened judicial interest has brought us to a point at which we are beginning to get some legal norms; but the course of reform will remain unclear for some time.

DETENTION AND INTERROGATION AFTER A "LAWFUL" ARREST

Once a person suspected of crime has been taken into custody the general problem is presented of determining what to do with him next. He cannot be immediately placed on trial; his case is not "in court," because at this point there is no charge against him. Someone has to decide whether a prosecution should be formally initiated by filing a charging paper in court, and if so, what specific offense or offenses should be charged. Typically, this is a job for the prosecutor; yet at this point he will ordinarily not even know that the suspect is in custody. Furthermore, there is a question whether the charge against the suspect ought not to be evaluated by some impartial authority in order to determine whether he should be held for judicial action. There is also a question about whether the suspect should be held in custody until his guilt is adjudicated or released pending that determination, and a time and place must be designated for making that decision. Both of these decisions—whether or not to hold for the institution of charges, and if so, whether or not to release pending further steps in the process—are, in theory at least, made at a preliminary hearing before a judicial officer who, when he sits in this capacity, is known as a magistrate. This occasion provides typically a terminal point for the initial investigatory and apprehending phase of the criminal process. We will later examine the differing views taken by our competing models of the scope and importance of this occasion, and consider possible resolutions of the differences. Suffice it to note at this point that any model must provide some kind of terminal point for what may be termed the "police" phase of the process, some mechanism for turning the criminal investigation into a criminal prosecution. This is not to say, of course, that the dividing line must in all cases be an absolute one; important issues remain about the extent to which police activity involving the suspect may go on after the prosecutorial phase has commenced, and conversely, about the extent to which prosecutorial activity may go on in the initial period of investigation and arrest. Leaving those complexities aside for the moment, a number of questions present themselves about the extent to which the accused may be required to cooperate in the investigation between the time of his arrest and the time that he is brought before a magistrate for preliminary hearing. May the police hold the accused indefinitely, or must they bring him before a magistrate at some particular time? If the latter, what sanctions, if any, should be imposed for failure to comply with the requisite time limits? May the suspect be interrogated by the police during this time, and if so, under what limitations? If the accused admits his guilt during this period, what restrictions, if any, are there on the use that may be made of this evidence at his trial? Should the accused be entitled to the assistance of counsel during the time between his arrest and the preliminary hearing, and if so, under what conditions and with what consequences for failure by the police to adhere to those conditions?

The Crime Control Model. The police cannot be expected to solve crimes by independent investigation alone. The best source of information is usually the suspect himself. Without the cooperation of suspects, many crimes could not be solved at all. The police must have a reasonable opportunity to interrogate the suspect in private before he has a chance to fabricate a story or to decide that he will not cooperate. The psychologically optimal time for getting this kind of cooperation from the suspect is immediately after his arrest, before he has had a chance to rally his forces. Any kind of outside interference is likely to diminish the prospect that the suspect will cooperate in the interrogation; therefore he should not be entitled to summon his family or friends, and most particularly, he should not be entitled to consult a lawyer. The first thing that a lawyer will tell him is to say nothing to the police. Once he gets that kind of reinforcement, the chances of getting any useful information out of him sink to zero.

Of course the police should not be entitled to hold the suspect for interrogation indefinitely, nor would they want to do so. The point of diminishing returns in interrogation is reached fairly soon, and anyway, the police don't have extensive enough resources to allow them to go on interrogating indefinitely. But no hard and fast rule can be laid down about how long the police should be permitted to interrogate the suspect before bringing him before a magistrate. The gravity of the crime, its complexity, the amount of criminal sophistication that the suspect appears to have—all of these are relevant factors in determining how long he should be held. The standard ought to be the length of time, given all the circumstances, during which it is reasonable to suppose that legitimate techniques of interrogation may be expected to produce useful information or that extrinsic investigation may be expected to produce convincing proof either of the suspect's innocence or of his guilt.

The suspect should not be held incommunicado under normal circumstances. His family is entitled to know where he is; but they should not be entitled to talk with him, because that may impair the effectiveness of the interrogation. Occasionally it may be justifiable not to notify them at all, as when a confederate is still at large and does not know that his partner in crime has been apprehended.

The point of all these illustrations, however, is that hard and fast rules cannot be laid down if police efficiency is not to be impaired. It follows that the rules must be flexible and that good-faith mistakes about their applicability in any given case should not be penalized. If the police err by holding a suspect too long, he has no complaint, because they would not be holding him unless they had some good basis for their belief that he had committed a crime. The public has a complaint to the extent that police resources are thereby shown to have been used inefficiently; but the redress for that is intradepartmental discipline in flagrant cases and a general program of administrative management that keeps such occasions to a minimum.

Any trustworthy statement obtained from a suspect during a period of police interrogation should of course be admissible into evidence against him. Criminal investigation is a search for truth, and anything that aids the search should be encouraged. There is, to be sure, a danger that occasionally police will not live up to professional standards, and will use coercive measures to elicit a confession from a suspect. That is not to be condoned, but at the same time we should keep in mind that the evil of a coerced confession is that it may result in the conviction of an innocent man. There is no way of laying down hard and fast rules about what kinds of police conduct are coercive. It is a factual question in each case whether the accused's confession is unreliable. A defendant against whom a confession is introduced into evidence should have to convince the jury that the circumstances under which it was elicited were so coercive that more probably than not the confession was untrue. In reaching a determination on that issue, the trier of fact should of course be entitled to consider the other evidence in the case, and if it points toward guilt and tends to corroborate the confession, should be entitled to take that into account in determining whether, more likely than not, the confession was untrue.

To say this is not to say that the unlawful use of force by the police on an accused is ever to be condoned. The point is simply that the use of force is not in itself determinative of the reliability of a confession and should therefore not be conclusive against the admissibility of a confession. The sanctions available for mistreating a person in custody are ample, if vigorously pursued, to ensure that this kind of conduct will be rare. It is by raising professional standards through internal administrative methods rather than by altering the outcome of randomly selected criminal prosecutions that improper police conduct is being eliminated. It follows from what has been said that practices less likely than the use of force to be coercive, such as an overlong period of detention unaccompanied by physical abuse, should not count conclusively against the admissibility of a confession.

The Due Process Model. The decision to arrest in order to be valid must be based on probable cause to believe that the suspect has committed a crime. To put it another way, the police should not arrest unless information in their hands at that time seems likely, subject to the vicissitudes of the litigation process, to provide a case that will result in a conviction. It follows that if proper arrest standards have been employed, there is no necessity to get additional evidence out of the mouth of the defendant. He is to be arrested so that he may be held to answer the case against him, not so that a case against him that does not exist at the time of his arrest can be developed.

Once a suspect has been arrested, he should be brought before a magistrate without unnecessary delay, which is to say as soon as it is physically possible to do so, once the preliminary formalities of recording his arrest have been completed. Anyone who is held in arrest has the right to test the legality of his arrest, i.e., whether there is probable cause to hold him, in a judicial proceeding. As a practical matter, that right is diluted through delay unless the accused is promptly brought before a magistrate. Since a suspect is entitled to be at liberty pending the judicial determination of his guilt or innocence, there must be as promptly as possible after arrest a proceeding in which the conditions of his release— for example release on bail—are determined. This right too is diluted by delay unless the suspect is promptly brought before a magistrate. And the suspect is entitled to the assistance of counsel, assistance that he needs most acutely as soon as he is arrested. As a practical matter, he is unlikely to receive that right unless he is promptly advised of it. Once again, his prompt production before an impartial judicial officer is necessary if his right is not to be diluted by delay.

It is never proper for the police to hold a suspect for the purpose of interrogation or investigation. Of course, some interval of time must always elapse between his arrest and his production before a magistrate, and it would be unrealistic to expect the police to maintain complete silence toward him during that period. However, there is all the difference in the world between an interrogation conducted during the relatively brief span of time necessary to get the suspect before a magistrate and an interrogation whose length is measured by the time necessary to get him to confess. Any such interrogation should, by that fact alone, be held illegal.

As soon as a suspect is arrested, he should be told by the police that he is under no obligation to answer questions, that he will suffer no detriment by refusing to answer questions, that he may answer questions in his own interest to clear himself of suspicion (but that anything he says may be used in evidence), and, above all, that he is entitled to see a lawyer if he wants to do so.

If the suspect does make self-incriminating statements while under arrest and before he is brought before a magistrate, their admissibility into evidence against him should be barred under any of the following conditions: (1) if the police failed to warn him of his rights, including his right to the assistance of a lawyer; (2) if he was questioned after the required warnings were given, unless he expressly waived his right to be silent and to see a lawyer; (3) if the confession was made during a period of detention that exceeded what was necessary to get him promptly before a magistrate; or (4) if the confession was made by other coercive means, such as the use of force. Any confession made under these circumstances should be regarded as "involuntary," and should be excluded at the trial in order to deprive the police of any incentive to obtain such a confession.

The rationale of exclusion is not that the confession is untrustworthy, but that it is at odds with the postulates of an accusatory system of criminal justice in which it is up to the state to make its case against a defendant without forcing him to cooperate in the process, and without capitalizing on his ignorance of his legal rights. It follows, then, that the existence of other evidence of guilt has no bearing on the admissibility of the confession or on the necessity for reversing a conviction based in part on such a confession. It also follows that the procedure for determining the admissibility of a confession must be such as to avoid any possibility of prejudice to the defendant through the process of determining admissibility. Specifically, in a jury trial the issue of the admissibility of a confession should be litigated on a record made before the judge and out of the hearing of the jury, so that the trial judge has the clear and undivided responsibility for deciding whether the jury should hear the confession and so that a reviewing court can have an unambiguous basis for deciding whether the trial judge reached the proper conclusion.

The Situation and the Trend. The power of the police to interrogate a suspect between his arrest and his production before a magistrate has until recently been generally recognized; but there is a strong and apparently accelerating judicial trend toward limiting both the duration and the prerequisites of such interrogation. In the early phase of this trend the Supreme Court laid down increasingly strict standards for determining when a confession is "involuntary" and therefore inadmissible in evidence against the accused. In these decisions the criterion of voluntariness was not the trustworthiness of the confession but rather its compatibility with the asserted postulates of an accusatory system in which the case against the accused must be established "by evidence independently and freely secured" and in which the state is not allowed "by its own coercion [to] prove its charge against an accused out of his own mouth."[8] Although the criterion was ostensibly applied on a case-by-case basis, a pattern of general and automatic standards for determining whether the circumstances of the interrogation were such as to be "inherently coercive" has developed. As a result, more recent decisions have been intended to preclude case-by-case scrutiny. This second phase manifested itself in federal criminal prosecutions where the Supreme Court, in an exercise of its supervisory power over the administration of federal criminal justice, laid down the so-called *Mallory* rule rejecting confessions that are secured during a period of detention that exceeds what is required to bring the accused before a magistrate "without unnecessary delay."[9] The states were left free of this requirement, and have in general not applied it to their criminal prosecutions. However, the length of detention was until recently a factor conspicuously stressed by the Supreme Court in reversing state criminal convictions based in part on a confession.

[8] Rogers v. Richmond, 365 U.S. 534, 541 (1961).
[9] Mallory v. United States, 354 U.S. 449 (1957).

Now, however, the Supreme Court has taken a sweeping new approach to the problem of police interrogation. Abandoning its traditional case-by-case approach to voluntariness and the limited duration approach of *Mallory,* the Court has invoked the Fifth Amendment's ban on compelled self-incrimination to limit severely the power of the police to interrogate a suspect in custody. In *Miranda* v. *Arizona,*[10] the Court held that the police may not interrogate a person in custody until he has been advised that he has the right to remain silent and to consult a lawyer; that if he indicates a desire to remain silent, the interrogation must cease; that if he indicates a desire to consult a lawyer, the interrogation must be suspended until his lawyer appears or, in the case of a person unable to retain a lawyer, until a lawyer has been engaged for him; and that if interrogation does continue without the presence of a lawyer and a statement is taken, "a heavy burden rests on the Government to demonstrate that the defendant knowingly and intelligently waived" the rights thus conferred upon him.

Other turns of the doctrinal screw have further tightened this new constitutional limitation. It has become a firmly established principle that convictions based in part on confessions deemed involuntary (for which one must now read illegal under *Miranda*) must be reversed regardless of how strong any other evidence of guilt may be. And the states have been told that they must establish procedures for litigating the admissibility of confessions that do not give juries a clandestine opportunity to hold against the defendant either the substance of a confession or the fact that one was made.[11] Except for the possibility of waiver, which leaves the door slightly but significantly ajar, it might seem that the Court has in effect ruled out of evidence any statement made by a suspect in custody during the period between his arrest and his production before a magistrate.

It is much too soon to know what effect the *Miranda* rule will actually have. Preliminary evidence suggests, however, that it has not appreciably diminished the proportion of self-incriminating statements made by suspects in custody. Suspects in large numbers have apparently been willing to "waive" the rights conferred

[10] 384 U.S. 436 (1966).
[11] Jackson v. Denno, 378 U.S. 368 (1964).

upon them and to make statements without obtaining the assistance of counsel. Whether and to what extent these "waivers" will serve to legitimate such statements remains to be seen. Unless the Supreme Court radically shifts its direction, however, it seems safe to predict that if the *Miranda* rule does not produce the intended effect of reducing the incidence of confessions, particularly by suspects who do not have the financial means to obtain counsel, the Court is likely to take the next step in the direction of the Due Process Model, which would be flatly to prohibit the use in evidence of statements given by suspects to the police. We shall consider at a later point whether this or some other resolution of the tension between the two models is desirable.

The confessions issue is probably the most dramatic now confronting the criminal process, although it is far from being the most important. The development of the issue exhibits characteristics that are typical of trends in the criminal process generally: (1) the substitution of broad, quasi-legislative rules of administration for the more traditional case-by-case adjudication; (2) reliance on the equality norm to reduce or eliminate disparities in treatment resulting from disparate financial means; (3) restriction of law enforcement discretion. What all of this seems to portend is a criminal process that is being forced increasingly to take on the contours of the Due Process Model, at least in terms of the norms that ostensibly govern it.

ELECTRONIC SURVEILLANCE

Beginning with the invention of the telephone wiretap and spurred by the extraordinary development of electronic technology, an ever more effective arsenal of surveillance devices has been built up. Mr. Justice Clark, writing for the Supreme Court in the important recent case of *Berger* v. *New York,* gives some vivid illustrations of what is now possible:

Sophisticated electronic devices have now been developed (commonly known as "bugging") which are capable of eavesdropping on anyone in most any given situation. They are to be distinguished from "wiretapping" which is confined to the interception of telegraphic and telephonic communications. Miniature in size—no larger than a postage stamp (⅜" x ⅜" x ⅛")—these gadgets pick up whispers within a room and broadcast them half a block away to a receiver. It is said that certain types of electronic rays beamed at walls or glass windows are capable of catching voice vibrations as they are bounced off the latter. Since 1940, eavesdropping has become a big business. Manufacturing concerns offer complete detection systems which automatically record voices under most any conditions by remote control. A microphone concealed in a book, a lamp, or other unsuspected place in a room, or made into a fountain pen, tie clasp, lapel button, or cuff link increases the range of these powerful wireless transmitters to a half mile. Receivers pick up the transmission with interference-free reception on a special wave frequency. And, of late, a combination mirror transmitter has been developed which permits not only sight but voice transmission up to 300 feet. Likewise, parabolic microphones, which can overhear conversations without being placed within the premises monitored, have been developed.[12]

Given the rate of scientific and technological change, it strains the imagination to visualize what may be possible only a few years hence.

These Orwellian prospects pose increasingly difficult problems for the criminal process as pressure from law enforcement for license to enlist these devices in the investigation of crime meets counterpressure from people who see the doom of individual freedom in a wholesale intrusion by government into the private lives of its citizens. All agree that the use of these devices for private snooping should be prevented. Beyond that, agreement ends. There is bitter and protracted controversy over whether law enforcement should be allowed to use these devices at all and, if at all, in what kinds of circumstances and under what kinds of controls.

The Crime Control Model. The war on organized crime demands the use of electronic surveillance. High-ranking members of organized crime syndicates are insulated by layers of structure from direct participation in the crimes committed by their underlings. If they are to be implicated, it must be by showing that they have directed a conspiracy. Since their role may not even be known to the immediate participants in any given illegal transaction of gambling or narcotics, the only way in which evidence

[12] 388 U.S. 41 (1967).

can be secured against them is by listening in on their telephone conversations and otherwise monitoring their discussions. Almost without exception, the conviction of top underworld figures has depended on the use of evidence or evidential leads obtained through electronic surveillance.

It is undeniable that abuses may occur, but their danger is greatly outweighed by the necessity for using these devices. Judicial control of the use of surveillance devices will probably not do much to protect against excesses of enforcement zeal because it is impossible for the judge to whom application is made for an authorizing order to do more than generally satisfy himself that the police have reasonable grounds for wishing to use the devices to overhear conversations on a particular telephone line or in a particular place. Judges cannot exercise continuous and detailed supervision over the monitoring. And the nature of the business is such that there is going to be a high ratio of chaff to wheat. However, we do not object in principle to having to obtain a court order, so long as judges do not require an impossible degree of specificity about what we are looking for. After all, if we knew precisely what we were looking for, we wouldn't have to look.

There should be no limitations on the kinds of criminal activity police are allowed to investigate using surveillance devices. Sometimes an important underworld figure can be tripped up on the basis of a relatively minor criminal charge. By the same token, we should be free to use what turns up whether it is what we were looking for or not. Law-abiding citizens have nothing to fear. If conversations that we overhear produce no leads to evidence of criminal activity, we are not interested in them. Law enforcement has neither the time nor the inclination to build up files of information about activity that is not criminal.

The Due Process Model. The right of privacy, as implied by the Fourth Amendment to the Constitution, cannot be forced to give way to the asserted exigencies of law enforcement. The use of electronic surveillance constitutes just the kind of indiscriminate general search that helped to bring on the American Revolution and that the framers of the Constitution were alert to guard against. In the name of necessity this grant of power would permit an unscrupulous policeman or prosecutor to pry into the private lives of people almost at will. Knowledge that this was so would certainly inhibit the free expression of thoughts and feelings that makes life in our society worth living. Electronic surveillance by anyone under any circumstances should be outlawed.

That is the optimal position. If it cannot be established, certainly it is essential that police authority for electronic surveillance be strictly limited to a small class of very serious cases. "The fight against organized crime" is far too vague and sweeping a rubric to provide adequate protection. And the offenses allegedly committed by organized criminals are committed by many others as well. The most that should be authorized is the use of electronic surveillance in cases of espionage, treason, or other crimes directly affecting national security. And even in such cases as these, there should be judicial control comparable to what would be exercised in deciding whether to issue a search warrant.

The Situation and the Trend. In the famous *Olmstead* case in 1928, the Supreme Court decided by a 5–4 margin that the admission into evidence of conversations overheard through a telephone wiretap did not violate the Fourth Amendment.[13] The closeness of that decision presaged the ambivalence that courts have expressed since that time. Congress in 1934 enacted Section 605 of the Federal Communications Act, which made it unlawful to intercept and divulge wire communications. This was subsequently interpreted by the Supreme Court to prohibit the introduction of wiretap evidence in federal courts. Thereafter a logically anomalous distinction developed between wiretapping and other forms of electronic surveillance that were not affected by the federal statute. The rule then developed that the legality of these other forms turned on whether or not a physical trespass was involved in the interception. In recent years the concept of what constitutes a trespass has been broadened, but there has remained until very recently a significant difference in treatment between wiretapping (which is unconditionally banned) and other, probably more intrusive, forms of electronic surveillance.

There have been a number of legislative attempts, usually in the wake of investigations of organized crime, to provide more

13 Olmstead v. United States, 277 U.S. 438 (1928).

or less limited authority for electronic eavesdropping by law enforcement officers. Recently, the National Crime Commission recommended that such legislation be passed. Interestingly enough, the Attorney General declined to endorse the Commission's plea, again demonstrating the extremely controversial nature of the issues involved. In the spring of 1967, the Supreme Court decided the important case of *Berger* v. *New York*,[14] testing the constitutionality of a New York statute permitting electronic surveillance upon court order. The Court held that the statute violated the Fourth Amendment, and the language of the decision raised substantial doubts whether any statute authorizing electronic surveillance except on the basis of a valid judicial warrant would now be upheld. Since it is rare that conversations sought to be overheard can be described in advance with the particularity required to sustain a search warrant for the seizure of tangible evidence, the Supreme Court's exception may not hold out much comfort to law enforcement. The Crime Control Act of 1968, recently enacted by Congress and reluctantly signed by the President, appears to validate electronic surveillance to a greater extent than would be approved by the Supreme Court under its most recent decisions. Law enforcement practices will, however, be governed by the Act's terms until a definitive ruling to the contrary comes from the Court. And that ruling, if it comes at all, may be several years off.

ILLEGALLY SECURED EVIDENCE

In any criminal process there are bound to be rules that delineate the circumstances under which the police may invade the privacy of the home in their search for evidence that will aid in convicting persons accused of crime. In our system these rules have tended to be linked with the rules governing the circumstances under which an arrest may be made, a familiar but by no means a necessary association. In this section we are not concerned with the considerations that ought, under one model or the other, to govern the legality of particular searches. Rather, the focus is on the positions that our contrasting models advance

14 388 U.S. 41 (1967).

on a narrower issue: assuming the illegality of a given search, what are the appropriate sanctions to redress the person whose privacy has been unlawfully invaded and to deter similar unlawful invasions in the future? The positions advanced by the competing models on this difficult issue are acutely different; and the rate of change in the real-world situation has been both rapid and dramatic.

The Crime Control Model. The police are bound to make mistakes, and it is of course desirable that these mistakes be minimized. Here, as elsewhere, the way to deal with mistakes is to afford a remedy for actual damages suffered by people whose privacy has been improperly invaded and to correct, by discipline and education, the future conduct of the officers who make the mistakes. It is unwise and unnecessary to provide the allegedly injured party with a windfall in the form of freedom from criminal conviction when his guilt is demonstrable.

There is no need for any special aid to private legal actions initiated for redress of illegal searches. The ordinary tort action that is available to law-abiding people when their interests have been invaded ought to be good enough for the criminal. Let him hire a lawyer, sue the police, and persuade a jury, if he can, that he has been actually damaged in a way that entitles him to monetary compensation. The discipline and education of the police is a matter, like any other problem of maintaining morale and standards in this large bureaucratic organization, for the police department itself. The "victim" is entitled to have his complaint considered; but he has no further interest, once the facts have been drawn to the attention of the proper departmental authorities.

In any event, there is no reason why evidence should not be used in the criminal process without regard to the manner in which it has been obtained. Here, unlike the problem of the confession, there is no question of trustworthiness or reliability. Physical evidence is physical evidence, regardless of how it is obtained. If one suspected of illegally possessing heroin is found to have heroin on the kitchen shelf, this supply of narcotics is reliable evidence of his guilt, whether the search that turned it up is later found by some judge to be legal or illegal.

The Due Process Model. The ordinary remedies for trespass upon one's property are totally deficient as a means for securing police compliance with rules regarding illegal searches and seizures. The victim usually is in no position to sue; even if he is, juries are notoriously unlikely to provide a remedy; and even if they do, police officers are often judgment-proof. Likewise, departmental discipline is an ineffective deterrent. The police are expected to get evidence upon which convictions may be obtained; if they do so, it is unlikely that their superiors will regard their illegal conduct as inefficient. The problem is that legality may mean inefficiency from the police standpoint, and efficiency is a value they tend to place above adherence to the finer points of constitutional law.

The only practical way to control illegal searches is to take the profit out of them. This means that any evidence illegally obtained cannot be permitted as evidence. It should be suppressed before or during trial; if it is not, convictions obtained in whole or in part on its basis should be reversed. Beyond that, any evidence obtained by leads provided by the result of an illegal search should also be banned so that there may be no easy evasion of the mandate. In doubtful cases, where it is unclear whether there is a connection or how strong it is, the standard should be one that resolves doubts most strongly against the proferred evidence whenever its discovery has been preceded by illegal searches. It may also be useful to enact a prophylactic rule that requires dismissal of the prosecution, not merely exclusion of the evidence, whenever an illegal search for evidence is shown to have taken place.

The Situation and the Trend. Until recently, there was a sharp division between the treatment of illegally obtained evidence in the state and federal courts. The exclusionary rule applied only to federal court cases. The states were free to ignore the rule and fashion whatever remedies they chose in order to deal with the problem of illegally secured evidence—this in spite of the fact that the Fourth Amendment's ban on unreasonable searches and seizures applied to state and federal cases alike. In the 1950's, a number of states that had previously not done so chose to apply the sanction of exclusion to evidence obtained through illegal search. Then, in 1961, the Supreme Court held in *Mapp* v. *Ohio*[15] that the states were constitutionally bound to apply the exclusionary rule in their criminal prosecutions, a decision that probably worked a greater change in state criminal procedure than any other that the Court had made up to that time.

The impact of the exclusionary rule on police practices is a matter for debate. There is no reliable comparative evidence about its deterrent efficacy. But whatever its effect on the primary conduct of the police, it undeniably has had and continues to have a profound effect on the criminal process itself. Particularly in cases involving so-called victimless crime, where the evidence of illegal activity typically comes from aggressive police work, there has been a sharp increase in the number of proscutions aborted by failure of proof. Given the difficulty of obtaining evidence in narcotics and gambling cases, it seems likely that there is some substance to police complaints that their efficiency in dealing with this kind of conduct has been impaired. Concomitantly, there has been an increase in the rigor with which evidence obtained subsequent to an illegal search has been examined for the taint of the prior illegality, an issue that now of course becomes increasingly important in state prosecutions.

ACCESS TO COUNSEL

Running through most of the issues that arise during this preliminary phase of the criminal process is the pervasive theme of access to counsel. It has a twofold relationship with the other issues on which our competing models of the process hold opposing views, acting as both their cause and effect. The importance of counsel is either enhanced or diminished, depending on the view one takes of the rules that ought to govern arrest, search, and interrogation. On the other hand, if one starts with a position on the utility or disutility of counsel at this stage of the process, that view is itself likely to be determinative of many of the other rules. And, as a practical matter, the availability of counsel is bound to have important consequences for the effectiveness with which the applicability of the governing rules, whatever they

[15] 367 U.S. 643 (1961).

may be, is challenged. It seems worthwhile, then, to reexamine briefly the question of access to counsel at this stage of the process, as an independent feature of the process.

The Crime Control Model. The period from the time that a suspect is arrested until he is brought before a magistrate is likely to be the crucial phase in the investigation of a crime. This phase is investigative, not judicial. There is nothing going on at this point that requires or can tolerate the intervention of a lawyer. The defendant's rights are sufficiently protected by the offer to see that his lawyer, if he has one, is notified that he is being held. If there is anything illegal about his detention, that can be remedied by his applying for habeas corpus. Otherwise, all issues that could conceivably arise from the police conduct during this phase are open to scrutiny at later stages of the proceeding. Particularly if the sanction of excluding evidence is to be applied, there is no reason at all for the accused to be given a chance to consult with his lawyer during this period. And, it should be noted, it is absolutely necessary for the police to question the suspect at this point without undue interference. This is their only chance to enlist the cooperation of the one person most likely to know the truth. Because the police do not arrest without probable cause, there is a high degree of probability that useful information can be learned from the suspect. If he is given an opportunity to consult a lawyer at this stage of the proceeding, he will invariably be told to say nothing. The most expeditious way of clearing a case will then be foreclosed, and the police will have to take the more laborious route of developing evidence unaided by leads supplied by the suspect. This foreclosure will also redound to the disadvantage of the innocent suspect, because he will be deterred from making statements that would otherwise lead to his early release. The only person benefiting from this procedure will be the guilty suspect, who is accordingly enabled to make it difficult, if not impossible, for a conviction to be obtained. If the police must conduct a full investigation without the suspect's aid in every case, trivial as well as serious, the number of cases that can be processed at a given level of police resources will sharply diminish. To put it more directly, the protection that the community enjoys against criminal activity will decline. A lawyer's place is in court. He should not enter a criminal case until it is in court.

The Due Process Model. A hardened and sophisticated criminal knows enough to keep silent in the face of police interrogation. He knows that self-exculpatory statements are often incriminating. He knows that he does not have to talk and that he is not likely to realize any advantage by talking. An inexperienced person in the toils of the law knows none of this. Unless the operative rules forbid it, the situations of these two categories of suspects are bound to be unequal.

Likewise, there is no moment in the criminal process when the disparity in resources between the state and the accused is greater than at the moment of arrest. There is every opportunity for overreaching and abuse on the part of the police. There is no limit to the extent to which these opportunities are taken advantage of except in the police's own sense of self-restraint. Later correctives palliate but do not suffice. What actually takes place in the police station is known only to the suspect and to the police. It is not hard to predict whose word will be taken if a contradiction arises.

The only way to ensure that these two equally obnoxious forms of inequality do not have a decisively malign impact on the criminal process is to require at the time of arrest (1) that the suspect be immediately apprised of his right to remain silent and to have a lawyer; (2) that he promptly be given access to a lawyer, either his own or one appointed for him; or (3) that failing the presence of a lawyer to protect the suspect's interest, he not be subjected to police interrogation.

The Situation and the Trend. We are rapidly moving toward a position in which no significant activity involving the suspect may go on after his arrest unless he has been given access to counsel. Although there is no generally recognized right to counsel upon arrest, in the sense that subsequent proceedings are not invalidated by failure to provide counsel, it is becoming an operational fact that denial of counsel at this stage is likely to nullify the results of any police investigatory activity. As we have already noted, the *Miranda* decision makes it very hazardous to obtain a statement from the suspect. And the Court has recently held that exposing the suspect to identification in a police lineup without giving his counsel an opportunity to be present will result in exclusion of eyewitness testimony based on an identification made in the course of a lineup.[16] As in the case of police interrogation, it remains to be seen how much of the practical effect of this decision is vitiated by "waiver" of the right to counsel at this stage of the process. It is certain that we are a long way from seeing counsel intervening on a large scale. The preliminary phase of the criminal process, from arrest to charge, still operates according to the Crime Control Model; but there are increasingly powerful propulsions in the direction of the Due Process Model.

[16] United States v. Wade, 388 U.S. 218 (1967).

CHAPTER TEN

The Models in Operation:

From Charge to Guilt Determination

THE DECISION TO CHARGE

Our suspect is still only a suspect so far as the formal operation of the process is concerned. He has been taken into custody, investigated, and possibly interrogated. If his is a typical case, the police by now know pretty much everything they are going to know about the circumstances. Someone must now decide what to do with the suspect. What is done with him depends on the answer to a number of subsidiary questions having to do both with decisions that have to be made and with the allocation of competences to make those decisions. Is there a reasonable probability of the suspect's factual guilt? Is there a sufficient amount of legally admissible evidence to establish his guilt in a trial? Who should be entitled to participate in deciding these questions? What challenges, if any, should the accused be able to offer to a decision (however made) that he should be held for further proceedings? If, on the other hand, there is substantial doubt about factual guilt or about the probability of establishing legal guilt, who should be entitled, and by what processes, to decide that the suspect should be released?

In broad terms, the principal issue at this point is whether the decision to hold the suspect—to convert him into a defendant by charging him with a crime—is one that should be arrived at in a primarily administrative way or one that should be made in a primarily adjudicative way. To simplify the issue we will assume that the police have satisfied themselves that the original decision

to arrest was sound and that the suspect is factually guilty, thereby
eliminating the question of the appropriate procedures and competences for deciding to release the suspect. It is clear that now
the initiative must pass from the police to the prosecutor, from
the expert in factual guilt to the expert in legal guilt. The decision to be made at this stage is a screening decision: should the
suspect be held for further stages of the process? Is this screening
decision one for the police and prosecutor alone, or is it one that
should be subjected to "impartial" scrutiny? If the latter, what
mechanisms should be provided to ensure that the scrutiny is
adequate, and what sanctions should be imposed if it is not?
These questions are greatly clouded in current practice, and we
may perhaps clarify them by considering what answers would be
given by each of our two models.

The Crime Control Model. The prosecutor is in the best possible position to evaluate the evidence amassed by the police and
to decide whether it warrants holding the suspect for a determination of guilt. The prosecutor must in any event do so in
every case; and it would be a waste of time and resources to
require that the job be done over again by a magistrate. The
prosecutor has no interest in pressing cases that are unlikely to
result in conviction; his professional reputation is generally based
on the proportion of convictions that he obtains in cases in which
a charge has been lodged against a suspect. Therefore, the interest
of the suspect in not being prosecuted on a completely groundless
charge is amply protected by confiding the screening decision at
this stage of the process entirely to the prosecutor's discretion.
Any system that required a preliminary judicial examination in
all criminal cases would collapse of its own weight. There are
simply not enough trained magistrates to go around. The most
that should be expected of the preliminary hearing is the appointment of counsel and the setting of bail.

There may be occasions when the prosecutor needs some support in the decision to charge a suspect. He may need to rally
community sentiment in a case that has aroused widespread
interest or in one where the suspect is a public official or otherwise prominent. Conversely, he may want to take a sounding of
general opinion to see whether it will back such a prosecution.

In this kind of situation a grand jury proves useful, providing as it does a kind of miniature public opinion poll for the prosecutor. If the grand jury disapproves, the prosecutor need press the case no further and can turn aside any criticism by pointing to the action of the grand jury. If, on the other hand, the grand jury approves, as it ordinarily will when the prosecutor voices a desire to press charges, any charge made is reinforced by the authority and prestige of the grand jury. Of course, the usefulness of the grand jury procedure depends on its secrecy. It is not an adversary proceeding, and the suspect is not entitled to be present, or to have the aid of counsel if he does testify, or to know what has gone on before the grand jury. If these conditions of secrecy are breached, the grand jury device simply provides another occasion for delaying or defeating the machinery of criminal justice.

In short, then, the prosecutor should control the decision to charge. He should be entitled to institute charges either by filing an information or by persuading the grand jury to return an indictment. In either case, he should not have to wait for a judicial officer to rule that the evidence is sufficient to support the institution of criminal charges against the suspect. The decision to convert a "suspect" into a "defendant" should be entirely up to the prosecutor.

The Due Process Model. It would be ridiculous to expect every arrest to produce a case sufficiently strong to warrant criminal prosecution. Some screening must take place. The appropriate forum for that screening process is a preliminary hearing before a magistrate, if the arrested person is not released before that stage is reached. The prosecutor cannot be trusted to do this screening job any more than the police can. Discretion at this stage of the process means substantial abandonment of an adversary system. Why should we expect the prosecutor, with nobody looking over his shoulder, to decide that there is insufficient evidence to hold the suspect for criminal charges? Why, in particular, should we do so in the large number of cases in which the evidence in the hands of the police is inadmissible but may lead to the discovery of other, possibly admissible evidence if the process is not terminated? Beyond this, any standard for deciding when the evidence at hand is sufficient to support a charge is bound to be too broad to be applied in a nondiscriminatory way unless it is applied inpartially and openly, two adverbs that do not describe the operations of a public prosecutor.

Consider the matter from the standpoint of the suspect. Typically, he is without funds to conduct an adequate defense and is substantially ignorant of his rights. If at this vital checkpoint in the process he is held to answer a criminal charge, the pressures from this point on build up toward extracting a plea of guilty from him, especially if he is likely, as his financial status makes him, to be kept in jail pending trial or entry of a plea on arraignment. If the criminal process afforded a speedy and noncoercive mechanism for guilt determination without pre-trial detention, there might be something more to be said for dispensing with the requirement of a preliminary hearing. As it is, such a screening operation by an impartial judicial official is necessary if suspects are to be given an adequate opportunity to challenge the processes being invoked against them.

The preliminary hearing should be held in public or in private at the option of the suspect. He should be entitled to be present and to have the assistance of counsel. The prosecution should be required to present enough testimony, of a kind and in a form admissible at the trial on the merits, to support a judgment that there is probable cause to charge the suspect with a specific crime or crimes. It is apparent that the traditional grand jury proceeding does not conform to these requirements. Although there is no objection to using the grand jury as an optional charging device, it is no substitute for an adequate preliminary examination and should therefore normally be preceded by a judicial hearing of the kind just described.

It is obvious that the effective implementation of these standards for "judicializing" the preliminary examination requires that counsel be available to the suspect at this stage of the proceeding. Indeed, if counsel is to be effective at this stage, he should probably enter the case at an earlier stage, as soon after arrest as possible, so that he may familiarize himself with the case before rather than during the hearing. It is equally obvious that the accused must be made to understand the function of the preliminary examination and of the assistance of counsel in connection with it. Without that understanding, no waiver of the right to preliminary examination should be allowed to stand. Indeed, it is doubtful that any waiver of preliminary examination should be allowed unless the suspect has had the assistance of counsel. The only effective sanction for ensuring that these procedures are followed is the sanction of nullity: a conviction obtained without adequate preliminary examination should not be allowed to stand.

The Situation and the Trend. It is hardly an oversimplification to say that the legal norms today tend strongly toward the Due Process Model while the factual situation tends even more strongly toward the Crime Control Model. The preliminary examination, although universally provided for, has fallen into disuse as a screening device. Its principal function today is setting bail. The screening function is in practice performed in the vast majority of cases by the prosecutor, aided and advised by the police.

The collapse of the preliminary examination as a screening device appears to be the result of two factors: the inadequacy of of the judicial resources at this level of the courts and the general unavailability of counsel at this stage of the process. In the American judicial system the committing magistrate is a relatively low-level official who may not even have legal training. In the larger cities his court is inundated daily by a stream of petty cases over which he exercises powers of summary disposition. He has neither the time nor the capacity to conduct an adequate preliminary examination in even the relatively serious cases that come before him in his committing capacity. Nor is he forced to do so by effective advocacy on behalf of the suspect. Comparatively few suspects appear to enjoy representation by counsel at the preliminary hearing, and even those that do are likely not to insist on what has become an unusual procedure.

The only external screening device that receives at all widespread use is the grand jury. However, it functions with rare exceptions simply as an extension of the prosecutor's office. The prosecutor who presents a case to the grand jury effectively dominates the proceeding. He examines the witnesses, and there is no opportunity for adversary challenge. The sufficiency of the evidence on which the grand jury acts tends to be immune from subsequent scrutiny both because of the relaxed standards applied to evaluate it and because of the difficulty of discovering what went on in the grand jury hearing. Although there appears to be some tendency toward easing the rules on grand jury secrecy, motivated essentially by a growing realization that the grand jury does not in fact perform a neutral role in the criminal process, it does not appear likely that the grand jury is going very soon to be transformed into the kind of neutral and judicial screening device called for by the Due Process Model.

The prospect for change appears stronger where the preliminary hearing is concerned. Courts have not directly required a judicial determination of probable cause to charge, and it may be doubted that any adequate constitutional basis can be found for requiring such a determination. However, there has been a growing recognition that the effective assistance of counsel requires intervention at an early stage of the proceedings. For example, the Criminal Justice Act of 1964, governing the provision of counsel in federal criminal proceedings, explicitly requires that counsel be appointed at the suspect's first appearance before the commissioner or court, which is the preliminary hearing stage. Effective aid by counsel at this stage would presumably provide much of the impetus necessary to bring the preliminary hearing back into use and make it a proceeding at which the prosecution is forced to submit its case to judicial scrutiny on pain of not being allowed to go on.

PRE-TRIAL DETENTION

Some interval of time must always elapse in the criminal process between the decision to hold a person for trial and the trial itself. (More accurately, this would be an interval between the decision that he may present a case for an adjudication of guilt and the adjudication itself. The adjudication need not, and under the arrangements most prevalent today usually does not, involve a trial, in the sense of a determination by an impartial tribunal that facts of sufficient reliability establish legal guilt.) What is to be done with the person who is charged with a crime

but not yet convicted of it? The answer has important consequences for the shape of the subsequent proceedings. Indeed, it
may determine whether there will be any subsequent proceedings, for a decision that the defendant will remain in custody
once he has been charged may itself act as an inducement for him
to plead guilty, thereby short-circuiting the part of the process
concerned with guilt determination and moving directly to the
stage at which the only remaining question is one of the ultimate
disposition.

In our system the question, baldly put, is bail or jail: will the
defendant be able to provide the required financial assurance
that he will appear for trial, or will he, for lack of such provision,
be kept in custody until the case against him has been prepared
for trial and he is brought before the court either to stand trial
or to plead guilty? The issues that divide the two models run
much deeper than this simple formulation suggests, posing as
they do questions that are begged by existing institutional arrangements. What reasons justify keeping a defendant in custody
before his guilt has been formally adjudicated? Is the only relevant consideration the likelihood that he will not appear for
trial? If so, are financial deterrents the only, or the most appropriate, means of assuring presence at trial? If not, what other considerations are relevant? The possibility that the defendant may
tamper with the evidence, as by intimidating prospective witnesses? The possibility that he may commit other offenses while
he is at large? The degree of probability that he is guilty of the
offense charged against him? Questions of this order, which are
blurred in the day-to-day administration of the criminal law, may
be clarified by examination in the context of our two models.

The Crime Control Model. The vast majority of persons
charged with crime are factually guilty. An arrest that results in
a formal charge has behind it a double assurance of reliability:
the judgment of the police officer who made the arrest is backed
up by that of the prosecutor, who has decided that there is enough
evidence to hold the defendant for trial. For all practical purposes, the defendant is a criminal. Just because the assembly line
cannot move fast enough for him to be immediately disposed of
is no reason for him to go free. If he does go free there is a risk

that he will not appear for trial, a risk that is heightened when he is well aware that he is guilty and has a lively expectation of probable punishment. If he does not appear voluntarily, we will have to devote some of our limited resources to tracking him down and bringing him in. That may be tolerable when it occurs sporadically and on a small scale; but if large numbers of people are turned loose before trial, the chances are that the problem will get out of hand and we will be faced with a vicious circle. The more people fail to appear, the more people will be encouraged not to appear, and the whole system will collapse.

Failure to appear is not the only risk involved in pre-trial liberty. The prospect that known criminals will commit further crimes while at large awaiting trial is in itself an adequate reason for not making pre-trial liberty the norm. The more hardened the criminal, the greater the likelihood that this will happen. Burglars will commit more burglaries; narcotics peddlers will sell more narcotics; gunmen will stage more robberies. The danger to property and to human life that results from letting known offenders go free even temporarily is inexcusable because it is so easily avoidable.

Even for first offenders and others who do not seem very likely to repeat their crimes while awaiting trial, there are good reasons why pre-trial liberty should not be available as a matter of right. Courts are inclined to be lenient with first and other minor offenders. Prosecutions of these offenders are likely to be dismissed in a large proportion of cases because it is not worthwhile to use the limited available resources to prosecute them. If their cases are not dismissed, the offenders may nonetheless be put on probation or fined or given suspended sentences—all dispositions that fall short of having any significant effect on their future conduct. For many such persons, a short period spent in jail awaiting trial is not only a useful reminder that crime does not pay but also the only such reminder they are likely to get.

Other considerations apart, it is likely that a significantly higher percentage of defendants who now plead guilty would elect to stand trial if they could be at liberty pending trial. People who know that they are guilty would just as soon get it over with and take what is coming to them if, in order to gamble on the off chance of an acquittal, they have to spend weeks or months in jail awaiting trial. But if they are released pending trial, the incentive to plead guilty is greatly reduced. The inevitable delays of the process, as well as those that are not so inevitable but can be brought about by carelessness or bad faith, would then work in favor of the defendant rather than, as is the situation when he is in custody, against him. It is unlikely that there would be a significant rise in the percentage of defendants eventually found not guilty because we are considering here only those people who are probably guilty. There would be some rise, partly attributable to the disappearance of witnesses through delays in bringing the case on for trial, partly attributable to the fact that some defendants, who we know are guilty, will get off through human error—mistakes by judges, jurors, or prosecutors. But the fact that some few defendants will get off who otherwise would not is only a secondary consideration. The main danger is that the increase in time required to litigate cases that don't really need to be litigated would put an intolerable strain on what is already an overburdened process. This consideration alone argues against a policy that makes pre-trial liberty the norm.

These arguments against automatic pre-trial liberty are not necessarily arguments in favor of the present bail system, under which there is a nominal right to pre-trial liberty. Acknowledging such a right would seem to place the bail system at odds with the postulates underlying our model. However, in practice there is no such "right" because of the discretion granted the committing magistrate, who can set bail in an amount that the defendant is unlikely to be able to afford. Such latitude is tantamount to the discretionary system required by our model—one that permits the courts, with the expert help of the police and the prosecutors, to select those people who—for whatever reason—ought not to be at liberty pending trial, and to see to it that they are not.

There are, it is true, injustices in the bail system that are not required by the demands of the Crime Control Model. There is no reason, for example, why defendants who are ultimately convicted and sentenced to prison terms should not have time spent in pre-trial custody credited against their post-conviction prison terms. And there may be many instances in which police efficiency would be promoted by not cluttering up station houses and detention centers with minor offenders. For these, the use of summons instead of arrest or release after arrest without the posting of bail may be desirable in the interest of cutting down on the use of police for convoy duty through the pre-trial pipeline. However, if pre-trial detention is to be mitigated for some people, it ought to be done explicitly for the purpose of promoting the efficiency of the criminal process rather than for the purpose of adhering to some abstract notion of a "right" to pre-trial liberty. Certainly in cases of serious crime the confinement of the defendant before adjudication of guilt serves the ends of the process and should be regarded as the norm. If the present system of requiring bail for some reason or other stopped producing a high rate of pre-trial confinement, it would have to be replaced by one that did.

The Due Process Model. A person accused of crime is not a criminal. The sharpest distinction must be observed between the status of a defendant and that of a person who has been duly convicted of committing a crime. Perhaps the most important, and certainly the most obvious, operational distinction between the two lies in the issue of physical restraint. Pending the formal adjudication of guilt by the only authority with the institutional competence to decree it—a court—the status of the accused cannot be assimilated to that of the convicted in this most important of respects. There are practical as well as ideological reasons why this should be so. An accused person who is confined pending trial is greatly impeded in the preparation of his defense. He needs to be able to confer on a free and unrestricted basis with his attorney, something that is notoriously hard to do in custody. He may be the most likely person to interview and track down witnesses in his own behalf—something he cannot do if he's in jail. His earning capacity is cut off; he may lose his job; his family may suffer extreme economic hardship. And all these things may happen before he is found to be guilty. Furthermore, the economic and other deprivations sustained as a result of pre-trial confinement all act as coercive measures that inhibit the accused person's will to resist. He is rendered more likely to plead guilty and, as a result, to waive the various safeguards against unjust conviction that the system provides. When this happens on a large scale, the adversary system as a whole suffers because its vitality depends on effective challenge.

A person accused of crime is entitled to remain free until judged guilty so long as his freedom does not threaten to subvert the orderly processes of criminal justice. His freedom could have this effect only if he deliberately failed to appear at the time and place appointed for trial. If persons accused of crime could with impunity fail to appear, the premise of cooperation on which a system of pre-trial liberty depends could not in practice be realized. Hence, it is important that the right to pre-trial liberty be exercised in a way that does not jeopardize the process as a whole.

The right to pre-trial liberty has been firmly established by the institution of bail. It has been thought that the requirement of a financial deterrent to flight will adequately protect the viability of the system while ensuring that the defendant can enjoy liberty before his trial. This judgment is expressed in the Eighth Amendment's guarantee that "excessive bail shall not be required," a formulation that may appear to some as merely an assurance that bail will be granted in noncapital cases and that it will be set at a reasonable amount. However, this literal interpretation ignores the spirit of the bail clause. The guarantee should be read to require that the defendant be released pending trial on the basis of bail or whatever other device or combination of devices will ensure his presence at the trial without denying him his freedom on grounds that have nothing to do with the assurance of his presence. Bail is simply one way—and not the only one—of assuring a defendant's presence at his trial. If the institution of bail does not adequately promote the desired combination of goals, then alternative means must be developed. These alternatives might include such deterrents to flight as criminal penalties for nonappearance, the use of summons rather than arrest (with its attendant physical custody) to initiate criminal prosecutions, release of arrested defendants on their own recognizance or in the custody of some responsible person, and use of cash bail instead of bail bonds.

Where bail is used, it must be set according to the circumstances of the individual case rather than on a mechanical basis. Thus, the nature of the offense charged is only one of several elements to be taken into account in making the bail decision. Setting bail mechanically on the basis of a schedule for certain offenses may in itself be an effective denial of the defendant's right. Essentially, a hearing for the setting of bail must be a fact-finding process in which the financial resources of the defendant, his roots in the community, the nature and circumstances of the offense charged, and other relevant factors are all taken into account in arriving at the minimum level of bail required to assure a reasonable probability of the particular defendant's appearance for trial. It is, of course, completely unacceptable to set bail at a figure that the defendant is thought to be unable to meet. Speedy appellate review must be available to correct errors of this sort, still another reason why the bail decision must initially be made on the basis of a record that others can subsequently appraise. To the extent that adequate investigative and other fact-finding resources are not brought to bear, the defendant should be entitled to go free on nominal bail or no bail. The period of custody should in no event exceed the minimum required after arrest to ascertain the relevant facts about the suspect's situation. Normally this should be done by the time the committing magistrate has made the decision to hold the arrested person for subsequent proceedings.

There remains, however, a large class of persons for whom any bail at all is "excessive bail." They are the people loosely referred to as "indigents." Studies of the operation of the bail system have demonstrated that even at the very lowest levels of bail—say $500, where the bail bond premium may be only $25 or $50—there is a very substantial percentage of persons who do not succeed in making bail and are therefore held in custody pending trial. It may be that the decision not to seek bail in many of these cases is a voluntary one: a man who knows that he is factually guilty may simply decide that it isn't worth his while to spend money on a bail bond premium. However, many people who are eventually adjudged guilty do post bond and are released pending trial. Their awareness that they are guilty may be just as great as the poor man's, but they avail themselves of their right to be free pending a formal adjudication of guilt. It is unfair to deny the poor the same right simply because for them the marginal utility of the bail money is higher than it is for the rich. At any rate, it is clear that if all persons in custody were informed of their right to be free on some basis other than the payment of bail premiums, many of those who now spend days or weeks or even months in custody awaiting trial would avail themselves of these other means. And if that is so, it seems to follow that a system that makes pre-trial freedom conditional on financial ability is discriminatory. Indeed, given the malfunctioning of the present system where the financially disadvantaged are concerned, it may well be that the bail system should be ruled out for rich and poor alike. One need not pursue the argument to that extreme, however, to recognize that a system that conditions pre-trial release exclusively or even predominantly on the provision of financial assurances of presence at trial is a seriously defective one.

Other asserted bases for pre-trial detention either are entirely without merit or present special problems that need to be handled on a more discriminating basis than a general rule permitting detention before determination of guilt. It is antithetical to our conceptions of justice to permit pre-trial detention to be used as a means of informal punishment in advance of (or instead of) a formal determination of guilt and sentence. And to speak of the possibility that the accused may commit further crimes if left at large is to beg the question; for it has not yet been determined that he has committed any crime at all. Many of the limitations on substantive criminal enactments safeguard us against being punished for a mere propensity to commit crime. The logic of preventive detention would extend to persons newly released from prison; why not re-arrest them and lock them up because they may commit another crime?

The problem of what to do with "dangerous" people who have not been convicted of committing crimes is a troublesome one. It far transcends the question of preventive detention of persons accused of crime. The solution, if there is one, must include setting up standards for determining who is "dangerous" and providing the minimal procedural due process safeguards of notice and a hearing for persons whom the state seeks to confine on this ground. Whatever the solution, it cannot bypass these basic due process requirements by permitting the indiscriminate preventive detention of people who are accused of crime. The problem can in any event be minimized by shortening the interval between charge and trial.

In some cases it is possible that the defendant if left at large will threaten witnesses, destroy evidence, or otherwise impede the preparation of the case against him. This is said to be particularly likely in the case of men involved in organized crime. The argument is a little hard to understand. The higher the degree of organization involved, the less likely it would seem to be that the personal attention of the defendant would be required to promote obstructive tactics. To the extent that there is a threat of this kind it can be dealt with in other ways: by giving witnesses police protection, by placing the accused under an injunction backed up by the contempt power, by providing criminal penalties for tampering with witnesses, and the like. The vice of detaining a defendant before he actually does anything bad is obvious: it penalizes him for a mere disposition, a totally unprovable thing, and it thus opens the way for the most widespread abuses. At the first concrete sign that the accused has engaged in obstructive activties, it is altogether proper to seek to confine him on the basis of proof that obstructive activities have taken place. But there is a great difference between doing this on the basis of proof after the fact and doing it on the basis of suspicion before the fact.

In summary, then, pre-trial liberty should be the norm. The only condition that the criminal process as such should impose ought to be the assurance of the accused's presence at trial. His presence ought to be assured by measures other than detention; and detention should never be resorted to merely because the accused is unable to make bail.

The Situation and the Trend. The legal norm established by the Eighth Amendment (forbidding the requirement of excessive bail) is construed to confer an absolute right to pre-trial release on reasonable bail in noncapital cases. Bail in turn is required to be set solely with respect to assuring a defendant's presence at trial; other considerations are inadmissible. The federal standards are echoed by those prevailing in the states. Although it has not been authoritatively ruled, it appears that the federal constitutional provision on bail would be held applicable to the states. There is at the present time very little appellate control over the setting of bail, and the court that performs this function has wide discretion. Bail reductions are usually ordered only when the bail set in a particular case is thought to be out of line for the particular offense charged. There is no general right to be free if one is unable to provide bail; and the remedy for an accused person who feels he is unfairly detained is said to be to move for prompt trial.

In practice, there is very little judicial control over bail practices. In the run of cases, bail is set mechanically, pretty much on the basis of the offense charged. There is almost never any investigation of the circumstances of a particular suspect or of the likelihood that he will appear for trial. Bail or jail is therefore a question answered solely on the basis of a defendant's financial resources and of his ability to get a professional bondsman to put up bail for him. On the whole it is the alleged gangster or hardened criminal who gets out on bail and the first or sporadic offender who stays in jail. Furthermore, the system in practice permits and even fosters the setting of bail in amounts that ensure that defendants will remain in jail. There is no question but that bail is sometimes used for purposes that are supposedly denied it by the legal norm, because of the unavailability of prompt remedial measures, the discretionary nature of the bail decision, and the lack of assistance of counsel in calling attention to infractions of the legal norms. It is a notable fact that the unbailed defendant is also to a large extent the unrepresented defendant. This combination of disadvantages makes the constitutional guarantee to a large extent useless in practice. If the legal norm is thought of as conforming in most respects to the Due Process Model, it is evident that the usual situation in practice is much closer to the Crime Control Model.

There exists today a widespread, vocal, and increasingly influential dissatisfaction with the operation of a system that places prime reliance on financial devices for assuring presence at trial. Unlike most of the other trends we are considering, this one is

not primarily judicial in character. There have been no landmark decisions creating new norms, as in the areas of investigatory practices or of right to counsel. Rather, the trend so far has
been given impetus primarily by people working in governmental and extra-governmental groups, who have described in
detail the present state of affairs and have framed new norms responsive to what are thought to be the needs indicated by the
factual revelations. Experiments are now under way that are designed to demonstrate the efficacy of other means of assuring presence at trial, among them: improved fact-finding mechanisms for
establishing whether an accused person is a good risk for release without financial conditions; the use of cash deposits in an
amount equal to what would otherwise be the bail bond premium, in order to reduce reliance on the professional bondsman;
and the use of summons rather than arrest to initiate prosecution
in minor cases. In 1966 Congress passed the Bail Reform Act,
which now governs in all criminal prosecutions in the federal
courts. Its stated purpose is "to revise the practices relating to
bail to assure that all persons, regardless of their financial status,
shall not needlessly be detained pending their appearance . . .
when detention serves neither the ends of justice nor the public
interest." The Act requires release without financial outlay unless the judge finds that "such a release will not reasonably assure
the appearance of the person as required." In that case, he is
directed to make use of any of a variety of devices, only one of
which is bail, to secure appearance. The President's Commission
on Law Enforcement and the Administration of Justice in its
1967 report urged the states to adopt comprehensive bail reform
legislation along the lines of the federal statute.

It is too soon to know whether the Bail Reform Act will have
an appreciable effect on bail practices in the federal courts. But
the ferment is there, and it seems safe to predict that in the foreseeable future state legislation and court rulings will strengthen
rather than retard the trend toward conformity with the Due
Process Model. There will be a significant increase in the percentage of criminal defendants who are at liberty pending trial,
accompanied by a significant increase in the number of criminal
defendants who do not plead guilty to the initial charge against

them. These defendants will instead either get the prosecutor to reduce the charge against them in exchange for their entering a plea of guilty ("plea-bargaining") or make the prosecution prove its case in court.

THE PLEA OF GUILTY

The vast majority of criminal prosecutions terminate with the entry of a plea of guilty. A guilty plea rather than a trial is the dominant mode of guilt-determination. It is widely asserted that any significant increase in the number of criminal prosecutions going to trial would result in a breakdown of the criminal justice system. The institution of the guilty plea is itself affected by factors operating at early stages of the criminal process, notably by whether or not pre-trial liberty and the assistance of counsel are available. It seems clear, both as a matter of logical inference and as one of demonstrable fact, that a defendant who is out on bail and who enjoys the services of a lawyer is less likely to plead guilty than one who lacks either or both of these advantages. It is of course possible that in many cases these advantages help the defendant bargain successfully for a reduced charge rather than lead him to insist on a trial on the merits. Nonetheless, it appears likely that there would be a substantial increase in the proportion of cases going to trial if procedures at earlier stages of the process customarily operated in favor of the defendant. The amount of increase is suggested by the fact that if there were a reduction of 25 per cent in the number of cases in federal courts disposed of on guilty pleas there would be roughly twice the number of trials that are now held. Approximately 80 per cent of criminal defendants disposed of in the federal courts from 1956 through 1962 entered pleas of guilty or *nolo contendere*. Assuming that the other 20 per cent stood trial and that all those included in the hypothesized reduction also were to stand trial, the present figure of 20 per cent for cases going to trial would double.

What do our two models tell us about the guilty plea? From the host of relevant aspects of this institution we will briefly examine three. Under what circumstances, if any, should a plea of guilty be set aside as "involuntary"? To what extent should a defendant who pleads guilty have the assistance of counsel? What obligation, if any, does the judge who receives the plea have to satisfy himself as to the factual and legal guilt of the accused?

The Crime Control Model. The purpose of the arraignment, at which the defendant is required to plead to the charge against him, is to dispose of as large a proportion of cases as possible without trial. It is in the interest of all—the prosecutor, the judge, the defendant—to terminate without trial every case in which there is no genuine doubt about the factual guilt of the defendant. If the earlier stages of the process have functioned as they should, only a very small proportion of cases should at this point remain in that category. There is also an irreducible minimum of cases where so much is at stake—either because of the gravity of the offense or the position of the defendant—that there is no reasonable possibility of compromise. The bank president charged with income tax evasion and the murderer have this in common: they have little to lose by going down fighting. Aside from those cases where the will to litigate is strong, all criminal cases ought normally to be terminated by a plea of guilty. If this general criterion is accepted, the details follow without much trouble.

There is a distinct social advantage to terminating criminal proceedings without trial whenever the defendant is willing to do so. Any number of subtle interacting factors may make a defendant willing; it would be an endless operation and one that might well defeat the objectives of the criminal process to inquire into the precise nature of these factors in any large number of cases. For example, the judge who is considering a plea of guilty may of course inquire whether any promises have been made to the defendant, since a promise of leniency by the police or the prosecutor is one that cannot be delivered on and is evidence that the prosecutor has not handled the case properly. But if the judge does discover that an improper promise has been made, the proper course is not to reject the plea but rather to set the defendant right about the legal situation and then to permit him to enter the plea if he wants to. In the overwhelming majority of cases, then, the function of an inquiry by the judge is to provide an assurance of regularity on the record, not to protect any special right of the defendant. It is also proper for the judge to make it clear that a defendant who pleads guilty can expect greater leniency in sentencing than one who insists on putting the state to the time and expense of a trial.

The general run of criminal defendants are perfectly capable of making up their own minds about whether they want to plead guilty. If a defendant has a lawyer and wants to consult him about the guilty plea, that is proper. But the state should be under no obligation to provide counsel for a defendant at arraignment. All that is required for a plea of guilty is that the defendant understand its nature and consequences in a general kind of way and that he enter it of his own free will. The judge's duty is to ensure that these conditions are met. It would involve a needless duplication of resources to insist that a defense lawyer as well as a judge participate in the entry of a guilty plea.

The judge need not inquire into the factual circumstances underlying the commission of the offense except to the extent that he thinks it will help him perform his sentencing function. Cases do not get to this stage of the criminal process unless there is substantial evidence of guilt. Any requirement that the judge inquire into the issue of guilt before accepting a plea would impair the efficiency of the process and undermine the purpose of the plea of guilty by converting the arraignment into an abbreviated trial on the merits. *A fortiori,* there should be no inquiry into the availability of defenses that have no relation to the issue of factual guilt. It is cause for congratulation, not alarm, when a defendant who is factually guilty is convicted and sentenced despite the existence of possible defenses that have nothing to do with the merits of the case. One of the great strengths of the guilty plea is that it serves to bypass issues that can only result in a weakening of effective criminal justice. If a defendant is conscious of his own guilt and willing to accept his punishment, it does neither him nor the community any service to inquire into possible errors made at earlier stages of the process that might enable him to escape his just deserts.

The Due Process Model. The arraignment is the fulcrum of the entire criminal process. It is at this point that one of two things happens: either the possible errors and abuses at the earlier, largely unscrutinized stages of the process are exposed to judicial scrutiny or they are forever submerged in a plea of guilty. The guilty plea is not only a device for expediting the handling of criminal cases; it is a kind of Iron Curtain that cuts off, almost always irrevocably, any disinterested scrutiny of the earlier stages of the process. Guilty pleas should therefore be discouraged. There may indeed be a serious question whether they should ever be permitted at all; but it is clear that they should be hedged about with safeguards designed both to cut down their incidence and to prevent their being used in cases where possibly meritorious challenges to the process exist.

No kind of pressure, either by the prosecutor or by the judge, should be brought to bear on a defendant to induce him to plead guilty. Plea-bargaining by a defendant who is adequately advised by counsel may, under careful supervision by the judge, be an acceptable way of terminating a criminal case. But the prosecutor, in order to avoid any possibility of coercive pressure, should never take the lead in proposing or suggesting a compromise plea. It is manifestly improper for a judge to use his sentencing discretion to coerce a guilty plea, either by threatening severe punishment in a particular case or by reserving lenient treatment, such as probation, for defendants who plead guilty. A criminal defendant is entitled to have the charges against him tried in the manner prescribed by law, no matter how overwhelming the evidence of guilt may be thought to be. A criminal trial should be viewed not as an undesirable burden but rather as the logical and proper culmination of the process. Accordingly, it can only defeat the ends of the system to penalize a defendant for insisting on a trial or to intimidate him by threatening him with unpleasant consequences if he does insist.

No one should be permitted to plead guilty without the assistance of counsel. If a criminal defendant cannot get a fair trial without counsel, how much less likely is he to have enjoyed due process if he has to resolve the highly technical and complex strategic problems involved in a guilty plea without expert assistance? It is doubtful whether waiver of counsel should ever be allowed at this stage. As a practical matter, there is unlikely to be such a waiver if the judge, on hearing that a defendant wishes to plead guilty, informs him that he is reluctant to accept a plea at this time, explains the advantages of consultation with counsel, and offers to appoint a lawyer immediately.

Despite these restrictions, even if they are faithfully observed, it is probable that a high proportion of criminal defendants will choose to plead guilty. The question then arises what guarantees of procedural regularity the judge should try to provide before, in effect, closing the door to further scrutiny by accepting the plea. He ought, in the first place, to require the prosecutor to summarize the evidence against the defendant, indicating what the testimony will be and by whom it will be provided. He should satisfy himself that there is probably sufficient evidence to sustain a conviction on the charge or charges against the defendant. He should also satisfy himself that the testimony the prosecution plans to elicit is admissible under applicable rules of evidence. Beyond satisfying himself about the evidence, the judge should also take this occasion to probe, with the assistance of the prosecutor and the defense counsel, the possible existence of abuses at earlier stages of the process, such as illegally obtained evidence, improper confessions, failure to provide counsel at an appropriate stage, and undue length of pre-trial detention, in order to determine any bearing such abuses might have on the defendant's plea of guilty. Only after he is satisfied that the record is clear in these two general respects—the establishment of guilt and the absence of abusive practices at earlier stages of the process— should the judge accept a plea of guilty. To the extent that these protective measures are not employed, the defendant should be entitled at a later time to move to set aside the plea of guilty and to stand trial.

The Situation and the Trend. Although reliable data are hard to come by, it is highly probable that any general view of the guilty plea in this country at the present time would disclose practices that conform far more closely to the Crime Control than to the Due Process Model. Pressures in the earlier phases of the process, particularly on those defendants who are not at liberty after arrest and who do not have the assistance of counsel, in addition to pressures exerted at or before the time of arraignment, tend strongly to militate toward the entry of pleas of guilty. The assistance of counsel, to the extent that it is available at the arraignment, is perfunctory in the majority of cases. Waiver is easily accomplished and widespread. And the role of the judge is a relatively passive one, with no generally effective pattern of inquiry into factual guilt or into the possibility of abuses at earlier stages of the process.

There are some signs, however, that the plea of guilty may receive increasingly close scrutiny. Some courts have taken the view that, if the prosecutor enters into a plea arrangement that depends on promises he is unable to fulfill, the resulting plea should be set aside as "involuntary." And a trend seems to be developing toward stricter standards for appraising the defendant's understanding of the nature and consequences of the plea. The full impact of *Gideon* v. *Wainwright* is yet to be determined, but it would appear that pleas of guilty entered without the assistance of counsel may prove vulnerable, quite apart from the probability that implementation of *Gideon* will ensure the participation of counsel in a higher proportion of guilty pleas than has hitherto been the case.

It seems unlikely that the practice of plea-bargaining will itself come under attack. Rather, the trend seems to be toward regulating and equalizing the conditions under which the bargaining takes place. Greater insistence on the participation of defense counsel and on a more active role for the trial judge will probably characterize the development of plea-bargaining. To the extent that this turns out to be an accurate forecast, the institution of the guilty plea will hold its place as the fulcrum of the criminal process only at the cost of a greater input of resources and, therefore, a diminution in "efficiency" as measured by the dictates of the Crime Control Model.

CHAPTER ELEVEN

The Models in Operation: Review of Errors

ALTHOUGH IT IS probably generally agreed today that any criminal process ought to provide some opportunity for correcting at least some of the errors that have occurred at earlier stages in the process, it should be kept in mind that the institution of appellate review in criminal cases is less than one hundred years old. If it would indeed "go against the grain, today, to make a matter as sensitive as a criminal conviction subject to unchecked determination by a single institution"[1] that fact is a striking testimonial to the dynamic character of the criminal process and to the consequent fluidity of what may usefully be regarded as the range of practical possibilities for change. Even if there is general agreement that in some sense appellate review is a standard feature of the process, many subsidiary issues concerning the terms on which review should be available divide the two models. What kinds of issues should be reviewable—"legal" issues only or "factual" determinations as well? What financial barriers to review, if any, should be allowed? Should review be automatically available, or should some screening devices be used to prevent frivolous appeals from being taken? If errors are found, what standards should determine the outcome of review? Must the defendant show that the outcome would probably have been different but for the error, or should some errors count as conclu-

---

[1] Paul Bator, *Finality in Criminal Law and Federal Habeas Corpus for State Prisoners*, 76 HARV. L. REV. 441, 453 (1963).

sive—and if so, which? What is the permissible timing of review, i.e., should review be limited to a continuation of the original process ("appeal"), or should it be permitted to take place also in a fresh proceeding ("collateral attack")?

It will be convenient to divide up the subject of review in accordance with the distinction just made between appeal and collateral attack, since the distinction has become thoroughly ingrained in our thinking about the criminal process. But there is also another reason for observing the distinction: the opportunity that it affords us to depart from the assumption that we are dealing with a unitary system of criminal justice and to examine in one hotly contested area the impact of federalism on the shape of the criminal process. For this purpose we will make the artificial and somewhat misleading assumption that review by appeal concerns review within a unitary system and that review by collateral attack concerns federal review of state criminal processes. We will classify the problems dealt with in this chapter accordingly.

APPEAL

The general role of an appeal system is of course strongly conditioned by assumptions about what has gone on in previous stages of the process. The Crime Control Model, as we have seen, places very heavy emphasis on the plea of guilty as the central guilt-determining device. The comparatively few cases that it confides to a more formal adjudicative process are those in which there is thought to be some doubt about the factual guilt of the accused. Those doubts are supposed to be resolved by the trier of fact. Accordingly, the role of an appellate review system is highly marginal: it is available to correct those occasional slips in which the trier of fact either makes a plain error about factual guilt or makes so gross a procedural mistake that the reliability of the guilt-determining process is called into question.

In contrast, the appellate stage in the Due Process Model is seen as having a much broader function. It operates, of course, to correct errors in the assessment of factual guilt (at least when they have hurt the defendant's case), but that is only the beginning of its function. It serves, more importantly, as the forum in which infringements on the rights of the accused (as laid down in the model) that have accumulated at earlier stages of the process can be redressed and their repetition in subsequent cases deterred. The appellate forum, seen as having distance from and independence of the police-prosecutor nexus into which the trial court is so often drawn, is both guardian and vindicator of the Due Process Model. Although the appellate stage is seen in the Crime Control Model as being a remote and marginal appendage of the process as a whole, it is perceived in the Due Process Model as being qualitatively crucial and quantitatively significant. The differences in these two views of the appellate stage are especially notable in the matters of how wide a scope should be permitted for review and how easily accessible such review should be.

The Crime Control Model. Once a determination of guilt has been made, either by entry of a plea or by adjudication, the paramount objective of the criminal process should be to carry out the sentence of the court as speedily as possible. We must be able to say that people who violate the law will be swiftly and certainly subjected to punishment. This end will be undermined if the process permits, and hence invites, delays in the serving of sentences. We should, therefore, evaluate any system of review primarily according to its effect on finality of guilt determination. To put the matter bluntly, appeals should be so effectively discouraged that merely taking an appeal will itself be a fairly reliable indicator that the case contains substantial possibility of error concerning factual guilt.

If appeal in criminal cases is available as a matter of right, restrictions must be imposed to ensure that the right is exercised responsibly. Specifically, the costs of an appeal—filing fees, printing costs for the record and briefs, and, most importantly, counsel fees—should not be waived or publicly defrayed unless the appeal is screened and determined to be probably meritorious. This screening power should be lodged in the court that made the determination of guilt, because it is the tribunal most likely to be familiar with the case and therefore best able to make an expeditious determination of probable merit. A decision not to permit an appeal by a person unable to finance it should be conclusive, subject only to review for gross abuse of discretion. Although in theory the same procedure should probably apply to all appeals, it may be sufficient to limit it in this way, because in practice the costs of the appeals process may discourage those who would have to pay them from taking frivolous appeals. Bail pending an appeal should be allowable only as a matter of grace, and should be withheld where the issues raised on appeal do not appear to be substantial.

No issue should be raisable on appeal that was not raised at an earlier stage of the process. No conviction should be reversed for insufficiency of evidence unless the appellate tribunal finds that no reasonable trier of fact could have convicted on the evidence presented. Appeals against a verdict of acquittal should be available to the prosecution to the same extent that appeals against a conviction are available to the defense. Errors not relating to the sufficiency of the evidence to establish factual guilt—errors in the admission or exclusion of evidence, in the trial court's instructions, in the conduct of the prosecutor or the trial judge—should not provide a basis for reversal of a conviction on appeal unless it is found that in the absence of the error or errors the result would probably have been different. Finally, no errors should suffice for reversal if the appellate court concludes on a review of all the evidence that the factual guilt of the accused was adequately established.

The Due Process Model. The first forum in which abuses of official power should be corrected in the criminal process is the trial. However, they are not always corrected there, and indeed the trial process may itself be a fertile source of additional abuses. If they are not corrected, they do not come to public attention, because the trial process is in the great run of cases only slightly more visible than the police and prosecutorial processes that precede it. The right of appeal is an important safeguard for the rights of the individual accused. Beyond this, it plays an essential role in the lawmaking process; for the steady flow of criminal cases on the appellate level provides the raw material for the elaboration of those very rights. If the Due Process Model is to retain its dynamic character, there must be full and unrestricted access to the appellate phase of the process.

There should be no limitations on the convicted defendant's

right to appeal. Financial restrictions are as much out of place here as they are at other levels of the process. If the appellant cannot afford to pay a filing fee, it must be waived; if he cannot afford to buy a transcript, it must be given to him; if he cannot afford to hire a lawyer, he must be assigned one. This last point is especially important: whether reversible errors justifying an appeal have occurred is certainly a matter on which the convicted defendant needs the help of a lawyer; there is no more technical aspect to the criminal process. No lawyer will advise an appeal where grounds for appeal are lacking, but only a lawyer can tell whether the grounds are there or not; for at this stage of the process it is legal errors rather than factual guilt that are primarily at issue. And, although bail pending appeal raises different and more restricted issues than does the question of liberty pending trial, it is important that the discretion to allow bail pending appeal not be manipulated coercively to discourage the pursuit of any appeal that has a semblance of merit. When discretionary judgments of this kind are inevitable, they ought to be lodged with the appellate court rather than with the trial court.

Although people should not be allowed to sit by silently and let errors go unchallenged at the trial level, appellants should not be held rigidly to a requirement that the errors of which they complain must have been challenged below. The appellate court should be entitled to notice any plain error prejudicial to the rights of an accused person. No single standard for determining reversible error can be advanced; even cumulative and repetitive errors of an insubstantial kind should suffice for reversal. Of course, any error abridging basic rights of the defendant—rights protecting him from illegal searches and seizures, coerced confessions, and unwilling self-incrimination—should be ground for reversal regardless of the strength of the rest of the case. To say this is simply to repeat that the criminal process itself must afford remedies for its abuse and deterrents against the misuse of official power. And the appellate process should afford similar sanctions against abuses that occur for the first time at the trial level, such as prosecutorial misconduct, prejudicial publicity, and ineffective counsel. The reversal of a criminal conviction is a small price to pay for an affirmation of proper values and a deterrent example of what will happen when those values are slighted. When an appellate court finds it necessary to castigate the conduct of the police, the prosecutor, or the trial court, but fails to reverse a conviction, it simply breeds disrespect for the very standards it is trying to affirm.

The Situation and the Trend. Appeals are taken in only a small proportion of criminal cases. The appeal is the apex of the pyramid, and represents a final selection from a group of cases whose number has been sharply reduced through previous screenings. Nonetheless, the appeal is important out of all proportion to numbers because the appellate level of the criminal process is where the governing legal norms are made explicit. There appears to be a fairly constant relationship between the number of appeals taken in criminal cases and the proportion of convictions that are reversed. Unsuccessful appeals are by and large not very significant legally; it is the successful appeal, in which reasons of more or less general applicability are given for reversing a conviction, that helps establish operative norms. Consequently, the greater the number of appeals taken, the greater the number of reversals there tends to be. And with an increase in the number of reversals, the inhibitory norms laid down tend to be more complex, precise, and thickly textured. In a very real sense, therefore, the question of access to the appellate process is strategically crucial to the struggle between the two models. The fewer appeals there are, the more likely it is that Crime Control norms will prevail; the more appeals there are, the more likely it is that Due Process norms will prevail.

There is no level of the criminal process at which the triumph of the Due Process Model, at least in terms of asserted norms, has been more speedily and more completely established than on the question of access to the appellate process. Only a decade ago the legal norm governing appeals by those who could afford to finance them was significantly different from the norm governing appeals by those who could not. The financial disparities doubtless remain; but the legal norms have been drastically pushed toward the Due Process end of the spectrum. In a series of landmark decisions, the Supreme Court has established the rule, on the state and federal levels alike, that the situation of financially incapable persons must be substantially equalized.[2] If a transcript of the trial proceedings is necessary for appellate purposes, the state must supply one to persons who cannot pay for their own. The screening of appeals as a prerequisite to relief from financial barriers has been greatly eased, perhaps virtually eliminated. And the right to counsel on appeal has been assured. Here as elsewhere, of course, the development of Due Process norms has preceded their translation into operative fact, and the process of providing the resources necessary to make the developing norms generally operative has barely begun.

On issues of scope and standards of review, the trend seems to be moving unmistakably toward the norms posited in the Due Process Model. Errors that are considered "constitutional" are more and more being viewed as grounds for automatic reversal without regard to the sufficiency of evidence of factual guilt. And even non-constitutional errors are being treated as requiring automatic reversal in the teeth of what have previously been regarded as well-established rules that forbid reversal without an assessment of the record as a whole. It is not surprising that this should be so. The appellate process is the forum *par excellence* for assertion of the norms that make up the Due Process Model, because this is the stage that has traditionally focused on legal rather than factual guilt. What can be observed on the appellate level today is simply the logical affirmation of the Supreme Court's increased emphasis on making Due Process norms govern earlier stages of the criminal process.

COLLATERAL ATTACK

When the criminal process ends with a determination of guilt, should that verdict be subject to review only on direct appeal within the court system in which the prosecution has been initiated? The question may arise even in cases where an appeal is not initially taken. It becomes particularly acute when the deter-

---

[2] Griffin v. Illinois, 351 U.S. 12 (1956); Coppedge v. United States, 369 U.S. 438 (1962); Douglas v. California, 372 U.S. 353 (1963); Draper v. Washington, 372 U.S. 487 (1963).

mination of guilt is made by a plea of guilty because in that situation any appeal is, as a practical matter, highly unlikely. The
issue is complicated by the coexistence of state and federal law
and of state and federal forums for deciding questions that arise
in criminal cases. For our present limited purpose of illustrating
the competition of the two models, we will focus on only a few
of the many questions that arise when a state's criminal process
has resulted in a guilty verdict and the accused, now a state
prisoner, asserts in a federal habeas corpus proceeding that he is
being held in custody in violation of the Constitution and laws of
the United States, alleging that rights established under the Fourteenth Amendment have been abridged at some stage of the state
criminal process.

It is obvious that one important dimension of the problem is
the delineation of what those Fourteenth Amendment rights are
thought to be. We can say with rough accuracy that the tenets of
the Due Process Model that have been translated into imperatives legally binding on state criminal courts have been based on
the requirements of the Fourteenth Amendment. The substantive questions raised on collateral attack, then, are those that have
been rapidly evolving as the core doctrines of the Due Process
Model that we have been examining. The procedural issues to
which we now turn are all aspects of a single basic problem: to
what extent should federal collateral attack on state criminal
convictions be permitted to nullify state criminal convictions on
the basis of the expanding rights of defendants as defined by the
Due Process Model? Two representative issues will serve to illustrate the distance between the two models with respect to this
crucial procedural problem. First, if a federal Fourteenth Amendment claim has been asserted by the habeas corpus petitioner in
the state criminal process—whether during trial, on appeal, or
in a state collateral proceeding if one was invoked—and has been
considered and rejected on the merits by a state court, may the
petitioner relitigate the issue in a federal habeas corpus proceeding? Second, if the federal habeas petitioner has failed to take his
opportunity to raise a Fourteenth Amendment issue in the state
criminal process and is therefore barred by state procedural rules
from now raising the issue, may he nonetheless secure a federal

determination? Affirmative answers to each of these questions tend to provide a broad scope for judicial vindication of the Due Process Model; negative answers tend to perpetuate the Crime Control Model, notwithstanding the fact that the norms now on the books incline toward the tenets of the Due Process Model. We need not spell out in detail the positions taken by the two models on these representative issues; they are implicit in what has been said earlier about the operations of the model at the appellate level.

Until 1953 it was doubtful at most whether federal constitutional claims raised and decided on the merits in state criminal cases could be reexamined by a federal court in a habeas corpus proceeding. The landmark decision in *Brown* v. *Allen*[3] held that they could be. Since that time there have been an increasing number of petitions for habeas corpus filed by state prisoners. In *Townsend* v. *Sain*[4] the Supreme Court has recently reaffirmed the doctrine of *Brown* v. *Allen,* and has laid down rules considerably more favorable to habeas petitioners than contemporary practice in the lower federal courts has provided for determining the circumstances under which they are entitled to have an evidentiary hearing on the underlying merits of their Fourteenth Amendment claims.

At the same time that the Court opened the door to determination of federal claims already heard in a state court, it appeared to close the door to a first determination in a federal court of a Fourteenth Amendment claim that state courts had refused to hear because of some state procedural default by the petitioner. In subsequent years there was lively controversy over the circumstances in which a procedural default by a state prisoner should not be counted against him for habeas purposes. The controversy has been at least temporarily resolved by the Supreme Court decision in *Fay* v. *Noia*,[5] which decrees in sweeping terms that a federal habeas court may (and in the ordinary case should) determine federal claims, even though the petitioner failed to avail himself of state remedies when they were still open to him. So, for exam-

[3] 344 U.S. 443 (1953).
[4] 372 U.S. 293 (1963).
[5] 372 U.S. 391 (1963).

ple, a state prisoner who contends that his conviction was based on a coerced confession but who failed to appeal from the conviction and was therefore barred from receiving a state determination is no longer barred from seeking release on federal habeas.

The combined effect of the doctrines of *Brown* v. *Allen* and *Fay* v. *Noia* has been to give the federal courts a broad supervisory power over the administration of state criminal justice. Of course, formidable obstacles stand in the way of any individual prisoner's success in pressing an application for habeas corpus. Working in most cases without the aid of counsel, he must convince a federal district judge, one of a notably unsentimental group of men, that there is arguable merit to his cause before he will even be given a hearing on his allegations. But with all the difficulties that collateral attack presents for the prisoner seeking to invoke it, it is undeniable that the remarkable expansion of its theoretical availability that has been taking place in recent years constitutes a powerful weapon for maintaining, capitalizing on, and expanding the influence of the Due Process Model on the criminal processes of the state and the nation.

ACCESS TO COUNSEL: A POSTSCRIPT

At every stage in the criminal process, as we have seen, our two models divide on the role to be played by counsel for the accused. In the Crime Control Model, with its administrative and managerial bias, he is a mere luxury; at no stage is he indispensable, and only in the very small proportion of cases that go to trial and the even smaller proportion that are reviewed on appeal is he to be regarded as more than merely tolerable. The Due Process Model, with its adversary and judicial bias makes counsel for the accused a crucial figure throughout the process; indeed, the viability of this model's prescriptions depends on his presence. The decision in *Gideon* v. *Wainwright*[6] that the states must provide counsel for criminal defendants who are financially unable to provide their own, is therefore the longest single step taken so far

[6] 372 U.S. 335 (1963).

by any institution of government in moving the norms of the criminal process toward the Due Process Model. Many issues posed by this development remain to be clarified. In what kinds of criminal prosecutions does the right to assigned counsel apply —in "serious" offenses only? If so, what are the criteria of "seriousness"? When does the right to counsel begin and end? Are the limits the same for assigned counsel as for privately retained counsel? Looming up behind these questions are even more portentous ones. Does the effective assistance of counsel require that the state provide financial compensation for the lawyers who serve? Must provision be made for other expenses of an effective defense? The emerging shape of the criminal process will be substantially affected by the answers given to questions such as these.

Without deprecating the importance of questions of this order, it can be asserted that *Gideon* v. *Wainwright* will remain for a long time the watershed decision in the evolution of the criminal process. It may also be the most durable. Even if the cycle of change turns out to be near its end, the norms of the process have been ineradicably changed, and in far more than the mere insistence that counsel must be provided. *Gideon* makes no sense except on the acceptance of premises, all the stronger for being unarticulated, about the adversary and judicial quality of the criminal process. As long as *Gideon* remains in the law, the normative content of state criminal processes will possess a core of meaning in common with the Due Process Model and will provide a base for the expansion of Due Process norms to other aspects of the process.

Yet *Gideon* and decisions like it do not alone determine the shape of the criminal process. The response of other institutions of government counts for as much when the question is one of providing the necessary resources to make the norm something more than a ground for reversing a few convictions. The implementation of *Gideon* may provide a paradigm of the tension between forces of change and those of inertia. No one can doubt that the norms of the criminal process have been moved rapidly and spectacularly across the spectrum toward the Due Process Model. But a parallel development in the real-world operation of the process remains for the future. No estimate of the direction and velocity of change in the criminal process can be realistic that fails to appraise not only the normative revolution that has occurred, but the competing forces of change and inertia that will govern the extent to which that revolution becomes a reality.

CHAPTER TWELVE

The Trend and Its Impact: A Tentative Appraisal

THE CRIMINAL PROCESS as it actually operates in the large majority of cases probably approximates fairly closely the dictates of the Crime Control Model. What systematically gathered evidence we have, reinforced as it is by the impressionistic "feel" for the situation that is widely current in our culture, suggests that the real-world criminal process tends to be far more administrative and managerial than adversary and judicial. Yet, as we have seen, the officially determined norms of the process are rapidly providing a standard that looks more and more like what has been described in these pages as the Due Process Model.

It would be unnecessarily repetitive at this point to recapitulate this development in detail. Its principal thrusts have been to "judicialize" each stage of the criminal process, to enhance the capacity of the accused to challenge the operation of the process (both at the time adverse action is taken or threatened and subsequently), and to equalize the capacity of all persons accused of crime to take advantage of the opportunities thus created. In theory at least, to revert to a figure suggested at an earlier point in Part II, the process is being turned from an assembly line into an obstacle course. This is by far the dominant normative trend. We must now try to appraise its durability.

There are some fairly obvious negative factors. First, the trend as it has so far developed is based almost exclusively on judicial decisions. Indeed, it has been derived from the lead taken by one judicial institution, the Supreme Court of the United States. Changes in attitude toward the criminal process or changes in personnel on the Court (which may come to the same thing) can slow or reverse the trend in two ways. First and more obviously, decisions can be overruled. Much of the development of the last decade has been accomplished by overruling earlier precedents; decisional instability has been a feature of its evolution, and there is no reason to suppose that this can work in only one direction. Some of the most crucial decisions have been the result of closely divided judgments, and minorities within the Court have made powerful appeals to the reason of another day. A second, subtler, and probably more serious, threat to the continued strengthening of the Due Process trend is that the justices will, out of a diminished enthusiasm either for the principles involved or for the continued combat their vindication entails, cease or slacken their scrutiny of the criminal process as it operates in both state and federal criminal courts. It is well to remember that the Court's jurisdiction in these matters is almost entirely discretionary and exemplary. Any perceptible slackening in the pace or tone of its overseeing functions will quickly convey a message to the lower courts, which are necessarily the first-line custodians of the norms for the process. That is not to say that the process of change can be maintained only if the Court continues to set new norms. We may well be coming to the point at which tightening the very open-textured pronouncements of the past decade will be the main task of a Court that remains committed to promoting the goals of the Due Process Model. But that sort of consolidating effort, no less than the innovating effort that has been going on, requires constant attention. Whether the Court will be willing and able to supply this steady and unspectacular kind of leadership remains to be seen.

Instability of decision and slowing of pace aside, there is another major reason why the predominantly judicial character of the trend we have been examining is a potential source of weakness. With insignificant exceptions the courts can intervene in the criminal process only to impose the sanction of nullity. That is powerful enough, especially when applied conscientiously by courts in which prosecutions are begun, but the sanction of nullity has its limitations. A court cannot ordain, administer, and finance an adequate system for providing lawyers for persons unable to afford their own. It can only refuse to validate criminal proceedings that are the product of inadequate systems or of no system at all. And, by and large, it can invalidate only those proceedings that happen to be brought before it for scrutiny, cases that typically require at some point the initiative of counsel. Hence, cases most in need of review because of lack of counsel may never be reviewed because of that very lack. If it is the strength of courts that they can deal only, as Professor Freund has said, at retail, it is their weakness too. The sanction of nullity applied on a retail basis may provide the goad for change; but it is not a sufficient instrument of change.

That brings us to a second and related cautionary note about the durability of the trend toward the Due Process Model. However diffused among governmental and extra-governmental agencies the authority for promoting change in the criminal process may be, few would be disposed to deny the centrality of legislative assistance. Yet the legislative response has been slow and grudging. A single instance will suffice. Thirty years have elapsed since the decision in *Johnson* v. *Zerbst*[1] that persons accused of crime in federal courts are entitled to have counsel appointed for them if they are unable to hire their own. Repeated attempts have been made to get the Congress to give practical content to this norm by setting up a system for appointing and compensating defense counsel in the various federal districts. Finally, and only after a President explicitly made this an aspect of his program and an Attorney General put the force of his office behind a specific set of plans (both for the first time), this reform was launched by passage of the Criminal Justice Act of 1964.

The lesson of this experience seems clear. The legislative process is not, even at best, a fast one. Powerful interests must normally be mobilized in order to get legislation approved. Reform in the criminal process has very little political appeal. There is no constituency of any consequence behind it, aside from a few professional organizations whose concern tends to exist in inverse ratio to their power. If it has taken 25 years to bring *John-*

[1] 304 U.S. 458 (1938).

son v. *Zerbst* to the brink of puberty, how long will the childhood of *Gideon* v. *Wainwright* have to last?

Inertia is not the only force to be contended with. Hostility toward the Due Process Model and the court rulings that give it expression is widely shared and is effectively mobilized by police and prosecutorial organizations. Every significant move in the Due Process direction has been greeted with dire predictions about an imminent breakdown in the criminal process. Because judicial activity has been based on the high ground of the Constitution, there have been not many instances of legislative riposte. But those who unhesitatingly give an affirmative answer to the rhetorical question "are the courts handcuffing the police?" need not get their prescriptions enacted into law; theirs is the status quo, and they can maintain it well enough by resisting legislative efforts to provide the resources required to translate Due Process prescriptions into operative fact.

Behind all this stands that enigmatic force, public opinion. Just where it stands we cannot know. Television and the other mass media seem to be making the defender of the accused into a folk hero. Yet one suspects that a substantial if not a preponderant segment of the public has little sympathy with the tenets of the Due Process Model. The fear of "crime in the streets" hardly goes hand in hand with solicitude for the rights of criminal defendants. It is hard to think that the balance of advantage in the criminal process, if that is a reckonable entity, now lies with the accused. Yet there is some evidence that at least a segment of the public believes both that the accused has most of the advantages and that the pendulum has swung dangerously away from order. When speculations of this sort become the stuff of political campaigns, it is evident that there are powerful currents running against the trend. Who can say what will happen to the Due Process Model?

All of this may conduce to a picture too one-sided for accuracy. One of the most powerful features of the Due Process Model is that it thrives on visibility. People are willing to be complacent about what goes on in the crminal process as long as they are not too often or too explicitly reminded of the gory details. The more frequently that specific cases are brought to light of invasions of privacy, of coerced confessions, of excessive bail, of lengthy periods of pre-trial detention, of deprivations of the assistance of counsel, the harder it becomes to maintain that the process should go on being primarily administrative and managerial. At root, the Due Process Model depends on the functioning of what has been called the sense of injustice. No one, Supreme Court justices included, is immune to the force of the horrible example. And therein lies the Due Process Model's peculiar strength. It is self-sustaining because its own operations uncover the raw material that fuels its continued growth. It would take a conspiracy of silence to check the mobilization of energies that perpetuates the Due Process revolution.

That is a conspiracy we are not likely to get. To start at the small end, the renaissance of criminal studies that has taken place in this country in the last fifteen or twenty years has produced a generation of scholars uniquely knowledgeable about and alert to the problems of the criminal process. They, in turn, are having an impact on students of the law that may well reverse the historic tendency of the American bar to ignore the problems of the criminal law and give us, if not a corps of professionals, at least a generation of dedicated amateurs. These tendencies are also producing a new journalism about the criminal process that will help to ensure that the subject does not drop out of sight. The Due Process Model is to a significant extent the model of the schools. As a result of cultural lag, we will not be seeing the full effects of this in the courts until the next generation of lawyers and judges, who will have cut their teeth on Due Process tenets, come into their own.

Beyond the immediate arena of the criminal law there are growing interests in national life that may be expected as a kind of by-product to foster the development of the Due Process Model. Two in particular may be mentioned—civil rights and poverty. The criminal process has been and will probably continue to be an important forum in the struggle over civil rights. Coercive uses of the criminal process—police brutality, arrests on inadequate grounds, excessively high bail, or the denial of bail, denial of access to counsel, prejudiced tribunals—have focused and will continue to focus attention on the problem of adequate challenge in the process, that mainspring of the Due Process Model. Just as the Jehovah's Witnesses made much of our law on free speech, so have the Negro demonstrators been making much of our law on the criminal process. Beyond this, the fact that the numbers of Negro criminal defendants are out of all proportion to their numbers in the population has already produced legislative and extra-governmental interest in the workings of the criminal process. The problem of poverty is not far removed. As we have seen, an important dimension of the Due Process ideology is its insistence upon equality in the operation of the criminal process. The problem of crime is to an important extent a problem of poverty. The current national interest in poverty cannot fail, first indirectly and then directly, to confront the manifold relationships between poverty and the criminal process. It has become part of the received doctrine that poverty and the administration of criminal justice must be dealt with together in the formulation of national policies. Thus unless the current that now appears to be running so strongly toward governmental concern in the problem of poverty is reversed, the exponents of the Due Process Model may expect to find powerful official support that has not hitherto been available for their cause.

One can do not more than venture a guess about the continuation of present trends in the criminal process. In the short run, at least, it seems probable that the development and consolidation of norms emerging from the Due Process Model will not slacken. In particular, norms requiring the equalization of opportunity to challenge the process are likely to become firmly established. This trend, as symbolized by the decisions on the right to assigned counsel, may in the end be a far more momentous one than trends expanding particular substantive rights of the accused. If those rights are not further extended, or even if they are curtailed, there will remain a number of opportunities to challenge the operation of the process that far exceeds the present capacity of criminal defendants to use it. If the recent trends toward the prescriptions of the Due Process Model in such matters as powers of arrest, use of illegally obtained evidence, confessions during police interrogation, pre-trial liberty, and early access to counsel were now to come to an abrupt halt—an unlikely eventuality—the theoretical operation of the process would still look very much like the Due Process Model. The burning question is whether the great mass of criminal defendants, who are financially unable to invoke the challenges now available to them, will find their capacity to do so materially improved by measures designed to assimilate their opportunities more closely to those presently enjoyed by the small minority of those who can afford counsel. The interest now being displayed by governmental and extra-governmental organizations in devising ways to implement this norm of the Due Process Model suggests that this trend is both durable and influential.

What are the implications for the criminal sanction of the trend toward the Due Process Model? If it tends to become not merely a legal norm but an operational fact that the accused will have a much better opportunity to challenge the operation of the process than he presently enjoys, what if anything should that fact have to say to our hypothetical rational legislator as he ponders the uses and limits of the criminal sanction? The problems are of course somewhat interdependent, in that official decision-makers will have a great deal to say about the extent to which the developing Due Process Model is allowed to become operational fact. Let us, nonetheless, make the simplifying assumption that to a degree the trend in the process is irreversible and that, for whatever reasons and however reluctantly, the rational legislator finds himself confronted by a given, so far as the changed mechanics of the criminal process are concerned.

The criminal process now appears to be changing into a somewhat unwieldy instrument of public policy, especially for dealing with large numbers of defendants. It may not remain to the same extent the low-cost, high-speed process envisioned in the Crime Control Model and reflected in the present real-world situation. At anything like the level of resources currently devoted to its operation, the capacity of the criminal process for dealing with its rapidly increasing annual intake will be seriously impaired.

One line of solution is to throw more resources into the operation of the process—more policemen, more prosecutors, more judges, more supporting services of all kinds. Although there has undoubtedly been an expansion in the public resources devoted to the criminal process, perhaps even greater than what would have been called for by increases in population or the so-called crime rate, we have not so far been notable for the steadiness of our attention to the resource needs of the process. Beyond that, even if the conscious choice were to lead us in that direction, there might come a point at which the quality of life in a free society would be adversely affected by increases in the proportion of public resources employed to detect, prosecute, and punish activity that had been defined as criminal. Some increase in the resources available for operation of the process is undoubtedly warranted, even apart from the demands of the shift toward the Due Process Model that we have been exploring; but a conscious choice to meet the problems created by that shift entirely or even predominantly through increasing the resources of crime control seems unwise if there is an alternative.

The alternative that I would commend to the rational legislator is to reexamine the uses now being made of the criminal sanction with a view to deciding which uses are relatively indispensable and which might with safety (and perhaps even with some net gain to the public welfare) be restricted or given up. Penal codes of particular times and places are never inherent in the nature of things. The behavior content of the criminal law has expanded enormously over the past century, mainly because declaring undesirable conduct to be criminal is the legislative line of least resistance for coping with the vexing problems of an increasingly complex and interdependent society. As a result we have inherited a strange mélange of criminal proscriptions, ranging from, on the one hand, conduct that offers the grossest kind of threat to important social interests to, on the other, conduct whose potentiality for harm is trivial or nonexistent.

It is always in order to question the uses made of this most awesome and coercive of sanctions. It is especially appropriate to do so at a time when the processes that are invoked to apply the criminal sanction are undergoing a profound change that renders them unsuitable for being lightly employed.

PART III

LIMITS

CHAPTER THIRTEEN

An Approach to the Problem of Limits

INTRODUCTION

In Part I we traced the rationale of the criminal sanction to its source in the inevitability and the moral ambiguity of punishment. In our present state of comparative ignorance about the sources and control of human conduct there is no escape from the use of punishment (whether criminal or not) as a device for reducing the incidence of behavior that we consider antisocial. There is also no escape from the conclusion that punishment is morally ambiguous: we cannot be sure that it does more good than it does harm. This tension between inevitability and ambiguity necessitates adherence to a set of doctrinal complexities that place certain limits on the means by which the system of criminal punishment may seek to prevent crime.

In Part II we inspected the clash of values that takes place at every level of the criminal process, and saw the emergence from that clash of a series of limiting norms that make the process an extraordinarily difficult and costly method of social control. These norms, which generally resemble the dictates of the Due Process Model, are the counterpart in the criminal process to the doctrines of culpability in the rationale of criminal law. In both cases, definite limits are placed on the power of the state over the individual, with the result that absolute efficiency in social control is sacrificed in the interests of fostering a reasonably free society.

Considerations of both rationale and process suggest that the criminal sanction, inflicting as it does a unique combination of stigma and loss of liberty, should be resorted to only sparingly in a society that regards itself as free and open. But what are the criteria that ought to guide the exercise of legislative judgment regarding the appropriate occasions for invoking the criminal sanction? How are we to decide what kinds of conduct should be made criminal? Part III of this book is designed to present some tentative answers to that difficult question, by way of both general argument and concrete example.

In a sense, all limiting criteria reduce themselves to a simple prescription: first things first. The criminal sanction is the law's ultimate threat. Being punished for a crime is different from being regulated in the public interest, or being forced to compensate another who has been injured by one's conduct, or being treated for a disease. The sanction is at once uniquely coercive and, in the broadest sense, uniquely expensive. It should be reserved for what really matters.

Considerations of several kinds enter into a determination of what "things" should be considered "first." On the credit side of the ledger are the social gains that will accrue from the successful prevention or reduction of the conduct in question, discounted by the prospects of achieving success (however defined). On the debit side are the moral and practical costs, reckoned in terms of values other than the prevention of antisocial conduct. Finally, there is the question of alternatives: what other means of social control are available to achieve the same ends? The question of alternatives is particularly crucial. If there are readily available alternatives that avoid or minimize the formidable battery of objections and obstacles we have been considering, they must be carefully weighed. If there are not, we must face, rather than reject out of hand, the alternative of doing nothing. Accordingly, it is to the question of alternatives that we will first turn in the rest of this chapter. There next follow two chapters in which we will examine the kinds of limiting criteria that our hypothetically rational or prudent lawmaker ought to take into account in determining what kinds of conduct should (or should not) be made criminal. Chapter Fourteen deals with criteria that emerge from the philosophic justifications for and limits on the use of criminal punishment. Chapter Fifteen canvasses a variety of criteria that relate to the practical or "social cost-accounting" aspects of the criminal process. The balance of the book is devoted to illustrative sketches of how the thesis of limitation propounded in Part III might be applied to some of the most troublesome problems in the criminal law.

THE QUESTION OF ALTERNATIVES

The prudent legislator, faced with the question of whether to make a certain kind of conduct criminal or (as it more frequently presents itself today) the question of whether to continue applying the criminal sanction to a certain kind of conduct, will ask himself what other means of control are available. When he asks himself this question, he is venturing into a neglected area of jurisprudence, the area of sanctions. The fact is that we do not have a systematic body of theory about the kinds of sanctions available to reinforce the primary norms of conduct that the law seeks to promote, or about their distinguishing characteristics, their strengths and weaknesses, the anticipated benefits from their use, and the social costs that their invocation incurs. One hopes that legal inquiry based on careful factual investigation will ultimately produce a workable jurisprudence of sanctions. As a tentative step toward mapping this *terra incognita,* I advanced, much earlier in this book, a rough classification of sanctions into four categories: compensation, regulation, punishment, and treatment. Each of these categories includes a variety of sanctioning devices, some of which we will now examine in an attempt to see how they relate to modes of criminal punishment in use at the present time and what objections may arise to the idea of substituting them, in the case of certain offenses, for the criminal sanction.

COMPENSATION AND REGULATION: THE CASE OF DRUNK DRIVING

Compensation involves the exaction of money or performance to recompense an identifiable beneficiary or class of beneficiaries for damage done or threatened by the action of another. Its purest form is seen in a civil court suit in which a person or a group of people obtain a money judgment for a breach of some legal obligation. If I am injured in an automobile accident through the negligence of a drunk driver, I can sue him to recover for my injuries. That is a useful sanctioning device, assuming that I can afford to sue and the defendant or his insurer can afford to pay. But no one would be satisfied to rest on this as the sole sanction for reducing the incidence of drunk driving. The vagaries of litigation between private parties leave the public interest in curbing drunk driving inadequately protected. Public prosecution of claims on behalf of private individuals who have been injured might reduce the hazards of litigation but would entail substantial public costs. Moreover, we have no reason to think that it would have anything but the most oblique and marginal effect on the objectionable conduct we are trying to alter, since our primary objective would be to afford compensation to the victims of drunk driving rather than to make people stop driving while drunk.

If we go one step further and levy fines for drunk driving which are then put into the public treasury, we are moving from compensation to punishment. There are many fields in which this sanctioning device is a useful one. Drunk driving is clearly not one of them. The drunk driver's perception of unpleasant consequences is not altered by making the public rather than the injured party the beneficiary of a monetary exaction. It is mainly in situations where economic gain is the objective of the antisocial conduct we seek to inhibit that monetary exactions are a useful sanction. Where that is the case, the question that needs to be asked is whether punishment (for that is what a monetary exaction in the public interest comes down to) needs to be *criminal* punishment. Must we burden ourselves with the apparatus of culpability requirements and with the cumbersome processes of the criminal law to apply a sanction whose end result is a monetary exaction rather than the combination of stigma and loss of liberty that comprises the usual form of criminal punishment? The answer is clear that we need not. There is a vast range of economic offenses, especially those in which a corporation rather than a natural person is the object of the law's attention, where the forms of the criminal sanction can and should be dispensed with. Minor traffic offenses, violations of food and drug laws, building code infractions, and the like are best dealt with through the agency of the civil rather than the criminal law. Legal theory has this problem well in hand: witness the proposed creation of a kind of intermediate category between the categories of civil compensation and criminal punishment, variously termed the civil offense, the violation, or the infraction. Unfortunately, legal practice has a long way to go in catching up with legal theory. We still burden the criminal process with a wide variety of conduct that could more expeditiously be handled on a civil basis. It may be expected that a desire to escape from the ever more burdensome dictates of the Due Process Model will hasten reform in some of these areas. Intermediate modes of sanctioning that blend compensation, regulation, and punishment will displace the use of the criminal sanction.

Regulation is a somewhat diffuse sanctioning category that embraces a constellation of devices used to bring the impact of public authority directly to bear on private conduct, both before and after the fact. Licensing, one of the most common devices of a regulatory nature, includes both before-the-fact and after-the-fact regulation. Once again, let us use the drunk driving problem as a concrete instance. There are many kinds of conduct in which one may not engage without having been individually "checked out" under some form of official scrutiny. Practicing medicine, flying commercial airplanes, barbering, and driving a car are just a few activities governed by this pervasive form of regulation. Its rigor and frequency vary over a wide range, depending on such factors as the number of people involved and the intensity of the public interest in screening out substandard performers. Tens of millions of people are licensed to drive cars after passing minimal tests of proficiency that in most states need never be repeated. By contrast, only a few thousand airline pilots are licensed to fly passenger planes. They are forced to undergo rigorous testing of technical proficiency, health, and emotional stability, all of which must be repeated at fairly frequent intervals. They must undergo continuous training designed to keep their skills up to date. Fur-

thermore, they are forced to submit to the surveillance of in-
spectors who observe and rate their performance. That is one way
to reduce "drunk driving." For obvious reasons, it is not a way
that may be practically employed to deal with the tens of millions
of automobile drivers on the nation's highways. Individualized
before-the-fact regulation is simply too expensive and too burdensome to be generally employed as a sanctioning technique. It is
also extremely abrasive when encountered by people who do not
expect it, as anyone who has ever been stopped at a police safety
roadblock can testify. The restrictive effect on the free flow of
private human activity exerted by before-the-fact regulation
counsels against its use in all but the most carefully chosen and
clearly important areas of conduct.

If individualized before-the-fact regulation is too costly, what
reliance might we put on after-the-fact regulatory activity, namely the suspension or revocation of a license? Today, of course, we
do resort to license revocation as a sanction against drunk driving, but it is not the sanction of first resort. We use the fact of
criminal conviction for drunk driving as a triggering event for
resort to the administrative process of license revocation. But we
might well ask: why not bypass the criminal process entirely? If
the object is to keep drunk drivers off the highways, why not attack that problem directly through license revocation rather than
obliquely through criminal punishment? Mechanically, that
would not be difficult to arrange. Whenever a driver was suspected of driving while drunk, the arresting officer could file a
complaint with the local office of the Department of Motor Ve-
hicles, which could then issue an order to show cause why the
driver's license should not be suspended or revoked. The hearing
would focus on the same evidentiary facts that would be involved
in a criminal prosecution, but it would do without the trappings
of the criminal law—including, most significantly for this purpose, the right to trial by jury and the standard of proof beyond a
reasonable doubt. The result would be an administrative order
suspending or revoking the driver's license. Drunken driving
would cease to be a crime for which punishment would be imposed; but driving with a suspended or revoked license would

take its place as a criminal offense. In short, criminal punishment would cease to be the first-line sanction and would become the sanction of last resort.

If we could be sure that people whose license had been suspended or revoked would stop driving cars, there would be obvious gains in this substitution of a regulatory sanction for criminal punishment. The combination of stigma and loss of liberty that inheres in criminal punishment represents a net loss in human dignity and autonomy. It is tempting to contemplate avoidance of that loss. License revocation is a punishment; but other things being equal, we should prefer punishments that do not entail stigma and loss of liberty to those that do. Of course, any punishment entails some loss of liberty, but there is more than a difference in degree between being deprived of the liberty to drive a car and being confined in the county jail. License revocation leaves the actor as a free participating member of society except to the extent that he poses a threat to the innocent.

Unfortunately, we have no assurance that license suspension or revocation would be an effective sanction. Failing some dramatic technological advance that would make it possible to identify unlicensed drivers without stopping and questioning them, there is every reason to believe that large numbers of people would simply accept the risk of being caught and would continue to drive. The use of criminal punishment would simply be postponed one step rather than avoided. There would be, if anything, a decrease in the deterrent efficacy of the law, because an unlicensed driver is less likely to be apprehended than one who is drunk. Paradoxically, it is the greater severity of license revocation that contributes to its relative ineffectiveness as a first-line sanction. The apparatus of the criminal law, for all its terror, usually produces a less onerous punishment than license revocation would be perceived as being. For many people, a couple of hundred dollars' fine or even thirty days in jail may impose less actual hardship than the permanent or extended loss of the privilege to drive a car. If people see it that way, they have very little inducement voluntarily to comply with the loss of a license. Only when severity of punishment is accompanied by certainty of detection is it likely to be effective. It seems, then, that workable alternatives are not easily come by. At best, the ones we have been considering simply postpone resort to the criminal sanction.

The most appealing alternative to criminal punishment would seem to be treatment. Every instinct of decency and compassion urges us to substitute helping for hurting. But we find it difficult to make the substitution without first going through certain symbolic motions. The principal symbolic cue for invoking treatment rather than punishment is the label "disease." And so it has become commonplace to assert that various aberrant forms of human conduct that we wish to discourage are not "really" crimes but are, rather, diseases. Narcotics addiction, drunkenness, and sexual deviation come immediately to mind as examples of the trend. These are all forms of behavior (or states of being) that the enlightened opinion of the day tells us should be regarded as diseases to be treated rather than as crimes to be punished. What conditions must be satisfied in order to permit this happy advance to be made?

There are only two: first, in order for the metaphor of disease to be at all appropriate we must have adequate measures of therapy; second, those who are afflicted must in the general run of cases view themselves as suffering from a disease of which they wish to be cured. It is obvious that these two conditions are closely linked. The more plausible a claim for adequate therapy can be made, the more likely it is that people will be willing to submit to its ministrations. More subtly, the climate in which claims for cure are accepted is a climate in which the predicate of disease will be assumed. Narcotics addicts are more likely to consider themselves in need of treatment and readier to submit to it if they can be told with a straight face that there is a reasonably specific therapy with a reasonably high probability of success. Only minimal compulsion, to deal with the singularly stupid or the singularly recalcitrant, is required when a believable therapy exists. One can devote considerable doctrinal ingenuity to explaining why involuntary hospitalization for a communicable disease like tuberculosis should or should not be classified as punishment; the important point is that very few "recalcitrant tuberculars" are subjected to punishment or treatment, as the case may be.

The tension between the humanitarian urge to treat and the absence of adequate measures of treatment has led to a spectacular rise, in the last decade, of the hybrid sanction of compulsory civil commitment. When we come to discuss the narcotics problem, we shall have occasion to consider it in detail. At this point, what needs to be said is that it simply cannot be seriously regarded as an *alternative* to the criminal sanction, for much the same reason that license revocation cannot be regarded as an alternative to criminal punishment for drunk driving. Civil commitment is either an outcome of the criminal process or a requirement whose flouting will require resort to the criminal process. On the one hand, certain people in the toils of the criminal process are sent to something called a hospital instead of something called a jail. This, at any rate, is the pattern of compulsory civil commitment in California and New York, the two states that have instituted programs. The transfer involves nothing more than a change of labels, especially if the people in question are not subjected to this mode of disposition until after they have been convicted of a crime. On the other hand, narcotics addicts could be required to turn themselves in for hospitalization without having been either arrested for or convicted of a crime. In that case, one might confidently predict that the criminal process would soon be applied to people for the offense of failing to report for treatment.

The most that can be said for civil commitment is that it represents a strategy for getting resources more adequately allocated to the punishment of one group of offenders than to other groups of offenders. Under whatever name, it is still punishment. And it is punishment that does not have even the minimal virtue of being labeled as what it is. Here as elsewhere we confront the hard fact that the criminal sanction has no adequate substitute as a sanction of last resort.

THE ALTERNATIVE OF DOING NOTHING

There is always the alternative of doing nothing. After a careful appraisal of costs and benefits, we may conclude that it is better not to impose any sanction at all than to resort to one of the available ones. No lawmaker can say that he has thought the problem through until he has considered that possibility. It is only when we confront this "null hypothesis" that we can squarely confront the central issue of how high on our scale of values the suppression of a given form of conduct ranks. To take an extreme example, although by no means a historically unrealistic one, let us hypothesize a lawmaker who decides that he wants to eliminate sexual intercourse between unmarried adults. A quick canvass of the sanctioning possibilities would reveal to him that criminal punishment is in fact the only method that gives promise of achieving the result. He would quickly realize that it would take very aggressive law enforcement techniques, amounting to snooping on an enormous scale, to provide anything like effective enforcement. Conversely, if it were hoped that a few exemplary prosecutions would significantly deter people from fornicating, he would be confronted with authorizing inescapably arbitrary decisions about whom to detect, apprehend, and prosecute. Before long, our lawmaker would conclude that the "costs" were too great to incur unless the suppression of fornication was near the top of his list of social objectives.

"Doing nothing" is not itself an all-or-nothing proposition. One can decide that an entire social problem is too vast to be attacked through use of the criminal sanction and that only selected aspects of it should be so attacked. If, for example, the social cost of dealing with narcotics addiction through criminal punishment or its thinly disguised counterpart, civil commitment, is thought to be too high, it is possible to narrow the reach of the criminal sanction by eliminating the crimes of use and possession that ensnare the great run of addicts, leaving only the prosecution of commercial traffickers to the criminal law. It may be doubtful that such a measure would have much impact on the illegal traffic, but the change would have the considerable virtue of eliminating significant enforcement expenditures, on the one hand, and significant human misery, on the other. The alternative of doing nothing, in short, always includes the intermediate alternative of doing less.

In the end, the question of alternatives, including the alternative of doing nothing (or less), is a question of resource allocation. We cannot have everything we want of the good things of this world; and that includes, unfortunately, the prevention of the bad things. We must weigh costs and assign priorities. This we have not done, as a glance at the calendar of crimes will readily demonstrate. After all the factors have been considered and somehow weighed, there always remains the question: what alternatives do we have, and finally, are we better off doing nothing? It goes very much against the American grain to adopt the alternative of doing nothing. We do not coexist easily with "evil." And yet it seems clear that in some contexts in which the use of the criminal sanction is at issue, the alternative of doing nothing provides the best available answer.

LIMITS AS A PROBLEM OF RESOURCE ALLOCATION

It has been estimated that public expenditures for law enforcement are currently running at the rate of about four billion dollars annually and that this figure will at least double over the next ten years. Incredible as it may seem, there are no data at all on how this amount is divided among various categories of criminal activity. The same is true for the people engaged in the criminal process, probably a more meaningful figure than dollar amounts. It is as if General Motors didn't know if it cost more per car to produce Cadillacs or Chevrolets, or as if the Secretary of Defense confessed ignorance about whether the Pentagon was spending more for ICBM's or paper clips. That being so, the rational lawmaker is quite at a loss to know what the most effective use of the marginal law enforcement dollar will be. In this lamentable state of ignorance, prudence suggests the imposition of some basic fiscal discipline.

We cannot have all the things we want, crime prevention included. Every hour of police, prosecutorial, judicial, and cor-

rectional time that is spent on marginal uses of the criminal sanction is an hour lost to the prevention of serious crime. Conversely, every trivial, imaginary, or otherwise dubious crime that is
removed from the list of criminal offenses represents the freeing
of substantial resources to deal more effectively with the high-
priority needs of the criminal justice system. Whether our rational legislator is engaged in revising an existing criminal code
or pondering a new proposal for invocation of the criminal sanction, he ought to remember that resources are limited, that every
dollar and every man-hour is the object of competition among
uses, and that (to end where we began) he should not only put
first things first, but also, what is perhaps harder, put last things
last.

CHAPTER FOURTEEN

The Search for Limits: Law and Morals

IMMORALITY: A NECESSARY CONDITION

The debate over the relationship between law and morals is perennial. It has rarely taken specific enough account, however, of what kind of law is at issue. The criminal sanction represents a very special kind of law, itself morally hazardous. As we have seen, the rationale of criminal punishment requires that no one should be treated as a criminal unless his conduct can be regarded as culpable. The flouting of this requirement that takes place when offenses are interpreted as being of "strict liability" contributes to the dilution of the criminal law's moral impact. The ends of the criminal sanction are disserved if the notion becomes widespread that being convicted of a crime is no worse than coming down with a bad cold. The question we now have to face is what role, if any, the moral force of the criminal sanction should have in determining what conduct should be treated as criminal. If individual instances of conduct may not be criminally punished without a finding of culpability, what does that say about categories of conduct?

The relationship is far from self-evident. The dictates of individual culpability are satisfied if a person engages in forbidden conduct without having a valid excuse for it. He is culpable because he has behaved in a way that the law has told him is unacceptable. If he knows that the law forbids him to sell oleomargarine, he is culpable if he sells it, regardless of whether—the law apart—the sale of oleomargarine is considered to be morally good, bad or indifferent. He is culpable because he has knowingly violated a legal prohibition. In this kind of situation, as we have seen, the actor's knowledge of the legal prohibition is crucial, which is why we view criminal punishment as inappropriate unless he has been warned that what he is doing is illegal. If he has been warned, punishment is justifiable, quite apart from the moral quality of the forbidden act.

Can we then assert that there is any kind of connection between the immorality of a category of conduct and the appropriate use of the criminal sanction? I think we can, but only on a prudential basis. Leaving aside for the moment the question of what we mean by immoral, we may discern an analogy between the requirement of culpability in the individual case and a limiting criterion for the legislative invocation of the criminal sanction: only conduct generally considered "immoral" should be treated as criminal. Several reasons support this prudential limitation. To begin with, the principles of selection we use in determining what kinds of undesirable conduct to treat as criminal should surely include at least one that is responsive to the basic character of the criminal sanction, i.e., its quality of moral condemnation. To put it another way, we should use the strengths of the sanction rather than ignore or undermine them. If the conduct with which the original sanction deals is already regarded as being morally wrong, the processes of the criminal law have, so to speak, a "leg up" on the job. This is a matter partly of public attitude and partly of the morale maintained by those who operate the criminal processes. The way to keep those processes running at peak efficiency is to ensure that those who operate them are convinced that what they are doing is right. The surest way to persuade them that what they are doing is right is to have them act only against what they think is wrong. If the criminal sanction is widely used to deal with morally neutral behavior, law enforcement officials are likely to be at least subconsciously defensive about their work, and the public will find the criminal law a confusing guide to moral, or even acceptable, behavior.

The argument that is often put against this prudential limitation on the use of the criminal sanction is that by accepting it we forgo an opportunity to condition people's view of what is immoral. "The very fact that a criminal statute has been enacted by the legislature is a powerful factor in making the proscribed conduct illegitimate in the eyes of a potential actor, even when the actor disagrees with the purpose of the law."[1] This argument misses much of the subtlety that must inform a wise use of the criminal sanction. Its use always involves a prediction about how people are likely to respond. As we know, they do not always respond to a new criminal prohibition by acquiescence. Sometimes their resistance is fatal to acceptance of the new norm, as was the case with Prohibition. When that happens, the effect is not confined to the immediate proscription but makes itself felt in the attitude that people take toward legal proscriptions in general. The risk that this will happen is a substantial one, but we can easily avoid it by observing the prudential limitation that I am contending for. Furthermore, while the opposing argument assumes that the criminal sanction is the only or the best sanction available for dealing with a particular category of conduct, that is rarely in fact the case. Finally, the criminal sanction seems to work best with new categories of conduct when its use has been preceded by other forms of conditioning. It is very doubtful, for example, whether our present vigorous enforcement of the criminal sanction against tax evaders would have been nearly as successful as it has been if it had not been preceded by the development of a tradition of self-assessment. To make conduct criminal is not necessarily to have people accept it as immoral. And even if it were, there would remain the question (which we have yet to canvass) of undesirable side effects resulting from attempts to condition public attitudes about what is immoral. Finally, it needs to be asked whether the building up of a body of opinion about morality is a function that a nontotalitarian society should entrust to the realm of law, especially criminal law.

The question remains: whose morality are we talking about? It is easy to slide into the assumption that somewhere in society there is an authoritative body of moral sentiment to which the law should look. That assumption becomes particularly dangerous, as we shall see, when it is used to buttress the assertion that

[1] Harry V. Ball and Lawrence M. Friedman, *The Use of Criminal Sanctions in the Enforcement of Economic Legislation,* 17 STAN. L. REV. 197, 217 (1965).

the immorality of a given form of conduct is a *sufficient* condition for declaring that conduct to be criminal. But when one is talking about immorality as a *necessary* condition for invocation of the criminal sanction, the inquiry should simply be whether there exists any significant body dissent from the proposition that the conduct in question is immoral. Is there any social group that will be alienated or offended by making (or keeping) the conduct in question criminal? If there is, then prudence dictates caution in employing the criminal sanction.

We can sum up this prudential limitation as follows: the criminal sanction should ordinarily be limited to conduct that is viewed, without significant social dissent, as immoral. The calendar of crimes should not be enlarged beyond that point and, as views about morality shift, should be contracted.

IMMORALITY: AN INSUFFICIENT CONDITION

If the immorality of conduct is a generally necessary condition for invocation of the criminal sanction, is it a generally sufficient one? That is the gist of the "law and morals" debate. Conventional morality, it is asserted, is what holds society together. It must be not only taught but enforced. The enforcement of morals needs no other justification. The usual lines of attack upon this argument are, first, that there is no easy way to determine what should count as immoral and, second, that other considerations (primarily of enforceability) should also be taken into account in determining whether immoral conduct should be made criminal. To these may be added a third: it simply is not true that we use the criminal law to deal with all conduct that we consider immoral; even the most extreme of legal moralists have never pressed for that. Therefore, unless the choice of proscribed conduct is to be purely whimsical, we must take other factors into consideration.

It is generally considered immoral to break a promise simply because it has become inconvenient to keep it. Not only is it regarded as immoral, but the conduct of the ordinary business of life would be greatly changed if the tendency to break promises frivolously became widespread. Yet we do not put promise-breakers in jail. What they do may be viewed as both immoral and harmful; but it does not result in the invocation of the criminal sanction. Examples could be multiplied, but the point is surely obvious. For whatever reasons—the availability of other sanctions (legal and extra-legal), the difficulty of agreeing about categories of excuse, the varying social importance attributed to different kinds of promises—we withhold the sanction of legal condemnation.

The extent of disagreement about moral judgments is an obvious reason for hesitancy about an automatic enforcement of morals. There have been monolithic societies in which a static and homogeneous ethnic, religious, and class structure conduces to widely shared acceptance of a value system. But that is hardly a description of the reality of twentieth-century American society, or of its pluralistic and liberal aspirations. In a society that neither has nor wants a unitary set of moral norms, the enforcement of morals carries a heavy cost in repression. We don't begin to agree about the "morality" of smoking, drinking, gambling, fornicating, or drug-taking, for example, quite apart from the gap between what we say and what we do. The more heterogeneous the society, the more repressive the enforcement of morals must be. And the more heterogeneous the society, the more foreign to its ethos that kind of repression is likely to be. Morals legislation is less likely to be socially damaging in, say, Portugal than it is in this country. In a society like ours, some tensions and some ambivalences are better left unmediated by the criminal law.

Much of what follows is devoted to showing that the enforcement of morals is a costly indulgence. Immorality clearly should not be viewed as a sufficient or even a principal reason for proscribing conduct as criminal. Morals belong to the home, the school, and the church; and we have many homes, many schools, many churches. Our moral universe is polycentric. The state, especially when the most coercive of sanctions is at issue, should not seek to impose a spurious unity upon it.

It can even be argued, as Professor Louis Henkin has done in a thoughtful essay, that the proscription of sin is not a permissible function of a government of limited powers in a secular society.[2]

[2] *Morals and the Constitution: The Sin of Obscenity*, 63 COLUM. L. REV. 391 (1963).

He suggests that there may be constitutional arguments against the use of the criminal sanction (or any other legal sanction) in fields like sexual conduct and obscenity except on a very narrow basis to deal with some valid secular concern. Of course, what constitutes a valid secular concern is not always easy to say, as we shall observe in the section immediately following this one. But the fact that a limiting criterion is not self-executing does not deprive it of utility. If a legislator can think of no better reason to proscribe conduct than that he (or his constituency) abhors it, he had better think twice about doing it.

"HARM TO OTHERS"

For the past hundred years, since the appearance of Mill's great essay *On Liberty*, the terms of the debate on law and morals have been set, almost immovably, by his declaration that "the only purpose for which power can be rightfully exercised over any member of a civilized community, against his will, is to prevent harm to others." This is the assertion that Sir James Fitzjames Stephen challenged, almost as soon as it was made, in *Liberty, Equality, Fraternity*. This is the ground on which Lord Devlin and Professor Hart have recently contended. There is, perhaps, not much further to be said about it. Nonetheless, we must ask how it fits into the search for limiting criteria.

To begin with, it has to be conceded that Mill's formula solves very little. Later in his essay Mill extends his concept of "harm to others" to include "risk of damage" to the interests of others, and it is usually possible to make a more or less plausible argument that any given form of conduct involves that risk in some way. The question is not one of whether or not there will be harm done; it is one of the remoteness and probability of the harm. Some things are more harmful than others. Homicide is more harmful than muttering voodoo incantations; rape is more harmful than reading dirty books. And in a world of limited resources, we need to draw discriminations about the gravity and remoteness of harms. Seen in this light, "harm to others" is a prudential criterion rather than a hard and fast distinction of principle.

"Harm to others" does not, of course, mean identifiable others. It has become fashionable to talk about "victimless crimes," meaning those in which there is no immediately identifiable victim to lodge a complaint. The absence of an identifiable victim can make enforcement difficult, and can encourage undesirable enforcement practices. But the prospect of these difficulties should not end the inquiry into the wisdom of any given use of the criminal sanction. Many offenses against the administration of government are "victimless crimes" in the sense that there is nobody to complain. Consensual transactions like bribery and espionage are admittedly difficult to detect because of the absence of an identifiable victim; yet they do not necessarily cause so little "harm to others" that we can forget about subjecting them to the criminal sanction.

The "harm to others" formula seems to me to have two uses that justify its inclusion in a list of limiting criteria for invocation of the criminal sanction. First, it is a way to make sure that a given form of conduct is not being subjected to the criminal sanction purely or even primarily because it is thought to be immoral. It forces an inquiry into precisely what bad effects are feared if the conduct in question is not suppressed by the criminal law. Second, it immediately brings into play a host of secular inquiries about the effects of subjecting the conduct in question to the criminal sanction. One cannot meaningfully deal with the question of "harm to others" without weighing benefits against detriments. In that sense, it is a kind of threshold question, important not so much in itself as in focusing attention on further considerations relevant to the ultimate decision. It is for these two instrumental reasons rather than for either its intrinsic rightness or its ease of application that it deserves inclusion.

GOALS OF PUNISHMENT

In Chapter Three and Chapter Four, we evaluated the utilitarian claims for punishment as they seem to apply to criminal conduct in general. But we have not yet related these claims to limiting criteria for the definition of specific offenses—a task with greater practical significance. What can we discern about the utilitarian modes of prevention—deterrence, intimidation, in-capacitation, and rehabilitation—that can help us decide what kinds of conduct to treat as criminal?

To begin with, there is the obvious point that unless at least *one* utilitarian mode of prevention is likely to be served by em-ploying the criminal sanction against a particular form of con-duct, we had better forget about it. Sneezing in church is a rela-tively uncontroversial example.

Intimidation is a potentially useful criterion but one that will require much more precise knowledge about the careers of crimi-nal offenders than we now possess. We do know something about the negative side of intimidation: there are repetitive and com-pulsive forms of criminal behavior, such as bad-check writing and prostitution, whose recurrence is not effectively inhibited by past punishment. We do not, however, have useful data on the affirmative side of intimidation. Are there offenses whose repetition can be shown to be inhibited by past punishment? Because of the difficulty in establishing a causal relationship be-tween past punishment and future conduct, it is unlikely that even more refined studies than are now available will provide useful clues for predicting whether given offenses are less likely to be repeated if the offenders have been punished.

Rehabilitation, to the extent that it means anything more than intimidation, is an attractive but dangerous basis for defining conduct as criminal. It is attractive because it plays down the negativism of punishment: we will reduce antisocial behavior by curing people of the bad traits that lead them to behave anti-socially. It is dangerous because it is so much easier to make the claim than to deliver on it. The illness analogy is a beguiling but misleading one. It is only in a loosely metaphorical sense that phenomena like alcoholism, narcotics addiction, and sexual de-viation can be termed "diseases." Yet there is a tendency to use the metaphor as though it were literally true and to follow it with the bold step of positing a duty to submit to being cured, the breach of which is then viewed as an adequate basis for invoking the criminal sanction. Other objections aside, this approach is deficient because of the unsatisfactory cure mechanisms available. If temporary detoxification represented a cure for alcoholism or narcotics addiction, there would be much to be said for requiring people to submit to detoxification and backing up the requirement with the threat of criminal prosecution, just as we do for tuberculosis or for vaccination against small pox. But when the "illness" turns out to be a part of the individual's total life situation and the "cure" requires drastic changes in that situation, the claim that rehabilitation is an adequate trigger for invocation of the criminal sanction quickly dissolves. One should be exceedingly wary of any proposal to make conduct criminal that is not now criminal, or of any justification for continuing to treat conduct as criminal that is based primarily on a rehabilitative claim.

Incapacitation is a relevant claim only if it can be shown that a high proportion of people who engage in a particular form of conduct are likely to go on doing so unless restrained. Very few murderers kill again; that incapacitative claim is weak. Higher proportions of burglars and armed robbers tend to repeat their offenses; the incapacitative claim is correspondingly stronger.

Deterrence, as we have seen, is the only justification that presents a generalized claim for recognition in terms of kinds of offenses (as opposed to kinds of offenders). But it evidently varies greatly in force. It is probably strongest in the case of conduct where the chance of being caught is high, where the actor is likely to weigh the risk, or where criminal conviction is especially feared although the risk is low. In other words, high-risk deliberate crimes and crimes committed by the law-abiding are the kinds of conduct most likely to be deterred by the criminal sanction.

It follows that a utilitarian case for defining conduct as criminal can best be made in situations where both deterrence and incapacitation are effective: where people are relatively likely to be deflected by the possibility of being caught *and* where punishment is likely to prevent the commission of further crimes. There are many situations in which the two are not correlated and, as we shall see, very few in which they are.

CHAPTER FIFTEEN

The Search for Limits: Profit and Loss

REMOTENESS AND TRIVIALITY

The conduct proscribed by any criminal code can be ranked in a hierarchy of remoteness from the ultimate harm that the law seeks to prevent. We prohibit the sale of liquor to an intoxicated person to lessen the likelihood that he will drive while drunk (an offense), crash into another car (an offense), injure an occupant of the other car (an offense), or cause the death of someone in the other car (an offense). There we have a spectrum of remoteness ranging from the illegal sale of liquor to manslaughter. Similarly, we make it an offense to possess tools specially adapted for burglary so that we may reduce the incidence of burglary (an offense), and thereby reduce the incidence of further offenses, such as larceny, robbery, rape, and even murder, that can ensue from burglary. Mayhem or murder might not be intended by most burglars, but they are nonetheless possible results of the confrontation between burglar and victim.

One of the most delicate problems in framing criminal proscriptions is to locate the point farthest removed from the ultimate harm apprehended at which meaningful preventive intervention can take place. If dangerous conduct can be deterred and dangerous persons identified well short of the point at which the danger becomes acute, so much the better. Or so it seems. Actually, increasing the radius of the criminal law in the interest of early intervention is a very risky business. The first question in every case is, or should be: how high is the probability that the preparatory conduct, if not inhibited by the threat of criminal punishment, will result in an ultimate harm of the sort that the law should try to prevent? A related consideration is whether the preparatory conduct is itself socially useful, or at least neutral, so that its proscription or curtailment might unduly inhibit people from doing what they should otherwise be free to do. To put the issue in terms that are familiar in the law, is the risk substantial and is it justifiable? We are well accustomed to seeing courts apply these criteria after the fact to determine whether a questioned instance of conduct was "reckless" or "negligent," so as to expose the actor to civil or criminal liability. There has not been an equivalent perception that the same calculus, applied before the fact, should be useful to the legislator in gauging when it is prudent to subject preparatory modes of conduct to the criminal sanction. Yet the need for good judgment is far greater in the legislative case than in the judicial.

Still another consideration relates to the problem of enforcement. By and large, the further removed the conduct in question is from the ultimate harm apprehended, the more difficult it is going to be to detect the occurrence of the conduct and to apprehend people who engage in it. Considerations of maximizing personal freedom and of minimizing the strain on law enforcement combine, then, to suggest considerable caution in the progression toward the remote end of the spectrum.

An example that is amusing because it is so extreme is a recent action of the New York City Council. At the urgent request of the Fire Commissioner, the Council voted to make it a criminal offense, punishable by a hundred-dollar fine, a thirty-day jail term or both, to smoke in bed in a hotel, motel, or other place of public abode. A subsidiary provision required that a notice to that effect be displayed by the proprietor of every place covered by the ban. Now, nobody doubts that a great many serious and sometimes fatal accidents are caused by people's smoking in bed and that it would be a far better thing if people did not smoke in bed. But consider the impossibility of enforcing such a prohibition without the most detailed kind of surveillance. Consider the invasions of privacy that such surveillance would entail. And, enforcement problems aside, consider the effect of announcing

that such commonly engaged in conduct has now become criminal. One wonders what was accomplished by the criminal prohibition that would not equally well be accomplished by requiring
hotels to display in each room a notice warning about the danger.
Alternatively, the solution might have been to make it criminal
to cause a fire by smoking in bed, regardless of the amount of
harm done. That kind of prohibition would at least have been
enforceable, whether or not it was enforced. As it is, given the
well-known relationship between intoxication and fires resulting
from smoking in bed, I suppose travelers should be grateful that
the City Council did not go one step further and make it a crime
to go to bed drunk in a New York hotel.

The idea of a criminal conviction no longer inspires the awe
that it once did, because of the tendency of legislative bodies
(like the New York City Council in this example) to prescribe
criminal penalties simply as a means of expressing their disap-
proval of conduct. This tendency results in two kinds of triviality: triviality of object and triviality of intention. By triviality
of object I mean the selection of behavior for which the regular
imposition of criminal punishment is disproportionate. By triviality of intention I mean an attitude of indifference or cynicism
on the part of legislators toward the actual enforcement of the
proscriptions they vote for. Both forms of triviality should be
carefully avoided. A rational legislator should not vote to subject previously legal conduct to criminal proscription unless he
is prepared to say, first, that the conduct being proscribed is so
threatening to important social interests that he is willing to see
people who engage in it subjected to criminal punishment and,
second, that he expects law enforcement to devote adequate
resources to detecting, apprehending, and convicting violators.
The two will tend in most cases to be complementary.

This principle is based largely on the idea of proportionality
in the relationship between conduct and punishment. If we were
free of that constraint, in practice as well as in theory, there
would be no reason for avoiding triviality. Indeed, there would
be no means of measuring it. Whenever we are unwilling to
impose punishment sufficiently severe to have a fair chance of
significantly reducing the incidence of the behavior in question,

we ought to take that reluctance as a warning and refrain from treating the behavior as criminal.

How severe is severe enough (or how lenient is too lenient) is an empirical question that is complicated by the difficulty of assessing how much deterrent efficacy resides in the mere fact of conviction of a criminal offense. That question in turn cannot be answered in a vacuum. It depends on how debased the currency has become. The more indiscriminate we are in treating conduct as criminal, the less stigma resides in the mere fact that a man has been convicted of something called a crime. We have fallen so far from the path of wisdom in this respect that it now takes considerable imagination to visualize how potent the mere fact of being labeled as criminal might become. But if we turn from conviction to punishment, we have available the crude benchmark of deprivation of liberty that inheres in an actual or potential sentence of imprisonment. If we are prepared to make that threat and to enforce it in enough cases to make the threat credible, then we have crossed the boundary of triviality. That a form of conduct can be seen as worthy of being punished to this extent is far from being a sufficient condition for treating it as criminal, but it should plainly be a necessary one.

Observance of this condition requires that we forgo primary reliance on such devices as monetary fines. If the most that we are prepared to exact in the great majority of occurrences of a particular form of reprehended conduct is the payment of money into the public treasury, we should not impose on ourselves the manifold burdens of invoking the criminal sanction. Whether the subject happens to be traffic offenses, or hunting out of season, or breaches of housing codes, or any one of the thousands of minor regulatory or sumptuary offenses with which the criminal sanction and its processes are presently encumbered, we ought to purge from the criminal calendar all offenses that we do not take seriously enough to punish by real criminal sanctions.[1]

There is readily available a conceptual tool for accomplishing this necessary purge. It is the category of a publicly instituted civil action for the recovery of a monetary penalty, which has been advocated by many legal scholars and which is beginning

---

[1] See above, pp. 130–31.

to be seriously studied by legislative bodies. Terms such as "civil offense," "infraction," and "violation" have been variously proposed for this category. Whatever the term, there are two criteria such a creation should meet. The first is well expressed by the Model Penal Code's prescription that "a violation does not constitute a crime and conviction of a violation shall not give rise to any disability or legal disadvantage based on conviction of a criminal offense.[2] The other, if scrupulously observed, might in time make the first unnecessary. It is that the machinery of the criminal process should be used as little as possible to enforce these laws. At the level of detection this stricture cannot be universally applied, because it is the general-purpose police force that will have to decide initially whether conduct is such that it should be processed criminally or civilly. Of course, if enforcement happens to be in the hands of a special-purpose police force, as it is in such regulatory areas as the control of food and drugs or the maintenance of housing standards, the separation is more easily accomplished. Even there, however, a decision will have to be made at some point about how conduct that carries both civil and criminal penalties should be treated. This point is typically reached in a public law office, which today may or may not be an office exclusively devoted to criminal prosecution. It is at this point that the separation should be clearly made, so that everything that follows can be kept separate. Once the decision to charge has been made by the appropriate legal officer, the forms and labels of the criminal process should be reserved for those cases in which the intention is to seek a criminal conviction. Otherwise, the pieces of paper that are filed should not be criminal pieces of paper: the defendant should be charged in a complaint, not an indictment; he should answer, not plead guilty or not guilty. The trial should not be held in a criminal court; even though the judge may be a judge before whom both criminal and civil cases are tried, this case should be on the civil calendar. The criminal burden of proof and the criminal doctrines of culpability should not be applied (which should be a substantial relief to the public prosecutor). At every stage of the process the strategy should be to minimize the possibility that what is being

2 MODEL PENAL CODE §1.04(5) (Proposed Official Draft, 1961).

done can in any way be confused with the operation of the criminal sanction.

If this prescription were rigorously and unsparingly applied, quite without regard to the restraints imposed by any other limiting criterion, the burden on the criminal process in this country would, on a conservative estimate, be cut in half. And aside from the beneficial economic effects of doing that, we would have achieved an immense gain in the clarity of purpose with which we employ the criminal sanction itself. I do not mean to suggest that every criminal conviction should result in a sentence of imprisonment. On the contrary, we need within the confines of the criminal sanction to make far greater use than we do of alternatives to imprisonment, particularly supervised release on probation. It may be enough to classify probation as a distinctively criminal sanction in that it involves a conditional loss of liberty. If the conditions of probation are violated, then the probationary status is revoked and imprisonment imposed instead. Probation aside, there will be a certain proportion of criminal convictions, particularly in cases involving illegal acquisitive conduct, where a monetary exaction will seem to be the most appropriate sanction. But this should always be a retrospective decision by the trial judge, looking back on what has been revealed about the defendant and his offense. From the prospective view of the prosecutor, particularly when the same conduct may offer the alternatives of criminal and civil treatment, the criminal process should be initiated only if there seems to be a substantial justification (with which, of course, the judge may ultimately disagree) for imposing a sentence of imprisonment.

I have been arguing that a wise legislature trying to distinguish between conduct that can be seen as trivial and conduct that cannot be so regarded will set the boundary line where imprisonment or the threat of it begins to seem clearly justifiable. Likewise, the judgment of people in law enforcement should be sensitive to this boundary. A far more difficult issue is presented when one considers whether the boundary should be more restricting. I have already mentioned the perplexities that attend our use of short-term imprisonment. It is far from clear that very short jail terms serve any of the goals of punishment, even deterrence, which is the only goal that it might plausibly serve. And it is all too clear that short-term imprisonment imposes severe social costs that we have not adequately confronted. Nonetheless, it would be dogmatic to assert that our reluctance to impose anything more than a short term of imprisonment is itself a reason for refusing to invoke the criminal sanction. However, it may consistently be regarded as a cautionary signal. If we are unwilling to embark seriously upon an enforcement program calling for a maximum penalty of, say, more than three months' imprisonment (the judicially developed dividing line for "petty offenses" under the Constitution), then we should consider seriously the possibility of not using the criminal sanction at all. Again, this does not mean that we must be prepared to impose a sentence of more than three months' imprisonment in all or even most cases but simply that we ought to be prepared to see that much used as the maximum in the worst cases of the conduct at issue.

A final point about the avoidance of triviality involves consideration of who is likely to be trivial. When we speak of the legislature we mean, generically, all those bodies that have the competence to declare that certain kinds of conduct shall be treated as criminal. In common parlance, this means the United States Congress and the legislatures of the several states. But it by no means exhausts the category of what might be called criminogenic governmental bodies. Two other kinds of governmental authorities have the power to create crimes: local governments (cities, counties, etc.) and administrative agencies. Local governments either are given that power by express legislative delegation or exercise it on the assumption that the power to define crimes inheres in "home rule." Generally speaking, this power is limited to employing relatively mild criminal penalties for violations of local ordinances. These ordinances must not be in conflict with state law, and there is a complicated and quite unsatisfactory body of legal doctrine that purports to regulate the "preemption" of local by state law. The issue is often sharply political, as it has been in California owing to efforts by the City of Los Angeles to regulate morals offenses more stringently than the state legislature has been willing to authorize on a statewide basis.

The power of administrative agencies to create crimes derives from specific legislative delegation. Typically, what happens is that an administrative agency is given the power to make rules and regulations within the area of its regulatory concern, and the legislature provides that all or certain kinds (i.e., repeated or "willful") of breaches of these rules and regulations may be prosecuted as criminal offenses. Since the legislative body exercises no routine review over the regulations adopted by the administrative agency, this means that as a practical matter the agency is defining what conduct is to be treated as criminal.

Considerable danger of triviality attaches to the criminogenic activities of both local governments and administrative agencies. Both tend to be myopic in their concerns; both legislate in the interstices of what has been done by the first-line legislative bodies. We have no studies of the nature or the volume of criminal business generated by these second-line legislative bodies. The administrative agencies probably generate very little; local governments clearly generate a great deal. Our routinely kept police, prosecutorial, and judicial statistics do not distinguish among sources of criminal proscription, and this omission makes study of the problem quite arduous. It seems plausible, however, that a disproportionate number of the offenses that these second-line legislatures, especially the local governments, feed into the criminal process are trivial. If this hypothesis turned out to be correct, part of a program for de-trivializing the criminal sanction would be to place some severe constraints on this proliferating criminogenic authority, if not to eliminate it altogether.

CRIME TARIFFS

There is an important economic dimension to the criminal sanction that can be illustrated by invoking the analogy of a protective tariff. The dictionary defines a tariff as "a schedule, system, or scheme of duties imposed by a government on goods imported or exported." If a tariff is imposed "for the artificial fostering of home industries," it is what we call a protective tariff.

Economists tell us that protective tariffs are uneconomic because they get in the way of the optimal allocation of resources that a free market is supposed to bring about. Protective tariffs have a bad name, but they continue to flourish, mainly because claims advanced in their behalf have considerable appeal to lawmakers. Some say that the appeal is essentially one of money and votes; the high-minded (or the committed) say that it is the health of the internal economy or, more fashionably these days, the demands of national defense. Whatever the basis really is, the protection of textiles, bicycles, watches, cheese, or what-have-you is always justified by the claim that it is desirable public policy to protect the commodity in question from the rigors of competition. Competition is good, but cheese is better, especially if it comes from Wisconsin.

Cheese is better, perhaps so. But are narcotics better? Is gambling better? Are abortions performed by terrified amateurs better? We do not ordinarily think of these blights as commodities protected by a tariff, but it is easy to demonstrate that they are just that. The tariff in question is the criminal law or, more precisely, the particular criminal statutes that make it illegal to do such things as traffic in narcotics, run a gambling enterprise, or perform abortions on pregnant women who don't want to have children. Of course, no one designed criminal enactments such as these to operate as a tariff. The object is not to enhance the profits of entrepreneurs in these particular lines of commerce by protecting them from competition. In fact, we rarely think of these activities as involving commerce because our emotionalism about crime gets in the way of our seeing that they are. We treat conduct as criminal and back the declaration up by threatening and, occasionally, inflicting punishment in order to prevent or at least reduce their incidence. That is far from providing a protective tariff; just the opposite, or so we think. But there is a common feature of some oddly disparate kinds of conduct covered by our criminal law that produces quite a different effect from that intended. It is very simply that the conduct in question, whatever else it may be and however heinous we may think it is, is traffic in a line of commerce.

Commerce involves transactions between willing buyers and willing sellers, each of whom gets what he wants from the deal. By making conduct that answers to this description criminal, what we are in effect doing is limiting the supply of the commodity in question by increasing the risk to the seller, thereby driving up the price of what he sells. It may be suggested that driving up the price is just what we want to do: make it so expensive to buy narcotics, for example, that people will stop buying them. As we know from current experience, it doesn't work that way. People go on buying narcotics even if they have to steal money to pay the price. Economic theory explains this phenomenon by introducing the concept of elasticity of demand. It is only when the demand is quite elastic that increases in price will reduce the amount demanded. People who are willing to pay two thousand dollars for a car will not ordinarily want the same car if its price is suddenly doubled. But the demand is inelastic when the commodity is something that people want so badly that they don't think much about price: something like salt, or medicine, or narcotics. And if the sale of the commodity in question happens to be illegal, the crime tariff goes into operation. Regardless of what we think we are trying to do, when we make it illegal to traffic in commodities for which there is an inelastic demand, the effect is to secure a kind of monopoly profit to the entrepreneur who is willing to break the law. In effect, we say to him: "We will set up a barrier to entry into this line of commerce by making it illegal and, therefore, risky; if you are willing to take the risk, you will be sheltered from the competition of those who are unwilling to do so. Of course, if we catch you, you may possibly (although not necessarily) be put out of business; but meanwhile you are free to gather the fruits that grow in the hothouse atmosphere we are providing for you."

Prohibition was a classic example of the operation of the crime tariff. Traffic in liquor became the monopoly of the lawbreakers, who proceeded to earn enormous monopoly profits and, behind the protective wall of the crime tariff on liquor, to build criminal organizations that could rapidly take advantage of any other crime tariffs with which we were willing to oblige them. With the disappearance of the crime tariff on liquor, a similarly profitable traffic in narcotics developed. This tariff is very high; we make it so hard on narcotics offenders that only the boldest venture into the field. It is far from clear that we have appreciably reduced the total supply of narcotics coming into the country.

What we have done is to channel the business into fewer and fewer hands (if the Narcotics Bureau and the F.B.I. are to be believed) and to drive the price of the commodity to new heights.

Opinions vary on what the effects would be if all controls on the sale of narcotics were removed overnight (a step, let it be said, that today lies outside the realm of the politically possible). One highly placed policeman of my acquaintance asserts that the addiction rate would show an immediate increase. A psychiatrist retorts that if narcotics become easily procurable, addiction will lose much of its allure. Who is to say which of them is right? By contrast, the economic effect of such a change is clearly predictable, if economics has anything to teach us at all. With the disappearance of controls the price of narcotics would plummet, and the financial ruin of the present illegal suppliers would quickly follow.

The case of narcotics is not unique. Consider, for example, the problem of abortions. By and large, it is illegal to perform an abortion in this country unless continuation of the pregnancy would be fatal to the mother. Comparatively few abortions are openly performed by reputable doctors in reputable hospitals on that ground or on the ground that the woman's mental health will be gravely impaired if she is forced to bear and raise a child. A much larger number of abortions—estimates range as high as one million per year—are performed clandestinely, with the knowledge that if they come to the attention of the police, arrest, conviction, and imprisonment will very likely follow. Not many do come to the attention of the police, of course. It is doubtful whether the arrest rate is as high as one per thousand abortions performed. Aside from sporadic police activity, the main threat to the abortionist is that something will go wrong and the patient (or her survivor) will complain to the authorities. But the threat is there; and it causes the crime tariff to operate. The case is plainly one of a highly inelastic demand. Women (and their husbands and lovers) who want an abortion do not care what the market price is; if they can possibly raise the money, they want the commodity regardless of price. Here the anticompetitive effect of the crime tariff operates not only on price but also on service. Because women cannot generally get abortions from those who are in the best position to do a satisfactory job—the members of the medical profession—they are driven to accept a product of inferior grade and quality from the hole-in-corner abortionist. They buy injury and even death from sellers who would be driven out of the market overnight if they did not have the protection of the crime tariff.

So far, we have treated the crime tariff from the buyer's standpoint. It can also be analyzed for its economic effect on the seller. Deterrence theory in one aspect is essentially economic in nature, although it has rarely been so described. In its Benthamite aspect, it views human conduct as involving the same kind of rational pursuit of satisfactions implicit in the concept of economic man. In that view, the risk of punishment is an offsetting factor that the intending criminal must weigh against the gain he hopes to realize from his criminal conduct. By reducing the potential gain, we hope and expect to reduce the incentive to engage in criminal activity. Deterrence works best, however, if the potential gain remains the same when the criminal is successful; the risk of loss then diminishes the attraction of the gain, which is a constant. We do not make bank robbery more attractive by punishing the bank robbers whom we manage to catch. The potential gain is unaffected by the offsetting risk of punishment. If murdering one's rich aunt in order to inherit a million dollars from her were legal, we would not increase the potential gain by making it illegal. The stake would still be the same million dollars. Or, to take a more realistic example, if a certain kind of sophisticated stock swindle happens to be legal, making it illegal will not increase the potential gain; the new risk of punishment will make the same old gain seem less attractive than it used to be. Swindlers will be, in a word, deterred.

But this assumption of a constant in potential gain, on which the successful operation of deterrence depends, does not hold for the category of "transactions" we have been examining. Because we are dealing with voluntary commerce in a commodity whose buyers are willing to submit to price increases, every increase in risk increases the potential gain to the seller. The harder we work to make the sale of abortions risky, the higher we drive the price that makes the risk worthwhile. The calculus of pleasure and

pain, to put it in Jeremy Bentham's terms, produces an equilib-
rium at a higher level of price. The theory of deterrence, however useful it may be in the ordinary run of crimes, breaks down.
In its place we get a crime tariff, which operates like any other
protective tariff.

Should we have crime tariffs? The question is not one that we
are likely to answer by focusing on economic factors alone. This
is simply one of several undesirable side effects that must be
taken into account in deciding when it is wise to use the criminal
sanction. Few are swayed by economic considerations alone. Just
as debates about the tariff on cheese are unlikely to be resolved
by economic arguments about the desirability of free competition
in cheese, so is it improbable that any demonstration, however
persuasive, that abortions cost more than they need to will carry
the day for free competition in abortion.

The concept is, however, a useful one in analyzing existing
uses of the criminal sanction and in thinking about proposed
new ones. The problem is by no means academic, given the pressure for extending measures of control like those we have for
narcotics to the newer "dangerous drugs." The rational lawmaker should hesitate before creating new crime tariffs. He
should require a persuasive demonstration that it will not produce the undesirable effects just described. Unfortunately, since
that kind of demonstration is so difficult to make, it is easy to
understand why it is rarely attempted.

TENSIONS BETWEEN POLICE AND PUBLIC

It is disturbing to observe the distrust bordering on hatred
with which the police are viewed by many segments of American
society. The most conspicuous such segment today is made up of
urban ghetto dwellers. Their hatred of the police is but a minor
symptom of a dangerous and deplorable alienation from society.
The divisions that threaten to tear our society apart will hardly
be healed by reform of the criminal law. But any program of
amelioration must surely attend to as obvious a source of trouble
as this one.

The urban poor are only the most notable of the groups who

see the police as the enemy. The same feelings of hostility, although on perhaps a less intense and less pervasive level, exist among other groups who fail in one way or another to conform with the whole range of values expressed by existing criminal law and, beyond that, with those who place a high value on freedom and privacy, whether for themselves or for others. These groups include intellectuals, bohemians, and to an increasing extent, the young. It is hard to know whether phenomena like the drug-taking fad are more a cause or an effect of this anti-authority mood.

A prominent cause of this prevalent hostility appears to be that the police (and hence the law, of which the police are the most immediate representative) are seen to be more intrusive than protective. The aggressively interventionist character of much of our criminal law thrusts the police into the role of snoopers and harassers. There is simply no way for the police to provide so much as a semblance of enforcement of laws against prostitution, sexual deviance, gambling, narcotics, and the like without widespread and visible intrusion into what people regard as their private lives. Ideally, the police should be seen as the people who keep the law of the jungle from taking over. Their predominant role should be to enforce, by prevention of offenses and detection of offenders, those proscriptions that guarantee the first requisite of social living: that people be reasonably secure in their persons and possessions against the grosser forms of depredation. If this were indeed their perceived role, it is doubtful that the slogan "support your local police" could ever have achieved its present divisive political significance. It is only when the police are seen, as they are in our society, as the guardians of conventional morality and ideological purity that such a slogan could become as emotive and divisive as that one has.

There is more at issue than "public relations." The confrontation between police and citizen is bound to be abrasive in a free society. The enforcement of criminal law is inherently coercive. Beyond that, there are special exacerbations that result from the clash of citizens, not merely with authority, but with authoritarian representatives of authority. Police work attracts people with a strong authoritarian bent, as we know from numerous sociological and psychological studies. This fact is neither sinister nor surprising. Nor does it mean that the police are "fascist beasts." But it does mean that men in police work are likely to be repressive rather than permissive, intolerant rather than tolerant, conforming rather than nonconforming. Contact with them when one appears to be a wrongdoer will be at least uncomfortable and anxiety-provoking. It may quickly become coercive and demeaning. The police, after all, are uniquely empowered to apply coercive physical restraint. The encounter is an unequal one that accordingly erodes one's sense of self-sufficiency and self-respect. Who does not, to mention the mildest of examples, become ingratiating and just a bit servile when the question of a speeding ticket is at issue? But if that kind of encounter—especially in more serious situations—becomes commonplace, as it may if one is poor, or black, or bearded, it produces either a rebel or a craven or both.

It is, of course, in the field of the victimless crime that aggressive, intrusive, and repeated police contacts are most apparent. It is an interesting paradox that the police are least visible when they are doing their most important work and most visible when they are doing their least important. If it is in fact desirable to minimize the occasions for police intervention, at least one knows where to begin looking. The most obvious clue is afforded by unsavory detection practices.

There are three generic types of police investigatory conduct that are so at odds with values of privacy and human dignity that we should resort to them only under the most exigent circumstances. They are physical intrusion, electronic surveillance, and the use of decoys. Although there arguably are circumstances under which each of the three can justifiably be employed, it is safe to say that any use of the criminal sanction that requires consistent use to be made of any of them should be suspect.

Physical intrusion can run the gamut from persistent stopping and questioning of people on the street to breaking into a man's dwelling. Prostitution and narcotics offenses are examples of crimes in which this mode of enforcement predominates. They share with each other, and with other offenses as well, the characteristic that it takes intrusive tactics by the police to discover whether a crime has been or is being committed. Quite without regard to the niceties of the constitutional law of search and seizure, there is the greatest difference between, on the one hand, breaking into a man's house to arrest him when you have probable cause to believe that he has already committed a crime (like robbery or burglary) and your interest is in arresting him, and, on the other, doing so when you have probable cause to believe that he is in the process of committing a crime there (like possession of narcotics) and your interest is in securing evidence that a crime is being committed. The second is much more of a bootstrap operation than the first. It is also much likelier to occur than the first, and the chances of making a mistake are far greater. No one doubts that there are times when the privacy of the home must be invaded for law enforcement purposes. There is no right of sanctuary. But serious questions about the use of the criminal sanction are raised when invasion of privacy is the routine price to be paid for vigorous enforcement.

A physical intrusion by the police is abrasive. An unnoticed intrusion, accomplished through electronic surveillance, is far more sinister. In the case of physical intrusion, you know when you have been injured. In the case of electronic surveillance you do not, and one inevitable by-product of that uncertainty, if the practice is thought to be generalized, is that people will feel constrained in their words and actions in the very place where they should feel most free. This is a very high price to pay for law enforcement; and one must ask what law enforcement uses are thereby advanced. It seems significant that there is no claim whatever that these techniques are of any use in the detection of the major and serious crimes against the person and property that represent the core uses of the criminal sanction. (The example of kidnapping, which used to figure conspicuously in arguments about wiretapping, now seems to have been abandoned, as it should be, since the monitoring of phone calls to the person from whom ransom was being sought could of course be legitimately accomplished with his consent.) Once again, the claim that devices of this sort are necessary in the detection of any given category of crime should produce the most careful inquiry into the importance of that particular use of the criminal sanction.

The use of decoys in police work raises two related problems. One is that people will be tempted into criminal conduct that they would otherwise be less likely to engage in: the problem of entrapment. The other is the degrading effect that putting oneself in the position of a shopper for illegal drugs or sex is bound to have on law enforcement officers. Once again, there is a substantial difference betwen occasionally using this kind of technique, as in the detection of espionage and bribery, and making it a way of life, as in the case of drug and sex offenses. Frequent resort to chicanery hardly conduces to respect for law. It would take a convincing demonstration that the object was especially important for law enforcement to rise above the stigma of these tactics. That demonstration has not been forthcoming, nor could it well be. Typically the use of unsavory detection practices has attended the suppression of conduct that, for other reasons as well as this, ranks low on any rational priority list for invocation of the criminal sanction.

SPORADIC ENFORCEMENT

It is of course impossible for every criminal event to become known to the police or for the identity of the actor in every known criminal event to be ascertained, or for every known criminal to be apprehended. And it is only theoretically possible for every known criminal to be prosecuted and convicted for his crimes. Full enforcement in any such absolute sense as this is a chimera. By the same token, objections to the idea of full enforcement, based on its literal impossibility, are a red herring. But, even if actual performance is bound to fall short of the ideal, there are compelling reasons why the ideal is one to which attention should be paid in determining the behavior content of the criminal law.

Paying attention to the ideal might mean taking care to avoid passing laws that seem very difficult to enforce and trying to avoid retaining laws that are being only sporadically enforced. Continued sporadic enforcement of a law is an indication that the community's sense of security is not being seriously threatened by the conduct in question; rates of enforcement therefore provide an index of relative priority among forms of antisocial conduct. Making and retaining criminal laws that can be only sporadically enforced not only is something of an exercise in futility but also can result in actual harm. It approaches futility because the knowledge that a given criminal proscription will be enforced in only a small proportion of the cases to which it applies is bound to affect the deterrent efficacy of the proscription. Among the harmful consequences, four are especially noteworthy. First, respect for law generally is likely to suffer if it is widely known that certain kinds of conduct, although nominally criminal, can be practiced with relative impunity. Second, enforcement officers aware that the enforcement rate for a particular offense is undesirably low may be tempted to use unsavory methods to raise the rate. Third, lack of full enforcement necessarily involves discretion in the choice of targets; this discretion is unlikely to be exercised in any but an arbitrary kind of way. Finally, this arbitrariness is bound to contribute to the unfortunate sense of alienation on the part of those who see themselves as its victims.

Each of these points requires some elaboration. First, however, we need to stop and consider what we mean by relatively full enforcement. Let us err on the side of conservatism. If more than one out of a hundred happenings that fit the description of a given form of criminal conduct come to the attention of the police and if more than one out of a thousand perpetrators of such acts are identified and introduced into the criminal process, I am willing to say that we have a case of relatively full enforcement. Of course, there are many kinds of criminal conduct that incur a higher rate of enforcement than these minimal figures represent. And, of course, full enforcement is not the only criterion that we need to take into account. For example, if the community's sense of security is heavily threatened by a form of conduct that cannot be subjected to a high degree of enforcement, there may be adequate reason for incurring the disadvantages that low enforcement rates bring. That possibility may be seen more clearly as we consider in detail just what the disadvantages of low enforcement are.

The most obvious disadvantage is its effect on deterrence. If, as we have seen, the strongest reason for proscribing conduct and on occasion punishing it is that in a variety of crude and subtle ways this may keep people from engaging in the proscribed conduct, then it surely follows that anything which substantially lessens that effect counts heavily against employing the threat. Many considerations may count against the threat, but none is more obvious than the weakness of the threat itself. The disastrous experience with Prohibition is only one of the many examples that might be cited. Prohibition failed for a number of reasons, but prime among them was the brute fact that people were able to violate the laws that forbade transporting, selling, and possessing intoxicating beverages with virtual impunity. Laws against gambling, against various forms of consensual sexual conduct, and (perhaps more arguably) against drug addiction exhibits something of the same shortcoming. An interesting side effect of this shortcoming is that, as the lack of deterrent efficacy becomes apparent, penalties are increased in the hope that they will make up in severity what they lack in certainty. As a consequence, the moral embarrassment inherent in the instrumental use of one person's suffering to affect the conduct of others is heightened by the perception that the punishment is not merely instrumental but also disproportionate. This side effect suggests the existence of an important practical clue to the existence of a full enforcement problem: sequential increases in the punishment prescribed for a given offense that cannot be explained by changes in public attitudes toward that offense. The successive increases in the penalties for trafficking in narcotics may be viewed as a fever chart of the deterrent inefficacy of that group of laws.

Respect for law is a somewhat vague concept at best, and the effect of deterrent inefficacy upon it cannot easily be estimated. There are at least two separable notions involved in the appraisal. First is the literal idea that because people recognize that the law is impotent to do A, they will be led to question its capacity to do B, C, and D. There might be something to this idea in a relatively simple and primitive society in which the authority of the law rested upon belief in its magical properties. Of course, to the extent that its authority rests upon that kind of belief in our society (and it may be more than a trivial consideration) the point may hold some force for us. On the whole, however, it seems somewhat implausible that the discovery of the law's impotence to control gambling is likely to have much effect on the deterrent efficacy of the criminal law prohibiting, say, bank robbery. More likely, this kind of diminution of respect for law in the literal sense affects attitudes toward proscriptions comparable to the one perceived as being relatively unenforced. If people realize that laws against gambling receive very low enforcement, their capacity to think analogically should lead them to see that the same will be true of laws against consensual sexual conduct and to act accordingly. A somewhat more sophisticated effect results, perhaps, when intending criminals recognize the strain on resource allocation that low enforcement proclaims, and are led to greater boldness in defying proscriptions that are relatively well enforced. This is the familiar "St. Patrick's Day effect," in which burglaries elsewhere in the city increase because of the concentration of the police in and around the parade area.

Finally, there is the impact of marginal enforcement upon the self-image of those subjected to it. Social deviance, however defined, is not limited to adopting illegal roles and engaging in illegal conduct. People will behave in mildly or grossly deviant ways and will group with others who are doing so, quite without regard to what the criminal law says, or to whether it says anything at all. One man's deviance is another man's pluralism. Yet there is a danger that this voluntary association of like-minded nonconformists may be turned into a deeply alienated and, on occasion, socially threatening subculture through the improvident use of the criminal sanction, especially when that use is arbitrary. Stigmatizing conduct and the people who engage in it as criminal imposes a powerful and often self-confirming identification, not simply from the standpoint of the rest of society but also, and very importantly, from the standpoint of the lawbreaker.

When a person's daily conduct, and therefore his entire life style, are labeled as criminal, he and his fellows are thrown together in a world against the world. Their potential as contributing members of society is diminished, whether or not their conduct itself disables them from performing useful social roles. There is some evidence that the narcotics addict can stay socially

integrated if the force of the criminal law does not thrust him
into a deviant subculture. The inhabitant of the homosexual
underworld might emerge from his cage if the threat of criminal
and para-criminal sanctions did not confirm his deviant identity.
There is also the problem of recruitment, about which we continue to know very little. How many people, especially young
people, are drawn into a deviant subculture in part because of its
illegality? When repetitive and compulsive conduct is the object
of the criminal sanction, the associated cost of "losing" people
from society is not one to be lightly dismissed.

ABUSE OF DISCRETION

It has been observed that if the criminal law were followed to
its strict letter the results would be intolerable, in part because
of the anarchic and archaic state of our substantive criminal law.
But even if our criminal proscriptions were framed with exqui-
site discrimination, it would still be necessary for the human beings who operate the criminal process to exercise judgment about
whether or not to arrest, release, prosecute, dismiss, or accept a
plea of guilty in a given case. The criminal law is neither a slot
machine nor a computer. But to admit the need for discretion is
not to make a virtue of it. And it is far from being a virtue in the
enforcement of the criminal sanction.

The basic trouble with discretion is simply that it is lawless,
in the literal sense of that term. If police or prosecutors find themselves free (or compelled) to pick and choose among known or
knowable instances of criminal conduct, they are making a judgment which in a society based on law should be made only by
those to whom the making of law is entrusted. For the rough approximation of community values that emerges from the legislative process there is substituted the personal and often idiosyn-
cratic values of the law enforcer. When victims of discriminatory
enforcement see what is happening, secondary effects subversive
of respect for law (like the effects discussed in the preceding section) are produced.

The worst abuses of discretion in enforcement occur in connection with those offenses that are just barely taken seriously,

like most consensual sex offenses. Here, especially in the case of fornication and adultery, enforcement is so sporadic as to be just one step short of complete cessation. And it is here that the greatest danger exists of using enforcement discretion in an abusive way: to pay off a score, to provide a basis for extortion, to stigmatize an otherwise deviant or unpopular figure.

When the proscription is taken seriously but resources are inadequate to provide anything like full enforcement, the discrimination becomes less flagrant but remains objectionable. Prostitution is a good example. The police take the line of least resistance, going after the more easily apprehended streetwalker and leaving her higher-status counterpart relatively undisturbed. When keeping high prostitution areas under surveillance, the police are likely to follow interracial couples, on the sound but obnoxious theory that theirs is more likely to be a commercial relationship.

The enforcement authorities, most often the public prosecutors, will sometimes mitigate the harsh effects of statutes that they believe to be overly broad. Social gambling is usually ignored, except on occasion when ulterior motives prompt a raid on a friendly poker game. But even this informal exemption is not uniformly applied. The lower-class counterpart to an evening of bridge at a tenth of a cent a point may be the back-alley crap game, which is far from being immune to arrests. Abortion provides another example of differential treatment. Reputable doctors performing illegal but "therapeutic" abortions in reputable hospitals are virtually immune from prosecution, although the availability of hospital records to prosecutorial inspection would appear to make this kind of illegal abortion uniquely easy to detect. Perhaps prosecutors are right to prefer bridge to craps and "therapeutic" to hole-in-the-corner abortions. But these are not choices that they should be free to make. It would not be so bad if this kind of differential enforcement were the harbinger of law reform. More often it is simply the substitute.

As we have previously seen,[3] there are well-established constitutional imperatives that restrict the scope of discretion delegable by legislatures to law enforcement authorities. These constitutional doctrines of void-for-vagueness and overbreadth serve to

[3] See above, pp. 91–96.

prevent only the most flagrant instances of abuse of discretion. We need to have these doctrines translated into prudential criteria of self-restraint on the legislative level. The criminal sanction requires a rifle rather than a blunderbuss; it takes legislative action as well as judicial scrutiny to meet that demand.

ASSEMBLY-LINE JUSTICE

One of the surest signs that the criminal sanction is being misapplied can be read in the endless procession of look-alike cases, especially through the lower criminal courts. Drunkenness and disorderly conduct are the major malefactors, accounting between them for almost half of all arrests. Vagrancy, gambling, and liquor law violations, are also conspicuous. In some major cities prostitution can be added to the list. These offenses are questionable under many of the criteria we have been discussing; but their particular vice in this respect is that they debase the process of dispensing justice. So great is the crush of cases and so little is the time available to deal with any given one that there is an almost total lack of attention to the situation of the individual defendant. The process is depersonalized and dehumanized. It offends against the basic precept that justice should not be rationed. For many people this assembly-line process is their only contact with the criminal law. It is hardly one that conduces to respect, either for the process or for the norms that the process seeks to enforce. The rationale of the criminal sanction demands that a judgment of conviction be both weighty and considered. With assembly-line crimes it is neither.

The rise of Due Process norms is making the assembly line harder to operate. A few determined defendants, enjoying the assistance of counsel, can bring the machine to a halt or, alternatively, force it to disgorge them. There are even today many courts in which a demand for a jury trial is likely to bring about a dismissal of charges, or at the least a negotiated plea that works to the defendant's advantage. This phenomenon is likely to become more prevalent as the numbers with which the process must deal continue to swell and as the opportunities for challenge to the process are enhanced. Much could be accomplished by eliminating a comparatively small number of relatively minor offenses. Until that is done, any additions to the list of criminal offenses should be rejected out of hand unless they are both serious enough and infrequent enough to give reasonable promise of not contributing to the assembly line.

COVERT FUNCTIONS

The function of the criminal sanction is to help prevent or reduce socially undesirable conduct through the detection, apprehension, prosecution, and punishment of offenders. This is the only function that its rationale permits and this is the only function with which its processes are adequately equipped to deal. However, a number of covert functions have made an appearance, in some cases coming close to monopolizing the resources devoted to enforcing particular criminal proscriptions.

One function that deviates least from the primary goal, but is nonetheless highly objectionable, is harassment. Police enforcement tactics are often aimed not at prosecution and conviction but at making life difficult for the object of their attentions so that he will either stop what he is doing or (more likely) go do it someplace else. This happens to a large extent in the enforcement of laws against gambling and prostitution in crowded metropolitan areas. The hallmark of this technique is the "raid," culminating in mass arrests followed by an almost total failure to prosecute. The technique may on occasion be quite effective in at least temporarily reducing the incidence of the conduct in question. But it is objectionable because it constitutes in effect punishment without determination of guilt.

Another covert function is exemplified by the use of vagrancy and disorderly conduct laws to provide the police with powers that they do not possess under the law of arrest. As we have seen, the police may arrest only on reasonable cause to believe that a specific crime has been committed by the person being arrested. Often the police will not have that basis for making an arrest but nonetheless will want to take someone into custody for some other purpose: to question him about a crime that he may have committed, to get information that may lead to the detection or apprehension of other possible criminals, to prevent his committing a crime, to get him off the streets, to persuade him to move on to another locality. Some of these purposes may be illegitimate under any view of proper police powers. Others may perhaps be purposes that the police should be given adequate power to effectuate. But it is wrong to use the substantive criminal law for this covert purpose. It is only the independently undesirable breadth and vagueness of these laws that permit them to be pressed into service to perform the covert function of supplementing the law of arrest.

Another, more benign but equally illegitimate, covert function is the use of the criminal sanction to perform needed social services that for one reason or another we are not prepared to perform directly and on their own merits. The drunkenness laws, for example, do nothing whatever to reduce the incidence of drunkenness, and nobody but the naive really suppose that that is what they are for. Rather, they serve two related social purposes: to provide temporary help and protection for the alcoholic and to remove an aesthetically offensive presence from the streets. The help is grossly inadequate, and the use of law enforcement time and effort to clean the streets is a conspicuous example of overkill. The use of the criminal sanction for this purpose is simply a compromise between taking measures that will deal with the problem effectively and acknowledging that we are really doing nothing, both of which we seem unwilling to do.

Use of the office of the public prosecutor as a kind of neighborhood law office for the settlement of family disputes and the collection of debts is a familiar phenomenon. The ostensible function being served is the enforcement of criminal statutes dealing with family nonsupport and with the writing of bad checks, but in both cases the leverage of possible criminal prosecution is used to compel the recalcitrant debtor to pay up. The service is very good from the complainant's standpoint. He gets free legal help. But it is a burden on the office of the public prosecutor to be called on to perform essentially civil law functions and, of at least equal seriousness, there is always the possibility of unfairness and abuse because of the coercive effect of the prosecutorial threat against a person who is typically not himself represented by a lawyer. Part of the solution to this problem lies in the provision of adequate social service help for dealing with family problems and for aiding people to get their financial affairs in order. Part of it lies in the provision of adequate legal assistance for the great mass of people who are unable to afford legal services at the going rate. These problems pose great challenges to the good will and resourcefulness of society; but they are not adequately met through the covert use of the criminal sanction.

These covert functions result, in every case, from the fact that criminal proscriptions are framed more broadly than is required for discharge of the overt function they can reasonably be expected to perform. In each case, narrowing of the reach of the criminal proscription rather than eliminating it is probably indicated. The point of this discussion, however, is not to frame a set of solutions but simply to suggest the existence of a problem. When an examination of what is really being done under the aegis of a particular proscription reveals that it is substantially devoted to the performance of covert functions, the prudent lawmaker should know that he is in the presence of a danger signal, or limiting criterion.

CHAPTER SIXTEEN

The Criteria Applied: Morals Offenses

THE CRIMINAL SANCTION AT ITS BEST

Most of the rest of this book is given over to a discussion of kinds of conduct that, on the basis of the limiting criteria we have been examining, do not seem clearly to warrant invocation of the criminal sanction. The examples given portray the criminal sanction working at considerably less than its optimal level. Before we turn to these examples it may be useful to try to establish some kind of bench mark for the optimal use of the criminal sanction. The criteria for choice seem so clear that it may be trite to rehearse them. They include the following:

(1) The conduct is prominent in most people's view of socially threatening behavior, and is not condoned by any significant segment of society.

(2) Subjecting it to the criminal sanction is not inconsistent with the goals of punishment.

(3) Suppressing it will not inhibit socially desirable conduct.

(4) It may be dealt with through even-handed and nondiscriminatory enforcement.

(5) Controlling it through the criminal process will not expose that process to severe qualitative or quantitative strains.

(6) There are no reasonable alternatives to the criminal sanction for dealing with it.

These criteria can be used in making up a kind of priority list of conduct for which the legislature might consider invoking the criminal sanction. Additions to the list (other than those that merely specify or fill in a genus already present) should be made with reserve, if at all. I do not propose in this book to attempt a comprehensive listing of conduct that qualifies under these criteria. Nor shall I try now to analyze the comparative weight that ought to be accorded these criteria in considering additions to the priority list. It will be enough for my present purpose to suggest a small sample of offenses that amply meet these criteria. It will not be necessary to reach very far to find them.

My list consists of the four crimes against the person that the F.B.I. uses (along with three property crimes) to make up its Index of Serious Crimes. These crimes are willful homicide, forcible rape, aggravated assault, and robbery. Willful homicide includes murder and non-negligent manslaughter. (This means, essentially, homicides in which the actor killed the victim either intentionally or recklessly.) Forcible rape is self-explanatory. Aggravated assault includes attacks in which the actor intended either to kill or to inflict serious bodily injury, whether or not he used a dangerous weapon; but for Index purposes it excludes cases in which bodily injury was inflicted in the course of forcible rape or robbery. Robbery is defined as the taking of property from a person by force or the threat of force, whether or not a weapon is used. In 1965 according to the F.B.I.'s Uniform Crime Reports there were about 10,000 willful homicides, about 22,000 forcible rapes, about 200,000 aggravated assaults, and about 120,000 robberies in the country.

No one would dispute the view that these offenses are the most threatening and the most strongly condemned in the entire criminal calendar. The crimes that concern people the most are those that involve the gravest threat to personal safety from the intentional conduct of others. There are five times as many deaths from automobile accidents as there are from willful homicides each year, but it is the intentional or reckless taking of life rather than its negligent or non-negligent taking that people fear. These four offenses are supremely threatening for differing reasons, but in each case one's physical security is placed at the mercy of a person intent on violating that security. Nothing makes either the victim or the community feel more helpless than an occasion on which someone has used force to work his will on another. Violent injury or the threat of it is the brute negation of the minimum that all of us—from the most self-sufficient to the most dependent—expect from life in organized society.

A recent survey has shown what has been intuitively apparent: what people fear most is physical attack by a stranger. Interestingly enough, and probably contrary to popular impression, only one of these four most serious crimes against the person is more often than not committed by a complete stranger. Various studies have shown that from 70 to 85 per cent of homicide victims were at least casually acquainted with their attackers. About two-thirds of aggravated assaults occur either within the family or among neighbors and acquaintances. Even forcible rape, which is thought by many to be the prototype of the attack by a stranger, is committed over half the time by a man who already knew his victim. Robbery is the only one of these major crimes in which attack by a stranger is the dominant pattern; about four-fifths of the robberies committed involve situations in which attacker and victim are not acquainted. Nevertheless, whether committed by a stranger, an acquaintance, or a member of the family, these offenses meet the first criterion as no others do.

The second criterion is stated negatively for the obvious reason that, although the goals are clear enough, we know little about the circumstances under which punishment effectively serves those goals. The strongest claim that can be made is that in relation to some kinds of antisocial conduct, punishment is not demonstrably ineffective. That appears to be the case with these four offenses. If the figures cited above with respect to reported crime accurately reflected the total number of offenses in these categories (which, as we shall presently see, they do not), the probability of a serious personal attack on an individual in this country would be on the order of 1 in 550. More significantly, despite a widespread impression to the contrary, the rate of reported serious crimes against the person in this country over the past thirty years has not been going up sharply, despite substantial improvements in the reporting of crime. No one knows how many people who might otherwise commit serious crimes against the person are deterred from doing so by the complex of factors that serve deterrent ends. However, given the supreme value that we attach to the safety of life and limb, it would take a wildly optimistic view of human nature to permit relaxation of the criminal law's intervention. We can be a little more nearly certain about the incapacitative effect of criminal punishment for these serious offenses. Substantial prison terms are served by persons convicted of these crimes. To the extent that the commission of a serious offense against the person is an indicator of danger— and we have no more reliable indicator—punishment in these cases protects society from repeated offenses of the same sort. And, unlike the only other class of cases in which we have been willing to impose substantial prison terms (narcotics offenses), we can be reasonably confident that a substantial proportion of those who commit these offenses are actually being apprehended, tried, convicted, and punished.

The third criterion is so clearly met that no comment is required.

The fourth criterion requires in the first instance a relatively high degree of efficiency in detecting the commission of offenses. The surest way to know that an offense has been committed is through the complaint of the victim. If there is no victim to complain, knowledge that an offense has been committed requires official detection, a necessarily haphazard process. Of course, not all victims complain. A pioneering survey conducted for the President's Commission on Law Enforcement and the Administration of Justice has shown a surprising degree of understatement in the reporting of serious crime. Significantly enough, however, the rate of understatement is lower for crimes against the person than it is for crimes against property, with the single expectable exception of forcible rape, the occurrence of which from the victim's standpoint is notoriously subjective.

The police vigorously investigate reports of these crimes. As one might expect, the "clearance rate"—the proportion of reported crimes solved by arrest—is higher for offenses in which the victim or a witness knows or can identify the culprit. Thus, the clearance rate for willful homicide runs about 90 per cent, for aggravated assault about 75 per cent, and for forcible rape about 65 per cent. All of these crimes, as we have noted, tend to be committed by people previously acquainted with the victim. Robbery, on the other hand, has a clearance rate of about 40 per cent, reflecting the greater proportion of robberies committed by strangers. Still, the chances of detection and apprehension are relatively high, as crimes in general go. This point has significance both for the probable deterrent effect of punishment for these offenses and for the even-handed enforcement of law by the police. The essential point is that these offenses are viewed so seriously that considerations of social class and other personal characteristics of the offender (or his victim) simply do not enter into a determination whether to investigate and arrest. Nor do considerations of resource allocation force the police to pick and choose the cases they will investigate. The ideal of full enforcement comes closer to realization for these offenses than for any others.

In considering the fifth criterion, we can note that the investigation of these offenses does not require the use of undesirable police practices. Illegal searches and seizures, wiretapping and other forms of electronic surveillance, entrapment and related decoy techniques are almost unknown in this branch of police work. Nor is this the kind of police work that encourages bribery and corruption. Overly aggressive pursuit of confessions is the only objectionable police practice that occurs frequently in the investigation of these offenses. And this is the one form of police misconduct most easily corrected through the operation of the criminal process itself.

The quantitative strains are no more pronounced than the qualitative ones. None of these offenses appears on the list of the ten criminal offenses for which arrests are most frequently made. Taken together, the four offenses comprise but a trivial fraction of the six million or more arrests made each year. It is precisely because their seriousness is out of all proportion to their numbers that these offenses cannot be said to impose a quantitative strain on the criminal process. Unhappily, it comes close to being true that there is an inverse ratio between seriousness and quantitative burden in the operation of our system of criminal justice.

The final criterion is perhaps the most important one. There is no reasonable alternative to the use of the criminal sanction in coping with these serious offenses. No other kind of legal control is even remotely relevant, with the possible exception of disarming the population. And the alternative of laissez-faire is unthinkable. The abandonment of the criminal sanction (or its counterpart under a different name) for dealing with these most basic of threats to human security would be tantamount to the dissolution of society.

This discussion may well be thought to have labored the obvious. But, as Holmes said in a different context, what we need most in our consideration of the criminal sanction is "education in the obvious." As we consider some of the malfunctions of the criminal sanction across a broad spectrum of human conduct, we must remember the serious offenses against personal security so that use of the criminal sanction against lesser offenses can be seen in a proper perspective. And we must remember that it is the same police, the same prosecutors, the same judges, the same correctional officers who must devote their time and energy to dealing with these lesser offenses. Resources are not infinite, nor are they spent with uniform prudence. Sometimes we may seem to buy only trouble with the resources we spend on the criminal sanction. But regardless of that, what we buy with our marginal dollar does not have equivalent marginal utility. Wisdom about the uses of the criminal sanction begins with recognition of that fact.

SEX OFFENSES

The debate over criminal laws forbidding certain varieties of sexual conduct has become the *locus classicus* of modern interest in the limits of criminal law. The recommendations both of the American Law Institute in this country and of the Wolfenden Report in England, the legislative revisions of the past few years in Illinois, New York, and England, and the famous debate between Professor H. L. A. Hart and Lord Devlin have all contributed to the impression that somehow this is *the* question in the criminal law. What the consenting adult does in private has become everybody's business to the precise extent that debate waxes hot over whether it is nobody's business.

It may not at this stage be possible to say anything new about the issues, but there are two prefatory observations that seem to be worth elaborating in the context of this examination of limiting criteria in the criminal law as a whole. The first is that, contrary to the supposition of many who have been engaged in the debate, the case of consensual sexual conduct is not a paradigm of the entire limits problem: it raises some issues that are quite atypical, and does not present others that tend to recur frequently in the field. The second is that the question is not whether certain kinds of sexual conduct should be subject to criminal punishment, but rather whether the laws in question are too broad: the issue is not whether to punish but when to do so.

One point that may well be unique to the problem of deviate consensual sexual relations is that by far the most powerful sanction is that of social stigma. There is little or no evidence to suggest that the criminal law exerts a deterrent influence that would not be present even if there were no criminal proscription. Although it is probable that there would be a substantial increase in the number of people who smoke marijuana or gamble or get abortions if those criminal prohibitions were relaxed, it seems implausible to suppose that a similar effect would occur if the laws against sexual deviation were changed. The reason is twofold: first, the strong pressures that impel people with homosexual tendencies to engage in deviate relations probably ensure that most who would do so are doing so already; second, the stigma that attaches even in so permissive a society as ours would militate against the advent of many new recruits. This is not to say that casual and situational experimentation might not increase if existing proscriptions were relaxed, but rather to suggest that it is unlikely that many people would change their predominant sexual patterns simply because of a change in the law. It is surely no coincidence that the strongest of human drives is matched by the strongest of social inhibitions. Law can no more suppress or divert the sexual drive than it can create it. These observations may perhaps be tested by the experience in jurisdictions that choose to change their laws, although even then, there will be the besetting difficulty of deciding whether correlates are causally connected.

There is also an important statistical difference between this problem and some of the others we will consider, particularly alcoholism and drug use. Although there is a qualitative enforcement cost in our present sex laws (whose dimensions we will shortly consider), it is improbable that enforcement activity in this field represents a quantitatively significant allocation of resources. We might have a more civilized criminal law by eliminating the sex squad, but it would be claiming too much to assert that we would thereby free significant additional resources for coping with the gross threats to security that should be the main business of the criminal law.

The other prefatory point that needs some elaboration is that the problem of sexual deviation and the law is not a problem of whether to eliminate the criminal sanction but rather of whether the definition of the offense should be narrowed to cover only those situations that enforcement actually deals with today. The question of "sexual conduct engaged in by consenting adults in private" is, with only trivial exceptions, an essentially symbolic one (leaving aside for the moment the question of what is meant by "in private"). If the law were changed in this one respect, the overwhelming majority of enforcement activity could go on unimpaired. Much enforcement activity is presently concentrated on offenses involving minors. And, as an important field study recently conducted in Los Angeles has shown, the vast majority of prosecutions are for sexual activity or solicitations conducted in places where no one would reasonably suppose that he was entitled to privacy.

I make these preliminary points not to denigrate the importance of the reform activity that has been taking place in this area but to suggest that the reform of the substantive criminal law is a very complex business in which sweeping generalizations are dangerous and the issues far from clear-cut. Nor do I mean to suggest the absence in this corner of the criminal law of issues that illustrate the pervasive importance of paying careful attention to the limits of criminal law. Let us now consider what some of those issues are.

Although the currently controversial issue arises in respect to deviate sexual conduct, the same considerations apply with almost equal force to "normal" sexual relations. For the criminal law to threaten the private sexual behavior of consenting adults, it must run afoul of many limiting criteria of the sort discussed in Chapter Fifteen. Some of the reasons listed below for not invoking the sanction where such behavior is concerned are self-explanatory; others will require some comment.

(1) Rarity of enforcement creates a problem of arbitrary police and prosecutorial discretion.

(2) The extreme difficulty of detecting such conduct leads to undesirable police practices.

(3) The existence of the proscription tends to create a deviant subculture.

(4) Widespread knowledge that the law is violated with impunity by thousands every day creates disrespect for law generally.

(5) No secular harm can be shown to result from such conduct.

(6) The theoretical availability of criminal sanctions creates a situation in which extortion and, on occasion, police corruption may take place.

(7) There is substantial evidence that the moral sense of the community no longer exerts strong pressure for the use of criminal sanctions.

(8) No utilitarian goal of criminal punishment is substantially advanced by proscribing private adult consensual sexual conduct.

The only countervailing argument is that relaxation of the criminal proscription will be taken to express social approval of the conduct at issue. There is little enough, as we have seen, to that general proposition. It becomes peculiarly vacuous when addressed to this issue, where the social taboo is so much stronger than the legal prohibition. It does not pay a statute much of a compliment, a justice of the Supreme Court once remarked, to say that it is not unconstitutional. It may also be said that it does not express much approval of a behavior pattern to say that it is not criminal.

The enforcement ratio of private consensual sex offenses must show incredibly heavy odds against arrest—perhaps one in ten million? There is an inherent unfairness in that situation regardless of how equitably discretion is exercised, which is to say, even if it is perfectly random. But it is not. The scanty available evidence suggests that enforcement takes place mainly in a context in which other mores, not reinforced by law, are being flouted, as, for example, where the partners are of different races. While this is outrageous, it is also understandable. If no systematic efforts are made to enforce these criminal proscriptions, their detection and prosecution must be triggered by something extrinsic to the conduct itself. With no guidance as to the social interests that ought to be protected (and there can be none), those enforcing the law must fall back on their own individual scheme of values.

Knowledge that the law is unenforced has a bad effect both on those who violate it and on the public at large. The violators are contemptuous of a law that they perceive to be both unjust and ineffectual. They react against it by strengthening their own identification as an outlaw group. As social stigma apart from the criminal law begins somewhat to relax, this isolating effect of the criminal proscription becomes even more objectionable than formerly. Otherwise law-abiding citizens see themselves as rebels against society, not because of society's deeds or even society's thoughts, but simply because of some words in a book. Imaginary offenses turn out to have effects that are far from imaginary.

The problem of criminal extortion against homosexuals was dramatically illustrated in 1967 with the indictment in New York of a nationwide ring of blackmailers who had secured large sums of money from prominent men—educators, military officers, entertainers—by posing as police officers and threatening criminal prosecution. The modus operandi is instructive. The threat was not merely to expose, but to prosecute. One wonders to what extent the vulnerability of homosexuals to extortion would be lessened by the removal of the criminal threat. It would hardly be total, given the existence of powerful motives for concealment having little or nothing to do with the criminal proscription.

The evaluation of undesirable police practices illuminates the difficulty of talking about the question of legalizing sexual conduct as if there were two mutually exclusive self-executing categories: private consensual conduct (which we mean to protect) and public indecency (which we mean to suppress). The notorious practices are two: the use of decoys to lure homosexuals into making advances; and surreptitious surveillance of places in which homosexual activity is likely to take place (public rest-rooms, baths, and the like). These are well-known evils, plainly degrading to the administration of criminal justice, at best un-dignified, at worst morally repulsive. The plea to eliminate them by legalizing private consensual activity is an appealing one, but it is misleading, at least in the short run. The police decoy would still be free to ply his unsavory trade. His job is to incite a sexual solicitation, verbal or physical. It does not matter that the solici-tation is to engage in conduct in private. It is itself criminal and remains so under proposals for reform such as the Wolfenden Report and the American Law Institute's Model Penal Code. Neither the law defining the offense nor the law of entrapment prevents decoy activity. As for surveillance, its legal vulnerability is based on the uncertain application of the constitutional pro-hibition against illegal searches and seizures rather than on any functional definition of privacy.

It may be that the long-run effect of legalizing private con-sensual conduct would be to abate the demand for aggressive police intervention in quasi-private areas of conduct, with the attendant evils of decoy activity and surveillance. However, it would be unwise for any program of legislative reform to place sole reliance on speculative long-run effects. We should there-fore consider what steps other than the largely symbolic one of legalizing private consensual conduct need to be taken in framing a program of legislative reform.

The first essential step is to determine what values might rationally be protected by the criminal law and what their rela-tive importance is. In my judgment there are three, two of prime importance and one of somewhat lesser significance. The first is protection against the use of force and equivalent means of coercion to secure sexual gratification. The second, closely re-lated to the first and equivalently important in precisely the degree that it is related to the first, is the protection of the im-mature against sexual exploitation. The third, less significant in the hierarchy of social values and also more difficult to secure without damaging side effects, is the prevention of conduct that gives offense or is likely to give offense to innocent bystanders.

These values would, I think, be generally agreed upon, although there might be less agreement that they are the only ones to be protected. They are all values that the criminal law is relatively well adapted to securing and that no other form of legal control is equally well adapted to securing.

The second step is to relate these values to the structure of a criminal code. If one inspects a typical criminal code in its impact upon sexual conduct, it becomes immediately apparent that there is no expression of a coherent value structure to be found. Prohibitions against the use of force (e.g., rape) and against the victimization of immaturity (e.g., "statutory rape") are interspersed with provisions banning particular forms of sexual expression (e.g., anal-genital contacts, oral-genital contacts) and particular kinds of sexual relationships (e.g., fornication and adultery). Then there are provisions dealing with solicitation and indecent exposure, backed up by vague and general prohibitions against disorderly conduct. There is total chaos in the penalty structure. One can rethink systematically only by proceeding as if the whole unwieldy apparatus did not exist and by resolving to begin afresh.

The first and most essential step in creating an adequately responsive structure for sexual offenses is to eliminate all distinctions based upon the sex of the participants. If force or threats of force are to be prohibited, it should make no difference whether a man assaults a woman or another man. If the sexual exploitation of minors is to be forbidden, it should not make any difference what the sexual identities of the exploiter and the exploited happen to be. Subjecting the construction of sexual prohibitions to this discipline goes a long distance toward ensuring that only the significant values identified above are protected.

Protection against the use of coercion presents interesting questions about what sorts of coercion should be, in effect, assimilated to the use of actual physical force. Threats of force that the actor is apparently in a position to carry out are by and large treated under existing law as the equivalent of force. Beyond this, existing law is somewhat equivocal. It seems clear, though, that sexual acts in all of the following circumstances should be assimilated, at least for criminal guilt if not for equal severity of punish-

ment: where the actor knows that the other person is unconscious; where he has surreptitiously administered drugs or other
intoxicants in order to impair the other person's ability to control his or her conduct; where he knows that the other person is
mentally ill and incapable of controlling his or her conduct; and
where he uses a threat other than one of force that would nonetheless be likely to be yielded to by an ordinarily resolute person,
such as a threat of discharge from employment.

These problems are quite easy in comparison to the problem
of giving content and limits to the protection of immaturity. The
first question is how immaturity is to be defined: subjectively, in
terms of the victim's actual state of physical or psychic experience
and development, or objectively, in terms of factors like age? The
subjective approach is more sensitively attuned to the values at
issue but is probably impractical. The processes of the criminal
law require that lines be drawn in advance, and this is incompatible with the kind of individualization that might in principle
be preferable. (One of the factors that ought to inspire restraint
in resort to the criminal sanction is a realization that the fit between criminal proscription and values to be protected by it is
often approximate.) Accordingly, it is necessary to fix upon an
objective datum like the victim's age. Here it is worthwhile to
make two distinctions: first, an age below which the use of a child
as a sexual object is so aberrant as to manifest a gross psychic
abnormality on the part of the actor; second, an age below which
the child, while a viable giver and receiver of sexual gratification,
is likely to have such poor judgment about the meaning of sexual
activity that he or she should be protected against it. Any selection of ages is bound to be arbitrary. Current legislative proposals
range all the way from 10 to 14 for the first category—what we
might call child molestation—and from 14 to 18 for the second,
which corresponds roughly to what, in the case of female victims,
has heretofore been known as statutory rape.

The next issue is whether the age of the "aggressor" in relation
to that of his victim should be relevant. It seems clear that it
should be. Adolescent sexual experimentation is inevitable and,
some would argue, desirable. In any event, it does not conform to
the model of a wily, experienced aggressor taking advantage of

the innocence and immaturity of his victim. Moreover, there is a subsidiary reason for giving some effect to relative age. There is often a question about who is the exploiter and who the victim. The closer the ages of the participants, the more ambiguous the situation is likely to be. Accordingly, it may be desirable to provide an age differential within which consensual activity, although involving at least one person below the "protected" age level, is free from criminal restraint. The variation can be increased or decreased depending on the strength of one's doubts about the reality of victim immaturity, and depending on where the outside limit for statutory rape is placed. On the whole, it would seem that the higher the "age of consent" is placed, the greater should be the zone within which the older partner is protected. If the age of consent is 18, a five-year differential would protect the older partner up to 23. If, however, the age of consent were as low as 14, or even 16, an age differential of more than three years would probably be excessive. Where the numbers are actually fixed will almost certainly be the product of legislative compromise. The important point is to observe the principle that some differential is required in order to avoid treating as criminal the conduct of persons who are roughly members of the same generation and hence unlikely to be involved in an exploitative situation.

It is also worth considering whether any additional attempt should be made to refine the category of the "innocent and immature." The principal available device is to provide a defense based on proof of the previous sexual promiscuity of the alleged victim. If the underage "victim" is in fact sexually experienced, it may be doubted that there is a significant value for the criminal law to protect. This may be one of the rare instances where the burden of proof with respect to the defense should perhaps be carried by the defendant. Otherwise it would be very easy in any prosecution for sexual misconduct with an immature girl or boy for the defendant to force the prosecution to undertake the difficult task of disproving the possibility of sexual promiscuity.

There are important subsidiary problems of determining gradations of seriousness in sexual offenses. Given the same attendant circumstances (the use of coercion or imposition on an im-

mature victim), should all forms of sexual expression be punished
with equal severity, or should some gradation be attempted?
These problems are interesting and important but somewhat
beside the point in the present discussion, which is concerned
with the question of what kinds of conduct should be treated as
criminal rather than how severely people who engage in criminal
conduct should be punished. Those problems of grading aside,
we have now canvassed the main problems that arise in determining the reach of the criminal law to protect the two most
important values with which it should be concerned in the sexual
sphere: freedom from coercion and freedom from the exploitation of immaturity.

There remains the question of public affront, the nuisance
aspect of sexual activity. In a society that has developed such
versatility at adapting sexual suggestiveness to serve the needs
of both entertainment and profit, it might seem that we could
pretty well dispense with any "protection" from sex-instigated
assaults on the eyes and ears. But consistency in these matters is
not that easy to come by. Sexual expression must still pay its way
in "redeeming social importance." Intercourse is in the process
of making its way out of the library onto the movie screen and
(more daringly because less controllably) the theater stage. But
we aren't quite ready for it yet in the village square. Privacy in
sexual conduct is still expected. And we continue to look to the
criminal sanction to help assure it. Yet the rationale for keeping
the criminal law out of the province of consensual sexual expression requires the exercise of great care in seeing to it that
claims for the protection of public decency do not provide the
impetus for negating that process of exclusion. Limiting questions need to be asked.

The first question is what we should mean by "private." People
may think they are alone and unobserved when they are not.
They may have selected a place for their activities where people
are unlikely to come, but where prurient interest has attracted
voyeurs, or the interest of law enforcement has attracted the
police. Or their sexual activities may go on in a mutually appre-
ciative group. How should the law respond? It seems to me that
the relevant criterion should not be what the actual effect was

but rather what effect the person or persons in question should reasonably have expected. Whether the locale is a lover's lane, a national park, a city street, or a wild party at someone's house, the criminal law should have no concern with consensual sexual conduct unless the trier of fact can say that the conduct took place under circumstances which created a substantial risk that someone might be offended.[1] The principle that I contend for would require an evaluation of the setting in which the sexual act took place in order to determine whether anyone (other than the police who were on the lookout for it and who found what they were looking for) who might reasonably have been expected to observe it would have been offended by what he saw. The adoption of such a criterion would probably mean that certain places would in time become known as the resort of persons having certain sexual proclivities. While this might superficially appear undesirable, it would have the beneficial result that people would know where to go and where not to go. So long as coercion or fraud were not practiced, and so long as minors were prevented from being corrupted, the results could hardly be objectionable.

A similar standard might also apply to the issue of sexual solicitation. Leaving aside the question of soliciting for prostitution, which is separately considered,[2] it seems clear that the mere fact of sexual solicitation should not be criminal. If the solicitation is successful and the two parties to the bargain then have sexual relations in private (as defined above), no criminal liability would result. In most American jurisdictions, however, the mere fact of sexual solicitation (and even the anomalous status of "loitering with intent to solicit") is treated as criminal. This is consistent to the extent that the completed conduct would also be criminal, as it almost universally is in the case of homosexual conduct and as it frequently is in the case of heterosexual conduct. However, once the principle is accepted that sexual relations carried on discreetly (a less misleading way of saying what is meant by "in private") by consenting adults fall outside the ambit of the criminal law, there is no intelligible reason for

---

[1] The same principle may be applicable in the area of obscenity. See below, pp. 316–28.

[2] See below, pp. 328–31.

making preparatory conduct looking toward that goal criminal. This is not to say, however, that all sexual solicitations should be immune to criminal prosecution. The question should be whether under all the circumstances the actor's conduct created a substantial risk that someone might be offended, either the person being solicited or passersby. In practice, of course, it is almost never a bona fide offended person who makes the complaint but rather a policeman who has put himself in a position to be solicited. Some courts have already begun to take the position that the police decoy is legally incapable of being offended—he is surely incapable of being startled—by the solicitation and that, therefore, statutes which presently include an "offensive or annoying" behavior criterion are not satisfied by a decoy's complaint. Whatever the increment of public annoyance that would result from total elimination of the solicitation offense, it would be more than justified by elimination of the odious and degrading decoy practices documented in detail by recent empirical studies.

The proposals in this section are designed to give realistic content to the proposition that private consensual sexual conduct among adults should not be the concern of the criminal law. The problem, as I pointed out at the beginning of this discussion, does not bulk large quantitatively in the misallocation of resources to the criminal sanction with which we are presently afflicted. It would bulk much larger if law enforcement were ever to undertake a really massive assault on illegal sexual conduct. The prevalence of the conduct bespeaks the futility of attempts to suppress it. From every rational perspective on the use of the criminal sanction, from the rule of "first things first" to the avoidance of useless suffering, to the civilizing of the police, these proposals have a capacity for betterment quite out of proportion to the amount of enforcement activity they would affect.

BIGAMY AND INCEST: TWO IMAGINARY CRIMES

The criminal codes of every state in the Union, of England and every country whose legal system derives from England, and of most of the rest of what we smugly refer to as the "civilized" world contain criminal prohibitions against bigamy and incest, and typically prescribe severe felony punishments for their breach. Yet it is extremely difficult to give a coherent account of why the conduct denounced by these offenses should be treated as criminal.

Bigamy is the act of contracting a marriage when one is not free to do so because he has another spouse living. The offense is not statistically significant but has presented many doctrinal difficulties; one might reasonably guess that it exhibits the lowest ratio of reported appellate court opinions to actual prosecutions of any crime on the books. Most of the difficulty has stemmed from persistent errors about whether and to what extent it is a defense that the alleged bigamist believed himself free to contract the questioned marriage, either because he thought that his first spouse was dead or (more commonly) that he and his first spouse had been validly divorced. Now that these doctrinal errors have been adequately exposed and the courts are beginning to come around to a clearer view of the problem, it remains to inquire what the offense is all about. The asserted rationales are, it has been said, more ingenious than convincing. They include the protection of public records from confusion, the prevention of public affront and provocation to the first spouse, and the assertion that cohabitation under color of matrimony is especially likely to result in desertion, nonsupport, and divorce. Professor H. L. A. Hart, who lists these reasons, rightly dismisses them as trivial, asserting that even if they were adequately taken care of by other specific offenses, there would still be pressure for retaining the offense.[3] Its gist, he suggests, lies in its protection of religious feelings from offense by a sham marriage that desecrates the marriage ceremony. But he tries to reconcile laws against bigamy with the view that it is wrong to punish conduct simply because it is irreligious or immoral by demonstrating that the bigamist is being punished as a nuisance, like anyone else who commits acts that publicly outrage decency. This too seems more ingenious than convincing. What about bigamous civil marriage ceremonies? What about bigamous church marriages that are not publicized?

If there is any coherent rationale for this offense, it is one re-

---

[3] H. L. A. Hart, *Law, Liberty, and Morality* (Stanford, 1963), pp. 38–43.

vealed by an inspection of the factual pattern in prosecutions actually brought. Almost without exception, they involve fraud on the second spouse, which she discovers after her apparent husband deserts her. Viewed in this light, the offense is essentially rape by deceit, inducing a woman to enter into sexual cohabitation by misrepresenting marital status. That kind of conduct is properly handled as an aspect of sexual imposition. Its gravamen has nothing to do with the irrelevant act of going through a marriage ceremony.

In addition to its utilitarian vacuity, the law is in practice enforced only sporadically, and then usually against members of minority groups or low-income people who are either culturally insensitive to the legal formalities attendant on family relationships or economically incapable of invoking them. There is substantial reason to believe that most bigamists ended their prior marriage with an informal "divorce by consent." The typical pattern is that the deserted second wife complains to a welfare agency about the absconder's nonsupport, and the ensuing investigation reveals that in addition to being a deserter he is a bigamist. The resulting mess is hardly helped by invocation of the criminal sanction. The offense is one we could do without.

Incest is an equally paradoxical offense. It represents one of the most nearly universal cultural taboos, yet its rationale and therefore its desirable definition are far from clear. It is typically defined as marriage, cohabitation, or sexual intercourse with a person to whom one is related within a specified degree of consanguinity. The prohibited relationships are typically parents and children, ancestors and descendants, brothers and sisters, uncles and nieces, and aunts and nephews. Some codes reflect a view of the relative heinousness of incest with various degrees of consanguinity by providing differential penalties. Louisiana prescribes fifteen-year prison sentences for incest between ancestor and descendant or brother and sister, but five-year sentences where it is between uncle and niece, or aunt and nephew. Illinois distinguishes in severity between father-daughter incest and all other forms (including mother-son!). The Model Penal Code draws no such distinctions but indicates doubts about whether uncle-niece, aunt-nephew relationships should be included at all.

By far the most frequent incestuous relationship is that between father and minor daughter. And a high proportion of such relationships involve stepfathers and stepdaughters. Typically, the man has married a woman with a daughter by a previous marriage whose sexual attractiveness to him is not damped down (as it might be in the case of a blood relationship) by years of regarding the growing child as a dependent to be nurtured rather than as a sexual object. Surely relationships of this kind should be inhibited by the criminal law. How can I possibly assert that incest is an imaginary offense? Very simply, because the conduct described above is covered by other criminal prohibitions and, in addition, much of it is not covered by the incest prohibition. Sexual abuse of a child below the "age of consent" is covered by statutes dealing with child molestation and statutory rape. Incest does not apply to sexual abuse other than intercourse, although much of the intrafamilial conduct that takes place consists of fondling or foreplay rather than actual intercourse. And incest in its traditional form is limited to consanguineous relationships, which makes it inapplicable to the sexual abuse of a stepdaughter. The most apparent utilitarian reasons for proscribing incest are therefore satisfied by other offenses. Prevention of sexual exploitation in the family setting and promotion of family solidarity by preventing internal sex rivalries are goals that are clearly defensible, but the offense of incest is not needed to promote them.

What values remain to be protected? There seem to be only two claims. One is the genetic risk that inbreeding leads to the birth of defective children. That reason is somewhat farfetched. Incestuous relationships are rarely carried on for the purpose of procreation. And geneticists are not at all agreed that inbreeding is dysgenic: its effect is only to accentuate the recessive traits of the parents. If they share unhealthy recessive traits, the effects will be bad; if they share healthy recessive traits, the effects will be good. The other claim is that criminal punishment is required to place a secular sanction behind a widely held religious or moral tenet; and a related assertion is that the community regards incest with such intense hostility that failure to condemn it will result in loss of respect for the criminal law generally. This is simply a stark claim for the enforcement of morals through the criminal law. It must be rejected on the ground that in the absence of any claim that the conduct in question is injurious to others or to those who engage in it, people should be free of the peculiar condemnatory restraint of the criminal law. If carrying on an open and notorious incestuous relationship gives offense to the community, there may be room for its prohibition as a nuisance, although it is questionable whether the community's injury is anything but self-inflicted, unless there is an exceptionally open flaunting of the sexual character of the relationship. Although it strikes most of us as bizarre and repugnant, there seems no good reason to prevent incestuous preferences from expressing themselves among adults. Civil sanctions such as the non-recognition of incestuous marriages should be sufficient.

THE SIN OF OBSCENITY

The problem of obscenity presents an interesting variant on the theme of enforcement discretion. In a series of superficially related "morals" offenses—fornication, adultery, homosexuality, prostitution—the question of discretion is but one of a group of practical enforcement issues, and it relates to the criteria by which a very few instances of a well-defined category of conduct are selected to be fed into the criminal process. By contrast, in the area of obscenity the problem of discretion is *the* practical problem, and it relates not to the selection of well-defined instances but to the process of official (which is to say, police, prosecutorial, and judicial) judgment by which instances of conduct are defined as falling into the prohibited category. Everybody knows what fornication is, but anybody who is sure he knows what obscenity is poses a threat to freedom of community thought and expression. This judgmental problem has plagued the Supreme Court for the past ten years, ever since its decision in the *Roth* case,[4] in which it attempted to lay down a standard that would accommodate its libertarian views about freedom of expression under the First Amendment with a strong but unarticulated perception

---

4 Roth v. United States, 354 U.S. 476 (1957).

that it is desirable (or politic) to afford the agencies of public order some latitude in suppressing obscenity. Our interest is in prudent legislative policy rather than constitutional limitations, but the rationales may be parallel if not identical. That the rationales are parallel is suggested by the fortuity that at the same time the Supreme Court began addressing itself to the problem, they found ready at hand the interesting attempt of the American Law Institute's Model Penal Code to solve the problem of standards and criteria. The tangles in which the Court has got itself are dramatic evidence of the difficulty of the problem; but they are less important than the continued freedom of police and prosecutors to legislate ad hoc every time they move to suppress an offensive book, magazine, or movie.

When the draftsmen of the Model Penal Code came to deal with the problem of obscenity, they had to confront the question of what social interests they were undertaking to promote or protect by invoking the criminal sanction. In the words of the principal draftsman of the obscenity provisions, their formulation expresses a "preference for an oblique approach to morals offenses, i.e., the effort to express the moral impulses of the community in a penal prohibition that is nevertheless pointed at and limited to something else than sin. In this case the target is not the 'sin of obscenity' but primarily a disapproved form of economic activity—commercial exploitation of the widespread weakness for titillation by pornography."[5] Note the ambivalence of this rationale. It does not look unambiguously toward the prevention of a defined secular harm. Rather, it gets at immorality by the ploy of attacking something else that the immorality in question is attached to, without directly confronting the issue of whether the "something else" is worth suppressing absent the immorality. In the legislative sphere as elsewhere, justifiable suspicion attaches to efforts to eat one's cake and have it too.

The Model Penal Code solution has four principal features. First is its definition of obscenity: "material is obscene if, considered as a whole, its predominant appeal is to prurient interest, that is, a shameful or morbid interest, in nudity, sex, or excretion,

[5] Schwartz, *Morals Offenses and the Model Penal Code* 63 COLUM. L. REV. 669, 677 (1963).

and if in addition it goes substantially beyond customary limits of candor in describing or representing such matters." Second, the Code defines forbidden conduct with respect to obscenity. It may not be sold, exhibited, advertised, or otherwise publicly disseminated. Third, it restricts the generality of these prohibitions by exempting dissemination to "institutions or persons having scientific, educational, governmental, or other similar justification for possessing obscene material" and "noncommercial dissemination to personal associates of the actor." Finally, it provides a number of evidentiary justifications that may be adduced to take material outside the realm of the obscene, which can be summed up as saying that if it isn't smut for its own sake, then it's all right.

These provisions must be appraised in the light of existing law on the subject of obscenity. The prevailing test for obscenity has been the tendency of the material to corrupt the morals of its consumer by arousing sexual thoughts and desires. Leaving aside the question of whether there is an intelligible sense in which the arousal of sexual thoughts and desires can be said to corrupt morals, thought control—even sexual thought control—hardly recommends itself as a goal of penal legislation. There must be something more at stake than that. The common-law background of obscenity suppression makes it clear that the "something more" is the asserted tendency of bad behavior to follow from bad thoughts.

Now, there is respectable precedent in the criminal law for outlawing things which, while not demonstrably harmful themselves, can be shown to have a causal relationship with things that are harmful. Drunken driving is a conspicuous example. In order to convict a man of drunken driving, we do not require a showing in each case that he was likely to cause harm to himself or others. Nobody thinks it arbitrary to dispense with that showing, because there is a valid experiential basis for believing that the risk is generally a substantial one. But no such experiential basis exists for believing that bad behavior, or any sort of predictable behavior, follows from having bad, i.e. sexual, thoughts. Indeed, there is some reason to believe that obscene literature acts as a substitute for rather than as a stimulus to aggressive sexual behavior. Consequently, obscenity regulation cannot be fitted into that familiar category of criminal prohibition in which it is the creation of risk rather than the ultimate harm that provides the valid basis for legislation.

If risk creation really were the thrust of obscenity legislation, there would be great appeal in the requirement that a substantial probability of harm, whether through incitement to commit crime or some other mode of causation, be shown in the particular case. Libertarian-minded judges, such as Curtis Bok and Jerome Frank, have sought to adapt the "clear and present danger" test from the law governing political expression as a limiting criterion for the application of obscenity statutes. Judge Bok would have required that "the causal connection between the book and the criminal behavior must appear beyond a reasonable doubt."[6] Judge Frank would have been satisfied with a test of reasonable probability.[7] It is difficult to know whether these suggestions were advanced seriously or tongue in cheek. It seems clear that, conscientiously applied, they would lead to exoneration in all but the most bizarre cases. I prefer to regard them as, in effect, calling the bluff of proponents of the traditional tests. "If you really are concerned," they seem to be saying, "with dangerous tendencies rather than with immorality as such, then put up or shut up." The gambit has been declined by, among others, the framers of the Model Penal Code, who rejected the "clear and present danger" approach on the candid ground of unenforceability. Their criterion, the "appeal to prurient interest," represents a substitute for "tendency to corrupt" adopted on the specific ground that "we prefer a test for criminal obscenity that is related to the nature of the attraction of the material *rather than to consequences that can hardly be demonstrated"* (emphasis added).[8] But if the consequences are not to be demonstrated, are they to be assumed? And if not, what is the interest that is being protected?

It seems that the Model Penal Code's approach is indeed "oblique," in a sense of the word that its draftsmen did not in-

---

[6] Commonwealth v. Gordon, 66 Pa. D. & C. 101, 156 (1949).
[7] United States v. Roth, 237 F2d 796, 806, 826 (2d Cir. 1956).
[8] MODEL PENAL CODE, Comment, p. 28 (Tent. Draft No. 6, 1957).

tend in the explanation quoted earlier. What it seems to do is to obscure the rationale for the proscription of obscenity by rejecting the secular harm connotations of "a tendency to corrupt morals" without explicitly avowing that it rests upon the denunciation of immorality as such. To repeat something that I have said earlier but that needs repetition, there is nothing wrong with a denunciation of immorality unaccompanied by identifiable secular goals if it is not backed up by the apparatus of the criminal process. The church, the school, and the home are all social institutions that exert coercive and condemnatory power; but it is a different, more limited kind of power than that entrusted to the law enforcers.

My characterization of the Model Penal Code's approach as essentially one of moral denunciation must be examined in the light of the second and third of its features. It might seem that a ban on sale, exhibition, advertising, or other public dissemination, qualified by exemptions for scholarly or personal use, falls considerably short of simple moral denunciation. However, it falls short of this by less than one might suppose. Although the proscriptions are motivated by an intention to focus on the commercial exploitation of the weakness for obscenity, they in fact go much further than that, as the principal draftsman has himself conceded.[9] A public exhibition or performance may be offered free or below its cost to the exhibitor, and a book may be ordered or sold as a convenience to the customer rather than from the bookseller's desire to profit; but all such transactions still fall within the ban of the proposed statute. The freedom of the individual to seek his own peculiar form of damnation is being inhibited not in the interest of preventing commercial exploitation but purely and simply because it is thought wrong that the individual should be allowed that latitude. As for the first exemption, there is a subtle form of philistinism in the notion that it is all right to dabble in erotica if it is business rather than pleasure, even when the business is "scientific, educational, or governmental." As for the second, it is hard to see any reason why one should not be permitted to make gifts of pornography to strangers if one

9 Schwartz, p. 681.

really wants to, except that the recipient may not appreciate it. But that is not a reason that seems to count in this statutory scheme. Perhaps it should, a thought to which we shall return.

There is a more fundamental objection that would still apply even if the Model Penal Code's recommendation remotely approached the target of commercial exploitation, which it clearly does not. That is the question whether if, assuming the thing being exploited commercially should not itself be suppressed, there is any reason to suppress its commercial exploitation. The explanation given by the Code's draftsmen can be read only as an assumed justification rather than as a demonstrated one. It is essentially that "if production and circulation of obscene material for gain could be eliminated, the supply would be cut off at the source." While private circulation would still take place, the "potential harm would be minimal because of the restricted scope of the activity." And this private circulation would tend to be limited to those "already 'corrupted.' "[10] The quotation marks around "corrupted" suggest that the draftsmen were aware that an important question was being begged. We have noted the acute difficulties that present themselves when the criminal law undertakes to prohibit consensual commercial transactions. Yet the framers of the Code were apparently willing to continue imposing that burden on an already burdened system in the interest of . . . what? They do not say. The answer can only be, on their own assumptions, the repression of sin.

The fourth conspicuous feature of the Code's treatment of obscenity is a series of evidentiary guidelines intended to channel enforcement discretion. They include the character of the audience for which the material was designed, the material's predominant appeal, its artistic or literary merit, the degree of its public acceptance in the United States, the good repute of the author or creator, and the appeal to prurient interest, or the lack thereof, in advertising or promoting the material. What they are all intended to say to the agencies exercising official discretion— the police, the prosecutors, and the courts—may be summed up in the phrase "redeeming social importance" used by the Su-

---

10 MODEL PENAL CODE, Comment, p. 13 (Tent. Draft No. 6, 1957).

preme Court in the *Roth* case to qualify what would otherwise
have been the excessively broad sweep of "appeal to prurient interest." And, until quite recently, the Court has seemed to be
moving steadily toward an application of First Amendment doctrine that would limit the reach of obscenity laws to "hard-core"
pornography, a category about which one Justice remarked that
he couldn't define it but he knew it when he saw it. Under this
regime of liberality we have in recent years been treated (or subjected) to an unparalleled flood of frankness in the literary and
artistic treatment of sexual themes. Very little remains to the
imagination, which may well be an aesthetic loss. But why should
the criminal law protect against aesthetic losses?

The members of the Supreme Court have had a liberal education in pornography, an education of the kind to which police
and prosecutors have long been subjected. Since the constitutional criteria that they uphold require them to scrutinize the
content of questioned works, the justices have had to wade
through hours of inspecting erotic books and magazines and even
movies. Eventually, it may be surmised, what happens to anyone
in the censorship business happened to them, or, at least, to a
majority of them. A reaction syndrome set in, compounded of
disgust at what they were forced to deal with and the development of a porno-centric outlook that exaggerated the prevalence
of smut. The result was the infamous *Ginsburg* decision,[11] in
which the Court retreated alike from its obligation to scrutinize
the allegedly obscene material and from its liberal stance.

Ralph Ginsburg was an entrepreneur of the new frankness
who decided to capitalize on this literary trend by publishing a
magazine called *Eros,* which was to serve as a kind of *Reader's
Digest* of legitimated quasi-pornography. Ginsburg was indicted
under the federal obscenity statute, convicted, and sentenced to
five years in prison, the maximum permissible. His conviction
was affirmed on appeal; but when the Supreme Court agreed to
review the case, Ginsburg must have thought that he was out of
trouble. The evidence of obscenity in the case was fairly thin, and
the sentence was unusually severe. To his surprise and that of

11 Ginsburg v. United States, 383 U.S. 463 (1966).

most other people, the Supreme Court affirmed his conviction. The rationale was even more startling than the result. The advertising and promotional methods that he used, said the majority, evidenced an intention to cater to prurient interest. Little if anything was said about the actual content of the magazine. It was enough that, having tried unsuccessfully to get mailing privileges from towns named Blueball and Intercourse, he had settled for Middlesex.

Few decisions of the Supreme Court in recent years have evoked such unanimous condemnation from the court's customary supporters. Yet it is not surprising that a reaction against the liberalism of the post-*Roth* years eventually set in. So long as the Court views the problem as one of accommodating the competing claims of freedom of expression and suppression of immorality, the line will be an uncertain and wavering one. An irony of the *Ginsburg* decision is that its result might have been foretold from the Model Penal Code's formulation of the offense of obscenity which, as we have seen, was the starting point for the Court's new liberalism. One of the Code's evidentiary guidelines, it will be recalled, deals with the appeal to prurient interest, or absence of any such appeal, in advertising or other promotion of the allegedly obscene material. And, just to close the trap more securely, another proposed provision of the Code would penalize one who advertises material "whether or not obscene, by representing or suggesting that it is obscene."[12] In this view, the wrapping in which the package comes is just as important as the package's contents. And this view is perfectly understandable, given the starting point of commercial exploitation.

I think that is the wrong starting point, for at least two reasons. The first has already been stated: the illogicality of undertaking to forbid selling what it is permissible to give away free. If obscenity itself should not be proscribed—and there seems to be no valid secular reason for doing so—it is hard to see why obscenity plus the profit motive is a fit subject for the criminal sanction. The second reason is that so long as the focus (even a slightly bootlegged focus) remains on the concept of obscenity as

---

[12] MODEL PENAL CODE §251.4(2)(e) (Proposed Official Draft, 1961).

a quality of the thing being appraised, there is no way out of the morass of ad hoc determinations whether this, that, or the other thing is "obscene." And as a result, policemen, prosecutors, and judges will continue to function as literary critics, some works of artistic merit will be repressed, and a substantial part of the intellectual community will continue to feel alienated from the system of law in general. (There is nothing easier to whip up a petition about than the latest censorship furor.)

The only valid purpose of obscenity law is to prevent public offense. It should be viewed, purely and simply, as the proscription of nuisance. People who do not wish to have erotic or other material that they find offensive foisted upon them are entitled to protection from it, just as they are arguably entitled to be protected against having to witness the real-life conduct of which pornography is the simulacrum. But it is hardly necessary in protecting that interest to forbid willing buyers and sellers to seek each other out. No one is forced to read *Fanny Hill,* or see a screening of *Un Chant d'Amour,* or attend a performance of *The Beard.* If to do so violates some moral or religious tenet that he holds important, he may keep the faith without requiring others, who do not share it, to follow suit.

In this view of the proper function of obscenity law, the *Ginsburg* decision is precisely wrong, as is the Model Penal Code legislation addressed to the advertising and promotion of obscenity. The more clearly the package advertises its contents, the more effectively the unwary consumer will be protected from exposure to what he is likely to find distasteful. Nor need it be feared that the advertising will itself be likely to give offense. No seller in his right mind is going to give away free what he wants to induce people to buy.

The nuisance rationale is recognized by the draftsmen of the Model Penal Code, but is illogically employed as the basis for the far broader ban on public dissemination that they propose. The example cited is intended to show why such a ban must go further than "pandering to an interest in obscenity," which is to say, exploiting such an interest primarily for pecuniary gain. The case is put that "a rich homosexual may not use a billboard on Times Square to promulgate to the general populace the techniques and pleasures of sodomy."[13] Of course he may not, but it is hardly necessary to shore up the whole ridiculous apparatus of censorship, as the Code's provisions would do, in order to prevent him from foisting upon an unwilling public portrayals of his deviational hobby. All that is required is treatment analogous to that given lewd conduct: a person may be punished for engaging in such conduct, the Code tells us, "which is likely to be observed by others who would be affronted or alarmed."[14] Indeed, since the representation of obscenity is one step removed from the conduct that it portrays, there seems less justification for treating it as anything but a public nuisance. The principle that forbids the rich homosexual himself to commit sodomy in Times Square, or to hire a troupe of strolling players to do so, ought to suffice to protect the public against the less dramatic outrage of a pro-sodomy billboard.

One of the subsidiary benefits of the nuisance approach is that it forces a sharper focus on the reality and gravity of the threatened offensiveness than is required when no well-defined secular harm is posited, as has been the case under the traditional approach and as would continue to be the case under the tidied-up version of the traditional approach contained in the Model Penal Code. Under a nuisance approach law enforcement officers would no longer have a roving commission to stamp out the unorthodox and the avant garde. Their job would be solely to keep the more obvious forms of public display under control. It would be the difference between a defensive and an aggressive war.

The paraphernalia of aggressive obscenity enforcement would likewise disappear. Breaking into premises to look for obscenity, making mass seizures of allegedly obscene material, and arresting people who attend allegedly obscene performances would be without purpose, and could be expected in time to die out as new habits of thought and new enforcement patterns responsive to them took hold. The question for the enforcement officers, and ultimately for the judges, would become narrower and easier than at present, shifting from the treacherously subjective judgment about the appeal or tendency of the material to the ob-

---

13 Schwartz, p. 681.
14 MODEL PENAL CODE §251.1 (Proposed Official Draft, 1961).

jective issue of whether under the circumstances of its exhibition
people were likely to be outraged or, better yet, had been outraged. Leaving aside the question of civil sanctions (such as actions for injunction), proof of a criminal violation of the obscenity laws would require a showing that a particular person or
persons had been subjected to psychic assault. It would, of course,
be a defense that the advertising or promotion of the publication
or performance had put people on notice that they might be so
assaulted.

Perhaps a special form of identification might come into being
to protect both sellers and buyers, like the skull and crossbones
used on poison. There might be a special section of the bookstore
or the art gallery, suitably posted for the warning of those who
would not want to subject themselves to what might be found
within. No one would be forced to sell what he found distasteful;
no one would be forced to sample offensive material, or to mingle
with people who wanted to. Freedom would reign, qualified only
by a ban on coerced attention.

What values would be lost under such a regime? It might be
thought that the protection of the immature, about which I have
so far not spoken, would suffer. That apparently was one of the
fears of the framers of the Model Penal Code. In a hypothetical
case, companion to that of the "rich homosexual," they noted
that "a zealot for sex education may not give away pamphlets at
the schoolyard gates containing illustrations of people engaged
in erotic practices."[15] Indeed he may not, under a nuisance rationale. The gist of that rationale as it applies to children is the
existence of a proxy complainant. Adults are deemed adequate
judges of their own capacity for smut. Children (however defined) are not. For their judgment is substituted that of the par-
ent, the teacher, or, *faute de mieux*, the policeman. So long as it
is deemed socially important to do so, children are to be kept
isolated from purveyors, whether commercial or not, of questionable material. We manage it, after a fashion, with liquor. We
should be able to do as much with hard-core pornography. The
problem of identifying it becomes less acute if its purveyors have
an economic incentive to advertise its availability to adults. They

[15] Schwartz, p. 681.

cannot, of course, have it both ways. What they promote for adults they may be forbidden to exhibit to children.

The nuisance approach would bring some problems of its own. It would not be easy to define the bounds of permissible solicitation, which would certainly become the main issue in deciding whether purveyors were giving offense. Would it be an obscene nuisance, for example, for a seller of blue movies to advertise his wares by mail? To refuse to remove a name from his mailing list upon request? To rent a mailing list from a supplier of Boy Scout equipment? The use of the mails obviously provides the most difficult problem because it is difficult to segregate recipients; but it may be that open availability of pornographic materials on the local market would preempt a very considerable part of the mail order supplier's business. He would then become a wholesale distributor for the local retail outlet, where the identity of the recipient would always be ascertainable. Once that stage was reached there could be no objection to banning mail order retail sales, because their only remaining purpose would be the illegitimate one of supplying minors who could not buy directly from retail outlets. Thus, after an initial period of adjustment, one of the most troubling problems in present-day obscenity enforcement might disappear or, at least, be substantially mitigated.

A final word needs to be said on the subject of alternatives to the criminal sanction. There is much to be said for the proposition that the after-the-fact method of control exerted by the criminal process is greatly preferable to administrative censorship and other forms of "prior restraint" of publication, sale, or exhibition. The diminution of personal freedom engendered by the method of the criminal sanction is far less sweeping than that involved in administrative censorship. The repressive attitudes of specialists in censorship are likely to be more pronounced than those of law enforcement officers, whose responsibilities cover a wider spectrum of antisocial conduct. This is likely to be the case no matter what the criminal law criterion is; but the difference would surely become much more pronounced if the thrust of the criminal sanction were limited, as I have suggested it should be, to the suppression of obscene nuisances.

There would be no net gain in personal freedom if the narrowing I have proposed in the criminal sanction were accompanied by a broadening in other forms of official obscenity control. A few sellers who might otherwise have been in jail would not be, but a far more significant form of freedom would suffer: the ability freely to exchange written and pictorial representations of "reality" without accounting to the orthodoxies of the day. Here, as elsewhere, the reform of the substantive criminal law is only a step in the direction of the free society, certainly not the whole journey.

PROSTITUTION: SIN OR NUISANCE

The offense of prostitution bears the same relation to the "sin" of fornication that the offense of commercially disseminating obscene material bears to the "sin" of obscenity. Both represent an attempt to secularize an essentially moralistic judgment about human conduct by fixing upon its commercial aspect as the "harm" to be eliminated.

There seems little reason to believe that the incidence of prostitution has been seriously reduced by criminal law enforcement, although the forms in which it is conducted have altered. It no longer appears to be true that prostitution is organized by criminal syndicates, apparently because the syndicates find other lines of business more profitable. Nor is the house of prostitution the familiar phenomenon that it was a generation or more ago. The business is conducted on more of an itinerant basis now. Its labor force covers the entire social and economic spectrum. As a recent New York survey put it, "they range from the girl who charges $1 to customers picked up in Grand Central Terminal to the socially prominent woman who grants her favors for up to $500 in a suite in one of New York's best hotels." In between are many gradations, ranging from streetwalking narcotics addicts up through bar girls and call girls to party girls. It is the ones at the lower end of the spectrum who most frequently come to the attention of the law. As one would expect, they include a disproportionate number of Negroes, Puerto Ricans, Mexican-Americans, and other members of the urban poor. The policing of streetwalkers in urban slums, as recent empirical studies have shown, is a persistent source of friction between the police and ghetto inhabitants.

As the courts become increasingly strict about the evidence that will satisfy a charge of prostitution or solicitation, the brunt of enforcement falls ever more heavily on those women who are so desperate that they will take the greatest risk. More often than not, they engage in prostitution to support a narcotics habit that is made expensive by yet another questionable policy of the substantive criminal law. Because judges are not moral monsters, they rarely give convicted prostitutes severe sentences. A short term in the county jail is the normal maximum. More often, a suspended jail sentence or a fine is imposed. The woman may soon be back in court again. The law is caught between unrealistic severity and triviality, with triviality winning the day. The whole tedious, expensive, degrading process of enforcement activity produces no results: no deterrence, very little incapacitation, and certainly no reform.

The side effects on law enforcement are unfortunate. Police corruption is closely associated with this kind of vice control. Contrary to popular opinion, the corruption does not usually take the form of bribes from the prostitute herself. She is regarded as too "untrustworthy," which is to say that she has little incentive to protect the police recipient of a bribe if an investigation takes place. Instead, the evidence is strong that extensive bribery is engaged in by the "businessmen" on the fringes of prostitution: the owners of bars where girls do their soliciting and of hotels where they take their customers.

An equally disgusting kind of enforcement practice is the use of the police or police-employed decoy to detect solicitation. A study by Professor Jerome Skolnick of enforcement practices in a large California city has shown that solicitation (as opposed to surveillance) accounted for over half the prostitution arrests, contradicting the police's own impression that the "cleaner" surveillance techniques were prevalent. Skolnick gives a vivid account of the technique of "trolling," by which potential customers (including police seeking to make arrests) drive slowly around a Negro area between midnight and 4 A.M. trying to pick up prostitutes without forcing them to appear to be soliciting. He describes how an elaborate and ever more sophisticated game develops in which

the prostitutes and the police try to overcome the others' latest
ploy. He concludes with this account of a conversation with a vice
patrolman about the difficulties of making a prostitution arrest:

> The broads are wisening up, getting real hanky. One of them told
> me she can always spot a cop because we never say, "Hey, baby, how
> would you like to turn a trick for ten bucks?" which is what a lot of
> these trollers say when one of these broads looks good to them. We
> got to wait for them to set the price, otherwise we don't stand a
> chance in court. It doesn't matter how many times a broad's been
> convicted for prostitution. If we set the price, we got no case. The
> law says we entrapped her.
> I was trolling one night and a broad walked over to the car and
> said, "Mister, I'm in trouble, I could use a little money."
> I said, "Well, I might be able to help you out, provided I get some-
> thing for my money."
> She said, "You'll get something, but how much you givin'?"
> I said, "How much you asking?"
> She said, "How much you offerin' to pay?"
> "Well," I said, "how's about a dollar?"
> "Oh, mister," she said, "you must be a policeman"—and walked
> off.
> You see, Jerry, we got to get them to set the price and for what,
> straight date, half-and-half, French or Greek. Otherwise we're doing
> the soliciting.[16]

One is surely impelled to wonder what substantive goals of law
enforcement can be so important as to justify this use of public
resources.

Although solicitation is the most popular charge, the act of
prostitution is, of course, criminal and is also the object of enforcement activity. The commonest technique is to observe what
appears to be a solicitation, follow the couple to a hotel, and then
arrest them as they leave. To make a case, the police must persuade the man to admit that the act was performed for pay, which
is rarely easy and will presumably become much harder in a jurisdiction like New York when the new rule goes into effect that the
buyer of commercial sex is also guilty of an offense. The surest
technique of discovery, however, is for the policeman to participate himself. Skolnick recounts the following incident:

[16] Jerome H. Skolnick, *Justice Without Trial* (New York, 1966), p. 103.

One of the now more experienced vice control officers reported that on his first night with the squad he used his own station wagon to pick up a girl, while an experienced vice control man was hidden in a large cardboard carton in the rear seat. He said that this was probably his most difficult arrest. As he put it:

"I took the car to a vacant lot that she picked out. After I stopped the car, I paid her the ten dollars that we'd agreed on for a straight fuck. She took the money and stashed it in her bra, and then pulled her Capri pants way the hell off. Just then Rogers stuck his head out of the cardboard box. Rogers was smiling and when she saw him she flipped. She began screaming and biting and scratching. She tore my shirt and she tore my jacket . . . we practically had to carry her into the station."[17]

What does society gain from this kind of law enforcement activity? If the effort is to stamp out prostitution, it is plainly doomed to failure. If it is to eradicate or curb the spread of venereal disease, that too is illusory, given the sporadic pattern of enforcement and the equally sporadic use of the power to quarantine persons suspected of having venereal disease. Indeed, there is persuasive evidence that that power is used not for its ostensible purpose at all, but rather as a bargaining counter in the game of criminal prosecution. As Skolnick explains: "The threat of a quarantine hold doubtless exerts some anticipatory pressure on the prostitute to 'cooperate' with police. The quarantine hold . . . can serve as a threat only if it is not uniformly administered."[18] To put it crudely but accurately, the law is perverted to serve goals for which it was never intended.

It seems that prostitution, like obscenity and like other sexual offenses, should be viewed as a nuisance offense whose gravamen is not the act itself, or even the accompanying commercial transaction, but rather its status as a public indecency. That is the approach taken in England, where law enforcement does not seem to be plagued with the self-imposed problems that our prostitution controls engender. In order to curb effectively the use of undesirable police techniques, it might also be desirable to provide that a conviction for public solicitation should require evidence that the person solicited was offended thereby and was neither a policeman nor someone in the hire of the police.

[17] *Ibid.,* pp. 105–6.
[18] *Ibid.,* p. 109.

CHAPTER SEVENTEEN

The Criteria Applied: Miscellaneous Offenses

THE CONTROL OF NARCOTICS AND OTHER DRUGS

For over fifty years the United States has been committed to a policy of suppressing the "abuse" of narcotic and other "dangerous" drugs. The primary instrument in carrying out this policy has been the criminal sanction. The results of this reliance on the criminal sanction have included the following:

(1) Several hundred thousand people, the overwhelming majority of whom have been primarily users rather than traffickers, have been subjected to severe criminal punishment.

(2) An immensely profitable illegal traffic in narcotic and other forbidden drugs has developed.

(3) This illegal traffic has contributed significantly to the growth and prosperity of organized criminal groups.

(4) A substantial number of all acquisitive crimes—burglary, robbery, auto theft, other forms of larceny—have been committed by drug users in order to get the wherewithal to pay the artificially high prices charged for drugs on the illegal market.

(5) Billions of dollars and a significant proportion of total law enforcement resources have been expended in all stages of the criminal process.

(6) A disturbingly large number of undesirable police practices—unconstitutional searches and seizures, entrapment, electronic surveillance—have become habitual because of the great difficulty that attends the detection of narcotics offenses.

(7) The burden of enforcement has fallen primarily on the urban poor, especially Negroes and Mexican-Americans.

(8) Research on the causes, effects, and cures of drug use has been stultified.

(9) The medical profession has been intimidated into neglecting its accustomed role of relieving this form of human misery.

(10) A large and well-entrenched enforcement bureaucracy has developed a vested interest in the status quo, and has effectively thwarted all but the most marginal reforms.

(11) Legislative invocations of the criminal sanction have automatically and unthinkingly been extended from narcotics to marijuana to the flood of new mind-altering drugs that have appeared in recent years, thereby compounding the preexisting problem.

A clearer case of misapplication of the criminal sanction would be difficult to imagine. We are very far indeed from having eradicated heroin addiction, that prototype of the drug use problem, even though the illegal market is entirely dependent on supplies smuggled in from abroad. The incidence of marijuana use has apparently risen sharply, although we have undertaken since 1937 to prevent its importation. And now we are confronted with a host of new drugs: stimulants, depressants, hallucinogens. Their use increases exponentially; they are much easier to manufacture and distribute than the traditional forbidden substances. It would appear that we are barely at the beginning of an era in which drugs that have the capacity to alter the mind will with increasing frequency be discovered, synthesized, and made available. What is to be done? The conventional answer is still the same: try to suppress it.

Civil Commitment for Narcotics Addiction. The conventional answer has been given a new twist lately. Instead of talking about criminal punishment, we now talk about civil commitment. This is conceived of as an alternative to the criminal sanction in which treatment takes the place of punishment. It has been available as an alternative to the criminal sanction since 1961, when California established a commitment program under the jurisdiction of the Department of Corrections, using a special facility known as the California Rehabilitation Center. New York and the federal jurisdiction have since followed suit, so that civil commitment programs are now available in the three enforcement systems that share the bulk of the narcotics problem.

As we have seen, civil commitment is a misnomer for these programs. What they all essentially involve is the suspension of criminal proceedings, either before or after conviction, and the involuntary commitment of these suspected or convicted criminals for an indeterminate period that may not, however, exceed a prescribed maximum. During the initial period of confinement the "patient" or "resident"—the word "inmate" is avoided as being too suggestive of a prison—is subjected to withdrawal of drugs. He is also, within the limits of available resources, given what is called "therapy" to assist him in overcoming his craving for drugs. This typically takes the form of group discussion sessions in which the patients are encouraged to help one another face up to their problems and to recognize the extent to which their dependence on drugs has been an unsatisfactory evasion of their problems rather than a solution. The patient is also put to work at learning a trade, usually one that fits in with the institution's need to perform essential services for itself. When he is judged ready, the patient is returned to the community in "outpatient" status, with some form of periodic supervision and chemical testing to determine whether he has reverted to drug use. If he has, he will be returned for further treatment, or if his relapse is recurrent or sufficiently serious, he may instead be sentenced to prison on the criminal charge of which he was originally convicted. If, however, he successfully completes a substantial period of drug-free life outside the institution, he will be discharged.

Confinement in a special purpose facility, detoxification, vocational training, group therapy, supervised release. These are the essential features of this "new" departure in dealing with narcotics addicts. There is no "treatment" involved except what has been referred to. Indeed how could there be? Medical progress is not made by changing legal labels. This much-vaunted program is simply criminal punishment with a new set of labels. It cannot be said whether it is more or less effective in helping addicts than the same regime under different labels.

The civil commitment movement may have the long-term effect of changing public attitudes about drug use so that more drastic and meaningful changes can ultimately be made. This is of course merely a surmise. It is also possible that it may have the effect of quieting our consciences about the problem. Small reforms, Lord Morley once remarked, are the enemy of great reforms. One effect is undeniable, although opinions may vary about whether it is good or bad. It has enabled us to believe that we really are changing, that we really are making progress. Listen to the President's Commission on Law Enforcement and the Administration of Justice: "There have been major innovations in legal procedures and medical techniques during the last few years. There are new Federal and State laws and programs designed to provide treatment. . . . These laws and programs signify that the Nation's approach to narcotic addiction has changed fundamentally."[1] Hypocrisy would be too strong a word, and probably unfair. Self-deception is about right.

The plain fact is that civil commitment changes nothing. If it were to be universally substituted for our presently predominant modes of dealing with the problem, none of the evils attendant on our use of the criminal sanction would be ameliorated. Large-scale deprivation of liberty would continue to take place, but now in the misleading name of treatment rather than punishment. The illegal market in drugs would continue to flourish, with attendant fostering of organized crime and inducement to users to commit property crimes to support their use. The economic costs of law enforcement would continue, as would the strain on decency in police work. Nothing would be different but the labels. This is not change; it is merely an excuse for not changing.

The Crime Commission's reference to "major innovations in . . . medical techniques" is an interesting one. I am aware of only two innovations, both of which have been tried on only the most limited of bases. One involves the daily administration of an opiate antagonist, cyclazocine, which in large doses apparently counters the effect of even relatively large doses of heroin. The other and better publicized technique involves the creation of a

1 *The Challenge of Crime in a Free Society* (Washington, D.C., 1967), p. 211.

substitute addiction to methadone, an opiate that leaves the user's capacity to function adequately in the community reasonably unimpaired. Preliminary reports on the methadone maintenance technique by Drs. Vincent Dole and Marie Nyswander at Manhattan General Hospital indicate a high degree of success in enabling addicts to shed their heroin addiction and lead relatively normal and useful lives in the community.

The methadone treatment runs head-on into the old controversy about the feasibility and propriety of supplying addicts with maintenance doses of addictive drugs on an ambulatory basis, the so-called "clinic plan." For many years the Bureau of Narcotics has harassed physicians who have undertaken to treat addicts on this basis. The Harrison Narcotic Act of 1914 exempts prescriptions issued by a physician "for legitimate medical uses" and dispensation to a patient by a physician "in the course of his professional practice only," without further definition of terms. Nonetheless, the Bureau of Narcotics has taken it upon itself to lay down a definition of what constitutes sound medical practice. For many years, in the face of strong but unorganized medical and lay opposition, the Bureau has continued to disseminate among doctors a regulation stating that it is unlawful for a physician to prescribe narcotics "not in the course of professional treatment but for the purpose of providing the user with narcotics sufficient to keep him comfortable by maintaining his customary use." Of course, the regulation begs the very question in issue by assuming that maintenance is "not in the course of professional treatment." It can be argued that the individual physician should be allowed to determine what is proper treatment for his patients. But doctors have allowed themselves to be deprived of that freedom by giving way to the threats of criminal prosecution repeatedly voiced by the Bureau when an individual medical practitioner, a little bolder than the rest, is found to be prescribing large quantities of narcotics for maintenance doses. After considerable vacillation on the subject, a joint committee of the American Medical Association and the National Research Council promulgated an ambiguous and unsatisfactory statement on the use of narcotics in medical practice in which, after issuing the customary ritualistic call for more research, they declared that on the basis of present knowledge, the administration of drugs on an ambulatory basis for maintenance purposes is medically unsound. And there the matter rests at present, although the New York civil commitment statute sheds a small ray of light by authorizing the administration of narcotics for maintenance purposes in research projects.

The prospects for significant change on the narcotics front appear slight. Despite the concentrated attention that it has received in recent years, especially on the federal level, there seems little evidence of any disposition to abandon the present approach. What pressure for change exists has been temporarily siphoned off into the delusive advocacy of civil commitment as a meaningful alternative to criminal sanctions for use and possession of narcotic drugs. The only effective short-run strategy appears to be to press for greater freedom in conducting research and experimentation, particularly on programs designed to test the prospects for ambulatory maintenance care for addicts. Even this will require some relaxation in the conventional enforcement viewpoint, which sees the habitual use of narcotics as threatening no matter what the surrounding circumstances may be. That relaxation will not easily be achieved.

Penalties for Marijuana Use. So far this discussion has concerned primarily the question of "hard" narcotics, as they are called to distinguish them from marijuana and the various new stimulants, depressants, and hallucinogens. Marijuana has been equated with narcotics by the federal government and most of the states for the past thirty years. Not merely importing (the hallmark of large-scale commercial operations) and selling (which may or may not be such a hallmark) but simple use or possession are the grounds for severe felony punishments, often with highly afflictive mandatory minimum sentences for second and subsequent offenses. In California, for example, simple possession of marijuana is a felony punishable by one to ten years' imprisonment; possession with intent to sell is punishable by two to ten years' imprisonment; sale of marijuana, quite without regard to quantity (a single cigarette will suffice) is punishable by a term of from five years to life imprisonment; and sale to a minor is punishable by a term of from ten years to life imprisonment. All of these are for first offenders. A variety of other sentencing statutes increase these terms, usually with an increase in the mandatory minimum for persons who have previously been convicted of other criminal offenses. And these provisions are not simply laws on the books. Substantial penitentiary sentences are served by large numbers of marijuana offenders. In 1965, for example, 138 persons were first released on parole from California prisons after having served institutional portions of their sentences. Roughly ten times that number were incarcerated in county jails, which in California are used for persons serving misdemeanor terms of less than one year.

These severe penalties are imposed despite the fact that the available scientific evidence strongly suggests that marijuana is less injurious than alcohol and may even be less injurious than ordinary cigarettes. Although the effect varies with the user, as is the case with any foreign substance introduced into the human system, it seems to be generally the case that marijuana produces a relatively mild intoxicating effect (or "high," as it is colloquially known) that does not stimulate aggression, lasts relatively briefly, does not have an aftereffect, and does not produce physical dependence. Although research on the effects of marijuana has been substantially inhibited by the existence of our rigid pattern of criminal controls, there appears to be a consensus among pharmacologists that there is nothing remotely approaching functional equivalence between marijuana and the narcotics or opiates. In terms of danger to the human organism there does not yet appear to be any substantial justifying reason for the invocation of severe criminal sanctions. Indeed, one may well ask whether putting people in prison is ever a desirable way of saving them from themselves. Although there is much dispute about the antisocial effects of marijuana use, mainly of a polemic nature, there is a total lack of solid evidence connecting its use with the commission of other crimes in a causative way. As for the familiar assertion that marijuana use leads to the use of narcotics, once again the evidence is simply not there. There is some reason to believe that the association between the two is cultural rather than physiological. High-use areas for marijuana are also high-use areas for narcotics. Those areas, as is well known, were until the 1960's concentrated in the urban ghettos. The ghetto child who early in life is introduced to marijuana becomes a prime candidate for narcotics addiction during adolescence or early adulthood not because of his having previously used marijuana but because the psychological and sociological constraints under which he lives place a premium on escape from reality, and narcotics addiction is a handy form of escape.

The plausibility of the cultural explanation for progression from marijuana to narcotics is greatly enhanced by the current phenomenon of widespread middle-class marijuana use. This phenomenon has many important implications that require analysis. But the point to be made here is that all observers of the situation agree on the absence of any progression to narcotics. The new marijuana smokers—college students, the new bohemians and their fellow travelers—consider it stupid to get involved with narcotics. To do so violates the ethos of "play it cool," which means moderation in all things, even in excess.

The startling increase in marijuana use has important implications for our inquiry. First and most obviously, it demonstrates (if further demonstration were needed) the inefficacy of the criminal sanction to control consensual behavior. Unlike the efforts of law enforcement to deal with such vice offenses as prostitution and gambling, the assault on marijuana has been neither sporadic nor trivial. Federal and state officials have made the most strenuous efforts to control the importation of marijuana and its subsequent distribution. Hardly a month goes by that some "major source" of marijuana is not arrested, with accompanying assertions that now, finally, the back of the problem has been broken. But the problem is a hydra-headed one. Nor has the imposition of really severe penalties made an impact. This, too, is to be expected. Severe penalties are not a deterrent to the professional organizations that supply the market. As the risk goes up for the hirelings, so does the reward. Severity of punishment unaccompanied by certainty of detection will not deter those who calculate the risk. Severe penalties are not a deterrent to the poverty-stricken, psychologically destitute slum-dweller. His life is the life of today, not of tomorrow. Gratifications are immediate or nonexistent. If he does pause to reflect, he may well conclude that nothing that happens will make him substantially worse off than he is. Severe penalties, accompanied by a high risk of detection, might serve to deter the new marijuana user, the middle-class man seeking a temporary escape from the middle class, or the college student seizing an attractive opportunity to rebel. But they do not, partly because the risk of detection is nowhere near high enough, even given the vigorous enforcement that prevails, and partly because the law in action is far more lenient toward these new and respectable users than it is toward the more traditional objects of its attention. Given the devastating consequences of a criminal conviction to a middle-class person and the growing ambivalence among law enforcement officers about the severe marijuana laws, every avenue of discretion is used to minimize the impact of the law. Although there have been notorious instances of severe sanctions imposed on college students caught in possession of marijuana, those instances are notorious at least in part because of their rarity. We may be witnessing the beginnings of the process of nullification, by which the community comes to terms with a law it does not believe in without actually repealing it.

Another implication of the current trend in marijuana use is that the costs of our existing policy are mounting. On the one hand, if differential leniency obtains between enforcement activities in the slums and those in the suburbs, an existing source of alienation in our culture will be enhanced. If, on the other hand, the trend toward nullification is checked, it will be at the price of wholesale law enforcement intrusion at levels of our society that are not accustomed to it and will probably not welcome it. Quite apart from the question of police practices, the continued use of criminal sanctions against marijuana users is very likely to hasten the erosion of respect for the law among the younger generation. We seem to be faced today with a particularly severe crisis of confidence on the part of youth toward the society in which they live. Its causes range far beyond the ambit of this discussion, and its course may well be irreversible. We may in truth be living in a revolutionary age the equal of which has not been seen, at least in the Atlantic world, for almost two hundred years. But those of us who are not prepared to act on apocalyptic premises may well consider whether the erosion of belief in law-abidingness is a phenomenon about which we can afford to be complacent, whether the laws regarding marijuana are not now a substantial contributor to that erosion, and whether we would not do well to prove again what can never stay proven for very long: that the law is made for the people, not the other way around.

Controls on Dangerous Drugs. We are confronted today with a peculiar by-product of our exploding technology: the development and proliferation of chemical substances that produce a wide variety of mind-altering characteristics, some of them of the highest therapeutic significance, others having no clear medical use, all of them exhibiting substantial possibilities for damaging abuse. Some of these substances, notably the psychic energizers and the tranquilizers, have revolutionized the treatment of emotional illnesses and made possible the restoration to useful functioning lives of people who only a decade ago were condemned to lifelong warehousing in the back wards of mental hospitals. Others, like LSD, have no generally accepted medical uses. There exists a disturbing trend toward subjecting all such "dangerous drugs" to the same kind of detailed controls that are presently imposed on narcotics and marijuana, with the same indiscriminate use of the criminal sanction for illegal distribution and possession. A number of states have recently adopted sweeping criminal proscriptions of LSD, following highly publicized instances of harmful effects to LSD users.

Our woeful experience with narcotics and marijuana controls should have made us a little more wary about this rush to invoke the criminal sanction. It seems particularly inappropriate in the case of drugs like the amphetamines, tranquilizers, and barbiturates, all of which have acceptable medical uses. Ours is a drug-using society, and self-medication is an important aspect of that use. Nothing but gratuitous misery will result from the occasional imposition of criminal conviction on a person who possesses for his own use drugs for which he does not have a medical prescription. Recent federal drug control legislation, although

probably more far-reaching than is desirable, sets a useful precedent by failing to make possession, unaccompanied by intent to
sell or use, a criminal offense. Unfortunately, many of the states
have ignored this precedent, and have passed highly restrictive
legislation of their own.

In addition to running counter to well-established habits in
the population, repressive criminal legislation in this field creates
an impossible enforcement problem. Heroin and marijuana, at
least, have to run the gauntlet of border control, since substantially all the supply comes in from abroad. The various "dangerous drugs" are all manufactured domestically. Furthermore,
many of these drugs can be synthesized at low cost in relatively
simple laboratory operations. There is, in short, very little prospect of effective control over the total supply and therefore no
prospect at all of keeping significant amounts of the supply out of
illegal channels of distribution. Although the greatest possible
control should be exerted through federal licensing and inspection of manufacturing facilities, record-keeping requirements
for manufacturers and distributors, and other regulatory devices,
it seems quite inexpedient to rely on the criminal sanction as the
primary means of control. Sanctions such as injunctions, license
revocations, and civil fines are much better adapted to backing
up those regulatory controls that can realistically be enforced.

ABORTION: THE CRIME TARIFF IN ACTION

The primary rationale of criminal laws prohibiting abortion
is the prevention of what is regarded as a form of homicide: the
destruction of an unborn fetus. Whether the fetus should be
regarded as fully human seems to be essentially a moral question.
In any event, the law has usually provided an exemption for an
abortion performed to save the life of the mother, a position generally contrary to that espoused by the Roman Catholic Church,
which is the principal organized moral system taking a doctrinal
stand on the matter. The law, then, has espoused a moral claim
except when there has seemed to be a good secular reason for not
doing so.

In recent years, the list of good secular reasons adopted by the
medical profession, if not by the law, has tended to expand. In a

field survey conducted in 1958–59, an associate and I demonstrated that among respectable members of the medical profession there exists a substantial consensus in favor of performing so-called therapeutic abortions on a variety of grounds short of saving or even lengthening the mother's life. They include preventing or alleviating severe emotional disturbance in the mother, preventing the birth of a probably deformed child, and relieving a woman whose pregnancy resulted from rape or incest. Even though abortions performed on these grounds were, and in most places still are, serious felonies, we were able to show that a substantial number of physicians not only approved performance of the operation under these circumstances but were prepared themselves to authorize or perform such operations. The Model Penal Code lent its prestige to the movement for abortion law reform at about the same time, and a long legislative struggle ensued in a number of states, with varying results to date. Both Illinois and New York rejected this liberalization of the abortion laws in the recent comprehensive revision of their penal codes. In 1967, however, California and Colorado passed statutes (although not without great difficulty) broadening the grounds on which abortions might lawfully be performed along the lines indicated above. There seems to be good reason to suppose that this process of reform will be followed elsewhere in the coming years.

It may be questioned, however, whether this kind of reform is adequately responsive to the seriousness of the abortion problem. On a conservative estimate, over one million abortions are performed in this country annually, most of them on married women. Perhaps one per cent of them are presently performed in hospitals. The rest are performed surreptitiously by "unethical" medical practitioners or, more commonly and with greater risk of maternal death or injury, by people without medical training and under conditions that are far from ideal. As a result, criminal proscriptions for which one might be tempted to claim the secular justification of protecting women against the bad effects of abortions actually produce just the opposite result.

Our abortion laws present a classic case of the operation of the crime tariff. Given the inelasticity of the demand for abortions, the legal prohibition has the effect of raising the risk and reward for the illegal practitioner and also of depressing the quality of the services offered. This phenomenon will not be relieved to any appreciable extent by the moderate or "therapeutic abortion" approach to law reform. Nor will that approach diminish the fact, nor the general knowledge of the fact, that every year upward of a million illegal and possibly dangerous abortions take place in this country. Most seriously, it must be recognized that moderate reform is essentially middle-class reform. It benefits those who are sufficiently well educated, well connected, and well financed to take advantage of the liberalized law. Where will the ghetto-dweller find a psychiatrist to testify that she runs a grave risk of emotional impairment if she is forced to give birth to her nth baby?

The reasons that impel people to seek abortions are reasons of overwhelming compulsion. In this sense, the offense violates the duress limitation, in that a substantial portion of the women who put themselves in the hands of an illegal abortionist do so out of a sense of desperation that will not be placated by less extreme measures. For the law to punish them is hypocritical; for it to punish those who supply the service they seek is inefficacious.

It may be that a greater diffusion of birth control information and ever-simpler means of contraception will combine to reduce the incidence of unwanted pregnancies. In addition, a more casual and accepting attitude toward contraception may engender a change in the still prevalent reprobation with which abortion is viewed. Indeed, hyperconsciousness of the population control problem may result in the acceptance of any and all measures, including abortion, that further the goal.

Whatever the future may hold, it seems a rational goal of reform to focus on the evils that result from illegal abortions and to give thought to ways of counteracting them. The conclusion seems irresistible that the only way to eliminate the illegal abortionist is to eliminate the illegal abortion, and to substitute for it a narrowly drawn criminal prohibition addressed to the real secular evil of abortions performed by unqualified practitioners, leaving to the evolving mores of the medical profession the determination of the circumstances under which its skills will be mobilized to perform abortions.

DRUNKENNESS: THE RIGHT TO BE "SICK"

Drunkenness is the paradigm case of an improvident use of the criminal sanction. It provides a classic illustration of the twofold evil that results from misusing the criminal sanction: we burden the operations of the criminal process to no avail, and we delude ourselves into believing that we have thereby solved a social problem. The burden is an especially dramatic one. Two million arrests in 1965, one out of every three, were for drunkenness offenses. The number of prosecutions is presumably much smaller, since many drunkenness arrests end with release after an overnight sobering-up in the "drunk tank." Nonetheless, both the police and the lower criminal courts, especially in large cities, are heavily burdened with a daily assembly line of drunkenness arrests, jailings (with all the attendant housekeeping), and appearances in court. The effect on the correctional system is, if anything, more severe. If the offender is given a jail term, it is typically spent in a short-term penal institution where he and his fellows contribute to an already severe overcrowding problem. Although reliable figures are lacking, it has been estimated that half the inmates of these institutions—city lockups, county jails, work farms, and the like—are serving sentences for drunkenness offenses.

Their incarceration does neither them nor anyone else any good. Nowhere else in the criminal law is the "revolving door" phenomenon more common. A very high proportion of these hapless people are chronic alcoholics. Some of them may be arrested as often as two or three times a week. Sending them to jail serves only the dubious social purpose of getting them out of sight for a while. It does not keep people from drinking, and it does nothing toward the rehabilitation of those subjected to imprisonment.

On one level, the alcoholism or drunkenness problem may be thought of as a public health problem. There is a good deal of merit in looking at it this way if the result is to channel resources into facilities where alcoholics can undergo detoxification, followed by a variety of counseling and therapeutic devices to help

them reduce their dependence on alcohol. That in essence is the
solution advocated by the President's Commission on Law Enforcement and the Administration of Justice. They recommend
that "drunkenness should not itself be a criminal offense. Disorderly and other criminal conduct accompanied by drunkenness
should remain punishable as separate crimes. The implementation of this recommendation requires the development of adequate civil detoxification procedures."[2] What they mean by detoxification is not altogether clear. If it is a euphemism for
sobering-up, the process is readily accomplished by an overnight
stay in a place where alcohol is unavailable. It may, however,
mean a longer-term process in which alcohol-induced nutritional
deficiencies and secondary withdrawal symptoms are also dealt
with. There is no question that this latter and more elaborate
form of short-term treatment is preferable. There is also no
doubt that it is vastly more expensive than simple "drying out,"
whether accomplished in a police station or in something called
a civil detoxification unit.

One question that must be asked is why the elimination of
drunkenness as a crime should have to wait upon the provision
of facilities that, however desirable, are going to call for increased
public expenditures and therefore are not going to be provided
on an adequate scale very soon. Is it because the public welfare
requires some form of short-term handling of the inebriate? And
does that in turn mean that compulsion should be used to require people who are drunk to undergo short-term detoxification? This seems an overly broad proposition at best; at worst, it
is a downright dangerous one.

The appropriate predicate for invoking compulsion against a
drunken person is that he poses a threat to himself or others, or
is a nuisance to others. The "threat" cases are few and far between. There may be instances when a drunk must be removed
from the streets for his own safety, lest he freeze to death or fall
into a river, or do something similarly dramatic. Far less often
will he pose a threat to others. As for the nuisance aspect of
drunkenness, it is very easy to overstate the extent to which the

---

2 *The Challenge of Crime in a Free Society*, p. 236.

alcoholic bothers others, especially if he is a part of skid row culture. In those cases, and they are probably a substantial majority, in which danger or offense is not a factor there is no solid case for compulsion. The alcoholic's submission to short-run detoxification measures should be on a voluntary basis. Experimental programs for dealing with the alcoholic outside the channels of the criminal process strongly suggest that an offer of help is usually accepted. As for more long-term measures involving residence in a controlled environment, the case for insisting on a limitation to voluntary treatment is even stronger. If compulsion is applied, social service becomes a tyranny both subtler and more coercive than the criminal sanction.

The claim that a given condition, such as alcoholism, is a "disease" must be carefully scrutinized if the corollary of an obligation to be cured is implied. It may be a useful rule of thumb that if people who are not frankly psychotic do not regard themselves as suffering from a disease of which they wish to be cured, it is questionable for the world to regard them as diseased. Alcoholism is a flight from the real world. Should the real world interdict such flights? Or, to put the question with precision, should it employ the coercion of formal social controls, whatever they are called, to interdict them? Is it useful, is it (if the concept may be invoked) moral to use social coercion to compel a surface acquiescence in values that the ego has not been able to accept? Is there not a right to the pursuit of unhappiness?

GAMBLING: THE CASE FOR EXPERIMENTATION

We are told that gambling is this country's largest and most profitable illegal industry. The amount of money that annually enters this market is said to be as high as fifty billion dollars, and the profits that accrue to the illegal entrepreneurs are estimated at six to seven billions. The sums involved in gambling are matched in impressiveness by the burden laid on the criminal process by our attempts to stop it. Gambling ranks ninth on the list of most frequent offenses by reported arrests. In 1965, according to the Uniform Crime Reports compiled by the F.B.I., there were about 115,000 arrests for gambling offenses, an understate-

ment since many arresting agencies do not report to the F.B.I.
and many arrests go unreported for one reason or another.

Our criminal prohibitions are so sweeping that all unregu-
lated gambling, with occasional insignificant exceptions, is illegal. Technically criminal conduct includes church bingo games,
social betting on card games, and friendly wagers on sporting
events. It is legal to lay pari-mutuel bets at the racetrack but
illegal for a group of people who have spent their day gambling
at the track to bet on the ball game that they listen to on the car
radio going home. Of course, middle-class people are almost
never prosecuted for social gambling; but knowledge that conduct widely engaged in by otherwise law-abiding people is criminal hardly conduces to respect for the moral force of the criminal
sanction.

The criminal sanction is peculiarly ineffective to prevent
people from engaging in gambling, as is demonstrated by the
magnitude of the figures cited at the beginning of this discussion.
The reasons are not hard to discern. Gambling is a consensual
transaction, having all the ease of concealment associated with
conduct that the parties involved do not complain about. Indeed,
the typical gambling transaction is probably more easily, quickly,
and privately consummated than is any other kind of illegal consensual transaction. It is much easier to place a bet with a bookie
than to buy heroin or have an abortion. Difficulties of detection
aside, the criminal sanction exerts little deterrent force. Penalties
for those occasional professional gamblers who are caught tend
to be very light, amounting to hardly more than a license tax for
carrying on the business. The consuming public does not regard
gambling as particularly wrongful, a sentiment both affected by
and reflected in the lenience with which gambling offenders are
treated. Social gambling is such a universal phenomenon that
people are not readily persuaded that a bet laid with a bookie is
any worse than one made with a friend at the office. There is a
moral ambivalence in our attitude toward gambling. It tends to
be reflected in resistance to proposals to reduce or eliminate reliance on the criminal sanctions, accompanied by equivalent
resistance to any but the most sporadic attempts at enforcement.
Sporadic enforcement is the hallmark of our efforts to deal with

gambling. A study of the files of any large metropolitan newspaper over a period of several years reveals the typical pattern. Once a year or thereabouts, a rash of stories appears about the prevalence of illegal betting in some part of the city, often accompanied by tales of police corruption. This is followed first by interviews with a grim-faced district attorney who vows war to the death against this plague, then by a wave of gambling raids and arrests, and finally by headlines reading "Bookie Ring Smashed" and editorials commending the authorities and urging continued vigilance. Then there is a period of silence. And in another year or so the whole thing starts again.

The frustration that law enforcement faces in trying to suppress gambling is matched by the intrusive tactics that, rightly or wrongly, the police feel called upon to use. Gambling offenses share with narcotics laws the distinction of having produced the major portion of the Supreme Court's decisions on illegal searches, wiretapping and other forms of electronic surveillance, and entrapment. Wiretapping and eavesdropping are particularly prevalent in gambling enforcement because of the fact that bookmaking operations are mainly conducted over the telephone. It is paradoxical indeed that police practices in violation of both federal law and the Fourth Amendment to the Constitution should be so heavily employed in the suppression of what, on any calculus, is one of the most trivial of crimes.

The necessarily indiscriminate tactics used by the police to detect and suppress gambling fall with grossly unequal force on the inhabitants of urban ghettos. In these areas, where the numbers game is the leading form of gambling activity, and where a host of small operators keeps the business going, the intrusive presence of the police is a constant feature of daily life. The middle-class businessman who places a bet with his bookie over the telephone is only dimly aware of the law enforcement activity directed at inhibiting his transaction. The slum resident who places a bet on the street corner or in the local bar or candy shop is highly conscious of the police threat. The difference is simply one more exacerbating distinction between being a middle-class and a lower-class American. I do not suggest that being poor or belonging to a minority group ought to confer immunity from law enforcement attention. But it is a cause for concern when enforcement has so much to do with class and race despite the widespread character of the behavior in question.

In gross financial terms, the laws against gambling represent our most generous subsidy to organized crime. The successful conduct of a gambling operation requires a high degree of organization, whether it is a casino where the customer plays games of chance at varying odds or a bookmaking service that takes bets on a wide variety of sports events. Particularly in the latter, there has to be a continuous flow of both information and money through the organization. Then, too, there must be a system of insuring against severe losses, through "lay-off" betting and other devices. To these complexities, which would exist even if gambling were legal, are added the intricate organizational devices required to insulate the enterprise from detection and to ensure that if a breach of security occurs at one level it will not compromise the higher levels. Thus, for example, the use of telephonic and other communications systems permits the efficient functioning of a compartmentalized structure in which the man who takes the bet may not know the identity of the person at the next echelon to whom he turns in the bets. In short, the illegal business demands a high degree of organization, a demand that has apparently been met with great success.

By responding to the economic logic of the situation, criminal organizations have arisen that take enormous monopoly profits out of the gambling business. The combination of illegality and the need for organization produces a classic operation of the crime tariff. These monopoly profits then become available to sustain the activities of the criminal organization on a wide variety of fronts, including the penetration of legitimate and quasi-legitimate economic markets. There is some evidence that gambling profits are reinvested in the loan shark business, which is said to be the second largest source of revenue for organized crime. In a neat reverse twist, this business may then be used to place small-time independent bookmakers under financial obligation and thus to coerce them into becoming part of a syndicated gambling operation, with resulting increases in the profits of the organization. These and similar market penetrations are facilitated by the use of extortion, violence, and other under-world tactics. And so the criminal law itself provides the base for the growing economic power of organized crime and for a net increase in criminality.

The effects of this subsidy go far beyond the merely economic. By making it worthwhile for criminal organizations to operate in the field of gambling, we provide the incentive for the wide-spread corruption of law enforcement processes and of the po-litical process generally. In order to secure protection for their activities, the forces of organized crime buy off police at the pre-cinct level. If they are a little more sophisticated, they buy off the chief of police. And if they are more sophisticated yet, they finance the election of local officials who then see to it that law enforcement is limited to a low and predictable level.

Finally, it must be noted that attempts to suppress illegal gam-bling, unproductive as they are, consume a large amount of law enforcement resources. Unfortunately, we have no studies show-ing a functional breakdown in law enforcement costs. We do not know, for example, what proportion of the manpower and tech-nical facilities of a metropolitan police department is employed in the detection of gambling offenses. We do not know how much prosecutorial time is involved in planning and conducting gam-bling prosecutions. Nor do we know how much court time is devoted to this kind of work. A simple count of numbers of cases is not very indicative because there is no uniformity in time spent per case. Studies of this kind are badly needed, but even in their absence we may be sure that the total figure is not insubstantial. Given an estimated total expenditure on law enforcement at all levels of four and a half billion dollars in 1965, it may not be unreasonable to suppose that a hundred million dollars is a con-servative estimate for gambling offenses. An extrapolation of past trends suggests that this figure will double in ten years. It is surely time to ask whether we are getting adequate value for these massive expenditures.

What is to be done? We have become familiar in recent years with proposals to legalize various forms of gambling, such as off-track bets on horse races. Some law enforcement officials have commended these proposals, including, most notably, former

Police Commissioner Murphy of New York. His reasons were interestingly responsive to the problem of the crime tariff. He stated, in testimony before a legislative committee considering Mayor Wagner's 1962 proposal to legalize off-track betting, that "it would reduce the flow of illegal gambling cash into syndicate-controlled enterprises by siphoning these funds out of the underworld reservoir." And again, "it would thus further weaken the racketeer's financial strength and narrow the area of exposure to possible corruption."

Opponents of the proposal made a number of points. The proposal would leave untouched most of illegal gambling, since racing bets amount to only about 15 per cent of the total amount bet illegally. Even with respect to off-track bets, the illegal operator would still be able to compete because the proposal did not call for certain extra services like parlays, back-to-back bets, round robins, and other exotic betting combinations. Legal bet shops would have to recruit in the underworld, since this is the only source of trained personnel. And the net amount of gambling would greatly increase.

These objections help to illustrate the difficulty of developing satisfactory alternatives to the use of the criminal sanction in any area. They don't, however, settle the matter. The first and second objections raise the difficult question of scale and pace of reform. The off-track betting proposal was designed not to eliminate but to reduce illegal gambling. Perhaps the proposal should have gone further and included betting on other sports events. Perhaps it needed to be more carefully tailored to assure that the consumer would get the services he really wanted. It requires a difficult legislative judgment to determine when a proposal goes far enough to be effective but not so far as to create risks, either that the proposal will not be acceptable or, if it is, that irreparable harm will be done if it turns out not to work well.

The objection about the recruitment of underworld characters needs to be seriously considered if it suggests that underworld habits of violence and corruption are inevitably associated with the recruitment of underworld characters. However, if it is meant to suggest that there is something intrinsically wrong with giving legitimate employment to people who have previously been engaged in illegal activity, it is surely misconceived. Finally, the question about the possibility of a net increase in the amount of gambling raises the general issue of the price that we are willing to pay to remove the evils that we have been discussing. There are important empirical questions here that have never been systematically investigated and that ought to be. But even if we had adequate measures of the increase in gambling activity to be expected in the wake of legislation, the question would remain: how much is too much? In order to answer that question we would need to know something about the extent to which gambling reduces other expenditures. Do the stakes come out of the grocery money? Or out of the recreation money? How accurate is the popular picture of gambling as the wrecker of the family economy?

What is needed here as elsewhere in the sanctioning field is a series of imaginative and carefully worked out social experiments. Gambling may be a particularly appropriate field in which to experiment because of its relatively low opprobrium. It may also be appropriate because it is so susceptible to rationalization and controlled study through modern technology. A publicly controlled or regulated computerized gambling operation would give us valuable clues about levels of use by various sectors of the consuming public, overhead costs, differential marginal returns, and other matters that it would be essential to know about in order to devise workable schemes for public regulation. One could also experiment with different forms of organization, both public and private. A plausible hypothesis is that because of their close affinities, gambling operations could best be carried on by insurance companies. The problem of take-over by organized crime could perhaps be minimized by entrusting the conduct of legalized gambling to enterprises with sufficient economic power to resist underworld pressures. A major insurance company or other existing financial institution might be better able to do this than a public agency organized for the specific purpose. In a fight to the finish between Cosa Nostra and, say, Transamerica it would be rash to bet on the former.

If the day for experimentation is still some distance off, there is still the possibility of closer study than we have so far had of the problems of conducting and regulating legalized gambling operations. Many examples are available, from England to the Bahamas, from New Hampshire to Nevada. It is an area totally untapped by serious students of social control. A final thought for students of the dynamics of legislative change. If a carefully devised and well-financed campaign were mounted in some state to secure sweeping measures of de-criminalization for gambling that minimized the chances for underworld take-over, it would be interesting to study the sources of opposition. Much of it, predictably, would come from highly moralistic quarters. The point of special interest is this: which side would the underworld be on?

THE BUSINESSMAN AS CRIMINAL

There is a vast area of criminal proscription that does not deal with either of the two principal kinds of antisocial activity we have so far been discussing: on the one hand, gross and immediate injuries or threats of injury to the security of person and property; on the other, vice crime, i.e., consensual sexual misconduct, drug abuse, and gambling. This area of proscription deals with legitimate economic activity, which in an acquisitive society like ours is the principal form of behavior that brings people and institutions into contact with each other and with more or less coercive forms of social control. In terms of our broad categories of sanctioning modes, this is the domain of compensation and, increasingly, of regulation; but it is also the domain of punishment, although in an interstitial and ancillary way. The term "white-collar crime" partially defines the area in question. As introduced by the sociologist E. H. Sutherland, the term refers to crimes that persons of respectability and high social status commit in the course of their occupations. It is a sociological concept that cuts across legal categories, and it is admittedly imprecise as a definition of categories of crime. The proper function of the term is probably connotative rather than denotative. Nonetheless, it has some usefulness as a boundary-setting term.

Another boundary-setting term is "regulatory offenses." This refers to the vast and disorganized set of proscriptions that are used for the job of regulating the mode in which business enterprise by individuals and corporations is carried on. These regulations touch every aspect of business life. The food and drug laws control the quality and safety of what the consumer buys by means of detailed regulation of both the end products and the processes by which the products are manufactured and distributed. Labor laws regulate the hours and conditions of employment over a wide spectrum of concerns that ranges from preventing the exploitation of children to requiring adequate toilet facilities. Housing codes contain detailed prescriptions of minimum standards for space, lighting, ventilation, heating, and sanitation. The skills of practitioners of arts as diverse as medicine and plumbing are checked out and guaranteed through elaborate systems of occupational licensing. Much of the financing of business enterprise is regulated through securities laws. The health of the competitive economy is safeguarded by the antitrust laws. In each of these cases, and in many others as well, the system of sanctions includes reliance on the criminal sanction. In none is it the primary reliance, and this feature serves at once to distinguish this category of crime from the others we have been discussing. Our inquiry is into the general utility of ancillary reliance on the criminal sanction in the economic sphere.

This focus entitles us to lay aside forms of economic conduct that are primarily controlled by the criminal sanction, of which the prototypes are cheating and embezzlement. If I sell you a piece of glass on the representation that it is a diamond, I am guilty of fraud or, as it is technically known, obtaining by false pretenses. If I collect your rent and pocket the money, I am guilty of embezzlement. Now it is true that I may be subject to a wide variety of other sanctions in either of these two prototype cases, depending on how heavily regulated my particular line of business happens to be. These may include such things as compensatory or penal damages, administrative cease and desist orders, judicial injunctions, civil fines, and revocation of occupational licenses. These may in certain areas become so effective that the criminal sanction itself lapses into disuse. Usually, however, these other sanctions operate to control kinds of conduct that are not

clearly criminal under general proscriptions of fraud or embezzlement. It may also be true that specific criminal proscriptions
ancillary to other forms of economic regulation are most effective
when they most closely resemble the prototype general offenses
of fraud and embezzlement. We will return to that possibility
when, later in the discussion, we compare tax fraud with criminal
violation of the antitrust laws.

What, generally speaking, are the purposes for which we invoke the criminal sanction to deal with economic offenses? There
is really only one. These proscriptions are uniquely deterrent in
their thrust. Through them we seek to maintain a high standard
of conformity among those who might be tempted to further
their own economic advantage by violating the law. These are,
generally speaking, sanctions addressed to the law-abiding. The
subsidiary goal of intimidation does not bulk large, partly because the criminal sanction is in fact invoked very infrequently
against economic offenders and partly because once a man has
been identified as an economic offender there is a range of other
regulatory devices, as well as strong informal pressure, to prevent
his repeating his offense. Incapacitation is not involved at all:
we do not send a tax evader to jail to keep him during that period
of time from engaging in continued tax evasion. And certainly
no one would claim any rehabilitative effect from the imposition
of criminal punishment on those pillars of the community who
happen to get convicted of economic offenses. The case for this
use of the criminal sanction rests squarely on deterrence.

The use of criminal sanctions in dealing with economic offenses could, if properly studied, be an excellent proving ground
for deterrence theory. Unfortunately, our ignorance in this area
is quite as profound as it is elsewhere in the study of sanctions.
Consequently, we can do little more than speculate. There is
much to be said in favor of a probable high deterrent efficacy for
criminal punishment in the field of economic activity. People
who value their standing in the community are likely to be especially sensitive to the stigma associated with a criminal conviction, as well as to the antecedent unpleasantnesses of the criminal
process. Furthermore, the kind of conduct that runs afoul of economic regulation is neither happenstance nor impulsive: people

who commit tax fraud, or conspire to rig prices, or knowingly sell adulterated foods have ample opportunity to calculate their courses of action, to weigh the risks against the advantages, and to take into account the possibility that their conduct will expose them to being branded as criminal. The other side of this coin is that it takes a substantial enforcement effort to make and keep the deterrent threat of the criminal sanction a potent one. It may be a close question whether the enforcement resources required to bring the threat up to its minimal level of credibility might not be better expended in noncriminal modes of regulation. Furthermore, there is the totally unexplored issue of what it takes to give the criminal sanction its bite when "respectable" offenders are involved. Is the fact of conviction enough? (Conversely, is the fact of accusation enough? If so, and especially if the conviction rate is not high, there may be a substantial question of fairness raised.) Or must there be a jail sentence? Must it actually be served, or is it enough that it be imposed? How important is publicity? Our information about this kind of issue is mere impression and anecdote.

Our comparative experience with federal criminal prosecutions in the tax fraud and in the antitrust fields may be instructive. For the past forty or more years, substantial felony penalties have been provided for federal income tax evasion. During most of that time, however, criminal enforcement was sporadic, being reserved essentially as an aid to the civil recovery of taxes due and as a means of prosecuting racketeers and other "public enemies" who were not otherwise easily within the reach of federal criminal law. Beginning in 1952 a new policy of across-the-board criminal enforcement was inaugurated by the Tax Division of the Department of Justice. Something on the order of six hundred to seven hundred criminal tax fraud cases are initiated each year, with a rate of conviction approaching 100 per cent and with about 40 per cent of those convicted receiving prison terms. Of course, nobody knows how effective this enforcement pattern has been in deterring potential violators. Common sense suggests, however, that it is more efficacious than is the case with criminal antitrust prosecutions. There are, to begin with, very few of these, since antitrust cases are invariably "big" cases. Twenty-five a year would be considered a lot. By no means all of these involve individual defendants. Of course, where only corporate defendants are charged or convicted, a fine is the only available sanction. The conviction rate is quite low, and prison sentences are remarkably rare. In fact, since the famous *Electrical Equipment* cases in 1960, in which seven corporate executives received and served jail sentences, no antitrust defendant has been imprisoned. In the flush of enthusiasm after that event, an official of the Antitrust Division wrote: ". . . similar sentences in a few cases each decade would almost cleanse our economy of the cancer of collusive price-fixing . . . ."[3] Whether that prediction would have been accurate no one can say; its factual predicate has not occurred.

We do not know whether criminal enforcement of the tax fraud laws has been "more effective" than criminal enforcement of the antitrust laws. We have no measures of effectiveness. But let us draw the commonsense inference that it has been, and speculate about why this should be presumptively so. First, and most obviously, there is a difference in the level of enforcement effort. Granted that tax fraud is a far more pervasive form of illegal activity than is collusive price-fixing, granted even that the ratio of prosecutions to actual incidents may not be different, there is probably a minimum threshold of enforcement activity above which one must rise in order to have a significant deterrent impact. Next, there is the fact that tax fraud is far more closely analogous to well-established and well-understood patterns of criminal behavior than is price-fixing. Tax fraud may be viewed as a special kind of obtaining by false pretenses, or of embezzlement, or both. The taxpayer makes false representations, either by affirmative misstatement or by omission, about the extent of his income. Or he may breach his fiduciary responsibility to account to the government for its share of his income. However it is viewed, the wrongfulness of his conduct is easily understood. The point is underlined by the fact that lots of people go to jail for tax fraud, but the relationship is a reciprocal one. Would they go to jail in such large numbers if juries and judges were not

3 Quoted in President's Commission on Law Enforcement, *Task Force Report: Crime and Its Impact—An Assessment* (Washington, D.C., 1967), p. 110.

persuaded that their conduct is deserving of criminal punishment? Antitrust defendants do not go to jail at least in part because judges and juries are not convinced that their conduct is morally bad. It is complicated conduct. Even when the fact of conspiracy is clear, with all the distinctive marks of concealment and the accompanying aura of wrongdoing, it is far from clear to all but the economically sophisticated what they are conspiring about and why it is so bad for them to be doing so. Their behavior is too close to the groove of what is accepted as conventional businessmen's activity for it to excite the sense of indignation and outrage that it takes for criminal sanctions to be unsparingly applied. We have seen over and over again that moral outrage ought not to be a sufficient condition for the imposition of criminal liability; this is one of the cases that should remind us that it is, after all, a necessary condition.

I mean to suggest that there is a complex and subtle relationship between the vigorous enforcement of a criminal prohibition and public acceptance of the propriety of employing criminal sanctions. It is by no means clear that we can persuade the public to view conduct as wrongful by making it criminal. Law, even criminal law, simply is not that potent a weapon of social control. Our experience with the use of the criminal sanction during the Prohibition period suggests that the reverse is true: far from stigmatizing hitherto morally neutral conduct as wrongful, the intensive application of the criminal sanction to such conduct has the effect of de-criminalizing the criminal law. If we make criminal that which people regard as acceptable, either nullification occurs or, more subtly, people's attitude toward the meaning of criminality undergoes a change.

There is, indeed, some reason to fear that sensitivity toward the criminal sanction has decreased as the formal apparatus of the criminal law has been called on to deal with a wide variety of morally neutral conduct. Typically, what takes place in these prosecutions is a compromise with the idea of criminality. The formal indications of criminality are all there, but the outcome is typically a fine, rather than an actual or even conditional sentence of imprisonment. One can observe a kind of trade-off at work in large areas of formally "criminal" enforcement of economic regulations. The conduct selected for treatment as criminal may be itself fairly trivial. Or, if it does carry a serious risk of harm, as in the adulteration or misbranding of drugs, the law may dispense with a showing that the violation occurred through any fault of the actor—through intentional, reckless, or even negligent conduct. In return, the penalties invoked are what one might call para-civil: they do not involve the distinctively criminal aspect of conditional or absolute loss of liberty. It is unclear what advantage enforcement derives from this kind of arrangement. It may be that the stigma of criminality is thereby somehow imposed on people who neither incurred the just condemnation of the criminal law nor suffered the ordinary penalties of that condemnation. We have no empirical basis, so far as I am aware, for knowing whether the advantage is real or apparent. What does seem clear is that it represents either an exercise in futility or the debasement of what should be the law's most powerful weapon.

I have not so far in these pages touched on some of the more technical problems that arise in the area of economic regulatory offenses, notably the question of corporate criminality. Economic enterprise is typically carried on through complex organizational structures. It is seldom easy to trace the threads of individual action and hence of individual responsibility through these structures. Often all that is patent will turn out to be the activity of some relatively low-placed member of the organization. The implication may be fairly strong that his activity was known to those in charge, but the fact of knowledge may be difficult to prove. Yet the criminal law does not ordinarily permit one person to be held criminally liable for the acts of another unless it can be shown that he aided in their commission or, at the very least, recklessly tolerated their commission by one whom he could have controlled, had he chosen to do so. There are two possible lines of solution. One is to relax the requirements for the imposition of vicarious liability. On the whole this has not been done with respect to serious offenses because of an understandable reluctance to expose a man to criminal punishment without convincing proof of personal guilt. The other course is to impose criminal liability on the corporation itself. This the law has regu-

larly done, and we are now accustomed to seeing corporate enti-
ties convicted of committing crimes. Often, indeed, the corporation is convicted while individual defendants are acquitted, even
where proof of individual guilt is strong. This differential treatment is often used as a justification for imposing criminal liability on corporations as well as on natural persons. The argument
is, however, of questionable merit, because we have no way of
knowing whether the individual defendants would have been
acquitted in the absence of a convenient corporate scapegoat.

Of course, the only punishment that can be imposed on a corporation is a fine, apart from the stigma of conviction itself. How
real that stigma is may be doubted. Sociologists of the Sutherland
persuasion talk about corporate recidivists; but there is very little
evidence to suggest that the stigma of criminality means anything
very substantial in the life of a corporation. John Doe has friends
and neighbors; a corporation has none. And the argument that
the fact of criminal conviction may have an adverse effect on a
corporation's economic position seems fanciful. A substantial
proportion of America's 500 largest industrial concerns have
been convicted of one or more economic regulatory offenses, but
it has never been shown to make any difference to their economic
position. The most famous corporate conviction in recent years
was that of the General Electric Company and three other concerns in the *Electrical Equipment* cases. It is true that the price of
G.E.'s stock declined following the conviction, but that was generally and, it seems, accurately attributed to the fear that substantial treble damage payments would have to be made to the
many buyers of heavy electrical equipment who had been forced
to pay higher than competitive prices as a result of the collusive
price-fixing activities of G.E. and the other corporate defendants.

Given the difficulty of attributing guilt to individuals for corporate crime and the rather ineffective sanctions available against
the corporation itself, one may well ask whether the present degree of reliance on the criminal sanction in the field of economic
regulation may not be misplaced. Here again the question of
alternatives presents itself, as it must always do in any examination of the usefulness of the criminal sanction. Where economic
gain is the motive for the infraction and where the ability to im-

pose significant economic deprivation on the offender exists, it may well be questioned whether the criminal sanction's contribution offers value equivalent to cost. To impose criminal standards of procedure and criminal criteria of proof for the end result of nothing more than a financial exaction may well be to pay a higher social cost than is necessary. Indeed, the conventional monetary fine structure of the criminal sanction may limit the deprivation far beyond what would be possible with a more flexible public or private damage action. There is also the possibility, exemplified in the enforcement of the antitrust laws, that extensive criminal prosecution simply diverts attention and resources away from the more fundamental task of assuring a competitive structure for industry. In this instance, as in others, the criminal sanction may be not only ineffective but diversionary. Its ready availability makes us less astute than we otherwise might be to devise sanctions that are better adapted to the exigencies of economic regulation than those to be found in the powerful, but limited and crude, repertory of the criminal sanction.

The problem may well be to devise sanctions that are not overly severe. Monetary exactions are presumably not too severe if some proportion is maintained between them and either the gain that has accrued or the loss that has been caused by the illegal activity in question. Forced dissolution, or "corporate capital punishment" is a remedy that might be reserved for repeated and flagrant instances of economic offenses. The concomitant for people might be a prohibition of continued work in certain lines. And then there is the unexploited sanction of publicity. If those who do business with the public were forced to expose the fact of their derelictions, through either labeling or advertising, a powerful deterrent to transgression might be added. Devices of this kind make conventional criminal sanctions pale by comparison. They suggest that thought needs to be given either to retreating from the criminal sanction in the economic regulatory sphere or to expanding its scope so as to achieve a better match between punishment and crime.

The doubts that I have raised about the use of criminal sanctions in the economic regulatory sphere are not by any means as all-encompassing as those that seem warranted in the realm of morals offenses. (There is, by the way, a certain affinity between the two. They are both economic at base and may perhaps both be characterized as exhibiting the wisdom of meddling as little as possible between willing buyers and sellers, assuming them to be reasonably well informed about what it is that they are bartering about.) It may be useful to summarize the several conditions which, to the extent that they obtain, conduce toward the prudent employment of criminal sanctions in the economic sphere. First, the actor should be a person who is clearly identifiable as the responsible party. Second, the nature of the conduct should be simple enough that it can be understood by a nonspecialized judge and jury. Third, it should be conduct that, when understood, will be viewed by a substantial segment of the community as wrongful—preferably wrongful because of its intrinsic nature, but as a minimum, wrongful if it is clear that the defendant knew or should have known that he was behaving contrary to an accepted standard. Finally, there should be some basis for believing that the enforcement of the economic regulation in question against this particular defendant is not arbitrary or discriminatory. If all of these conditions are met, it cannot be said that the invocation of the criminal sanction is unwise.

Conclusion: Means and Ends

WE HAVE reached the end of our inquiry, although we are far from having solved the problems into which we have been inquiring. Where does it leave us?

The dilemma of the criminal sanction urgently confronts us today. Although its premises have never seemed shakier, it is actually being resorted to more than ever before. While its processes are being forced to conform to values that reduce its efficiency, we place heavier and heavier demands on those processes. In sum, society is relying more heavily than it ever has before on a means of social control whose philosophic basis and actual operation have come under severe attack.

The argument of this book has been that both the reliance and the attack are largely misconceived. The criminal sanction is indispensable; we could not, now or in the foreseeable future, get along without it. Yet we resort to it in far too indiscriminate a way, thereby weakening some of the important bases upon which its efficacy rests and threatening social values that far transcend the prevention of crime.

We need to keep steadily in view the fact that all uses of the criminal sanction are not equal. We have not kept this fact steadily or even intermittently in view. Crime is a sociopolitical artifact, not a natural phenomenon. We can have as much or as little crime as we please, depending on what we choose to count as criminal. Only when this basic fact is understood can we begin to deal rationally with the problem of choice by applying relevant criteria for proper uses of the sanction. I have tried to provide some of these needed criteria. What they all have in common is their relationship with the distinctive features of the criminal sanction—its characteristic strengths and weaknesses.

The criminal sanction is the best available device we have for dealing with gross and immediate harms and threats of harm. It becomes less useful as the harms become less gross and immediate. It becomes largely inefficacious when it is used to enforce morality rather than to deal with conduct that is generally seen as harmful. Efficacy aside, the less threatening the conduct with which it is called upon to deal, the greater the social costs that enforcement incurs. We alienate people from the society in which they live. We drive enforcement authorities to more extreme measures of intrusion and coercion. We taint the quality of life for free men.

The revolution that is taking place in the criminal process is a response to the special threat that the criminal sanction poses to values of privacy and autonomy, to the maintenance of a decent distance between the individual and constituted authority. Although it is largely a judge-made revolution, it has called general attention to the need for reforms. But reforms in the process are largely pointless unless accompanied by equivalent attention to the ends for which the process is being used. As our discussion has shown, means and ends interact. But simple interaction is not enough: means ought to be subservient to ends. We have not been able as a society to face that obvious point. Only recently we have had a massive inquiry into the operation of our criminal process under the auspices of a presidential commission. It found many weaknesses, deficiencies, and strains in the system. It proposed many remedies. Yet the commission's proposals utterly failed to come to grips with the simple proposition that is the subject of this book: all uses of the criminal sanction are not equal.

That mistake has not always been made. When Sir Robert Peel set about creating the modern police force as we know it, he recognized the relationship between what the criminal process has to work on and the way it works. Charles Reith, the historian of the British police, describes Peel's insight as follows:

Peel realized what the Criminal Law reformers had never done, that Police reform and Criminal Law reform were wholly interdependent; that a reformed Criminal Code required a reformed police to enable it to function beneficially; and that a reformed police could not function effectively until the criminal and other laws which they were to enforce had been made capable of being respected by the public and administered with simplicity and clarity. He postponed for some years his boldly announced plans for police, and concentrated his energies on reform of the law.[1]

What Peel saw as true about the police is true about all the agencies and operations of the criminal process. The process cannot function effectively unless the subject matter with which it deals is appropriately shaped to take advantage of its strengths and to minimize its weaknesses. The prospect of spending billions of dollars, as the federal government now seems prepared to do, on improving the capacity of the nation's system of criminal justice to deal with gamblers, narcotics addicts, prostitutes, homosexuals, abortionists, and other producers and consumers of illegal goods and services would be seen for the absurdity that it is if we were not so inured to similar spectacles. Our national talent runs much more to how-to-do-it than to what-to-do. We sorely need to redress the balance, to ask "what" and "why" before we ask "how."

There is no easy recourse to alternative sanctions. Most alternatives turn out on inspection either to require the backup of the criminal sanction or themselves to be thinly disguised versions of the criminal sanction. The real alternative in many cases will turn out to be doing nothing (as a matter of legal compulsion), or at any rate doing less. Distasteful as that alternative may sometimes seem, we need to press the inquiry whether it is not preferable to doing what we are now doing.

The criminal sanction is at once prime guarantor and prime threatener of human freedom. Used providently and humanely it is guarantor; used indiscriminately and coercively, it is threatener. The tensions that inhere in the criminal sanction can never be wholly resolved in favor of guaranty and against threat. But we can begin to try.

[1] *The Police Idea* (London, 1938), p. 236.

BIBLIOGRAPHICAL NOTE

Bibliographical Note

THIS NOTE is intended to provide the reader (who, it will be recalled, is supposed to be the Common Reader) with what I called in the Preface "a map of the intellectual terrain." This book is an extended argument; the Note is simply an attempt to identify the sources of the principal facts and ideas from which the argument has been constructed. As such, it has no pretense to being a bibliography, definitive or otherwise, of the various fields touched on in the argument.

Let me start by identifying the works that have most strongly influenced my views. As I have said earlier, the intellectual tradition with which I claim kinship is that of Bentham and Mill. But I am a lawyer, not a philosopher, and my perspective here is that of a student of the legal system. My general views about law have been greatly influenced by Henry M. Hart and Albert M. Sacks, *The Legal Process* (Tent. ed., 1958). My views about criminal law owe much to the work of Herbert Wechsler and Louis B. Schwartz, especially in their capacity as Reporters for the American Law Institute's MODEL PENAL CODE, my constant recourse when I began to teach the subject over a decade ago. It is unfortunate that this invaluable work, our best treatise on the substantive criminal law, remains inaccessible to all but the most determined, scattered as it is throughout thirteen tentative drafts. My views on the rationale of criminal punishment have been greatly clarified by the work of H. L. A. Hart, particularly his papers entitled *Prolegomenon to the Principles of Punishment* and *Punishment and the Elimination of Responsibility*, recently reprinted in a collection of his writings entitled *Punishment and Responsibility* (London, 1968). Finally, my skepticism about substitutes for the criminal law as an instrument of social control rests in part on the conviction that no one has adequately answered the challenge to the "new learning" laid down by Jerome Michael and Mortimer Adler in *Crime, Law, and Social Science* (New York, 1933).

The first four chapters of the book are devoted to an attempted resolution, at least for the needs of the criminal law, of the great philosophical debate over the morality of punishment, a debate whose classic protagonists are Kant and Bentham. Kant's *Rechtslehre* and Bentham's *Principles of Morals and Legislation* are the basic texts. The classic phase of the controversy is succinctly recapitulated in Jerome Michael and Herbert Wechsler, *Criminal Law and Its Administration* (Chicago, 1940), pp. 6–11, and in greater detail in Edmund L. Pincoffs, *The Rationale of Legal Punishment* (New York, 1966). In addition to Professor Hart, a number of philosophers on both sides of the Atlantic have influenced my thinking about the morality of punishment. They include J. L. Austin, A. C. Ewing, Joel Feinberg, John Rawls, Herbert Morris, and Richard A. Wasserstrom.

The elaboration of deterrence theory that I have undertaken owes much to Johannes Andenaes, *General Prevention—Illusion or Reality?*, 43 J. CRIM. L., C. & P.S. 176 (1952). My first exposure to the pitfalls of the "rehabilitative ideal" came through reading Francis A. Allen's essay "Criminal Justice, Legal Values and the Rehabilitative Ideal," which gave currency to that term; this perceptive essay has recently been collected with several of Allen's other papers in *The Borderland of Criminal Justice* (Chicago, 1964). What I have termed the behavioral branch of the utilitarian position receives its most carefully reasoned statement in Barbara Wootton, *Crime and the Criminal Law* (London, 1963); the same author's *Social Science and Social Pathology* (London, 1959) is also of interest. The range of contemporary sociological and psychological theories is judiciously surveyed in Leon Radzinowicz, *In Search of Criminology* (London, 1961).

Chapters 5 through 7 constitute a reinterpretation of basic criminal law doctrine in the light of the integrated theory of criminal punishment developed in the first four chapters. Only within the last generation has the task of doctrinal clarification been satisfactorily pursued. The starting point is Herbert Wechsler and Jerome Michael, *A Rationale of the Law of Homicide*, 37 COLUM. L. REV. 701, 1261 (1937). The major works in England and the United States, respectively, are Jerome Hall, *General Principles of Criminal Law* (2d ed., Indianapolis, 1960), and Glanville Williams, *Criminal Law: The General Part* (2d ed., London, 1961). The results of modern scholarship in this field have been translated into statutory form with useful commentary in the American Law Institute's MODEL PENAL CODE, particularly Tent. Draft No. 4 (1955).

The neglect of basic doctrine by legislatures and courts has been extensively documented in the periodical literature. Examples include Henry M. Hart, *The Aims of the Criminal Law*, 23 LAW AND CONTEMP. PROB. 401 (1958); Gerhard O. W. Mueller, *On Common Law and Mens Rea*, 42 MINN. L. REV. 1043 (1958); and Herbert L. Packer, *Mens Rea and the Supreme Court*, 1962 SUPREME COURT REV. 107. The rise of strict liability is recorded in Francis B. Sayre, *Public Welfare Offenses*, 33 COLUM. L. REV. 55 (1933). The insanity defense and related issues have provided the basis for an enormous literature, much of it polemic. Representative polar examples are Henry Weihofen, *Mental Disorder as a Criminal Defense* (Buffalo, 1954), and Thomas S. Szasz, *Law, Liberty, and Psychiatry* (New York, 1963). A balanced treatment that may well be the definitive work on the subject is Abraham S. Goldstein, *The Insanity Defense* (New Haven, 1967).

There is no adequate overview of the stages of the criminal process, a lack for which I have tried to compensate in Chapters 8–12. Specific aspects of the procedural revolution have been extensively treated in the legal literature. Perhaps the best introduction to the underlying legal data can be found in the casebooks from which law students study the subject of criminal procedure. Of these, the most satisfactory are Livingston Hall and Yale Kamisar, *Modern Criminal Procedure* (St. Paul, 1966), and Monrad Paulsen and Sanford H. Kadish, *Criminal Law and Its Processes* (Boston, 1962). The best source for general information about the criminal process as it operates today is the report of the President's Commission on Law Enforcement and Administration of Justice, *The Challenge of Crime in a Free Society* (Washington, D.C., 1967), and the Commission's various task force reports, particularly those on *The Police* and *The Courts*. Many legal scholars have devoted their efforts to studying phases of the procedural revolution. Those whose work I have found consistently useful include Francis A. Allen, Anthony G. Amsterdam, Edward L. Barrett, Jr., Paul M. Bator, Caleb Foote, Abraham S. Goldstein, Joseph Goldstein, Sanford H. Kadish, Yale Kamisar, Curtis R. Reitz, Louis B. Schwartz, Murray L. Schwartz, and Alan R. Westin. Some of their work is cited below. Most of what they have written is published in the form of law review articles and may be located through the *Index to Legal Periodicals*.

The police phase of the criminal process has been the subject of extensive empirical investigation in recent years. Two excellent studies are Edward L. Barrett, Jr., *Police Practices and the Law— From Arrest to Release or Charge*, 50 CALIF. L. REV. 11 (1962), and Joseph Goldstein, *Police Discretion Not to Invoke the Criminal Process: Low-Visibility Decisions in the Administration of Justice*, 69 YALE L. J. 543 (1960). The results of the American Bar Foundation's Survey of the Administration of Criminal Justice, conducted in the mid-1950's, are gradually finding their way into print. Survey data relating to the police are treated in Wayne R. La Fave, *Arrest: The Decision to Take a Suspect into Custody* (Boston, 1965). The problem of arrests for investigation is analyzed and a legislative solution proposed in American Law Institute, A MODEL CODE OF PRE-ARRAIGNMENT PROCEDURE (Tent. Draft No. 1, 1966). By far the best empirical study of police work that has so far been published is Jerome Skolnick, *Justice Without Trial* (New York, 1966). There is no equivalent study of the work of public prosecutors, a lack that legal and sociological scholars might well try to remedy.

The pervasive issue of access to counsel has been the subject of a number of studies, official and private. A representative example is *Report of the Attorney General's Committee on Poverty and the Administration of Federal Criminal Justice* (Washington, D.C., 1963). The landmark case of *Gideon* v. *Wainwright* is discerningly described in Anthony Lewis, *Gideon's Trumpet* (New York, 1964). The bail problem is dealt with in a number of studies, many of them sparked by the Vera Foundation in New York City, which has been a great force for reform. Daniel J. Freed and Patricia M. Wald, *Bail in the United States: 1964* (Washington, D.C., 1964), is a good introduction to the subject. The leading American scholar in the field, Caleb Foote, has collected his papers on the subject in *Studies on Bail* (Philadelphia, 1966). The growing recognition that the guilty plea is strategically crucial to the criminal process is reflected in Donald J. Newman, *Conviction: The Determination of Guilt or Innocence Without Trial* (Boston, 1966), a study based on data collected in the American Bar Foundation's Survey of the Administration of Criminal Justice. An extreme example of how costly the full panoply of the criminal process can be is afforded by John Kaplan and Jon R. Waltz, *The Trial of Jack Ruby* (New York, 1965).

Chapters 13 to 15 seek to define limiting criteria responsive to the characteristics of the criminal sanction discussed earlier. The question of limits has been almost entirely ignored since Bentham's classic exposition of the subject in Chapter 13 of the *Principles of Morals and Legislation*. The major exception to this generalization is Hermann Mannheim, *Criminal Justice and Social Reconstruction* (London, 1946), an original and highly penetrating work that examines from a socialist point of view the role of the criminal law in the reshaping of modern society. There have been many *ad hoc* attacks on particular uses of the criminal sanction, and there have been oblique discussions of its use in the debate over the relation of law and morals. Examples of both are noted below. The subject has not been treated as a whole, however, with one important recent exception: Sanford H. Kadish, *The Crisis of Overcriminalization*, 374 ANNALS OF THE AMERICAN ACADEMY OF POLITICAL AND SOCIAL SCIENCE 157 (Nov. 1967), a revised version of a paper originally prepared for the President's Commission on Law Enforcement and Administration of Justice.

The modern debate on the relationship of law and morals was incited by the Wolfenden Report's famous recommendation that sexual relations between consenting adults should not be the concern of the criminal law: Great Britain, Committee on Homosexual Offenses and Prostitution, *Report*, Cmd. No. 247 (1957). The terms of that debate were set, however, by John Stuart Mill's *On Liberty* (London, 1859) and Sir James Fitzjames Stephen's rejoinder, *Liberty, Equality, Fraternity* (London, 1872). They are refined but not really changed in the modern debate between Lord Devlin, *The Enforcement of Morals* (Oxford, 1959), and Professor H. L. A. Hart, *Law, Liberty, and Morality* (Stanford, 1963).

The economic approach to the problem of limiting criteria, aside from earlier work of my own that has been incorporated into Chapter 15, is exemplified by Thomas C. Schelling, "Economic Analysis and Organized Crime," a paper prepared for the President's Commission on Law Enforcement and printed in the Commision's task force report on *Organized Crime* in 1967. A sense of the problem of assembly-line justice is given in Abraham Blumberg, *Criminal Justice* (Chicago, 1967). The problem of police relations with the urban poor is hardly one that needs documentation today.

In contrast to the paucity of literature on the general and theoretical aspects of limitations on the use of the criminal sanction, there are a number of works that deal with the specific criminal offenses used as examples in Chapters 16 and 17. Many of them are touched upon in the various task force reports issued by the President's Commission in 1967, notably *Assessment of Crime, Drunkenness, Nar-*

cotics, and Drug Abuse and *Organized Crime*. The former is a particularly useful compilation of quantitative data not easily accessible
elsewhere.

For the problem of sex offenses, the best single source is the discussion in the American Law Institute's MODEL PENAL CODE (Tent.
Draft No. 4, 1955). A representative collection of papers on various
aspects of sex offenses is Ralph Slovenko, ed., *Sexual Behavior and the
Law* (Springfield, Ill., 1965). A useful discussion of these and other
"victimless" crimes is Edwin M. Schur, *Crimes Without Victims*
(Englewood Cliffs, N.J., 1965). A superb field study that documents
in detail the enforcement difficulties that beset this area of the criminal law is *The Consenting Adult Homosexual and the Law: An
Empirical Study of Enforcement in Los Angeles County*, 13 U.C.L.A.
LAW REV. 643 (1966).

Background materials on bigamy and incest may be found in Tent.
Draft No. 4 of the MODEL PENAL CODE. I have relied heavily on the
treatment of obscenity in Tent. Draft No. 6, although I disagree with
the draftsmen's statutory proposals. In addition to that treatment,
stimulating discussions of the obscenity problem from the perspective
of the courts may be found in Louis Henkin, *Morals and the Constitution: The Sin of Obscenity*, 63 COLUM. L. REV. 391 (1963), and
Harry Kalven, *The Metaphysics of the Law of Obscenity*, 1960 SU-
PREME COURT REV. 1. James C. N. Paul and Murray L. Schwartz, *Federal Censorship: Obscenity in the Mail* (New York, 1961), is an important empirical study of enforcement problems. The enforcement
of laws against prostitution is dealt with in Paul W. Tappan, *Delinquent Girls in Court* (New York, 1947), as well as in Jerome Skolnick's *Justice Without Trial*, previously cited.

The leading treatment of the legal aspects of narcotics control is
William Butler Eldridge, *Narcotics and the Law* (2d ed., Chicago,
1967). Among the many empirical and policy studies on the narcotics
problem, Isidor Chein et al., *The Road to H: Narcotics, Delinquency,
and Social Policy* (New York, 1964), is by far the best. The contemporary state of medical and other relevant knowledge about narcotics,
marijuana, and dangerous drugs is assessed in a series of papers by
Richard H. Blum printed as appendixes in the Presidential Commission's task force report on *Narcotics and Drug Abuse*.

Literature on the abortion problem is canvassed in Tent. Draft No.
9 (1959) of the MODEL PENAL CODE. The historical and legal background of abortion is splendidly treated in Glanville Williams, *The
Sanctity of Life and the Criminal Law* (New York, 1957). Herbert L.

Packer and Ralph J. Gampell, *Therapeutic Abortion: A Problem in Law and Medicine*, 11 STAN. L. REV. 417 (1959), is a field study that documents the tension between legals norms and reputable medical practice in the abortion field. Quantitative data on the abortion problem are presented in Paul Gebhard et al., *Pregnancy, Birth, and Abortion* (New York, 1958). A collection of recent writings on the subject is found in Alan F. Guttmacher, *The Case for Legalized Abortion Now* (Berkeley, Calif., 1967).

Much of the contemporary lore on alcoholism is reflected in the Presidential Commission's task force report on *Drunkenness*. The results of an ambitious scholarly effort to attack the problem, the work of the Cooperative Commission on the Study of Alcoholism, are reported in Thomas F. A. Plaut, *Alcohol Problems: A Report to the Nation* (New York, 1967). There is, unfortunately, no good scholarly work on gambling and its social control. For the time being, we have to make do with the official demonology, currently reflected in the Presidential Commission's task force report on *Organized Crime*.

The phenomenon of the businessman as criminal is documented and theorized about in an extensive sociological literature, notably Edwin H. Sutherland, *White Collar Crime* (New York, 1949), and Marshall Clinard, *The Black Market* (New York, 1952). The problems are ably discussed and the literature collected in Chapter 8 of the Presidential Commission's task force report on *Assessment of Crime*, which also contains two valuable attachments on criminal antitrust and tax fraud enforcement, prepared, respectively, by the Antitrust and Tax Divisions of the Department of Justice.

INDEX

Index